The Book of Shen

fourth edition

Mark Tarver

The Book Of Shen - Fourth Edition
Copyright © (Mark Tarver 2021)

All rights reserved

ISBN: 978-191501-211-1
Paperback

Published 2021 by Upfront Publishing
Peterborough, England.

An environmentally friendly book printed and bound in England
by www.printondemand-worldwide.com

Dedicated to Magdalena Pamesa (1940-2010)

Contents

Part II Working with Types

Appendices

How to Read this Book

The source for the Shen is remarkably small; the Shen kernel is just over 3,700 lines of Shen code. However the ideas integrated within the kernel cover several modules in university computer science: functional programming, logic programming, type theory, formal language theory and compiler theory being some of them.

The Book of Shen (*TBoS*) covers all the material needed to program in Shen and to understand the code in the kernel. *TBoS* presupposes no special knowledge, in that nothing is assumed, but it does demand talent and commitment to derive complete understanding from it.

There are two levels of understanding with respect to Shen. The first is the understanding of how to program in Shen. The second is the understanding of how the kernel works and the logical foundations of Shen. A newcomer will first wish to attain the first level of understanding, before deciding if he wishes to attain to the level of the second.

Accordingly the chapters in this book are partitioned into starred and unstarred chapters. The unstarred chapters deal with how to program in Shen and contain application programs which can be downloaded from the Shen website. The starred chapters deal with computational and logical foundations of Shen. These starred chapters are for those who want to attain the second level of understanding.

Since *TBoS* covers many years of research and development, it is unlikely the reader will vault through these pages in any short time. It is suggested that the logical way to read *TBoS* is to read the unstarred chapters first and then the starred ones.

A Conceptual Dependency Table

The following table indicates the immediate dependencies between the chapters of this book. A dependency of chapter *m* on chapter *n* means that chapter *m* cannot be understood without a grasp of the material in chapter *n*.

Chapter	Title	Dependencies
1	Beginnings	
2	Starting Shen	
3	Recursion	2
4	Lists	3
5	Strings	2-4
6	Higher Order Functions	2-4
7	Assignments	2, 3
8	Vectors	2-4
9	I/O	2-5
10	Macros and Packages	2-4
11	Exceptions and Continuations	2-5, 9
12	Non-determinism	2-4
13	Shen YACC	2-4, 12
14	Lambda Calculus	2-4
15	Kλ	2-4, 10, 11, 14
16	Writing Good Programs	2-4
17	Types	2-9, 11
18	Sequent Calculus	2-4, 12
19	Concrete Types	2- 9, 11, 17, 18
20	Proof and Control	2-11, 17-19
21	Abstract and Algebraic Datatypes	2-11, 17-19
22	Typed Shen YACC	2-4, 12, 17-19
23	A Model Checker	2-4, 12, 18
24	An Interpreter for Kλ	2-9, 11, 14, 15, 17, 18
25	Shen Prolog	2-4, 12, 18
26	Compiling Sequent Calculus	2-4, 8, 11, 12, 18, 25
27	Compiling Prolog	2-4, 12, 18, 25
28	The Semantics of 𝓛	2-9, 15, 17, 18
29	System 𝓢	2-9, 15, 17, 18, 28
30	Type Safety	2-9, 15, 17, 18, 28, 29

Preface to the Fourth Edition

The fourth edition of *The Book of Shen* follows six years after its predecessor and is longer by nearly 100 pages. A further 80 pages or so from the third edition have been rewritten, so that in total around a third of the fourth edition is new or revised material.

The new material deals with the compilation of sequent calculus notation, Shen Prolog and Shen YACC which went through big changes between 2019 to 2021. The same applies to Shen itself which saw the introduction of a simplified optimising compiler in 2019. I have also included in this book, a rather nice study of computational model theory that was present in the second edition but dropped from the third.

A feature of the fourth edition, which was missing in the previous three, is the use of kernel code to explain the algorithms within Shen. A functional language is more than a means of getting a computer to do what we want. A functional language is also a specification of what the computer does. The inclusion of kernel code in this text is an expression of confidence in Shen as a specification language and in the implementation. I hope this will lead to greater understanding of Shen.

Acknowledgements

I'd like to thank David Holdcroft and Rod Burstall, many moons ago, for hiring me.

I'd also like to thank the sponsors of this work and the members of the 2011 committee who helped make Shen possible on all the platforms on which it has appeared. I'd like to single out the following people for special appreciation.

Vasil Diadov; for supporting Shen financially from 2011-2012.

Ramil Farkshatov, not only for his ports to Python and Javascript, but for his important contribution to chapter 9 in arguing successfully for an approach to I/O based on bytes.

Bruno Deferrari for his excellent web work in maintaining OS Shen.

Willi Riha for long discussions on Shen.

Neal Alexander for his financial support and his intellectual input.

Carl Shapiro for his wisdom on Lisp.

And finally Magdalena Pamesa, who did not understand computers, but whose devotion made all this possible.

Mark Tarver
April 2021

1 Beginnings

1.1 Declarative Programming

One of the first skills that every student acquires in learning to program is to use **assignments**. An assignment has the form "let X = X+1", whereby a variable is given a value in a program. In most languages, assignments are foundational; programs cannot be written without them. If we take a language like C or Fortran, and subtract the ability to write assignments, then the result is no longer a viable programming language. These languages are called **imperative**, **procedural** or **non-declarative** languages.

Declarative languages can survive this kind of subtraction. If we take a language like Shen and subtract assignments, then the result is still a viable programming language. In the case of **pure declarative programming languages** like Miranda^{TM}, where there are no assignments, this subtraction leaves the language unchanged. So in a declarative programming language, any computation can be described without the use of an assignment statement. Declarative languages are themselves partitioned into **functional programming languages**, like Shen and Miranda^{TM}, and **logic programming languages**, of which **Prolog** is the most widely used.[1]

This gives an accurate, but shallow characterisation of the procedural/declarative distinction. It does not explain why some programmers have been attracted to the declarative paradigm; as John Hughes (1990) puts it.

It says a lot about what functional programming isn't (it has no assignments....) but not much about what it is. The functional programmer sounds rather like a mediaeval monk, denying himself the pleasures of life in the hope it will make him virtuous. To those more interested in material benefits, these advantages are totally unconvincing.... It is a logical impossibility to make a language more powerful by omitting features, no matter how bad they may be. Clearly this

---

[1] The partition is a little fuzzy; during the '80s several experimental languages explored the connection between logic and functional programming and the result was a series of hybrid languages such as LOGLISP (Robinson and Sibert (1980)) and LIFE (Ait-Kaci and Podelski (1993)) that shared features of both paradigms. Other systems like POPLOG (Sloman (1985)), provide an environment for communicating between programs written in both styles.

1

characterisation of functional programming is inadequate. We must find something to put in its place - something that not only explains the power of functional programming but also gives a clear indication of what the functional programmer should strive towards.

To begin to meet Hughes' requirements, it is necessary to understand how functional programming originated and how the split between procedural and declarative programming began. We have to return to the beginning of computer science.

1.2 Mathematical Foundations

Computer science theory began with the attempt to make precise the idea of an **algorithm**. The name derives from the ninth-century Persian mathematician Mohammed ibn Musa al-Khowarizmi who described simple procedures for carrying out addition, subtraction, multiplication and division in the new Indian decimal system. The Cambridge English Dictionary defines an algorithm as

a set of mathematical instructions that must be followed in a fixed order, and that, especially if given to a computer, will help to calculate an answer to a mathematical problem

In ordinary speech, an algorithm is sometimes expressed in the native tongue of the speaker. So the rules for subtracting numbers are taught to us using conversation and examples. Conversational vocabulary is often imprecise and frequently rather verbose at the task of describing algorithms. Take this example, of an explanation of how to find square roots using Newton's Method of Approximation (a method studied in chapter 6 of this book).

Take the number you want to find the square root of and take a guess at the square root. If you are happy with your guess, then fine. If you want to have a better approximation than this guess, then take the average of the guess together with the result of dividing the number you want to find the square root of by that guess. That will give you a better guess. Keep on doing this until you have a guess you're happy with.

These instructions might serve their purpose, but they are vague, long-winded and difficult to follow. The example shows very clearly the weakness of relying on English, or any other conversational language, to express algorithms. Though the Cambridge definition is good enough for casual use, it is not formally precise. But not until the twentieth century did mathematicians try to construct a definition of an algorithm that was formally precise.

When they did so, two leading mathematicians, Alan Turing in England and Alonzo Church in America, came up with different answers. However, the answers, though different, later proved equivalent, in the sense that any procedure that could be represented as an algorithm according to Church's answer, could be represented as an algorithm according to Turing's answer. It was rather as if two biologists trying to characterise the species of tigers, had defined them as "the species of which the largest land carnivore native to India are members" and as "the members of the species *Panthera tigris*". In a similar way, the definitions of Church and Turing were different, but they characterised the same group of processes.

The **Church-Turing thesis** is that any adequate definition of an algorithm will prove equivalent in this way to the definitions provided by Church and Turing. Since the idea of "adequate" is not formally precise, the Church-Turing thesis is not mathematically provable. However, in practice other definitions of "algorithm" offered since Church and Turing, by for example, Post (1943), have proved equivalent to Church and Turing's versions in exactly the way that the Church-Turing thesis predicts. So most computer scientists are happy to accept that these definitions of "algorithm" capture what is important for them about this word.

Both Church and Turing realised that trying to characterise algorithms in terms of what could be said in English was a waste of time. Instead, they both invented different formal languages in which algorithms could be more clearly expressed. In addition, both men provided a series of rules for manipulating this formal language in a set manner. An algorithm was defined by both men as a procedure that could be expressed in their chosen language. However, the language that each chose was very different, and the differences were the foundation for the later procedural-declarative split in programming.

Turing's idea was that an algorithm could be represented as a series of instructions that could be executed by a rather simple machine, that later became known as a **Turing Machine** (figure 1.1). A Turing machine consists of three components.

1. An endless stream of tape segmented into an infinite number of adjacent squares. Some of these squares may have symbols on them.

2. A mechanical head that positions itself over a square and which can read the symbol on that square or overwrite it. The head can also move to the square to the left of the square it is currently over or to the square to the right.

3. A program or series of instructions that tell the mechanical head what to do. It is assumed that a Turing machine is always in an internal state. These states are usually identified by the natural numbers 0,1,2, 3.... An instruction has the form

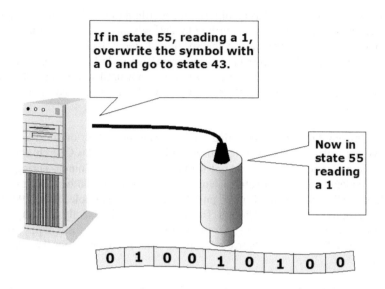

Figure 1.1 A Turing Machine Executing a Program Instruction

If in state n, reading symbol S_j, then execute action A_k and jump to state q_l.

Action A_k could be the action of halting (the computation ends), or of overwriting the scanned symbol by another symbol or of moving to the left adjacent square or the right adjacent square. A program for a Turing machine is a set S of instructions or quadruples $<n, s_j, a_k, q_l>$ such that if $<n, s_j, a_k, q_l> \in$ S and $<n, s_j, a_k', q_l'> \in$ S, then $a_k = a_k'$ and $q_l = q_l'$ (i.e. there are no conflicting instructions about what the machine should doing any given situation). The machine halts when it is reading symbol s_j in state n where for all a_k and for all q_l, $<n, s_j, a_k, q_l> \notin$ S (i.e. the machine has no instructions about what to do when reading symbol s_j in state n).

Turing's machine contains no restrictions on the number of symbols it can read or print, but only two are necessary - conventionally they are 0 and 1. To set a Turing machine running, the machine is started in its lowest state, scanning the leftmost of a series of 0s and 1s; this series represents the input to the machine. The output is what is left on the tape when the machine halts. An algorithm is defined as any terminating procedure that a Turing machine can be programmed to perform.

Turing's approach is easily appreciated by anybody with a simple working knowledge of the architecture of a computer. The states of the Turing machine correspond to the line numbers of a conventional program; the action of jumping to a new state is mirrored in the JUMP of assembly language. The endless tape is just a model of the bounded memory of the computer and the head of the Turing

4

machine becomes the CPU of the digital computer. When World War II began a few years after Turing published his paper on the Turing machine, there was a demand for real computing engines that could tackle the difficult tasks of cracking enemy codes and calculating bomb and shell trajectories. Turing's pencil-and-paper creation provided a blueprint for engineers, and consequently became immensely influential in the design of the modern digital computer.

Across the Atlantic in America, Church had very different ideas. For many years, mathematicians had worked with the idea of a **function**. Put simply, a function is a mathematical object that receives one or more inputs and delivers an output. Algorithms too, receive inputs and deliver an output, so it is natural to consider that algorithms are a subclass of the class of functions. Usually when mathematicians wish to explain the properties of a function, they use equations to do it. Here is an equation that converts Fahrenheit to Centigrade.

$$C = 5/9 \times (F - 32)$$

We can easily distil a procedure from this equation that reads.

To convert Fahrenheit to Centigrade, subtract 32 from Fahrenheit and multiply by 5/9.

A more complex example comes from Boyle's Law, which relates the pressure of a confined gas to the volume it occupies and its temperature. According to Boyle's Law, if a confined gas is kept at pressure P_1, occupying volume V_1 at temperature T_1, and then the gas has its pressure, volume or temperature changed so that it then has pressure P_2, volume V_2 and temperature T_2, the change will satisfy the equation.

$$(P_1 \times V_1) / T_1 = (P_2 \times V_2) / T_2$$

So, from Boyle's Law, it is possible to construct a function that given the old temperature of the gas, its pressure and volume, and the new pressure and volume, will produce as output the new temperature. The equation is

$$T_2 = (P_2 \times V_2 \times T_1) / (P_1 \times V_1)$$

Again, we could easily distil a procedure from this equation. Here is one.

To calculate T_2, first multiply P_1 by V_1 to give a result R. Then multiply P_2 by V_2 by T_1 to give a result S. Then divide S by R.

However, we could also distil this procedure.

To calculate T_2, first multiply P_2 by V_2 by T_1 to give a result S. Then multiply P_1 by V_1 to give a result R. Then divide S by R.

5

The result is the same whichever procedure we choose. The point about calculations involving Boyle's Law is that they are algorithmic or mechanical, whichever order we choose to do them in, and we should always get the same result. This gives another way of looking at algorithms. *Rather than identify an algorithm with a procedure consisting of a fixed series of steps, we can think of an algorithm as a function that can be characterised in a certain way.* What marks the function as computable is not that the way we compute with it is predetermined (because in the case of Boyle's Law this is not true), but the fact in that the function can be described in logical and mathematical terms.

This insight is the beginning of functional programming. It captures an important idea, which is that a program can be viewed as more than just a series of commands to a computer. A program can be viewed as a mathematical description of an algorithm: a description, which, as a bonus, can also be executed by the computer. In computing this is known as an **executable specification**.

Nevertheless, things are not so simple. For though all algorithms can be represented as functions, not all functions are algorithms. Consider this function over the natural numbers.

$(f n)$ = *1 if there are n successive 7s in the decimal expansion of* π.
  0 otherwise

This describes a function, but not one we can easily use to compute because the decimal expansion of π is infinitely long.   If we wanted to compute the value of $(f$ 1000$)$ we would have to search for 1000 successive 7s in the decimal expansion of π. So far 1000 successive 7s have not been detected in the decimal expansion of π, but this does not mean that they are not there. At best, all we can do is expand π looking for 1000 successive 7s and this may take forever. However the concept of an algorithm requires a terminating procedure that is guaranteed to return a definite answer. Plainly, the function f does not define any such procedure. f is a **non-computable** function.

Once we begin to look for non-computable functions, they swarm in number. Some are bizarre, for example the function that maps a person to 1 if his maternal grandfather hated boiled eggs is still a function (though a queer one); but obviously there is no algorithm for determining one's ancestors' egg-eating habits. The problem is that ordinary language allows us to concoct functions in a very unrestricted way. If the class of computable functions, to which algorithms correspond, is to be isolated from the broader class of functions as a whole, we need a special language and vocabulary to do it.

This is what Church provided in devising the **lambda calculus**[2] as a notation for describing computable functions. Along with this formalism, Church gave a

---

[2] Which we study in chapter 14 of this book

precise set of rules for reasoning with and for simplifying expressions of this notation. To perform a computation, in Church's terms, was to apply a function to an input, and to derive a result. By formally stating the rules for deriving results, Church defined a model of computability. An algorithm was just a computable function. A computable function was an expression that could be written in the lambda calculus so that when it was supplied an input (again written in lambda calculus), by a fixed and finite series of applications of the rules of lambda calculus, an expression could be derived which could be simplified no further and which represented the solution.

In contrasting the approaches of Turing and Church, it is easy to see why Turing, rather than Church, was immediately influential in shaping the course of computing. Turing provided an actual model of a computing engine. Church's definition of computability gave little clue as to how the lambda calculus was to be implemented. Moreover, some of Church's constructions, like his representation of the natural numbers as lambda expressions, were very convoluted. Here, for example, is Barendregt's representation of 2 in pure lambda calculus.

$$(((\lambda x\,(\lambda y\,(\lambda z\,((z\,x)\,y)))) \,(\lambda x\,(\lambda y\,y)))$$
$$(((\lambda x\,(\lambda y\,(\lambda z\,((z\,x)\,y)))) \,(\lambda x\,(\lambda y\,y)))\,(\lambda x\,x)))$$

The example is a little unfair, because functional programming languages do not use pure lambda calculus to represent numbers. However, it is easy to understand why an observer would conclude that Church's definition of computability was of no practical use in computer science. Not until the '60s did computer scientists begin to explore the consequences of applying Church's ideas. In the intervening 20 years, engineers and programmers built their work on the paradigm given by Turing. This was to be fateful in the development of programming as a discipline.

1.3 The American Experience

When World War II ended, America emerged as the richest and most powerful nation on the planet, producing at one point 40% of the world's GDP. Computer engineering gravitated naturally to a country that was rich in émigré scientists and natural resources. Consequently the early years of functional programming belong to America.

These early years are the early years of the American work into **Lisp**. Lisp was the offspring of an intellectual marriage conducted by John McCarthy between Church's work on the lambda calculus and an earlier language called **IPL** (Information Processing Language) that was invented by two American scientists Newell and Simon. Newell and Simon were pioneering the study of automated deduction and needed a flexible language in which to program the computer to simulate human thought. Conventional languages require all information to be predeclared in variables or arrays of fixed size. What Newell and Simon wanted

7

was a language in which structures could be dynamically built up and broken down in response to the intellectual requirements of the program. They struck upon the idea of using the list as the fundamental data structure on which to organise their procedures.

The basic idea is that, whenever a piece of information is stored in memory, additional information should be stored with it telling where to find the next (associated) piece of information. In this way the entire memory could be organised like a long string of beads, but with the individual beads of the string stored in arbitrary locations. "Nextness" was not determined by physical propinquity but by an address, or pointer, stored with each item, showing where the associated item was located. Then a bead could be added to a string or omitted from a string simply by changing a pair of addresses, without disturbing the rest of the memory.[3]

In fact, the pair consisting of an item of a list and the pointer to the address where the next item is stored is known as a **cons cell pair**. Functional programming languages were to copy IPL in making lists the central data structure in programming. The pointer representation of Newell and Simon is the machine basis of the cons representation of a list discussed in chapter 4.

About that time, John McCarthy, then a young mathematician at MIT, was doing preliminary work on a program called 'Advice Taker' that would allow a computer to receive instructions in English. McCarthy knew about IPL and had read Church's work. McCarthy observed that many computable functions could be defined by equations, but only by equations that mentioned that function on both sides of the = sign. One simple example is the function.

$(factorial\ 0) = 1$
$(factorial\ n) = n \times (factorial\ n\text{-}1)$ where $n > 0$

These equations are not circular (unlike $(factorial\ n) = (factorial\ n)$) because they enable the calculation of a factorial by the calculation of the factorial of the number preceding it. Eventually the simplest case (0) is reached and the computation ends. Such functions are called **recursive** and in McCarthy's new language, recursion was the principal means of defining computable functions. McCarthy also borrowed on use of lists by IPL. But he improved on IPL by adding a reclamation program that allowed the computer to reclaim memory when it was running short, by marking out the symbol structures that the computer no longer needed. This process became known as **garbage collection**.

The resulting language, called **Lisp**[4] (McCarthy 1960), was remarkable. Lisp programs were themselves written as lists of symbols, which meant that Lisp

---

[3] Simon (1991), p 212.
[4] Short for LISt Processing Language.

programs could be written which would write Lisp programs. A Lisp program could even modify itself while it was running, or receive as part of its input some other Lisp program and apply it to another part of its input.[5]

Lisp freed the programmer from having to consider the architecture of the computer. By allowing the programmer to define algorithms as functions, and abstracting away from the need to consider allocating or reclaiming memory, Lisp left the programmer free to work on the problems that interested him.

To give an analogy, Lisp was transparent as regards the architecture of the machine on which it ran: writing Lisp code was like looking at the problem through a clear window. Writing in a procedural language like assembler requires not only thinking about the problem, but also thinking about the architecture of the underlying machine which is explicit in assembly language. Looking at a problem through assembler is like looking at it through a stained or dirty window, or trying to see to the bottom of a pond on which there is a lot of surface glare and reflection.

So it turned out that the very feature of functional programming that kept Church's ideas in the shadow of Turing's, that is the lack of a specific machine for executing computations, was also its greatest strength. But it was strength purchased at a high price. The structure of a procedural language is dictated by the design of the digital computer, which works by executing a series of commands and shifting data from one address to another. In a programming language like assembler, which reflects the internal architecture of the computer, programs are likely to run quickly. In contrast, a language that ignores the architecture of the machine needs a very sophisticated compiler to relate the language to the computer.

In the early years of Lisp, such sophisticated compilers did not exist. Moreover the garbage collection process was itself expensive, causing the computer to hang for vital seconds while memory was reclaimed. Even the list processing feature, one of the most important ideas to come from computer science, was costly because a lot of the computer's memory was tied up in storing pointers from one address to the next. Functional programming acquired an immediate reputation for inefficiency that confined it to research labs for another 20 years. In the value scales of the '60s, when machines were slow and CPU time was expensive, inefficiency was a serious charge.

By the early '70s, Lisp programmers recognised that the performance lag in Lisp programs was a serious bother, and that the foundation of the problem was the distance of the architecture of the computer from the actual Lisp. Clever compilation was one answer and this was done with versions of Lisp like

---

[5] This is called **higher-order programming** and was implicit in Church's lambda calculus; we study this technique in chapter 6.

MacLisp (developed for the DEC-10 mainframe); but another was to design the architecture of the machine around the Lisp language. These machines became famous as the **Lisp machines**.

In the context of their times, the Lisp machines were startlingly innovative, and they introduced many ideas that have since become part of high street computing; such as windows and the mouse (developed for the Xerox Lisp machine). The first serious Lisp machine was **CADR,** which anticipated the personal computer years before the IBM XT.[6] High tech companies like Symbolics and Lisp Machines Incorporated mushroomed around research into Lisp machines and larger companies like Xerox and Texas Instruments also fielded their own Lisp machines.

But Lisp machines were in the end to fail. At the time of writing, no manufacturer is engaged in the production of Lisp machines. Ironically, these machines were to operate to the detriment of the spread of Lisp as a commonly used programming language. By choosing to work on Lisp machines, whose cost confined their use to favoured researchers in well-funded laboratories, the Lisp machine community isolated their work from mainstream computing. Ordinary programmers could not afford to run programs that used 10Mb of memory, when 1Mb was seen as a lot. While Lispers worked in ivory towers, always looking to the future, procedural programmers working in **C** (another product of the '70s) concentrated on developing programs that ran on shoebox machines. By directing their efforts to standard computer architecture, the procedural programmers established a near unchallengeable dominance on conventional machines.

Stimulated by the investment of billions of dollars that the Lisp machine vendors did not have, these shoeboxes were eventually to surpass the performance of the dedicated Lisp machine. By 1990, conventional workstations running efficient Lisp compilers could equal the performance of Lisp machines. By 1996, the humble PC could rival the performance of the workstation. Lisp machine vendors went bankrupt.

Lisp itself survived and in 1984 Lisp was standardised into **Common Lisp**. This had the advantage of providing a common language standard for Lisp implementers to work with, and one that was largely downwards compatible with several existing Lisp dialects. The disadvantages were that the resulting language was very large and many of the bad features of Lisp, that McCarthy himself later acknowledged were in the language, were frozen in the Common Lisp language definition. Across the Atlantic, British computer scientists like David Turner were finding fault with Lisp and British computer science was making its own contribution to the history of functional programming.

---

[6] At the top of CADR's microcode listing was a quote from the rock opera *Tommy* "Here comes a man to bring you a machine all of your own".

1.4 The British Experience

One of the earliest workers in functional programming this side of the Atlantic was Peter Landin who in 1964 published a paper describing a method for mechanically evaluating lambda calculus expressions on a computer. The design, called the **SECD machine** (short for Stack-Environment-Control-Dump), examined in chapter 24, influenced many later compilation strategies, including the **Functional Abstract Machine** (Cardelli, 1983) that was used to compile Standard ML.

Lisp was designed as a functional language that supported a model of computation called **eager evaluation**. In eager evaluation, all the inputs to a function are first evaluated before the function is set to work computing the final answer. Sometimes this is not a sensible strategy; a simple example is the problem of computing $f(factorial(100))$, where f is defined as $f(n) = 0$. Since f always returns 0, no matter what the input, computing the value of *(factorial* 100) is a waste of time. In an eager language like Lisp, *(factorial* 100) would be computed, but in a language that uses **lazy evaluation** it might not. The defining characteristic of lazy evaluation is *procrastination* - only evaluate when you have to. **SASL**, developed by David Turner (1976, 1979), was a functional programming language that was driven by lazy evaluation.

Automated deduction had already provided an important input into functional programming through Newell and Simon's work on IPL. In 1979, it provided another. In that year Milner, Gordon and Wadsworth published their work with the **Edinburgh LCF** marking an important development in both functional programming and automated reasoning. In 1976, Milner had published a paper describing how functional programs could be proved free of **type errors** in a way that was entirely mechanical. A type error is an error that arises when a function is applied to an input whose type is unsuitable (the multiplication of two strings is an example).

To accomplish this, Milner used the **unification algorithm,** studied here in chapter 25, and developed for automated reasoning by Robinson in 1965. Using Milner's algorithm (called the $\mathcal{W}^e$ algorithm), a proof that a program was free from type errors could be executed by a computer. This was an important advance in the production of reliable software and in their 1979 publication, Milner, Gordon and Wadsworth introduced the first functional programming language to incorporate this new technology - the Edinburgh MetaLanguage or **Edinburgh ML**. Since Edinburgh ML, nearly every new functional programming language has incorporated some form of type checking and these languages form the class of what is called **statically typed languages**. .

Edinburgh ML became upgraded and standardised as **Standard ML**. An important addition to the upgraded version was **pattern matching**, which was an old idea that went back as far as **SNOBOL** that was invented in Bell Labs in

1962. SNOBOL was a text processing language that allowed the programmer to isolate pieces of text by searching for patterns. Since all functional languages exploit the use of lists, it is much easier to use patterns to isolate the needed elements than to write functions which search for them. The use of **pattern-directed programming** is common in functional programming today and is used throughout this book.

The '80s in Britain were a very fertile time for the implementation of new models for compiling functional languages. This area is rather outside the ambit of this book, but we shall mention David Turner's (1979) paper, which suggested that **combinatory logic** could be used to implement functional languages as an alternative to lambda calculus. In many ways, combinators are even simpler than lambda calculus. Following Turner, scientists experimented with new models for compiling functional programming languages; **combinators, supercombinators, graph reduction**, and **dataflow machines** were researched in this decade. The result was that the performance gap between functional and procedural languages was narrowed in that decade.

But while implementers of functional languages poured their efforts into building better compilers and new functional programming languages such as Haskell, procedural programming proceeded to capitalise on its lead by expanding into new application areas. An important step in the spread of the procedural paradigm was the invention of the language **C** by Dennis Ritchie and Ken Thompson in 1973. Ritchie and Thompson were working in Bell labs on the first release of the **UNIX** operating system and they needed a fast, portable programming language that was close to assembler but not tied to specific machines. They designed C - a functional programmer's bad dream. Riddled with assignments, and clinging close to the architecture of the computer, C programs run extremely quickly. The success of the UNIX operating system allowed C to spread to nearly every computer, and its good performance meant that programmers took it up as the language of choice when writing CPU-intensive programs for machines of limited power.

The success of the procedural paradigm at a time when machines were too slow to support the functional approach, left computing with a culture that is recognisably procedural. UNIX and **Windows** are built on the foundations of C, and the shell languages that support these systems are recognisably procedural. The **X-windows** system is likewise C-based and the paradigms for building graphical user interfaces are based on procedural languages like **Visual Basic**. **Java** has emerged as a leading language for building Internet applications, and its antecedents are C and **C++.** The 21st century programmer expects access to graphical interface builders, numerical packages, debugging tools, Internet capability, electronic mail, multi-user capability, sound and graphics to be within reach inside his chosen medium. At the end of the twentieth century, functional languages, for all their mathematical sophistication, still presented the user with a cursor and a command line that was recognisably '70s in style.

Luckily in the first decade of the twenty-first century, much ground was made up outside of academia. The creation of **Python** (van Rossum, 1990) provided a language which, if not purely functional, had a core and approach that was recognisably functional and a syntax that was more immediately appealing than Lisp. In contrast to Lisp and other functional languages, Python has a well-supported library with a large and active commercial community and a great deal of support amongst service providers.

In 2007, Rich Hickey introduced **Clojure** which was viewed by many as an overdue modernisation of Lisp. Clojure offered tight integration of a Lisp-like language to **Java** and Java libraries and compilation into the **Java Virtual Machine.** In addition, Hickey developed fast vector manipulation algorithms and provision for multiprocessing which made Clojure a hit for many users. Consequently many programmers rediscovered the power of Lisp through working with Clojure.

The result is that functional programming has experienced something of a renaissance in the opening years of the twenty-first century and the future of the discipline looks bright. It is fairly certain, as the new multiprocessor machines come into common usage, that the clean computational model of functional programming will offer one of the best ways of utilising this power without becoming trapped in the complexities of assignments.

1.5 The Forerunners of Shen: SEQUEL

The history of Shen began in 1989, when I was working as a research assistant at the LFCS in Edinburgh. At that time, I worked in Lisp, and to improve my productivity, I wrote a 700 line Lisp program which translated pattern-directed functional code into reasonably efficient Lisp.

While cycling in the Lake district in the spring of 1990, I had the insight that since type checking was inherently deductive in nature, the type discipline of a language could be specified as a series of deduction rules. Using the techniques of high-performance theorem-proving, these rules could be compiled down into an efficient type checker. The type-discipline would be free from the procedural baggage of low-level encoding and presented in a form that was clear, concise, and accessible to experimentation and extension by researchers in type theory. This was a bold conception that seemed eminently reasonable, but which in fact took a further 15 years of development to realise completely.

The prototype development was the language SEQUEL (**SEQUE**nt processing **Language**), written in Lisp and introduced publicly in 1992 and to the International Joint Conference on Artificial Intelligence in 1993. SEQUEL anticipated many of the features of Shen, in particular the use of Gentzen's sequent notation to formulate the type rules. SEQUEL actually contained the type theory for a substantial portion of Common Lisp (over 300 Common Lisp system functions were represented in SEQUEL) necessitating a sizeable source code program of more than 23,000 lines. SEQUEL was not only designed to support type secure Common Lisp programming, it was also supposed to support direct encoding of theorem-provers by giving the user the power to enter logic rules in sequent notation to the SEQUEL system.

SEQUEL sustained Andrew Adams's (1994) reimplementation INDUCT of the Boyer-Moore theorem-prover. His M.Sc. project was written in 6,000 lines of SEQUEL, and generated nearly 30,000 lines of Common Lisp, and gained him a distinction. In 1993, state-of-the-art was a SPARC II, so power was limited. Loading and type checking INDUCT took several minutes.

SEQUEL was a compromise of the ideals of deductive typing for several reasons.

1. The sequent compiler was inefficient.
2. Since SEQUEL was heavily configured to support Common Lisp, the language was not consistent with lambda calculus (since Common Lisp does not support lambda calculus features like currying and partial applications).
3. SEQUEL inherited case-insensitivity from Common Lisp and the use of the empty list NIL to mean false.
4. SEQUEL lacked a formal semantics.
5. SEQUEL also lacked a proof of type correctness.

Over ten years and two countries all these problems were eliminated.

Until 1996, SEQUEL stayed in operation with minor amendments. Most of my creative time from 1993-1996 was spent writing poetry. SEQUEL continued to support final year projects, but late 1996, I returned to computer science research.

1.6 The Forerunners of Shen: Qi

The first modest change was to introduce case-sensitivity and the use of proper booleans in place of T and NIL. Large parts of the implementation were rewritten, reducing the source code by several thousand lines. In 1998 overloading in SEQUEL was dropped and the entire list of function types was placed on a hash table. This was in a sense a move away from Lisp and towards a cleaner model and a smaller language. The plus was the elimination of 10,000 lines of code.

In late 1997, I applied for three years unpaid leave from my job as a lecturer in order to concentrate on finishing this work. One year was granted, and from 1998 to 1999 a lot of work was expended in providing the new language with a formal type theory. After a false start, the current type theory was evolved in 1999 and the semantics was developed between 1999 and 2000.

14

During that same period, a lot of work was done in testing whether deductive typing was really a practical option. Early results were not encouraging, 30 line programs could take as many seconds to type check. The goals of deductive typing - complete declarative specification and a type checking procedure that was conceptually distinct from the rules that drove it - meant that performance-enhancing hardwired hacks were not allowed. Eventually a technology was developed and the performance benchmarks showed that a 166MHz Pentium under CLisp could just about run the system. In 2020, 4.7 GHz machines are on sale, which make these old challenges into programming molehills.[7]

The implementation went through two complete rewrites. The first rewrite was very thoroughgoing and introduced partial applications and currying into the language, making it lambda calculus consistent.

As a Taoist, feeling the need for a name for the new implementation, I called it *Qi* – the name for the life-force in Taoism.

In 2001 a robust version of a compiler-compiler (first devised by my colleague Dr Gyuri Lajos) was built and used to encode some of the complex parsing routines needed in Qi. This was the compiler-compiler **Qi-YACC** which was later used in Qi.

In 2002 I left the UK for America bearing Qi 1.4 with me. Qi 1.4 was used to build almost the whole of Qi 2.0 which was a clean rebuild of the whole system. Qi 2.0 was never released however, because of an improvement to the type checking algorithm $\mathcal{T}$ used in Qi 1.4.

In 2003, I developed the experimental algorithm $\mathcal{T}*$ and type checking gained a factor of 7 speedup over 1.4. In late 2003 I put the finishing touches on a correctness proof for the type theory and $\mathcal{T}$ and $\mathcal{T}*$. In 2003 Qi won me the Promising Inventor Award from the State University of New York. Carl Shapiro, currently of Google, attended my functional programming class at Stony Brook that same year. He was to exert a significant influence on development of Qi.

In 2004, Qi 2.0 was revised to work with $\mathcal{T}*$ and the result was Qi 3.2. After some more debugging and revisions, Qi 4.0 emerged. Carl's interest in SEQUEL made me revisit my old work. In 2005 I constructed a new model for compiling Horn clauses called the **Abstract Unification Machine**. The AUM compiled Prolog into virtual machine instructions for a functional language. AUM

---

[7] It is worth noticing though, that a 166MHz Pentium is about the slowest machine that could feasibly run Qi 1.4 and that this machine appeared about 1997. Therefore the goals of deductive typing that were formulated in my 1990 paper were about seven years short of having the technology they needed to work.

technology gave 100 KLIPS under CLisp and 400 KLIPS under the faster CMU Lisp and quadrupled the speed of the type checker. The beta version, Qi 5.0, used prototype AUM technology. Qi 6.1, which used the AUM, again improved performance.

Qi 6.1 was also the first version of Qi to use the **preclude** and **include** commands for managing large type theories. Qi 6.1 was released in April 2005, along with the web publication of *Functional Programming in Qi* and at the same time as the creation of **Lambda Associates**. At 6,500 lines of machine-generated Lisp, Qi 6.1 was three times smaller than the SEQUEL of 1993 and was placed online in April 2005.

The appearance of Qi was swiftly followed by a serious illness that laid me up for 2006 and most of 2007. Following a partial recovery in 2008, a factorising version of the Qi compiler was introduced which made Qi competitive with the fastest hand-compiled Lisp code.[8] The revised language, Qi II, corresponding to the text *Functional Programming in Qi* was released in 2008.

1.7 Shen

The chain of events that precipitated Shen began with an invitation to address the European Conference on Lisp in Milan in 2009. The invitation came about because the invited speaker, Kent Pitman, had been himself taken ill with cancer which meant, understandably, that he had to withdraw. I was invited to take his place.

Ironically I was ill too and at first declined, since I was healing at that time. But the organiser was frantic and I finally accepted. My address proposed a language like Qi but based on a primitive instruction set that was so small that it could be translated onto almost any platform. Qi had been implemented in Common Lisp, which has over 700 system functions. But of that large number, Qi only used 118 system functions in its implementation.

I estimated that Qi could be implemented in an even smaller instruction set no more than 50 primitive functions, and that they should be so carefully chosen as to be easily implemented and widely portable. This instruction set defined a very simple Lisp, closer in spirit to Lisp 1.5, the original Lisp from which the gargantuan Common Lisp descended. This micro-Lisp was later to be called **Kλ**.

This idea was the subject of my talk at the conference, but it was ignored since my criticisms of Common Lisp were not well received. Feeling I was wasting my time, I left computer science in 2009 and journeyed to India. Shen therefore

---

[8] See section 15.6.

remained a dream until my partner Dr Pamesa called me back and asked that I complete the work. She died before this was done.

In 2010 an appeal was launched to fund this research and happily it succeeded. Armed with some means of subsistence, I returned to designing and building the new implementation during 2011. Eventually what emerged in September 2011 was a clean, portable language under a $free license, implemented initially in 43 primitive Kλ instructions running under Common Lisp. The new language was named *Shen*, the highest form of energy in Taoism and the Chinese for *spirit*.

Shen introduced quite a number of features not found in Qi; including string and vector handling through pattern matching, the capacity to read streams from non-text files through an 8 bit reader and an advanced and powerful macro system. Designed for portability, Shen was slower than Qi[9] which was optimised for Lisp, but vindicated itself rapidly and within 18 months Shen had been ported to Common Lisp, Scheme, Clojure, JavaScript, Java, Python, JVM and Ruby. During this process Kλ acquired four more primitives.

The first edition of this book was written during the first part of 2012 and was a fairly hasty rehash of *Functional Programming in Qi*, adapted to meet the needs of the new language standard. The resulting text was accurate, but rather improvised during a period when I was in and out of clinics.

Following an improvement in 2013, I decided to rewrite the text to cover more carefully the details of Shen and to impart more flow and depth to the treatment of the language. The more leisured approach and the value of being able to see the results of the early work into Shen allowed me make additions and improvement to the work. The second edition was published in 2014.

Later that same year, I revised two chapters in the second edition, focusing on the practical techniques for controlling type checking and the relation between Shen and languages like SML. These changes eventually made their way into the third edition which was published in 2015.

In 2018, Neal Alexander raised an interesting issue of the definition of polyadic type operators which led me to add a new section on list handling in sequent calculus and revise some of the Shen kernel code. Since dependent types are something of a hot topic, I also added a section on this subject. In the hot summer of 2018, during a spell of insomnia, I created a version of Shen YACC that generated statically typable code and this led to a new chapter. Another new chapter came from a revised version of model checking (first discussed in the second edition).

---

[9] This difference in performance was made up in the later versions of Shen.

From 2019-2021, I completely revised the code for the entire kernel introducing a new Prolog and YACC compiler. These changes were substantial enough to warrant a fourth edition in 2021.

Further Reading

A discussion of the Turing machine and its properties is found in Boolos, Burgess and Jeffrey (2002). The lambda calculus is discussed in chapter 14 of this book, and references can be found at the end of that chapter. McCarthy (1960) describes the genesis of Lisp. Backus (1978), in his famous Turing award lecture, argues for the declarative paradigm, criticising imperative languages as "fat and weak". Turner (1982) develops the case for functional programming. Gabriel (1990) has an interesting discussion about why declarative programming (in the shape of Lisp) has not displaced the procedural paradigm. Introductions to functional programming and functional programming theory can be found in Bird and Wadler (1998) and Field and Harrison (1988). Introductions to Lisp are provided in Winston and Horn (1989) and Schapiro (1986). Abelson's and Sussmann (1996) is an excellent introduction to functional programming in Scheme - a dialect of Lisp. Shrobe (1988) is a good review of the history of the Lisp machines just before their demise. Wikstrom (1987) and Paulson (1996) introduce SML. An overview of Miranda^{TM} is given in Turner (1990) and Thompson (1995) is a book length introduction to Miranda^{TM}. **Haskell** from the University of Glasgow is a recent and popular addition to the functional programming family, Thompson (1999) is a good introduction.

Tarver (1990) reviews some of the earliest thoughts that led to SEQUEL. Tarver (1993) was an early principal publication of this approach and Tarver (2008) describes Qi.

Web Sites

The life and work of Alan Turing is beautifully presented in a web site dedicated to that purpose; Andrew Hodges' The Alan Turing Home Page (http://www.turing.org.uk/turing/) contains a wealth of information. The University of Arizona (http://www.math.arizona.edu/~dsl/tmachine.htm) provides links to several sites containing downloadable software and applets for simulating Turing machines. http://cm.bell-labs.com/cm/cs/who/dmr/chist.html offers an account of the development of C. The Association of Lisp Users (http://www.lisp.org/table/contents.htm) provides an extensive web site for Internet sources on Lisp including links to original papers on the history of Lisp. New Jersey SML offers a free high-performance ML (http://www.smlnj.org/). http://www.haskell.org is the web address for all things Haskell.

www.lambdassociates.org was the web site for Qi and the site is now archived. A 2008 address explaining Qi was recorded as an audio file http://www.lambdassociates.org/blog/l21.wmv. My 2009 address in Italy was postwritten and appears in Appendix C and this explains the motivation for Shen.

Part I

The Core Language

2 Starting Shen

2.1 Starting Up

If Shen has been configured according to the installation instructions, then the top level looks similar to figure 2.1

```
Shen, copyright (C) 2010-2021 Mark Tarver
Shen Language Foundation, version 30
running under Common Lisp, implementation: SBCL
port 3.1 ported by Mark Tarver

(0-)
```

Figure 2.1 The Shen top level

The italicised portions may vary according to release and platform. The figure shows the SBCL implementation of Shen 30; should you be using another platform or a different version, the italicised text may be different.

The integer prompt shows that you are in the **read-evaluate-print loop** (REPL). Functional programming languages interact with the user at this level. The purpose of this loop is to receive the expressions that you enter, to evaluate them, and to print a response.[10]   These expressions can be of various kinds.   The simplest expressions that Shen evaluates are the **self-evaluating expressions** that evaluate to themselves. There are four kinds of self-evaluating expression.

1. **Numbers:** this includes integers (-3, 78, 45), floating point numbers (2.89, -0.7) and e-numbers (12.6e14).
2. **Symbols:** this includes any unbroken series of symbols (except booleans, numbers, and strings) such as Mynameisjack, catch22.
3. **Booleans:** true and false.
4. **Strings:** a string is any series of symbols enclosed between a pair of double quotes such as "my name is jack", "catch 22".   Notice that strings permit spaces whereas symbols do not.

---

[10] The symbol ^ within any input, followed by carriage return, will abort the current line input.

An expression is evaluated by typing it to the Shen top level and hitting the return key. Figure 2.2 shows some self-evaluating expressions entered to Shen.

```
(0-) 9
9

(1-) "foobar"
"foobar"

(2-) hello
hello
```

Figure 2.2 Some self-evaluating expressions typed to the top level

Every time an expression is evaluated, the Shen top prompt reappears with an integer in parentheses which is the input number.

2.2 Applying Functions

Since typing self-evaluating expressions is not an exciting pastime, we will consider how to apply functions to inputs in Shen. There are three principal ways of writing functional expressions.

1. **Infix**; where the sign for the function comes between the bound variables. This is the usual practice in arithmetic where we write "2 – 1"; the minus sign comes between the "2" and the "1".

2. **Prefix**; the sign comes before the bound variables. So in prefix "2 – 1" would be written "- 2 1".

3. **Postfix**; the sign comes after the bound variables. So in postfix "2 – 1" would be written "2 1 –".

Shen functions are usually written in prefix form.[11] To apply a function f to inputs $x_1,...,x_n$, we enter $(f\ x_1,..,x_n)$ (figure 2.3).

```
(0-) (+ 1 2)
3

(1-) (+ (* 3 4) (+ 1 1))
14
```

Figure 2.3 Some simple applications typed to the top level

---

[11] However functions can be written to Shen in infix form using macros (see chapter 10).

21

There are several ways of evaluating expressions in functional programming languages; one widely used model is **applicative order evaluation**, which is the one Shen usually uses. The evaluation procedure of applicative order evaluation is to first evaluate, from left to right, $x_1,..,x_n$ before applying f to the results of this evaluation.

Thus in figure 2.3, Shen first evaluates (* 3 4) to 12 and then (+ 1 1) to 2 before adding the two together. The result 14 is the **normal form** of the expression (+ (* 3 4) (+ 1 1)); that is, the result produced when the evaluation has completed itself without any error being raised. The **arity** of a function is the number of inputs it is designed to receive. In the case of * and + this is 2, and these are referred to as **2-place** functions. A function like + that is built in to Shen is a **system function**.

2.3 Repeating Evaluations

Typing ! followed by an integer n will repeat the input whose input number is n. !! repeats the last input. ! followed by a symbol s will repeat the last input $(f x_1,.., x_n)$ where s is a prefix of f (figure 2.4).

```
(0-) (+ 5.6 9.0)
14.6

(1-) !+
(+ 5.6 9.0)
14.6

(2-) !!
(+ 5.6 9.0)
14.6
```

Figure 2.4 Using ! to repeat evaluations

The % command will print (without evaluating) every previous expression whose prefix matches what follows %. % on its own will print off all functional expressions typed to the top level since the session began. Where n is a natural number, %n will print off the nth expression typed to the top level since logging in to Shen.

```
(3-) %+
0. (+ 5.6 9.0)
1. (+ 5.6 9.0)
2. (+ 5.6 9.0)
```

Figure 2.5 Using % to print past inputs

2.4 Strict and Non-Strict Evaluation

All computer languages have some provision for detecting conditions operating within the program and then diverting the control of the program depending on whether these conditions are realised. The classic example is the conditional expression *if ... then ... else ...* which in one form or another is found in every computer language. Use of conditional expressions requires the use of **boolean expressions**, where a boolean expression is one that evaluates to either true or false. The *if ... then .. else ...* construction is found in Shen as a 3-place function if that receives

1. A boolean expression x.
2. An expression y whose normal form is returned if x evaluates to true.
3. An expression z whose normal form is returned if x evaluates to false.

Though this is all quite simple, it is important to know that conditional expressions are not evaluated using applicative order evaluation. The reason why is easily brought out by example. The 2-place function = returns true if the normal forms of its two inputs are the same, and false if are they are different. Suppose we evaluate (if (= 1 0) (* 3 4) 3) by applicative order evaluation.

(if (= 1 0) (* 3 4) 3)
$\Rightarrow$ (if false (* 3 4) 3)
$\Rightarrow$ (if false 12 3)
$\Rightarrow$ 3

The reduction of (* 3 4) to 12 in the penultimate step is quite unnecessary, because the result of evaluating (if false (* 3 4) 3) cannot depend on the evaluation of (* 3 4). A better evaluation strategy evaluates (= 1 0) to its normal form, and then evaluates the appropriate expression.

This latter form of evaluation is an example of **non-strict evaluation.** A strict evaluation strategy requires that every input to a function to be evaluated before the function is applied to the results. In a non-strict evaluation strategy, it is possible to return a normal form from an expression x even when there is a subexpression of x that has no normal form. The expression (if (= 1 0) (+ a a) no) evaluates to no in Shen, though the evaluation of (+ a a) will raise an error.

The cases function allows the concise expression of nested 'if's; for instance for any *a b c d* the expression (if *a b* (if *c d e*)) can be written as

(cases *a b*
      c d
         true *e*)

If no cases apply an error is raised.

if is one of the **primitive functions** of Kλ from which Shen is built (all the rest being definable in terms of these primitives) and we shall point out these functions as we proceed.

2.5 Boolean Operations

A **boolean operation** is a function that receives booleans as inputs, and returns a boolean as a result. The function and is a boolean operation which, on receiving boolean inputs x and y, returns true if the normal forms of x and y are true and returns false otherwise (figure 2.10).

```
(0-) (and (= 1 1) (= 2 2))
true

(1-) (and (= 1 2) (= 2 2))
false

(2-) (and true 4)
error: 4 is not a boolean
```

Figure 2.6 Using and

Again and expressions are not evaluated by applicative order evaluation. In the second input in figure 2.6, since (= 1 2) is evaluated to false, the value of (= 2 2) is immaterial. and is a **polyadic** function (i.e. it can receive a variable number of inputs) so that (and true true ….. false) is a legitimate construction.

The polyadic function or receives boolean inputs and returns true if at least one evaluates to true, and returns false otherwise. For similar reasons, applicative order evaluation is suspended here too.

```
(3-) (or (= 1 0) (= 2 2))
true

(4-) (or (= 1 0) (= 2 1))
false
```

Figure 2.7 Using or

and and or are also primitive. not returns true if its input evaluates to false and false if its input evaluates to true.

```
(6-) (not (= 1 1))
false
```

```
(7-) (not (= 1 2))
true
```

Figure 2.8 Using not

All other Shen function applications are evaluated by applicative order evaluation, which is a strict evaluation strategy.

2.6 Defining New Functions

Equational specifications are a simple way to begin to understand how functions are defined in Shen. For instance, the equation (*return-b a*) = *b* defines a function *return-b* that receives *a* and returns *b*. The domain of *return-b* is the set {*a*} and the range of *return-b* is the set {*b*}. Both the range and the domain are finite in size. If we want to add new elements to the domain and range then we add new equations. Often a function can be represented to Shen in the manner of a series of equations. The syntax is slightly different from the one used by mathematicians. First, the = is replaced by a -> and the bracket (is placed before the function symbol, so the first equation would appear more as:-

(return-b a) -> b

Second, all those equations that relate to the same function are grouped in brackets.

((return-b a) -> b
 (return-b c) -> b)

Third, since all the equations bracketed together must relate to the same function, it is tedious to keep typing the name of this function for each such equation. The name of the function is instead given at the top of its definition (figure 2.9). The entries a -> b and c -> b are **rewrite rules** within the Shen function definition (we shall see shortly that they differ a little from equations).

Entering the definition of return-b causes Shen to compile it into its **environment**. The environment can be considered to be a set of function names and their associated definitions. Once the definition of a function has been entered to the Shen environment, Shen will allow the use of this function in evaluation.

```
(15-) (define return-b
        a -> b
        c -> b)
(fn return-b)

(16-) (return-b c)
b
```

```
(17-) (return-b d)
error: partial function return-b
Track return-b ?  (y/n) n
```

Figure 2.9 Defining and using a simple function in Shen

Supplying an input for which there is no covering rule generates an error message. A function which is not defined for all its inputs is called a **partial function**. Here Shen signals that return-b is partial, accompanied by an offer to track the function which we refuse for now.[12]

But, suppose we want to say that *whatever* the input, return-b will return b. Since the domain of the function is now infinite in size, we cannot produce an equation for every possible input. Mathematicians use variables like x to cope with cases like this. In Shen, a variable is any symbol beginning with an uppercase letter. Using variables, one equation can state that whatever the input, return-b will return b. If we remedy the definition of return-b then Shen overwrites the old definition.

```
(19-) (define return-b
       X -> b)
(fn return-b)

(20-) (return-b d)
b
```

Figure 2.10 Overwriting an older definition

2.7 Equations and Priority Rewrite Systems

Equational specifications are a useful way of getting to grips with the task of defining functions. But there are significant differences between a set of equations and a series of rewrite rules in a Shen function definition. Consider the following equations.

$$(f\,a) = b$$
$$(f\,a) = c$$

Entering this directly into Shen produces the following definition.

```
(define f
  a -> b
  a -> c)
```

---

[12] In the next chapter we see how to gainfully accept this offer.

26

Evaluating (f a) produces b and never c. The second rewrite rule a -> c behaves as if it did not exist; the reason being that Shen tries rewrite rules from top to bottom. First a -> b is used and then a -> c. As soon as a -> b is tried with the input a, of course b is returned. The second rewrite rule is irrelevant and is **starved** by the first rule. This feature, of ordering rewrite rules so that some are tried in preference to others, is a characterising feature of **priority rewrite systems**. If we wanted to show that (f a) was identical to c, we could easily do this using the equations above, but in Shen (= (f a) c) would evaluate to false. We could amend the definition of f to allow (= (f a) c) to be true as follows.

```
(define f
  a -> c
  b -> c)
```

The amended definition now gives (f a) and c the same normal form. Nevertheless, the price for achieving this is that we have abandoned a simple transcription of the original equations. The problem of fairly transcribing a set of equations into rewrite rules has been intensively studied and it is known that there is no decision procedure for deriving a fair representation of an arbitrary set of equations.[13]

Equations are, in a sense, more powerful and less controlled than rewrite rules. But the same sensitivity to ordering gives Shen capacities that a purely equational specification does not have. For example, suppose we want to define a function identical that returns true given two inputs with the same normal form, and returns false otherwise. Using our equational specification approach, we write:-

$$(identical\ x\ x) = true$$

This is fine for the positive case. x has been used twice indicating that the two inputs must be the same for true to be returned. But what of the negative case? We cannot write

$$(identical\ x\ y) = false$$

This says that for *all* x and y, *identical*$(x,\ y) = false$. If we want express this function using equations, we have to expand our vocabulary and allow ourselves to use **conditional equations**.

$$(identical\ x\ x) = true$$
$$(identical\ x\ y) = false\ if\ x \neq y$$

---

[13] Meaning by "fair", a set R of rewrite rules, so that $a = b$ follows from the equations when and only when both a and b have unique normal forms a' and b' under R, such that a' and b' are syntactically identical. There is a semi-decision procedure, the **Knuth-Bendix procedure** (see Further Reading), which, when it terminates, will deliver a fair set of rewrite rules from a set of equations.

Shen's priority ordering allows identical to be defined in terms of rewrite rules.

```
(define identical
   X X -> true
   X Y -> false)
```

Since the rule X X -> true is tried first, any identical inputs must return true. If the second rule is tried, it can only be because the first rule failed, in which case the output must be false. In the final rule, the variables X and Y do not appear to the right of ->. Another way of writing this function is to use a **wildcard** _, to indicate that the nature and computation of the values of these variables is of no interest.

```
(define identical
   X X -> true
   _ _ -> false)
```

Another significant difference between rewrite rules and equations is that rewrite rules, unlike equations, must obey the **variable occurrence restriction**. The variable occurrence restriction requires that a variable that appears on the right-hand side of a rule must appear on the left-hand side. So the equation f(X,Y) = g(X) cannot be oriented into the rewrite rule (g X) -> (f X Y). Shen definitions that violate this restriction produce a free variable error (figure 2.11).

```
(0-) (define g
        X -> (f X Y))
error: the following variables are free in g: Y
```

Figure 2.11 A function that violates the variable occurrence condition

Since free variables often result from clerical errors, Shen raises an error. If we want Shen to accept the free variable we use protect (figure 2.12).

```
(0-) (define g
        X -> (f X (protect Y)))
(fn g)

(1-) (define f
        A B -> B)
(fn f)
```

Figure 2.12 Protecting free variables

Here for all values of X, (g X) will evaluate to the variable Y.

28

2.8 A Bible Studies Program

A mid-western millionaire has commissioned a project to build an intelligent question-and-answer program for material from the Bible. Part of the task is to encode the genealogies in the Book of Genesis; the relevant verses are as follows.

... Adam ... begat a son ... called ... Seth: .... and all the days that Adam lived were nine hundred and thirty years.... And Seth ... begat Enos: ...and all the days of Seth were nine hundred and twelve years: and he died.   And Enos ... begat Ca-i'nan: .... and all the days of Enos were nine hundred and five years: .... And Ca-i'nan ... begat Mahal'aleel: ... and all the days of Ca-i'nan were nine hundred and ten years: ..... And Mahal'aleel ... begat Jared: ... and all the days of Mahal'aleel were eight hundred ninety and five years: ... And Jared ... begat Enoch::... and all the days of Jared were nine hundred sixty and two years .... And Enoch ... begat Methu'selah: and all the days of Enoch were three hundred sixty and five years: .... And Methu'selah ... begat Lamech: ... and all the days of Methu'selah were nine hundred sixty and nine years: ... And Lamech ... begat a son: and he called his name Noah, ... And ... all the days of Lamech were seven hundred seventy and seven years: and he died.

King James Bible, Genesis, Chapter 5 verses 3-31

Much of this information can be captured in two functions **begat** and **lived** given on the next page. **begat** says who begat who and **lived** how long they lived. Since the names are capitalised, to avoid confusion with variables, we use strings for names.

The code introduces comments. A single line comment begins with a \\ and is deemed to continue until a new line begins. A multiline comment begins with * and continues until *\. Here are two examples.

```
\\ This is a single line comment
\* This is a multiline comment which can go on and on and on and on and on and
on and on until terminated by *\
```

First the lived function.

```
(define lived
  \\ the ages of the patriarchs!
  "Adam" -> 930
  "Seth" -> 912
  "Enos" -> 905
  "Ca-i'nan" -> 910
  "Mahal'aleel" -> 895
  "Jared" -> 962
  "Enoch" -> 365
  "Methu'selah" -> 969
  "Lamech" -> 777)
```

The begetting part is more potentially more difficult because begat is not a function but a relation, that is, begat does not map a person to one unique person unless the person has only one offspring.[14]   Luckily the Bible only traces the direct line.

```
(define begat
  "Adam" -> "Seth"
  "Seth" -> "Enos"
  "Enos" -> "Ca-i'nan"
  "Ca-i'nan" -> "Mahal'aleel"
  "Mahal'aleel" -> "Jared"
  "Jared" -> "Enoch"
  "Enoch" -> "Methu'selah"
  "Methu'selah" -> "Lamech")
```

Rather than typing this into the top level, it is more logical to enter it into a file "bible.shen" and save the file; the function load loads the file.

```
(0-) (load "bible.shen")
(fn lived)
(fn begat)
run time: 0.02635635635s
loaded

(1-) (begat "Enoch")
"Methu'selah"

(2-) (lived (begat "Adam"))
912
```

Figure 2.13 Loading and running the Bible program

All operations involving reading and writing to files, including loading files, are conducted relative to the **home directory** which by default is the directory in which Shen is situated. The command (load "myfile") will load a file from the directory in which Shen is located.

The function cd changes this home directory to allow files to be read from elsewhere without the user having to enter the full pathname. cd takes a string argument indicating the pathname; if the string is empty ("") then the home directory defaults again to the directory in which Shen is situated. The directory pathname may be **absolute** or **relative** where the pathname is interpreted relative to the directory in which Shen is situated.[15]   Figure 2.14 shows a session with cd

---

[14] In chapter 4 we will be able to solve this by grouping objects into lists. Logic programming, studied in chapter 25, deals with relations directly.

[15] The behaviour is partly dependent on platform and the operating system .

using first an absolute pathname under Windows 7, and then a relative pathname, and ends with resetting the home directory back to the default.

```
(5-) (cd "C:/Users/Mark Tarver/Documents/CS/Languages/Bible")
"C:/Users/Mark Tarver/Documents/CS/Languages/Bible/"

(6-) (load "bible.shen") \\ load a file in the above directory
(fn lived)
(fn begat)
run time: 0.04680030047893524 secs
loaded

(7-) (cd "") \\ change the directory to the home directory
""
```

Figure 2.14 Changing the home directory

Exercise 2

1. The Centigrade to Fahrenheit conversion is given by the equation $xF° = (9/5 \times x) + 32C°$. Write a function cent-to-fahr that calculates the equivalent Fahrenheit from the Centigrade. Write the inverse function fahr-to-cent that calculates the equivalent Centigrade from the Fahrenheit.

2. An **and-gate** is an electronic device that receives two electrical signals that are either high (1) or low (0) and outputs a high (1) signal if and only if both inputs are 1 and outputs 0 otherwise. An **or-gate** is an electronic device that receives two electrical signals that are either high (1) or low (0), outputs a 1 signal if and only if at least one input is 1, and outputs 0 otherwise. An **inverter** is an electronic device that receives an electrical signal that is either high (1) or low (0) and outputs a 1 signal if and only if the input is 0 and outputs 0 otherwise. Write down the Shen definitions of and-gate, or-gate and inverter as functions.

3. In neural nets, a neuron is a device that receives a number of numerical inputs $i_1,...i_n$ each of which it multiplies the corresponding weight $w_1,...,w_n$. If the sum of $(w_1 \times i_1)$ $+ ... (w_n \times i_n)$ is greater than a threshold K then the neurone produces a 1 and if the sum is less than K it produces a 0. Design a function that simulates a neurone designed to receive inputs i_1 and i_2, multiplies them by w_1 and w_2 respectively, and produces an output 0 or 1 depending on K. Your encoding should allow the user to fix the values of w_1 w_2 and K.

4. During the Vietnam War, an American pilot jumped from his downed B-52 from a height of 60,000 feet. Encode the formula $d = ½ at^2$, where d = distance travelled, a = acceleration and t = time elapsed, into a function and calculate the distance the pilot fell in 10 seconds. You can take a to be 30 ft/sec^2.

5. *The speed of light is 186,282 miles per second. The nearest star outside our solar system is *Proxima Centauri* which is 4.243 light years away. How long would the following objects take to travel to that star from earth?

a.   A jumbo jet, travelling at 550 mph.
b.   An Apollo rocket travelling at 23,000 mph.
c.   The Voyager probe travelling at 50,000 mph.

Your program should allow the traveller to fix his destination distance in light years and enter the speed in miles per hour.

7. Build a currency converter in Shen. Your currency converter will convert dollars, pounds and yen. To help you get started, here is the 2008 exchange scale for all these currencies into Euros.

$$1 \text{ US Dollar} = 0.84104 \text{ Euro}$$
$$1 \text{ British Pound} = 1.43266 \text{ Euro}$$
$$1 \text{ Japanese Yen} = 0.007725 \text{ Euro}$$

Your converter will receive any positive quantity of money in any of the above currencies and convert it into the target currency chosen by the user. Your program will allow the conversion rates to be reset, but only after password authorisation has been given to the system.

Further Reading

O'Donnell (1985) (pp 20-29, 90-97) gives a detailed study of the design and implementation of a programming language based on equations. The Knuth-Bendix procedure is a classic method for transforming arbitrary sets of equations into rewrite rules and is described in Knuth and Bendix (1970). The original account is not very readable and Bundy (1983) and Duffy (1991) provide more readable introductions. Plaisted (1993) gives a nice overview on the field of rewriting. There are regular conferences, devoted specifically to rewrite systems, published in the LNCS series, amongst which a paper by Baeten and Bergstra (1986) details the properties of priority rewrite systems. There has been a lot of discussion in functional programming circles about the advisability of using priority rewriting in the definition of functions. Priority rewriting leads to shorter and simpler programs, but it also separates the definition from its equational representation because these rules can overlap and then prioritising must be used to determine which rule is actually used. In mathematics, changing the order of the equations does not affect what is stated. Order insensitivity is also useful in implementing parallel functional programming languages, since each rule can be tested independently. Jorrand (1987) is a study of FP2; an experimental parallel functional programming language based on term rewriting. Wadler in Peyton-Jones (1987), chapter 5, gives a useful discussion of the conditions under which a set of rewrite rules is order-insensitive.

Web Sites

The Lawrence Livermore National Laboratory (http://www.llnl.gov/sisal/) ran the SISAL project, whose goal is "to develop high-performance functional compilers and runtime systems to simplify the process of writing scientific programs on parallel supercomputers and to help programmers develop functional scientific applications." The result was the SISAL functional programming language available through Sourceforge http://sisal.sourceforge.net that is available for UNIX and Windows. pLisp designed by Thomas Maher (http://www.techno.net/pcl/tm/plisp/) is an experimental implementation of parallel functional programming for a Lisp-like language. IEEE's

Parascope site (http://computer.org/parascope/) is the best place for links to the world of parallel computing.

Stand-alone implementations of the Knuth-Bendix completion procedure are very difficult to find; generally the procedure is embedded as proper part of larger systems designed to handle equational problems. The theorem prover OTTER (http://www-unix.mcs.anl.gov/AR/otter/) contains a Knuth-Bendix completion procedure as does MIT's Larch system (http://www.sds.lcs.mit.edu/Larch/index.html).

3 Recursion

3.1 Of Numbers

Numbers in Shen are either integers (...-3,-2,-1,0,1,2,3, ...) or floating point numbers (48.6464, -6776.5) or e numbers (4.5e3, 1.84e-4, 34e20). .9 and .67 etc. are acceptable shorthands for 0.9 and 0.67. Shen automatically recognises the cancellation of repeated subtraction when parsing, so --9 is parsed as 9.

All floating point numbers are treated and parsed as expressing sums of products; thus 434.78 is parsed as

$$434.78 = (10^2 \times 4) + (10^1 \times 3) + (10^0 \times 4) + (10^{-1} \times 7) + (10^{-2} \times 8)$$

e numbers are similarly parsed as products

$$1.84e\text{-}4 = 1.84 \times 10^{-4}$$

The precision of the computation depends very much on the platform. By preference Shen uses **double precision arithmetic** which means that the memory assigned to represent a number spans 64 bits on a modern 32 bit computer. This is the recommended IEEE standard for representing floating point numbers. Any Shen implementation running under Common Lisp, JavaScript, Clojure or Scheme will meet this standard. This gives accuracy to around fifteen places. By default Shen gives the most accurate representation of any numerical computation, and the computation can introduce inaccuracies in the least significant place.[16]

An interesting question concerns the comparison of floats and integers - is (= 1 1.0) true or not? If as in Shen, we treat the decimal notation as shorthand for a sum, then the answer is 'yes'; i.e. $1.0 = (1 \times 10^0) + (0 \times 10^{-1}) = 1$

---

[16] However the representation returned by a computation may vary according to platform. Under Common Lisp, Shen computes 56565e34 to 565650000000000000000000000000000000000, whereas under Javascript it is printed as 5.6564999999999995e+38. The standard maths library contains a rounding function for those who are bothered by extraneous digits.

Therefore if = represents identity then (= 1 1.0) is true. This is the verdict Shen returns.

```
(0-) (= 1 1.0)
true
```

This verdict opens up the differences between languages in their treatment of numbers and reaches down into the philosophy of mathematics. In Prolog 1 = 1.0 is false. In ML the comparison is meaningless (returns an error) because 1.0 and 1 belong to different types - *real* and *int*.

Strictly this is wrong. Computing has fogged the issues here and committed the traditional error of confusing *use* and *mention* in its treatment of integers and floats, in other words, between *numbers* and the signs (*numerals*) we use to represent them. The number 11 can be represented in various ways; as 11 in decimal, B in hexadecimal, XI in Roman numerals and so on.

We should not confuse the identity of two numbers with the identity of their representation. If we want to say that 1.0 is not an integer and 1 is, we commit an error, because 1.0 = 1; unless we mean by "integer" an expression which is applied to the numeral itself i.e. "1.0". In which case the expression "integer" is predicated of something which is a numeral, in computing terms, it is a string test. In Shen, the integer? test is taken as predicating of numbers and 1.0 is treated as an integer.

However there are often pragmatic grounds for distinguishing numbers as distinct that traditional mathematics has regarded as identical. In computing it is sometimes *convenient* to treat these alternative representations as different in kind. A case in point are the rational numbers, treated since Pythagoras as a ratio of two whole numbers 1/3, 5/8 etc. Every schoolboy is taught to replace 2/1 by 2 in his calculations and 2/1 and 2 are regarded as the same number.

However finite floating point numbers cannot, with complete accuracy, capture a rational; 1/3 is not 0.3 or even 0.333333 but 0.3 repeated. Hence there is a case for retaining rational numbers as a special type.[17] If we introduce rational numbers as objects composed of two elements it is awkward to maintain that 2/1 = 2 because computationally they are utterly different objects. So some languages either omit the rationals or regard them as distinct in all cases from integers. However the degree to these distinctions are enforced in computing varies according to platform.[18]

---

[17] Shen lacks them but in chapter 8 we show how to construct them.

[18] The nature and identity of numbers is an old philosophical question over which men have argued for centuries. Regarding the identity of 1.0 and 1, we have kept the traditional view that floating point numbers are simply a representation of numbers of which integers are a special case. The view that 1,

Our excursion into the foundation of number theory being done for now; we will now look at how numerical computation is performed in Shen. In Shen there are four basic numerical operations.

1. Addition +
2. Subtraction -
3. Multiplication *
4. Division /

Both addition and multiplication are **polyadic operations** in Shen, meaning that these operators can take any number of inputs or **arguments** as they are called in functional parlance. The polyadicity arises from the fact that both these functions are associative so that (+ X (+ Y Z)) and (+ (+ X Y) Z) are equivalent. Hence the Shen reader treats the internal bracketing as unwanted hair and accepts (+ X Y Z). Shen division is true division and not integer division so that (/ 5 2) will produce 2.5 and not 2. All these functions are members of the set of **primitive functions** from which Shen is assembled.

In addition there are four numerical relations which are also primitive.

1. Greater than >
2. Less than <
3. Greater than or equal to >=
4. Less than or equal to <=

The generic equality relation = will operate between numbers. The function number? will return true for all and only numbers and both of these are primitive. Shen accepts zero-place functions so that we can define constants like π as follows

---

1/1 and 1.0 are alternative representations of the same number was probably characteristic of mathematics until the early C20; the change in perspective came through two historical sources; the first in mathematical logic and the second in computing.

The basis in mathematical logic lies in Bertrand Russell's reductionist analysis of numbers whereby a number tower is built from the natural numbers (which are themselves reduced to cardinal numbers) consisting of more and more complex set theoretical constructions. In Russell's analysis, rational numbers are quite distinct entities from natural numbers and if you want to compare them, you cannot do so through an equality relation but have to do so through constructing an equivalence relation of the appropriate kind.

Hence 2/1 is not the same object as 2 in Russellian mathematics (though it is in traditional maths) because preserving this identity introduced awkward special cases. However, it is important to note that Russell *completely disavowed* that he was trying to analyse the meaning of mathematical assertions in his work on logical atomism. Rather he was attempting to reconstruct mathematics by providing a mapping from conventional maths into Russellian arithmetic. As in computing, mathematical logic followed the line of convenience.

```
(6-) (define pi
  -> 3.14159)
(fn pi)

(7-)  (+ (pi) 1)
4.14159
```

Figure 3.1 Defining π as a zero place function

3.2 Recursion and the Factorial Function

The factorial of a natural number *n* is the result of multiplying *n* by the all the positive integers less than *n*. By convention *(factorial* 0) = 1. We start writing a series of equations to define factorial (figure 3.2).

$$(factorial\ 0) = 1$$
$$(factorial\ 1) = 1 \times 1 = 1$$
$$(factorial\ 2) = 2 \times 1 = 2$$
$$(factorial\ 3) = 3 \times 2 \times 1 = 6$$
$$(factorial\ 4) = 4 \times 3 \times 2 \times 1 = 24$$
....

Figure 3.2 Part of an infinite series of equations for the factorial function

The problem is that there are an infinite number of such equations. Can we somehow reduce this infinite set of equations to something finite and of a manageable size?

We can through the device of **recursion**. If we examine these equations, they all fit a common pattern. Above 0, the factorial of any integer is the result of multiplying that integer by the factorial of the integer one less than it.

$$(factorial\ 0) = 1$$
$$(factorial\ 1) = 1 \times (factorial\ 0) = 1 \times 1 = 1$$
$$(factorial\ 2) = 2 \times (factorial\ 1) = 2 \times 1 = 2$$
$$(factorial\ 3) = 3 \times (factorial\ 2) = 3 \times 2 = 6$$
$$(factorial\ 4) = 4 \times (factorial\ 3) = 4 \times 6 = 24$$
....

Figure 3.3 Isolating the pattern within the equations in 3.2

This allows us to use two equations in place of the infinite list we started with (figure 3.4). The second equation includes the proviso that $x \neq 0$.

$$(factorial\ 0) = 1$$
$$\text{where } x \neq 0, (factorial\ x) = x \times (factorial\ x\text{-}1)$$

Figure 3.4 The equations that define the factorial function

37

In representing these equations in Shen, we take advantage of the fact that Shen tries rewrite rules in the order in which they appear in a function definition. If the first and second equations become the first and second rewrite rules in the definition of factorial, the ordering guarantees that Shen tries the second rule only when the input is not equal to 0. Hence the two equations can be combined into one definition without having to explicitly say that $x \neq 0$ (figure 3.5).

```
(define factorial
  0 -> 1
  X -> (* X (factorial (- X 1)))))
```

Figure 3.5 The factorial function in Shen

Entering this function to Shen shows it to work.

```
(59-) (factorial 6)
720
```

The calculation of the factorial of any natural number > 0 depends on calculating the factorial of the integer one less than it. Thus, the Shen factorial function calls itself $n+1$ times for any natural number n and having reached zero, executes all the deferred multiplications.

3.3 Forms of Recursion

The equational definition of *factorial* in figure 3.3 shows the typical anatomy of a recursive function. The first equation - (*factorial* 0) = 1 - gives the **base case** of the recursive definition; this provides a point where the function ceases to call itself. The base case corresponds to a condition within a procedural loop that causes the loop to be exited.

The second equation - where $x \neq 0$, (*factorial*(x) = $x \times$ (*factorial x*-1) - corresponds to the **recursive case** where the function calls itself. The recursive case corresponds to the condition within a loop that causes the loop to be repeated. In the example there is one base case and one recursive case, though in other definitions there can be several of each.

Once the base case 0 is reached, the computation does not cease since the recursive outputs of factorial have to be multiplied to give the answer. We can rewrite our definition of *factorial* so that the answer is returned on reaching the base case (figure 3.6).

```
(define factorial
  X -> (factorialh X 1))

(define factorialh
  0 Accum -> Accum
  X Accum -> (factorialh (- X 1) (* X Accum)))
```

Figure 3.6 A tail recursive definition of factorial

38

Our new definition of *factorial* passes its input X to an **auxiliary** or **help function** factorialh that helps to define *factorial*. The definition of factorialh contains an extra input (an **accumulator**) Accum, which totals the value calculated for factorial. When the base case 0 is reached, returning the accumulator gives the correct answer.

The two different versions of *factorial* are almost identical, and yet they display different patterns of computation. In the first version, the necessary multiplications are postponed till the end of the recursion. Carrying out this process requires that the computer remember the multiplications to be performed later. The length of the chain of operations, and hence the amount of information needed to keep account of the computation, grows in linear proportion to the value n of *(factorial n)*. Such a recursion is called **linear recursion**.

In the second kind of recursion, **tail recursion**, the necessary multiplications are performed during the recursion, and the memory used to keep track of the computation is virtually constant. The difference becomes significant if the chain of deferred calculations made by linear recursion becomes larger than the available memory set aside to store them. In that case the computer may raise an error.[19] For this reason functional programmers generally write computationally intensive recursive functions to be tail recursive.

Addition is another example of a recursive arithmetic function. The problem is to recursively define an addition function *plus* over natural numbers, using only operations which add 1 to or subtract 1 from a number. To begin we write a series of equations giving specific inputs to *plus* and the corresponding results.

$$(plus \; x \; 0) = x$$
$$(plus \; x \; 1) = 1 + (plus \; x \; 0)$$
$$(plus \; x \; 2) = 1 + (plus \; x \; 1)$$
$$(plus \; x \; 3) = 1 + (plus \; x \; 2)$$

Figure 3.7 Part of an infinite series of equations for addition

Apart from the first equation (the model for the base case), all the other equations have the form

$$(plus \; x \; y) = 1 + (plus \; x \; y\text{-}1).$$

Using the equations $(plus \; x \; 0) = x$ and $(plus \; x \; y) = 1 + (plus \; x \; y\text{-}1)$, we define a recursive function plus in Shen (figure 3.8).

---

[19] The distinction between tail and linear recursion is built into many optimising compilers in functional programming languages though not all (e.g. Python). The limit at which linear recursion fails due to memory overflow depends on the size of the **call stack**, which is the area of memeory devoted to storing these deferred computations.

```
(define plus
  X 0 -> X
  X Y -> (+ 1 (plus X (- Y 1)))))
```

Figure 3.8 The plus function in Shen

This definition is linear recursive; we leave the tail recursive version as an exercise for the reader.

The Fibonacci function over the natural numbers is defined through the equations in figure 3.9.

$$(fib\ 0) = 0$$
$$(fib\ 1) = 1$$
$$\text{if } x > 1, \text{ then } (fib\ x) = (fib\ x\text{-}1) + (fib\ x\text{-}2)$$

Figure 3.9 The equations defining the Fibonacci function

The transcription into Shen is easy (figure 3.10).

```
(define fib
  0 -> 0
  1 -> 1
  X -> (+ (fib (- X 1)) (fib (- X 2)))))
```

Figure 3.10 The Fibonacci function in Shen

One point of note is that fib is invoked twice in the recursion. Recursive functions that call themselves more than once in one recursive call are called **tree recursive** functions, since the computation branches at such a call into two or more calls to the same function.

1 is odd and not even. For any natural number x, which is greater than 1, x is even if its predecessor is odd and odd if its predecessor is even. This definition is used in figure 3.11 to create a program that recognises odd and even numbers. The odd? function calls even and the even? function calls odd? Functions which are defined in terms of each other are **mutually recursive**.

```
(define even?
  1 -> false
  X -> (odd? (- X 1)))

(define odd?
  1 -> true
  X -> (even? (- X 1)))
```

Figure 3.11 A mutual recursion between even? and odd?

40

3.4 Tracing Function Calls

These different patterns of execution can be traced through the Shen tracking package. The package allows us to trace the input to any user-defined function and the corresponding output. When a function *f* is tracked, each time *f* is called, the inputs to *f* are printed and so is the normal form of the output *f* returns. untrack untracks a function. Figure 3.12 shows a trace of the factorial function.

```
(62-) (track factorial)
factorial

(63-) (factorial 3)
 <1> Input to factorial
 3 ==>
  <2> Input to factorial
  2 ==>
   <3> Input to factorial
   1 ==>
    <4> Input to factorial
    0 ==>
    <4> Output of factorial
    ==> 1
   <3> Output of factorial
   ==> 1
  <2> Output of factorial
  ==> 2
 <1> Output of factorial
==> 6

(64-) (untrack factorial)
```

Figure 3.12 Using the Shen trace program

(step +) typed to the top level will cause the tracking package to pause after each Inputs to ... and wait for a keystroke from the user. Typing ^ (abort) at this point will abort the computation. The trace package query is triggered whenever a function *f* is called with an input for which there is no rule in the definition of *f* to determine how that input is to be treated.

3.5 Guards

A prime number is a whole number > 1, divisible only by itself and 1 to give another whole number. Our task is to construct a prime number detector which returns true if *x* is a prime number and false otherwise.

One way to construct such a detector is to start with 2, if *x* is 2 then it is prime. If not, we begin with $x = 3$ and try to divide 2 into *x*. If the result is a whole number > 1, then *x* is not prime. If the result is not a whole number then we repeat the

41

test, incrementing 3 to 5. We continue, and if we have incremented the divisor to a number greater than the integer square root (*isqrt*) of *x*; then we know we have found a prime. This algorithm requires a function that:

1. holds the number *x*,
2. holds the integer square root of *x* and ..
3. holds the divisor that is initially set to 2.

Call this function *prime-h?*. We define the function *prime?* in terms of *prime-h?* (and *prime-h* itself) in four equations (figure 3.13).[20]

(*prime? x*) = (*prime-h? x* (*isqrt x*) 2)
(*prime-h? x max div*) = false   if *x*/*div* is an integer and 1< *div* ≤ *max*
(*prime-h? x max div*) = true   if *div* > *max*
(*prime-h? x max div*) = *y*   if *x*/*div* is not an integer
                                and *max* ≥ *div*
                                and (*prime-h? x max* 1+*div*) = *y*

Figure 3.13 Defining a prime detector in equations

The definition of *prime?* is easy - merely a transcription of the equation. The definition of *prime-h?* is trickier. The equations have conditions attached to them that must be represented. Shen represents these conditions by **guards**. A guard is a functional expression that evaluates to true or false, which is placed after the rule and preceded by the keyword where, and which must evaluate to true for the rule to apply (figure 3.14).

```
(define prime?
  X -> (prime-h? X (isqrt X) 2))

(define isqrt
  X -> (isqrt-help X 1))

(define isqrt-help
  X Y -> Y                          where (= (* Y Y) X)
  X Y -> (- Y 1)                    where (> (* Y Y) X)
  X Y -> (isqrt-help X (+ Y 1)))

(define prime-h?
  X Max Div -> true     where (> Div Max)
  X Max Div -> false    where (and (integer? (/ X Div))
                              (< 1 Div)  (<= Div Max))
  X Max Div -> (prime-h? X Max (+ 1 Div))
          where (and (not (integer? (/ X Div)))(>= Max Div)))
```

Figure 3.14 An unoptimised encoding of the prime detector

---

[20] This is not an efficient way of testing for primes, and is simply used as a teaching example. See question 2. in the attached exercises to this chapter for a hint on how to improve this program.

Using our knowledge of the evaluation strategy of this program, some of the code in figure 3.12 can be eliminated. The (< 1 Div) test is redundant, because prime-h? is started with a divisor of 2. The (<= Div Max) is redundant too, because if (> Div Max), the program would have terminated. Similarly the (not (integer? (/ X Div))) (>= Max Div) tests can be dropped (they must be satisfied if the first two rules fail). After eliminating redundant code, the resulting program appears in 3.15.

```
(define prime?
  X -> (prime-h? X (isqrt X) 2))

(define isqrt
  X -> (isqrt-help X 1))

(define isqrt-help
  X Y -> Y                          where (= (* Y Y) X)
  X Y -> (- Y 1)                    where (> (* Y Y) X)
  X Y -> (isqrt-help X (+ Y 1)))

(define prime-h?
  X Max Div -> true                 where (> Div Max)
  X Max Div -> false                where (integer?²¹ (/ X Div))
  X Max Div -> (prime-h? X Max (+ 1 Div)))
```

Figure 3.15 An optimised encoding of the prime detector

Guards do not give Shen any extra computational power; they are merely a convenient device for clarifying the control within a program. In fact all Shen function definitions can be coded with only one rewrite rule in each function! To do this, we transfer all the control information that appears to the left of the ->, to the right in the form of a nested case statement. What is left on the left of the -> is simply a series of variables called **formal parameters**. Here is a recoding of prime-h? along these lines.

```
(define prime-h?
  X Max Div -> (if (integer? (/ X Div))
                   false
                   (if (> Div Max) true (prime-h? X Max (+ 1  Div)))))
```

Some functional languages such as Lisp, Scheme and Python require programs to be written in this style. The introduction of significant structure to the left of -> is what pattern-directed or **pattern-matching** functional programming is about. The translation of Shen programs into this form is both purely mechanical and also an important stage in the compilation of Shen.²²

---

²¹ See appendix A; integer? is a system function.

²² See chapter 15 for more on this.

3.6 Counting Change

How many ways can a one pound coin be changed? We can generalise the question and ask *"Given a sum of n pence, in how many ways can it be converted into coin change?"* To begin, we identify the units of coin currency existing in Britain of 2020; they are the 2 pound coin, the pound coin and the 50p, 20p, 10p, 5p, 2p and 1p coins. The problem has a simple recursive solution. Let d be the value of the highest denomination, and n be the value of the money, which we are trying to break down. Then the number of ways c of breaking n into change is c where

c = the number of ways of breaking $n-d$ pence into change +
  the number of ways of breaking n pence into change using all
  remaining denominations *except* the highest denomination d.

What stops the recursion? We say that

1. There is one way of changing 0 pence (give nothing back!).
2. There are no (zero) ways of changing less than 0 pence.
3. If there is no available denomination to use, there are 0 ways of changing any sum of money.

Putting this reasoning together gives the function count-change.

```
(define count-change
   Amount -> (count-change-h Amount 200))

(define count-change-h
  0 _ -> 1
  _ 0 -> 0
  Amount _ -> 0  where (> 0 Amount)
  Amount Fst_Denom
  -> (+ (count-change-h (- Amount Fst_Denom) Fst_Denom)
        (count-change-h Amount (next-denom Fst_Denom))))

(define next-denom
  200 -> 100
  100 -> 50
  50 -> 20
  20 -> 10
  10 -> 5
  5 -> 2
  2 -> 1
  1 -> 0)
```

Figure 3.16 Counting change in Shen

(count-change 100) provides the answer, 4563, to the original question.

3.7 Non-Terminating Functions

Recursion gives the ability to define **non-terminating** functions such as

```
(define silly
  X -> (silly X))
```

which calls itself forever. Here (silly X) is undefined for all values of X, since whatever input is submitted to silly, no normal form is computed.

There are other examples of functions, which are non-terminating only for certain inputs; for example the expression (factorial -1) has no normal form. The last example shows that functions that fail to terminate for all inputs are not always silly. To avoid non-termination we must ensure the input is a natural number.

However, there remain functions whose computation is not guaranteed to terminate and which are resistant to all safeguards.[23] A good example comes from number theory. Goldbach's conjecture suggests that every even number > 2 is the sum of two primes. The following program tests the conjecture.

```
(define slow-goldbachs-conjecture
  -> (slow-goldbachs-conjecture-h 4))

(define slow-goldbachs-conjecture-h
  N -> (slow-goldbachs-conjecture-h (+ N 2)) where (sum-of-two-primes? N)
  N -> N)

(define sum-of-two-primes?
  N -> (sum-of-two-primes-h? 2 N))

(define sum-of-two-primes-h?
  P N -> false                                  where (> P N)
  P N -> true                                   where (sum-of? P 2 N)
  P N -> (sum-of-two-primes-h? (next-prime (+ 1 P)) N))

(define sum-of?
  P1 P2 N  -> true                              where (= N (+ P1 P2))
  P1 P2 N  -> false                             where (> (+ P1 P2) N)
  P1 P2 N  -> (sum-of? P1 (next-prime (+ 1 P2)) N))

(define next-prime
  X -> X                                        where (prime? X)
  X -> (next-prime (+ 1 X)))
```

Figure 3.17 Goldbach's Conjecture in Shen

---

[23] It was proved in 1936 by Alan Turing there is no algorithm for detecting all programs which may fail to terminate; a result known as the *Unsolvability of the Halting Problem*.

Currently the truth of Goldbach's conjecture is open to proof or disproof.[24] If conjecture is true, then the program in 3.17 will not terminate. If it is false, then it will halt and print out an integer that will refute the conjecture. Currently, mathematicians do not know what would happen. But from a programmer's viewpoint, the program is very inefficient because it uses next-prime to recalculate the same primes repeatedly. In the next chapter, we look at how lists can be used to store results for programs like this.

Exercise 3

1. Define the following functions.
   a. expt, that raises a number M to a natural number power N.
   b. round_n, that rounds a floating point number M to N places, rounding downwards.
   c. square?, that returns true if N is a perfect square. A perfect square is the result of multiplying a natural number by itself.
   d. gcd, which computes the greatest common divisor of two natural numbers a and b. This function returns the largest divisor common to a and b. The gcd of 12 and 16 is 4.
   e. lcm, which computes the least common multiple of two natural numbers a and b. This function returns the smallest number into which a and b both divide to give whole numbers. The lcm of 12 and 15 is 60.

2. Show how the prime detector program can be easily optimised to improve performance. Hint: think how the search can be improved to eliminate looking at even numbers.

3. *Define the 3-place function nth_root that receives the natural number N, the positive number M and the natural number P, where P > 0. nth_root finds the Nth root of M to an accuracy proportional to P as follows. Fix the conjectured value C for $\sqrt[N]{M}$ at M/2. Raise C to the power N and determine if C^N rounded to P places equals M. If so, return C. If C^N rounded to P places > M, reduce the value of C and repeat. If C^N rounded to P places < M, increase the value of C and repeat. The trick is seeing how to increase or decrease the value of C to converge on a solution.

4. Melvin Micro has defined his own version of if as follows:-

   ```
   (define melvins_if
     true X _ -> X
     false _ Y -> Y
     Test _ _ -> (error "test ~A must be true or false.~%" Test))
   ```

   He defines factorial as

   ```
   (define factorial
     X -> (melvins_if (= X 0) 1 (* X (factorial (- X 1)))))
   ```

[24] The Prussian mathematician Christian Goldbach suggested Goldbach's conjecture in 1742. It has been tested up to 4×10^{18} (April 2012). In 2001 a $1 million prize was announced in the Chicago Sun-Times for the first proof of Goldbach's conjecture. Two major publishers funded the money and the competition remained open until March 15th 2002. The prize was not won.

What happens when Melvin tries to use this function to compute factorials? Give reasons.

5.   Melvin Micro has deposited $10,000 in a long term account in the year 2000. At 5% interest per year, he hopes to collect on this account for his retirement. Assuming he takes no money from his account, what will it be worth in 2040?

6.   In 2005, the USA produced 10,900 billion dollars of goods and services with a growth rate of around 2.5% per annum. The same year China produced 6,400 billion dollars of goods and services with a growth rate of 9% per annum. Assuming these rates are maintained, at what year does the GNP of China exceed that of America?

7.   In probability theory, the probability $P(A \vee B)$ of either or both of two independent events A or B occurring is given by the equation.

$$P(A \vee B) = 1 - ((1 - P(A)) \times (1 - P(B)))$$

P(A) is the probability of A occurring and P(B) is the probability of B occurring. 1 indicates certainty, 0 impossibility. Assume that the probability of a major global catastrophe in any one year is 1/200. What is the probability of a major global catastrophe in the next fifty years?

8.   The factorisation of very large numbers is a key element in computer security. The prime factors of a number n are those primes which when multiplied together give n. Devise a program to compute the prime factors of the number 123456789.

9.   *Two regiments of riflemen are facing each other. One side has 1000 men, the other 800. The smaller side fires first and then the larger and so on alternately. A riflemen hits and kills his enemy once in every 10 shots. Once a man is hit and killed he cannot fire back. The fight is to the finish. How many men are left in the stronger side at the end of the fight? What happens if the stronger side fires first?

10. *Implement a calendar program which determines what day of the week a particular date falls on. Use your program to calculate the day of the week on 13th July 2113.

11. A high-speed reconnaissance plane weighs 105,000 lb of which 70,000 lb is fuel. At a cruise speed of 1,800 mph, the plane uses 3lb of fuel per 10,000lb of weight per mile. The airforce need to know how long the plane will cruise and hence what is its effective radius of action. Write a program to compute a solution. Your program should allow the user to set the parameters of this problem for different aircraft.

Further Reading

The Fibonacci function in this chapter executes in exponential space relative to the input n. Henson (1987, chapter 4) shows how to derive a linear Fibonacci function definition from the tree recursive version using the rules for manipulating function definitions in Burstall and Darlington (1977). Bird (1984) and Wand (1980) extend this technique. Abelson and Sussman (1996) explain how to detect prime numbers using the square-root method used here and also present a much faster method based on the Fermat test. This book also has a good discussion of various types of recursion and the compilation strategies for dealing with them. The problem of showing that the evaluation of an arbitrary expression halts or showing it does not is, of course, unsolvable (being a corollary of the Halting Problem).

The problem of counting change is an old one. Kac and Ulam (1971) p.34-39 show how to calculate the number of ways of splitting a dollar without the use of a computer; their method uses simultaneous equations and polynomials. The computation used in this book is not particularly efficient since identical computations are repeated. Memoisation is a technique for recording the results of a computation so it need not be performed more than once. For more on memoisation see Field and Harrison (1988).

Web Sites

Chris Caldwell (http://www.utm.edu/research/primes/) maintains a site devoted to primes. http://www.fortunecity.com/meltingpot/manchaca/799/prime.html is a less detailed, but a more accessible account of primes.

4 Lists

4.1 Representing Lists in Shen

In Shen, a list begins with a [and ends with a]. So the list composed of 1, 2 and 3 would be written as [1 2 3]. Spaces are used to separate items; the list [123] is not the same as the list [1 2 3], since [123] is the list containing the single number 123. Shen evaluates lists according to the **list evaluation rule**.

The List Evaluation Rule

The normal form of a list $L = [x_1,...,x_n]$ is the list $[x'_1,...,x'_n]$ arrived at by evaluating the contents of L from left to right where for each x_j $(1 \leq j \leq n)$, x'_j is the normal form of x_j.

Suppose we wish to find the normal form of [(* 8 9) (+ 46 89) (- 67 43)] using the list evaluation rule. We evaluate (* 8 9) first.

(* 8 9) $\Rightarrow$ 72

Second we evaluate (+ 46 89)

(+ 46 89)❙ $\Rightarrow$ 135

Last we evaluate (- 67 43).

(- 67 43) $\Rightarrow$ 24

So the result is [72 135 24].

Lists can be placed within lists (figure 4.1). The last example in that figure features one rather special sort of list - the empty list [ ]; a list which contains nothing and which evaluates to itself.[25] Shen requires all brackets to balance before undertaking an evaluation. If there are unequal numbers of (s and)s, or [s and]s, then Shen will wait for the user to balance them. ^ can be used to abort the line input in periods of confusion.

---

[25] The empty list can also be written as ( ) in Shen.

[[1]] ⇒ [[1]]
[tom dick harry] ⇒ [tom dick harry]
[[1 dick [3]]] ⇒ [[1 dick [3]]]
[(+ 1 2) [(+ 2 3)]] ⇒ [3 [5]]
[(+ 34 34) [(* 7 8) "foobar" [(- 9 8)]]] ⇒ [72 [56 "foobar" [1]]]
[] ⇒ []

Figure 4.1 Some examples of lists and their normal forms

4.2 Building Lists with cons

There is one primitive function for building up lists - cons. The function cons receives two inputs, an object x and a list L and builds a list L' through adding x to the front of L; this is **consing** x to L (figure 4.2).

```
(0-) (cons 1 [2 3])
[1 2 3]

(1-) (cons tom [dick harry])
[tom dick harry]

(2-) (cons tom (cons dick (cons harry [ ])))
[tom dick harry]
```

Figure 4.2 Using the cons function

Using cons, a supply of self-evaluating expressions, and the empty list [], any finite list can be built up. For instance, suppose we wish to construct the list [[a b] c [d e]]. The list [a b] is formed by consing a to the result of consing b to [].

$$[a\ b] = (cons\ a\ (cons\ b\ [\ ]))$$

[d e] is the result of consing d to the result of consing e to [ ]

$$[d\ e] = (cons\ d\ (cons\ e\ [\ ]))$$

The list [[d e]] is formed by consing [d e] to [ ].

$$[[d\ e]] = (cons\ [d\ e]\ [\ ])$$

The list [[a b] c [d e]] is the result of consing [a b] to consing c to [[d e]].

$$[[a\ b]\ c\ [d\ e]] = (cons\ [a\ b]\ (cons\ c\ [[d\ e]]))$$

Thus [[a b] c [d e]] is expressed in terms of consing operations.

[[a b] c [d e]] = (cons (cons a (cons b [ ])) (cons c (cons (cons d (cons e [ ])) [ ])))

When a list is described like this, using only cons, [ ] and self-evaluating expressions we say that it is in **cons form**. For practical purposes, writing lists in cons form is tedious and unnecessary. However, when we come to reason about programs, it is important to know that any list can be recast in cons form. The translation of a list to its cons form version is purely mechanical. Simply keep applying the following rules throughout any list representation until they can no longer be applied.

Cons Form Translation Rules

(i)   [ ] is translated as [ ].
(ii)   A non-list e remains the same.
(iii) $[e_1,...,e_n]$ where $(n \geq 1)$ is translated as (cons e_1 $[,...,e_n]$).

A shorter way of expressing consing (as an alternative to writing "cons") is to use |; every expression to the left of | is consed in turn to the list on the right of | (figure 4.3).

(0-) [1 | [2 3]]
[1 2 3]

(1-) [tom dick harry | [ ]]
[tom dick harry]

Figure 4.3 Using | in Shen to cons expressions

We explain how to evaluate expressions containing | by showing how such expressions can be translated into expressions not containing |, but cons instead. The translation involves applying the following rules to every part of any given expression until the |s are gone.

| Elimination Rules

(i) $[e_1 \mid e_2]$ is translated to (cons e_1 e_2).
(ii) $[e_1 ,..., e_n \mid e_{n+1}]$ $(n \geq 2)$ is translated to (cons e_1 $[..., e_n \mid e_{n+1}]$).

We apply these rules to [tom dick harry | [ ]].

[tom dick harry | [ ]]
= (cons tom [dick harry | [ ]])   by rule (ii)
= (cons tom (cons dick [harry | [ ]]))   by rule (ii)
= (cons tom (cons dick (cons harry [ ])))   by rule (i)
$\Rightarrow$ [tom dick harry].

51

4.3 hd and tl Access List Components

cons builds lists out of component parts. hd and tl allow these component parts to be extracted from the assembled lists. hd receives a non-empty list and returns the first element in it; tl receives a non-empty list and returns all *but* the first element of that list (figure 4.4). hd and tl satisfy these equations.

$$hd(cons(x, y)) = x$$
$$tl(cons(x, y)) = y$$

Using hd and tl in composition, we can access any element in a list.

```
(0-) (hd [1 2 3])
1

(1-) (tl [1 2 3])
[2 3]

(2-) (hd (tl (tl [1 2 3])))
3
```

Figure 4.4 Using hd *and* tl *to extract elements from a list*

What happens if hd and tl are applied to the empty list? In this case the behaviour is platform dependent and unpredictable. There are two functions head and tail in Shen which are more predictable; they raise an error in that case. Both these function depend on testing the list to see if it is empty before applying hd or tl respectively.

The test for a non-empty list in Shen is cons? (another primitive function) which returns true to a non-empty list and false to anything else; so (cons? []) returns false, as does (cons? 67) etc. Obviously hd and tl are a little faster than head and tail.

An unusual feature of Shen (shared by another language Common Lisp) is that it is possible to cons together two objects neither of which are lists. The result is known as a **dotted pair**. This is printed in Shen using a bar |.

```
(0-) (cons 1 2)
[1 | 2]

(1-) [1 | 2]
[1 | 2]

(2-) (tl [1 | 2])
2
```

52

The utility of a dotted pair D versus a two element list L is that accessing the second element of a dotted pair requires only one operation (tl D) whereas for L it requires two (hd (tl L)).

A **lookup table** is an association of elements organised for the purpose of retrieving information. If a lookup table is coded as list in which various items are grouped together according to some criteria of interest then the list is called an **association list**. A telephone directory can be treated as a lookup table in which the leading item is a surname. A relational database for a hospital is functionally representable as a lookup table in which the leading item is (say) the patient's National Insurance number and the details associated with that are the medical details and identity of the patient.

Here is a simple association list for the capitals of the world and the respective countries, encoded as a list of dotted pairs in Shen.

[["London" | "Great Britain"] ["Paris" | "France"] ["Madrid" | "Spain"] ["Amsterdam" | "Holland"] ["Berlin" | "Germany"] ["Warsaw" | "Poland"] ["Vienna" | "Austria"]]

A function country maps a capital to a country using this list. In order to do that, the list has to be traversed. Our initial code begins easily.

```
(define country
   Capital -> (traverse Capital [["London" | "Great Britain"]
                                 ["Paris" | "France"]
                                 ["Madrid" | "Spain"]
                                 ["Amsterdam" | "Holland"]
                                 ["Berlin" | "Germany"]
                                 ["Warsaw" | "Poland"]
                                 ["Vienna" | "Austria"]]))
```

The definition of traverse comes next; plainly if the list is empty there is nothing constructive to return except "don't know". If the capital is found at the head of the table we return the country otherwise we recurse down the table.

```
(define traverse
   Capital Table -> (cases (= Table []) "don't know"
                           (= Capital (hd (hd Table))) (tl (hd Table))
                           true (traverse Capital (tl Table))))
```

In traditional functional languages like Lisp, Python and Scheme, programs are written in this way and what occurs to the left of the arrow is a series of variables or formal parameters. In fact in chapter 15 we shall see that all Shen programs are in fact compiled into this sort of idiom.

However in the previous chapter we got used to the idea that in Shen we could write other expressions to the left of the arrow and not just formal parameters. This is characteristic of **pattern-matching** found in modern functional programming languages like Shen, ML and Haskell. Let us see how to do this for lists in Shen. The first lines of our program were

```
(define traverse
  Capital Table -> (cases (= Table []) "don't know"
```

This can be replaced by a pattern directed invocation

```
(define traverse
  _ [] -> "don't know"
```

The second case was

```
(= Capital (hd (hd Table))) (tl (hd Table))
```

which can be replaced by several patterns; writing in cons form we can have

```
Capital (cons (cons Capital Country) _) -> Country
```

But practically the bar notation is far easier to use and we leave the task of compiling from bar notation to cons form to the Shen reader. Here is the sensible version. Note that Capital occurs twice indicating that the lead element has to be identical to the capital.

```
Capital [[Capital | Country] | _] -> Country
```

And the final case was

```
true (traverse Capital (tl Table))
```

which comes out as

```
Capital [_ | Table] -> (traverse Capital Table)
```

Putting it all together, here is the traverse function.

```
(define traverse
  _ [] -> "don't know"
  Capital [[Capital | Country] | _] -> Country
  Capital [_ | Table] -> (traverse Capital Table))
```

Now let's consider a slightly more complex problem; we have a set of 100 students all taking six compulsory exams; discrete maths, Java programming, algorithms and data structures, functional programming, databases and computer ethics. We have the task of printing out a sheet containing their names against each of these exams and later this sheet will be annotated with their marks. We have the 100 names to hand on the computer and the six compulsory exams are easy to write down in a list. We have to generate a 600 element list in which their names are set against the exam and this we do not want to do by hand.

What we actually need is to find the **Cartesian product** of the two lists. The Cartesian product of X and Y is formed by pairing every element of X with every element of Y. So (cartesian-product [1 2 3] [a b]) evaluates to [[1 | a] [1 | b] [2 | a] [2 | b] [3 | a] [3 | b]].

To compute the Cartesian product we take the first element of X and form all possible dotted pairs with the elements of Y; then the next element of X in the same way, and so on until X is emptied. The sets of pairs are then joined into one set. So to compute (cartesian-product [1 2 3] [a b]) we need to join [[1 | a] [1 | b]], [[2 | a] [2 | b]] and [[3 | a] [3 | b]] to make [[1 | a] [1 | b] [2 | a] [2 | b] [3 | a] [3 | b]].

'Joining' in this context means that the lists are *appended* together so that (e.g.) joining [1 2 3] with [4 5 6] produces [1 2 3 4 5 6]. Note that appending is *not* the same as consing; consing [1 2 3] to [4 5 6] will produce [[1 2 3] 4 5 6]. append is a Shen system function. The code for Cartesian product is given in figure 4.5.

```
(0-) (define cartesian-product
      [] _ -> []
      [X | Y] Z -> (append (pairs X Z) (cartesian-product Y Z)))
(fn cartesian-product)

(1-) (define pairs
      _ [] -> []
      X [Y | Z] -> [[X Y] | (pairs X Z)])
(fn pairs)

(2-) (cartesian-product ["Harold Abelson" "John Backus"
                          "Rudolf Carnap" "Richard Dawkins"]
        ["discrete maths" "Java programming"
        "algorithms and data structures" "functional programming"
        "databases" "computer ethics"])
```

Figure 4.5 Cartesian products in Shen

The response is

[["Harold Abelson" "discrete maths"] ["Harold Abelson" "Java programming"] ["Harold Abelson" "algorithms and data structures"] ["Harold Abelson" "functional programming"] ["Harold Abelson" "databases"] ["Harold Abelson" "computer ethics"] ["John Backus" "discrete maths"] ["John Backus" "Java programming"] ["John Backus" "algorithms and data structures"] ["John Backus" "functional programming"] ["John Backus" "databases"] ["John Backus" "computer ethics"] ["Rudolf Carnap" "discrete maths"] ["Rudolf Carnap" "Java programming"] ["Rudolf Carnap" "algorithms and data structures"] ["Rudolf Carnap" "functional programming"] ["Rudolf Carnap" "databases"] ["Rudolf Carnap" "computer ethics"] ["Richard Dawkins" "discrete maths"] ["Richard Dawkins" "Java programming"] ["Richard Dawkins" "algorithms and data structures"]... etc]

55

Shen prints ... etc if list structures are so long that printing them in full seems unacceptably tedious.[26]

Combinatorial computations involving lists are not uncommon. Melvin Micro, an avid first year student of CS, decides to make a drink called a *porchcrawler* which consists of quantities of beer, gin, vodka, rum, and whisky sweetened perhaps with lemonade. Being devoid of plausible party conversation, but long on science and with an iron constitution, he decides to try all possible combinations of these ingredients in search of the perfect porchcrawler. The number of combinations being large, Melvin decides to compute them all and work through the list.

Melvin's problem is to compute the **powerset** of a set S; the set of all subsets of S. Thus *powerset*($\{a, b, c\}$) = $\{\{a, b, c\}, \{a, b\}, \{a, c\}, \{b, c\}, \{a\}, \{b\}, \{c\}, \{\}\}$. Melvin represents a set as a list that contains no duplicated elements. Since no spaces are involved in the names of the items he is manipulating, Melvin writes them as symbols and not strings. Here is his program (figure 4.6).

```
(define powerset
    [ ] -> [[ ]]
    [X | Y] -> (append (subsets X (powerset Y)) (powerset Y)))

(define subsets
    _ [ ] -> [ ]
    X [Y | Z] -> [[X | Y] | (subsets X Z)])
```

Figure 4.6 Melvin's coding of powerset

The response to (powerset [beer gin vodka rum whisky lemonade]) is

[[beer gin vodka rum whisky lemonade] [beer gin vodka rum whisky] [beer gin vodka rum lemonade] [beer gin vodka rum] [beer gin vodka whisky lemonade] [beer gin vodka whisky] [beer gin vodka lemonade] [beer gin vodka] [beer gin rum whisky lemonade] [beer gin rum whisky] [beer gin rum lemonade] [beer gin rum] [beer gin whisky lemonade] [beer gin whisky] [beer gin lemonade] [beer gin] [beer vodka rum whisky lemonade] [beer vodka rum whisky] [beer vodka rum lemonade] [beer vodka rum] [beer vodka whisky lemonade]... etc]

4.4 Local Assignments

Melvin's definition of *powerset* is inefficient because (powerset Y) is computed twice within the same expression. A better strategy is to compute the normal form of (powerset Y) once and store it for use the second time. This is done with **local assignments** using let.[27] (let V E A) receives three inputs V, E and A where;

---

[26] By default the maximum length for printing is set at 20 elements though this can be changed for any positive integer n by (set *maximum-print-sequence-size* n).

[27] Another primitive of the 46.

56

1. V is a variable, which is assigned a value which is ...
2. the normal form N of E, and (let V E A) returns ......
3. the normal form of the expression that results from substituting N for all free instances of V within A.

Here is *powerset* redefined in figure 4.7 using let.

```
(define powerset
  [ ] -> [[ ]]
  [X | Y] -> (let Powerset (powerset Y)
               (append (subsets X Powerset) Powerset)))
```

Figure 4.7 An efficient coding of powerset using local assignments

The assignment of (powerset Y) to Powerset is local because the assignment works within the scope of let. We cannot usefully employ Powerset outside the local assignment because Powerset would have no value attached to it and a free variable warning would be raised.

let allows multiple local assignments without nested parentheses. Thus

```
(let X 4
     Y 5
     Z 6
     (+ X (* Y Z)))
```

means exactly the same as (let X 4 (let Y 5 (let Z 6 (+ X (* Y Z))))).

4.5 Goldbach's Conjecture Revisited

The previous chapter closed with an example of a possibly non-terminating program to test Goldbach's conjecture. The wasteful recalculation of primes meant that the program ran unfeasibly slowly given even a three digit number on which to test the conjecture. Lists provide the solution; we carry around in the program a list of all the primes calculated up to the number being tested. We refactor this program using lists.

```
(define goldbachs-conjecture
  \\ begin with 4 and the list of primes < 4
  -> (goldbachs-conjecture-help 4 [3 2]))

(define goldbachs-conjecture-help
  N Primes -> N    where (not (sum-of-two? Primes N))
  N Primes  -> (if (prime? (+ N 1))
                 (goldbachs-conjecture-help (+ N 2) [(+ 1 N) | Primes])
                 (goldbachs-conjecture-help (+ N 2) Primes)))
```

```
(define sum-of-two?
  \\ no primes left?  then return false
  [] _ -> false
  \\ If the X + any other prime = N return true
  [X | Primes] N -> true       where (x+prime=n X [X | Primes] N)
  \* no?  then recurse.  *\
  [_ | Primes] N -> (sum-of-two? Primes N))

(define x+prime=n
  \\ no primes left, return false
  _ [] _ -> false
  \\ X + the first prime = N?, so return true
  X [Prime | _] N -> true       where (= (+ X Prime) N)
  \\ recurse and try the other primes
  X [_ | Primes] N -> (x+prime=n X Primes N))
```

Figure 4.8 A more efficient coding of Goldbach's Conjecture

Exercise 4

1. Give the cons-form representation of each of the following.
   [a b c], [[a] [b] [c]], [a [b [c]]], [[a | [b]] c], [a | [b | [c]]]

2. Using only hd and tl, isolate c in each of the expressions in question 1.

3. Define each of the following.
   a. A function total that returns the total of a list of numbers.
   b. A function remdup that removes all duplicated elements in a list.
   c. A function first_n that receives a list L and a natural number N and returns the list of the first N elements of L.
   d. A function flatten that receives a list L and flattens it by removing all internal brackets - so (flatten [a [b] [[c]]]) ⇒ [a b c].
   e. *A function permute that returns all the permutations of a list; (permute [a b c]) = [[a b c] [a c b] [b a c] [b c a] [c a b] [c b a]]. The order of the permutation does not matter.
   f. *A function exchange that exchanges the *m*th and *n*th elements of a list L; so (exchange 3 5 [a b c d e f]) ⇒ [a b e d c f].

4. Classify the recursive function definitions used to answer the previous question as tail-recursive, tree-recursive, mutually recursive or linear recursive.

5. Define a binary number as a non-empty list of 0s and 1s.

   a. *Define binary-add that adds two binary numbers.
   b. *Define binary-subtract that subtracts two binary numbers.
   c. Write a function decimal-to-binary that converts a decimal natural number into binary.
   d. Write a function binary-to-decimal that converts a binary number into decimal.

```
```

e. Define perfect?, that returns true if N is perfect. A perfect number is a natural number > 1 that is the sum of its divisors. 28 is perfect since 28 = 1 + 14 + 2 + 7. 6 is perfect since 6 = 1 + 2 + 3.

f. Define triangular?, that returns true if N is a triangular number. A triangular number is a natural number > 0 that is the sum of the first n natural numbers for some n. 1, 3, 6, 10, 15, 21 are all triangular since 1 = 0 + 1, 3 = 0 + 1 + 2, 6 = 0 + 1 + 2 + 3 and so on.

6. Rewrite the counting change program of the previous chapter so that it receives a list of the denominations in use and returns the answer. So our original result of 4563 would be returned by (count-change 100 [200 100 50 20 10 5 2 1]).

7. *Write a program that enumerates the powerset of a set [1,2,3,....20] by printing the elements of this powerset down the screen. Your program will also supply the millionth element of this enumeration in a second or less. The order of the elements in the enumeration does not matter.

8. *The ancient English game of *cribbage* is played in five and six card variations. We shall ignore some of the subtleties of scoring in this question. In cribbage a hand is scored as follows. Sets of cards whose total pip value is 15 score 2. Any number of cards can be in a set. For the purpose of totalling, face cards count as 10, ace as 1. Three or more cards in sequence (called a *run*) count 1 point for each card in the sequence. An ace is low in cribbage, so ace, two, three is a run, but not queen, king, ace. In five card cribbage, three or more cards of the same suit (called a *flush*) count one point for each card in the flush. In six card cribbage, *four* or more cards of the same suit count one point for each card in the flush. A *pair* (two cards of the same rank) counts 2 points. Here is a hand in six card cribbage.

J♥, Q♥, K♥, K♠, K♣, 5♥

The value of this hand is as follows. 10 points for cards totalling 15 (pair the 5 off with every other card); 6 points for runs (two runs of J, Q, K); 4 points for a flush (the four hearts) and 6 points for pairs (three distinct pairs made from the three kings) giving 26 points in all. Devise a program that scores hands in five and six card cribbage.

9. Cribbage requires the player to discard two cards from his hand. In six card cribbage this gives 30 possible discards and in five card cribbage, 20 possible discards. Devise a function that goes through all the possible discards and works out which is the best discard. The best discard will maximise the value of the remaining cards left in the player's hand (three cards in the case of five card cribbage and four in the case of six card cribbage).

10. *The Roman numeral system was used for many centuries in the ancient world. The table below shows Roman numerals and their decimal equivalents.

Roman	Decimal
I	1
V	5
X	10
L	50
C	100
D	500
M	1000

"The Roman counting system used tallies for numbers ending in 3 (III = 3, 33 = XXXIII). However, four strokes seemed like too many, so the Romans moved on to the symbol for 5 - V. Placing I in front of the V, or placing any smaller number in front of any larger number, indicates subtraction. So IV means 4. After V comes a series of additions - VI means 6, VII means 7, VIII means 8. IX means to subtract I from X, leaving 9. Numbers in the teens, twenties and thirties follow the same form as the first set, only with X's indicating the number of tens. So XXXI is 31, and XXIV is 24. 40 is XL, and 60, 70, and 80 are LX, LXX and LXXX. CCCLXIX is 369. As you can probably guess by this time, CD means 400. So CDXLVIII is 448." Implement a program that takes a Roman numeral from 1-3000 as a list and outputs the corresponding decimal number. (From www.novaroma.org/via_romana/numbers.html).

11. *(For readers with some logic). Implement a tautology tester which, by use of truth-tables, returns true if the input is a tautology and false if not. Thus (tautology? [[p & q] => q]) should return true.

Further Reading

The cons-cell representation of a list is the basis for the representation of a list within the architecture of the digital computer. Allen (1978) contains an account of cons-cell representations. There are other alternatives. Abelson & Sussman (1996) has a discussion of streams which can emulate lists of infinite length. Miranda[TM] uses schemas based on set comprehension as well as lists. The language SETL discussed in Schwartz J.T., Dewar R.B.K., Dubinsky, E., and Schonberg, E., (1986) uses the set instead of the list as its basic data structure. http://galt.cs.nyu.edu/~bacon/other-setl.html provides many links to ongoing work with SETL.

5 Strings

5.1 Strings and Symbols

A string is any series of characters flanked by double quotes ("). Strings behave ostensibly rather like symbols but with a greater degree of flexibility in allowing any standard keyboard character within the double quotes. Thus [a is not an acceptable symbol but "[a" is an acceptable string. In fact any symbol can be turned into a string by simply flanking it by double quotes.

In many languages, but not Shen, strings perform many of the duties of symbols as inputs to functions. Symbols which are simply used as inputs, without any intent to designate a variable or a function are called **idle symbols** in this text. Why allow symbols unless they are working as variables or calling functions? There are several reasons for freeing symbols from such roles.

First, an intellectually trivial but significant reason is that using symbols instead of strings saves time at the keyboard and the result is easier to type and prettier to read. If we are coding an algebra program then [x + [3 - y]] is easier to read and type than ["x" "+" [3 "-" "y"]].

The second reason for allowing idle symbols is that we can make effective use of a powerful idea called **programs as data**. As we shall see in chapter 10, we can represent Shen programs as complex lists containing symbols and write **metaprograms** (or programs that generate programs) which grab those lists and turn them directly into programs using either macros or a function called eval.

In contrast languages which do not allow idle symbols generally have to represent native programs as strings and this requires complex string parsing techniques which are generally more cumbersome to write and slower to execute than the list based ones. In effect, by having a pool of idle symbols to hand we can recruit them as needed for the various tasks which as programmers we might feel inclined to get them to perform.[28] Having established then, the right of idle

---

[28] In Shen, not only can symbols can be recruited for various purposes, but the same symbol can be recruited for different purposes making it a **multiple namespace** language. In a **single namespace** language like Scheme, ML or Python a symbol can only be recruited to mean one thing. The significance of this will become clearer in chapter 21.

symbols and strings to coexist in the same language, we now return to the subject of strings.

Any symbol can be turned into a string by means of the str function which is a primitive function. Thus (str cheese) returns "cheese". str, being one of the primitives, is fast in execution but limited in scope. In fact str is designed to work on Shen **atoms** – that is to say, either symbols, booleans, numbers or strings. (str "cheese") returns ""cheese"".

There is a converse function, intern, for turning a string into a symbol. (intern "cheese") produces cheese. intern is another primitive and will work on symbols and booleans that are effectively embedded within quotes. It can, depending on platform, sometimes extract from quotes objects that are not symbols, (e.g. numbers) but this is not guaranteed.

The basic recognisor for strings is string?, and cn will concatenate (join) two strings together. Both of these are primitive functions and are relatively fast. The correlate of the empty list [] is the **empty string ""**.

```
(0-) (string? "hello world")
true

(1-) (cn "H" (cn "i!" ""))
"Hi!"
```

Figure 5.1 Basic string operations

The set of acceptable strings is actually larger than the set of strings that we can construct from the keyboard characters. The **standard ASCII** character set (figure 5.2) evolved from a set of characters that are expressible within seven bits or 128 (2^7) combinations. Each character is associated with a number which is its **code point**. Later **extended ASCII** representing a set of characters expressible within eight bits or 256 (2^8) combinations was evolved. Still later **32-bit Unicode** was evolved providing enough space to encode the currently recognised 1,112,064 characters with room to spare.

All commonly used computer languages have provision to represent the standard ASCII character set and this includes Shen. Since some of these characters cannot be found on the keyboard, they are referred to through their code points.

ASCII	String	ASCII	String	ASCII	String	ASCII	String
0	blank	36	$	72	H	108	l
1	☺	37	%	73	I	109	m
2	●	38	&	74	J	110	n
3	♥	39	'	75	K	111	o
4	♦	40	(	76	L	112	p
5	♣	41	)	77	M	113	q
6	♠	42	*	78	N	114	r
7	bell	43	+	79	O	115	s
8	"	44	,	80	P	116	t
9	tab	45	-	81	Q	117	u
10	newline	46	.	82	R	118	v
11	♂	47	/	83	S	119	w
12	♂	48	0	84	T	120	x
13	newline	49	1	85	U	121	y
14	♫	50	2	86	V	122	z
15	☼	51	3	87	W	123	{
16	►	52	4	88	X	124		
17	◄	53	5	89	Y	125	}
18	↕	54	6	90	Z	126	~
19	‼	55	7	91	[	127	⌂
20	¶	56	8	92	\		
21	§	57	9	93	]		
22	▬	58	:	94	^		
23	↨	59	;	95	_		
24	↑	60	<	96	`		
25	↓	61	=	97	a		
26	→	62	>	98	b		
27	←	63	?	99	c		
28	∟	64	@	100	d		
29	↔	65	A	101	e		
30	▲	66	B	102	f		
31	▼	67	C	103	g		
32	blank	68	D	104	h		
33	!	69	E	105	i		
34	"	70	F	106	j		
35	#	71	G	107	k		

Figure 5.2 The ASCII Character Table for Windows

Shen allows non-keyboard characters to be embedded into strings by use of the c#*n*; notation; where *n* is a natural number. Thus in Windows the string "c#16;" is read and printed as "▶" because ▶ has the ASCII code point 16.[29] The table previous shows the list of ASCII code points and their associated characters.

The function n->string maps any ASCII code point to the corresponding **unit string**[30]. The domain of this function includes all of the ASCII codes from 0-127 and may, depending on the platform, incorporate a wider character set beyond 127, such as Unicode; however this is not guaranteed. For cases outside the ASCII code point space, this function may return an error. The inverse of n->string is string->n; both of these are primitive (figure 5.3).

```
(0-) "c#16;"
"▶"

(1-) (string->n "c#15;")
15

(2-) (n->string 67)
"C"

(3-) (string->n "G")
71
```

Figure 5.3 Using ASCII character codes

5.2 Building strings with make-string

The polyadic function make-string is rather more sophisticated than str; it accepts a string and a series of zero or more following arguments. One of these is ~%, which forces a new line (figure 5.4).

```
(4-) (make-string "goodbye cruel world,~%I bid you adieu.~%")
"goodbye cruel world,
I bid you adieu."
```

Figure 5.4 Using make-string

~A creates slots in the message, which can be filled in any way by placing expressions after the message string. The expressions are evaluated to their normal forms, and these normal forms are placed in the slots of the message and the result is printed. Figure 5.5 shows an example.

---

[29] For Linux and other operating systems, the appearance of non-keyboard characters may differ from those under Windows.

[30] A unit string is a single character flanked by quotes; such as "e" or "7".

```
(10-) (make-string "~A in ~A ~A made ~A ~A.~%" God his wisdom the fly)
"God in his wisdom made the fly."
```

Figure 5.5 Filling the slots in a string

The slots are determined by the following key sequences; ~A, ~S and ~R. ~A and ~S are identical except that when slot value is a string, ~A embeds it in the slot without quotes and ~S embeds it with quotes. ~R embeds a list into the slot using (...)s for [...]s which is useful for printing formulae.

```
(4-) (make-string "~S, said the fly.~%" "Why?")
""Why?" said the fly."

(5-) (make-string "~A, said the fly.~%" "Why?")
"Why? said the fly."

(6-) (make-string "~A = ~A~%" [1 + 1] 2)
"[1 + 1] = 2"

(7-) (make-string "~R = ~R~%" [1 + 1] 2)
"(1 + 1) = 2"
```

Figure 5.6 Building strings using different slots

5.3 Coercing Strings to Lists

A slower, but again more general function than intern, is read-from-string[31] which will take any series of readable objects embedded in a string and return them as a list (figure 5.7).

```
(0-) (read-from-string "hello world")
[hello world]

(1-) (read-from-string "[hi there")
read error here:

[hi there
```

Figure 5.7 Reading from a string

explode is a useful function which explodes any object (including lists etc) into a list of unit strings. The expression (explode "hello") delivers ["h" "e" "l" "l" "o"]. Exploding [1 2 3] delivers ["[" "1" " " "2" " " "3" "]"] (the gaps between the numbers are marked by blank strings).

---

[31] This function is covered in more depth in 9.4.

The expression ($ hello) is superficially similar in exploding its argument; however the exploding is done by the reader and ($ hello) is read in as if the user had typed in "h" "e" "l" "l" "o". This is useful to avoid typing multiple quotes. Thus the definition

```
(define remove-hello
  [($ hello) | X] -> X)
```

is equivalent to and is parsed as

```
(define remove-hello
  ["h" "e" "l" "l" "o" | X] -> X)
```

5.4 Programming with Strings

There are two basic primitives pos and tlstr for processing strings. pos takes two arguments, a string *s* and an integer *n* and returns the *n*th character of *s* counting from zero. tlstr returns all but the first character of *s*. Again both of these are primitive.

It is significant that hdstr, which returns the first element of a string, is not a primitive though it is provided as a courtesy (being equivalent to (pos *string* 0)). The reason for this is that many languages store strings in the form of vectors of characters, and in a vector *v* the *n*th element of *v* can be located in constant time. Hence it is just a quick to locate the 100th element of a string as the first and hence pos is a primitive and hdstr is not. A vector-based representation of strings has profound consequences for the speed of string handling operations and we will understand this better in chapter 8 on vectors.

Shen incorporates a function @s which acts as a polyadic version of cn. Thus (cn "H" (cn "i!" "")) can be written as (@s "H" "i!" "") or (@s "Hi" ""). The polyadicity is created by the Shen reader. Internally, the Shen reader inserts the missing brackets, and @s is read as a concatenation of *unit strings*. So the expression (@s "Hi!" "")) is read as (@s "H" (@s "i" (@s "!" ""))).

@s can be used in pattern-matching over strings and nearly all complex string manipulation programs are written in this style. Used in a function, (@s X Y) matches X to the head of the string and Y to the tail. @s therefore suffices to define all the primitive string operations. One such function tests a string to see if it is the prefix of another string.

```
(0-) (define string-prefix?
      "" _ -> true
      (@s S Str1) (@s S Str2) -> (string-prefix? Str1 Str2)
      _ _ -> false)
(fn string-prefix?)

(1-) (string-prefix? "123" "1234")
true

(2-) (string-prefix? "1234" "123")
false
```

Figure 5.8 Testing one string to see if it is a prefix of another

Now we have got the idea of string handling, let us consider again a problem we dealt with in the previous chapter; that of computing a list of students and the exams they had taken.

In order to do that we computed the Cartesian product of the students' names and the exams they took. In our scenario we had 100 names and 6 exams, but there was no supposition that the names were ordered alphabetically. If they are not ordered alphabetically then the Cartesian product will itself not be ordered alphabetically and we will end up with an unsorted 600 element list. Hence the student list should first be sorted alphabetically before the Cartesian product is computed.

Bubble sort is one of the simplest and least efficient sorting algorithms but it is sufficient for a 100 element list. Bubble sorting a list L into ascending or descending order works by traversing L comparing each item x with its successor y. If y is prior to x according to the sort relation, then the positions of x and y are exchanged. Bubble sorting is repeated until no change occurs, at which point L is sorted. Here it is in Shen.

```
(define bubble-sort
  X -> (bubble-again-perhaps (bubble X) X))

(define bubble
  [ ] -> [ ]
  [X] -> [X]
  [X Y | Z] -> [Y | (bubble [X | Z])]          where (prior? Y X)
  [X Y | Z] -> [X | (bubble [Y | Z])])

(define bubble-again-perhaps
  X X -> X
  X _ -> (bubble-sort X))
```

Figure 5.9 Bubble sort

One name is prior to another if the surname is prior.

```
(define prior?
  Name1 Name2 -> (string< (surname Name1) (surname Name2)))
```

The surname will be the series of characters that follow the last whitespace in a string. Whitespace is located by the code point, being either a new line, a tab or a blank.

```
(define surname
  Name -> (surname-help Name ""))

(define surname-help
  "" Surname -> Surname
  (@s S Name) _ -> (surname-help Name "") where (whitespace? S)
  (@s S Name) Surname ->  (surname-help Name (cn Surname S)))

(define whitespace?
  S -> (let N (string->n S) (element? N [9 10 13 32])))

(define string<
  (@s S _) (@s S# _) -> true        where (< (string->n S) (string->n S#))
  (@s S Ss) (@s S Ss#) -> (string< Ss Ss#)
  "" (@s _ _) -> true
  _ _ -> false)
```

We test the program on a list of names.

```
(9 -) (bubble-sort ["Rudolf Carnap"  "Richard Dawkins"
                "John Backus"  "Harold Abelson" ])
["Harold Abelson" "John Backus" "Rudolf Carnap" "Richard Dawkins"]
```

Exercise 5

1. Write a program that computes your initials from a string containing your full name and displays them as a list of unit strings.

2. An **anagram** is a word or a phrase made by transposing the letters of another word or phrase; for example, "parliament" is an anagram of "partial men," and "software" is an anagram of "swear oft." Write a program that figures out whether one string is an anagram of another string. The program should ignore white space and punctuation.

3. Design, then implement a program that sums the ASCII codes of all the letters of any string.

4. Divide a string into two halves. If the length is even, the front and back halves are the same length. If the length is odd, the extra character goes in the front half.

5. Write a program that given a natural number *n*, outputs a string in which *n* is embedded in an *n×n* square. For example, for the input 3 the square would be (numbers line up).

    a.   "3 3 3
    b.   3 3 3
    c.   3 3 3"

6. Generalise intern to gen-intern so that you can read an expression of the form "[1 2 3]" and return [1 2 3]. Whether your platform already does this is not important.*

7. Write a function trimr to remove all trailing whitespace from the right of a string.

8. Write a function triml to remove all leading whitespace from the left of a string.

9. Write a function padr to add extra whitespace to the right end of a string to make it length *n*. If the string is already *n* characters or longer, do not change the string.

10. Write a function padl to add extra whitespace to the left end of a string to make it length *n*. If the string is already *n* characters or longer, do not change the string.

11. Write a function padc to centre a string by adding blanks to the front and back. If the string is already *n* characters or longer, do not change the string. If an odd number of blanks have to be added, put the extra blank on the right.

12. Write a function shorten which shortens a string to *n* characters. If the string is already shorter than *n*, the function should not change the string.

13. Write a function capitalise which capitalises the first letter in every word. Assume the first letter is any letter at the beginning or preceded by a blank. All other letters should be turned into lowercase.

14. Write a function count which counts the occurrences in a string, *a*, of the single character which is the second argument, *b*.

15. Write a function delete which deletes any occurrence in the first argument, *a*, of the single character which is the second argument, *c*.

Further Reading

String processing languages began with SNOBOL (string oriented and symbolic language) in 1962 (Emmer, 1985) developed by AT&T. More recent successors include TCL/tk (Ousterhout, 2006) and Perl (Wall et al., 2012). TCL/tk was popular in the '90s and Perl remains the language of choice for many people involved in text processing. The main feature of Perl in relation to strings is its regex pattern matching which allows the programmer write a single line to search for a string in a body of text.

6 Higher Order Functions

6.1 Higher Order Functions

Functions often seem insubstantial since they have no physical existence; the square root function, for instance, cannot be given a location; there is no moment when it was created, since it stands outside time and space. For people of a philosophical persuasion, this makes functions very strange objects. However a willingness to countenance functions as substantial objects is implicit in functional programming, where functions are treated as potential inputs or outputs to other functions, just as other objects like numbers or strings. In functional programming, functions enjoy the same rights of processing as other data objects; i.e. functions are **first-class objects**.

Higher-order functions receive functions as inputs or return them amongst the output. In Shen map is a higher-order system function. Its definition is:

```
(define map
  F [ ] -> [ ]
  F [X | Y] -> [(F X) | (map F Y)])
```

map receives a 1-place function F and a list L. If L is empty, then L is returned. But if L is of the form [X | Y] then the function F is applied to the first element X and the result is consed to the effect of recursing on the tail of the list using map. Figure 6.1 shows the use of map.

```
(0 -) (define double
         X -> (* X 2))
(fn double)

(1-) (map (fn double) [1 2 3 4])
[2 4 6 8]
```

Figure 6.1 Using the map function

70

fn maps the symbol double to the function it designates. [32] In Shen a symbol may moonlight in a number of roles and it is necessary to be clear what we are asking of it. In this case we are asking for the function associated with that name. [33]

6.2 Abstractions, Currying and Partial Applications

The function that doubles a number is represented in Shen as (/. X (* X 2)). /. is the Shen ASCII substitute for the Greek lambda, and (/. X (* X 2)) is referred to as an **abstraction** or a **lambda expression**. We can most easily read the notation of abstractions by taking /. to mean "the function that receives an input...". Thus (/. X (* X 2)) is read as "the function that receives an input X and returns the result of multiplying X by 2". Figure 6.2 shows the use of an abstraction.

```
(1-) (/. X (* X 2))
#<CLOSURE :LAMBDA [X] [* X 2]>

(2-) ((/. X (* X 2)) 5)
10
```

Figure 6.2 Using abstractions

The evaluation of an abstraction in Shen delivers an object called a **closure**, which is a compiled representation of the original abstraction with zero or more pieces of data attached to it. [34] In Shen, closures are represented as expressions beginning #<CLOSURE ...>. [35] These expressions are **internal expressions**; they cannot be read and evaluated in their computer-printed form (i.e. typing #<CLOSURE :LAMBDA [X] [* X 2]> will generate an error).

As shown, abstractions can be applied to expressions just like normal functions. They differ from conventional Shen functions in being applicable to only one input, for in these examples exactly one variable follows the /.. However it is possible to represent *n*-place functions with abstractions, where *n* is any value.

An example with the 2-place function + will illustrate the idea.

---

[32] function was used instead of fn in older versions of Shen and this will still work.

[33] This brings out the difference between Shen and single namespace languages mentioned earlier. In a single namespace language such as Python. ML or Haskell, a global symbol may only have a single role and hence the disambiguating function is not needed. Note that in the Lisp platform, the compiler may be clever enough to figure out that the symbol is being used to denote a function. However this is not a portable feature and good practice requires us to use fn.

[34] More precisely, a closure is a function represented as a pair composed of a lambda abstraction together with an assignment of values to the free variables of that abstraction. See chapter 14 of this book for a discussion of lambda expressions and chapter 24 for a discussion of closures.

[35] This representation may vary according to the platform being used. There is no obligation in Shen to print closures or streams or native objects of the platform in a specific form and if Shen cannot print such an object it is printed as a *funex* in the form funex*n* where *n* is a number. See chapter 9 on printing..

The 2-place function + can be represented as an interaction of two 1-place functions *f* and *g*. *f* receives a number *x* and produces a function *g* that waits to receive another number *y*. Whatever number *y* is supplied to *g*, *y* is added to *x* to produce the result $x + y$. Thus the function + is denoted by the expression

"the function that receives an input *x* and returns a function that receives an input *y* that then returns $x + y$".

Translating this into the notation of abstractions gives (/. X (/. Y (+ X Y))). Now suppose we tell Shen to apply this expression to the number 5.

```
(1-) ((/. X (/. Y (+ X Y))) 5)
#<CLOSURE :LAMBDA [Y] [+ X Y]>
```

Figure 6.3 Applying an abstraction to produce a function

Shen returns a closure which represents a function that adds 5 to its input.   If ((/. X (/. Y (+ X Y))) 5) is itself applied to 3, then the result is the same as applying this closure to 3, which produces 8. (/. X Y (+ X Y)) is an accepted abbreviation for (/. X (/. Y (+ X Y))).

```
(2-) (((/. X  Y (+ X Y)) 5) 3)
8
```

Figure 6.4 Using an abstraction to add two numbers

When an abstraction is applied to an input to produce a function (as in 6.3) then the application is called a **partial application**. Since the 2-place function symbol '+' and the abstraction '(/. X Y (+ X Y))' both denote the same operation of addition, it is reasonable to expect that we should be able to enter '(+ 5)' as a partial application in Shen and return a closure just as in figure 6.3.   This is correct; we can substitute '+' for '(/. X Y (+ X Y))' and gain the same function.

```
(3-) (+ 5)
partial application of *
#<FUNCTION (LAMBDA (Y11607)) {100709824B}>

(4+) ((+ 5) 3)
8
```

Figure 6.5 Currying + to add two numbers

Nearly every application[36] can be written to Shen in the form (*f i*), consisting of a function *f* and a single input *i*. When an expression in this form is **curried** and the operation of placing it in this form is **currying**.[37]

---

[36] With few exceptions; the functions cons, let, output, make-string, error, @p, @v, @s, input are not curried or curryable in Shen and are referred to as **special forms**. The partial application warning can be disabled by (warnings -); see appendix A.

Partial applications can be incorporated into function definitions. This function, xn-map, when supplied with a number N and a list L, multiplies every element of L by N.

```
(define xn-map
   N L -> (map (* N) L))
```

This loads with a note 'partial application of *', since partial applications often result from clerical errors.

6.3 fn and Abstractions

The Shen reader treats an 'fn' call as shorthand for the corresponding abstraction. So (map (fn double) [1 2 3]) is compiled into (map (/. X (double X)) [1 2 3]). This compilation depends on Shen having access to the arity of double.

If *f* is used as a function in a definition *d before* Shen has access to the definition of *f* (that is *d* is typed to the REPL before *f* is defined or else *d* is defined in one file *A* and *f* in another *B* and *A* is loaded before *B*) then the elimination in favour of a lambda expression is not possible. In that case Shen leaves (fn *f*) in place. When *f* is defined, the value for (fn *f*) is stored in a table as a lambda function. The value for (fn *f*) is computed dynamically by an association list search and the relevant abstraction is retrieved. If no entry for *f* can be found in the table, an error is then raised.[38]

6.4 Overapplications

An **overapplication** occurs when an *n*-ary function is applied to *m* arguments where $m > n$, e.g. (reverse [1] [2]). This is an error in nearly all cases and Shen will issue a warning (e.g. 'reverse might not like 2 arguments') when compiling. There are rare cases where it is not. Consider the following higher-order function compose which forms the composition of a list of functions.

```
(define compose
   [F] -> F
   [F | Fs] -> (/. X ((compose Fs) (F X))))
```

The overapplication (compose (let F (* 2) [F F]) 3) does not return an error but actually computes 12. The reason being that the curried form is ((compose (let F (* 2) [F F])) 3). The composition (compose (let F (* 2) [F F])) produces a function that when applied to 3 multiplies it by 4.

---

[37] After Haskell B. Curry, the mathematical logician who is usually credited with inventing this technique, although Schonfinkel was the first to use it.

[38] When *f* is defined externally to Shen (e.g. in the host platform), this information must be supplied by the user. Thus if square is externally defined as a 1-place function that squares a number then the declaration (add-lambda-table square 1) should be used. Alternatively (specialise square 1) will exempt the application of square from being 'fn'ed by Shen.

Activating type checking, as discussed in the second part of this book, guards against pathological misuse of partial and overapplications due to programmer error.

6.5 Programming with Higher Order Functions

Programming with higher-order functions enables us to

1. Get rid of unnecessary definitions using abstractions.
2. Use similarities in different processes to shorten our code.
3. Pass functions as data.

The Cartesian product program of 4.5 invoked a function pairs that paired an element X with each element of a list L. Rather than define a function like pairs, we use an abstraction; a similar optimisation works for the powerset function.

```
(define cartesian-product
  [] _ -> []
  [X | Y] Z -> (append (map (/. E [X E]) Z) (cartesian-product Y Z)))

(define powerset
  [] -> [[]]
  [X | Y] -> (let Powerset (powerset Y)
                  Sets (map (/. Z [X | Z]) Powerset)
               (append Sets Powerset)))
```

Figure 6.6 Cartesian product and powerset recoded using abstractions

If two programs both share properties then rather than encode them separately, we can draw out the similarities using higher-order functions. Our case study compares the bubble sort algorithm of the last chapter with **Newton's method of approximations**. Just to remind us, figure 6.7 gives the code for bubble sort again, but now as a higher-order program in which the priority relation is a parameter.

```
(define bubble-sort
  R X -> (bubble-again-perhaps R (bubble R X) X))

(define bubble
  _ [] -> []
  _ [X] -> [X]
  R [X Y | Z] -> [Y | (bubble R [X | Z])]        where (R Y X)
  R [X Y | Z] -> [X | (bubble R [Y | Z])])

(define bubble-again-perhaps
  _ X X -> X
  R X _ -> (bubble-sort R X))
```

Figure 6.7 Bubble sort as a higher order program in Shen

Newton's method of approximations is a common way is to compute square roots. The method says that if we want to find the square root of N, we take a guess Guess and average the result with N/Guess. This average will then be a better estimate of the value of √N than the original Guess. By repeating the process as many times as desired, we will derive the value of √N to a given degree of accuracy.

Suppose we decide to use Newton's method of approximations to derive the value of √N to three decimal places. We start our guess at √N by guessing that √N = N/2.0. Every time we derive a better value for √N using Newton's method, we compare the two values. Eventually the better value will be different from the old one by an absolute difference of less than (say) .001 which will be good enough. This value will be returned as our value for √N (figure 6.8).

```
(define newtons-method
  N -> (let Guess (/ N 2.0)
          (run-newtons-method N (average Guess (/ N Guess)) Guess)))

(define run-newtons-method
  _ BetterGuess Guess -> BetterGuess
            where (close-enough? Better_Guess Guess)
  N Better_Guess _
  -> (run-newtons-method  N
              (average BetterGuess  (/ N BetterGuess))
              BetterGuess))

(define average
  M N -> (/ (+ M N) 2.0))

(define close-enough?
  BetterGuess Guess -> (< (abs (- BetterGuess Guess)) .001))

(define abs
  N -> (if (> 0 N) (- 0 N) N))
```

Figure 6.8 Newton's method in Shen

The code for bubble sort and Newton's method share a common element in that they both apply a procedure to their input until no significant change is produced in the output. To make use of this observation to shorten the code we need to formalise the idea of *converging on a value*.

The basic idea of convergence is that we have a function F which is iteratively applied to a value X until the result differs from the result of the previous iteration within some agreed tolerance R. When that point is reached we have converged on a solution within the bounds of R. Figure 6.9 shows the higher-order function converge, that computes this.

```
(define converge
  F X R -> (converge-help F (F X) X R))

(define converge-help
  _ New Old R -> New  where (R New Old)
  F New _ R -> (converge-help F (F New) New R))
```

Figure 6.9 The converge function

Using converge, the top level of the bubble sort program can be rewritten; the bubble-again-perhaps function is now redundant (figure 6.10).

```
(define bubble-sort
  R X -> (converge (/. Y (bubble R Y)) X (fn =)))
```

Figure 6.10 Rewriting the top level of the bubble sort program

Applying converge to Newton's method is a little more difficult since run-newtons-method is a 3-place function, not a 1-place function like bubble. However the number N whose square root we are to find is fixed when newtons-method is called and it always stays the same while the program is running. The newtons-method function can use a specialised version of run-newtons-method for that particular value of N. Since N is fixed, this specialised function could be a 2-place function.

Still one too many places! However, consider that run-newtons-method carries both the old value and the better value around in order to compare them for equality. If we use converge to derive the final value, such a comparison is not needed. Since the specialised version of run-newtons-method is defined only when newtons-method is called, it must be created "on the fly". Creating functions on the fly is a job for abstractions and so we use them to recode the original Shen program (figure 6.11). The recursion and comparison is driven by converge.

```
(define newtons-method
  N -> (converge (/. M (average M (/ N M)))
                 (/ N 2.0)
                 (fn close-enough?)))
```

Figure 6.11 Newton's method recoded using a higher order function

The combined length of the two revised programs is less than half that of the originals. Higher-order functions can save us a lot of tedious code if we can learn to recognise the cases in which they are applicable. But if we want to seize these opportunities, we must be alert for high-level similarities between algorithms.

Higher order functions allow us to treat functions as data just like numbers or lists. This technique, called **procedural attachment,** is used in the next example - how to build a spreadsheet.

Imagine that we want to maintain a list of details about an employee Jim, including his salary and the amount he pays in tax. Suppose that he pays 25% of his wages in tax. If we enter his tax as a cash figure, then if he has a wage increase then the cash figure for tax will be wrong. Business managers cope with problems like this using *spreadsheets*; Jim's tax is stored, not as a number, but as a function that allows the calculation of his tax from other details on the spreadsheet. Our task is to model a spreadsheet in Shen.

Our spreadsheet will consist of a series of *rows*, each row consisting of an *index* and a series of *cells*. The index is a unique name that marks out that row and a cell is composed of an *attribute* (like tax or job) and a *value*. Values can be either *fixed values* which are **atoms** (booleans, numbers. strings or symbols) or they can be *dependent values* (functions) which when applied to the appropriate inputs, will return fixed values. To assess a spreadsheet, we replace all the dependent values by fixed values.

Figure 6.12 shows a sample spreadsheet in which Jim's wages are pegged to Frank's and his tax is pegged to .8 of whatever Frank pays. Frank is down as earning £20,000 a year and paying .25 of this in tax. We want to evaluate this expression so that the dependent values are replaced by fixed values, giving figures for wage and tax for both Jim and Frank.

```
[[jim [wages (/. Spreadsheet (get-val frank wages Spreadsheet))]
     [tax (/. Spreadsheet (* (get-val frank tax Spreadsheet) .8))]]
 [frank [wages 20000]
     [tax (/. Spreadsheet (* .25 (get-val frank wages Spreadsheet)))]]]]
```

Figure 6.12 A sample spreadsheet in Shen

Figure 6.13 shows a spreadsheet program in Shen. The top level function **assess-spreadsheet** works along each row in turn, assigning fixed values to the cells; the entire spreadsheet is carried in this process, since a dependent value may access any part of the spreadsheet. **assign-fixed-values** takes a row and assigns a fixed value to every cell. **assign-fixed-values** will receive a cell and a spreadsheet; if the value in the cell is fixed, the cell remains the same. If it is dependent, then the value in the cell is applied to the spreadsheet to derive a fixed value.

```
(define assess-spreadsheet
  Spreadsheet
  -> (map (/. Row (assign-fixed-values Row Spreadsheet))
               Spreadsheet))

(define assign-fixed-values
  [Index | Cells] Spreadsheet
  -> [Index |  (map (/. Cell (assign-cell-value Cell Spreadsheet))
                    Cells)])

(define assign-cell-value
  [Attribute Value] _ -> [Attribute Value]
                              where (fixed-value? Value)
  [Attribute Value] Spreadsheet
           -> [Attribute (Value Spreadsheet)]])

(define fixed-value?
  Value -> (or (number? Value) (symbol? Value) (string? Value)))

(define get-val
  Index Attribute Spreadsheet
  -> (get-row Index Attribute Spreadsheet Spreadsheet))

(define get-row
  \\ looks for the right row using the index
  Index Attribute [[Index | Cells] | _] Spreadsheet
  -> (get-cell Attribute Cells Spreadsheet)
  Index Attribute [_ | Rows] Spreadsheet
  -> (get-row Index Attribute Rows Spreadsheet)
  Index _ _ _ -> (error "Index ~A not found" Index))

(define get-cell
  Attribute [[Attribute Value] | _] Spreadsheet
  -> (if (fixed-value? Value) Value (Value Spreadsheet))
  Attribute [_ | Cells] Spreadsheet
  -> (get-cell Attribute Cells Spreadsheet)
  Attribute _ _ -> (error "Attribute ~A not found" Attribute))
```

Figure 6.13 A spreadsheet program in Shen

The get function works along each row, carrying the full spreadsheet with it. We need to do this because a dependent value will access other values before returning a fixed value, and we will then need the spreadsheet again (e.g. Jim's tax accesses Frank's tax which accesses Frank's wages). We cope with this by creating two copies of the spreadsheet, one to work through row by row, and the other to hold in memory in case the whole spreadsheet is needed. This technique, of duplicating inputs to keep one for processing and one to remember, is called **spreading the input**. Finally get-cell looks for a cell corresponding to the attribute, and retrieves the value. If the value is fixed, then it is returned, if not then it is applied to the spreadsheet to retrieve the appropriate value.

Figure 6.14 shows our spreadsheet program in action.

```
(5-) (assess-spreadsheet
    [[jim  [wages (/. Spreadsheet (get-val frank wages Spreadsheet))]
       [tax (/. Spreadsheet (* (get-val frank tax Spreadsheet) .8))]]
     [frank  [wages 20000]
       [tax (/. Spreadsheet (* .25 (get-val frank wages Spreadsheet)))]]])

[[jim [wages 20000] [tax 4000.0]] [frank [wages 20000] [tax 5000.0]]]
```

Figure 6.14 Assessing a spreadsheet

Exercise 6

1. Define the following higher-order functions.

   a. A function count which takes a 1-place boolean function F and a list L and returns the number of elements in L that have the property F.
   b. A function some? which takes a 1-place boolean function F and a list L and returns true if some element of L has the property F and false otherwise.
   c. A function all? which takes a 1-place boolean function F and a list L and returns true if every element of L has the property F and false otherwise.
   d. A function compose that receives a non-empty list of 1-place functions and forms their composition. Thus (compose [(/. X (+ 1 X)) (fn sqrt)]) would generate a function that added one to the square root of a number.
   e. A function test-speed that receives a list input L and a natural number N. The list L is composed of a function symbol F followed by a series of elements $X_1,...,X_j$. test-speed should apply F to the inputs $X_1,...,X_j$, performing this operation N times, and timing the whole computation (hint: look at the function time in Appendix A).
   f. A function partition that receives a list L and an equivalence relation R on that list and generates the partition of L by R as a list of lists.

2. A progression is an object that mimics a possibly infinitely long list and can be represented as a three-element list [X F E]. X is the first element in the progression and F is the function that applied to any element of the progression gives the next element and E tests if the progression is exhausted. So the progression of natural numbers can be represented as [0 (/. X (+ 1 X)) (/. X false)].

   a. Write a function, lazy-nth, that given any progression P, gets the *n*th element of L.
   b. Devise a 2-place function some? that receives a 1-place boolean function *f* and a progression P, returning true if there is an object *x* in P such that $(f\,x)$ = true.
   c. If two progressions A and B have an infinite number of elements, then appending them together makes no computational sense because the stream that is tagged at the end will remain inaccessible to stream-nth. But we can interleave them by generating a progression composed of two-element lists where the *n*th element of this progression is composed of a list containing the *n*th element of A and the *n*th element of B . Write a function interleave which does just that.

79

d.   Write a function all? that receives a 1-place boolean function f and a progression, returning true if every object x in the stream is such that $(f x)$ = true.

e.   Write a function expand that takes a progression and generates the list that corresponds to it. So (expand [0 [(/. X (+ 1 X)) (/. X (= X 1000))]]) generates the list of numbers [0 1 2 3 .... 1000].

4.   It is natural to think of lists as data objects and functions like head and tail as procedures which act on data-objects. But we can change this perception.

a.   Implement the list [1 2 3] as a higher-order function that receives the message head and returns 1 and the message tail and returns the corresponding higher-order function that represents the list [2 3]. Implement [ ] as a function that returns an error given the message head or the message tail.

b.   Now implement the functions first and rest. first receives the higher-order function that represents the list and derives the first element from it. rest receives the higher-order function that represents the list and derives the corresponding higher-order function that represents the tail of the list.

c.   Finally define constr as the analogue of cons that builds a new list representing function from an old one. Show that (first (constr X Y)) = X.

Further Reading

Hughes (1990) defends functional programming because of its ability to support higher-order programming. Abelson and Sussman (1996) has a very good discussion of higher-order programming. The classic reference for sorting algorithms is Knuth (1998).

Web Sites

Alejo   Hausner   (http://www.cs.princeton.edu/~ah/alg_anim/version2/sorts.html)   at Princeton includes a description of several classical sorting algorithms (including bubble sort) which are implemented in Java.

7 Assignments

7.1 Simple Assignments

An assignment is an expression whose evaluation causes an object to be associated with a symbol in the environment so that we can call upon this object through invoking the symbol in an appropriate way. These objects are called **global values**.

If *s* is a symbol and *e* an expression, the simple assignment (set *s e*) does two things.

1. The normal form *e** of *e* is returned.
2. As a side-effect, *e** becomes the value of the global variable *s;* so that the expression (value *s*) will return *e**.

Figure 7.1 shows a short script that uses set and value. We follow the Lisp tradition of asterixing global variables.

```
(0-) (set *number* 6)
6

(1-) (+ (value *number*) 6)
12

(2-) (set *number* 5)
5

(3-) (+ (value *number*) 6)
11
```

Figure 7.1 Using simple assignments

Although conventionally, when computer scientists talk about assignment statements, they generally do not include function definitions under that category, the use of define is, strictly speaking, another example of an assignment. The effect of define is to change the environment in which the computation is carried out and in that sense it is an assignment.

The important difference between function definitions and other assignments is that, generally, function definitions do not and cannot change during the execution of a program, whereas simple assignments can change the value assigned. The basic similarity between assignments and function definitions can be brought out by assigning an abstraction to a global variable. The variable can then be used to invoke the function in almost the same way as a regular function definition. Figure 7.2 shows how a simple assignment can do this.

```
(0-) (set *factorial* (/. X (if (= X 0) 1 (* X ((value *factorial*) (- X 1))))))
#<CLOSURE :LAMBDA [X]  [if [= X 0] 1 [* X [apply [value '*factorial*] [- X 1]]]]>

(1-) ((value *factorial*) 9)
362880
```

Figure 7.2 Using a simple assignment to hold an abstraction

Simple assignments can make programs shorter. For example, the get-val function of the previous chapter required the spreading of the input, 'Spreadsheet', in order to retain some memory of what the entire spreadsheet was like. However, if we assign the spreadsheet to a global variable (called *spreadsheet*), then this spreading is unnecessary and the program sheds an auxiliary function and becomes simpler (figure 7.3).

```
(define get-val
    Index Attribute [[Index | Cells] | _] -> (get-cell Attribute Cells)
    Index Attribute [_ | Rows] -> (get-val Index Attribute Rows)
    Index _ _ -> (error "Index ~A not found" Index))

(define get-cell
    Attribute [[Attribute Value] | _]
    -> (if (fixed-value? Value) Value (Value (value *spreadsheet*)))
    Attribute [_ | Cells] -> (get-cell Attribute Cells)
    Attribute _ -> (error "Attribute ~A not found" Attribute))
```

Figure 7.3 Using simple assignments in place of spreading

7.2 Destructive Operations

The function set used to perform simple assignment is an example of a **destructive function** because the effect of applying the operation is to change the global environment in which the computation is carried out by destroying or overwriting any previous value attached to the assigned symbol.

Destructive operations are a topic of contention in computer science. Pragmatically, as we shall see, being able to perform destructive operations on data allows us to simplify certain programs and can radically improve the performance of programs that are forced to modify large data structures.

82

On the minus side, there are several disadvantages to destructive operations. The first is that that there is no possibility of returning to the premodified version of the data structure unless we take care to keep it in memory.

The second is that the mathematical purity of functional programming is no longer maintained. We cannot reason about such programs using conventional logic because basic mathematical principles *apparently* break down. One such is self identity; i.e.

$$\textit{for all } x, x = x$$

Interpreted *de re*[39], as a statement about objects, this principle is universally true; everything is itself. But interpreted *de dicto*, as a statement about languages, it is false. *De dicto* the principle reads that all substitution instances of '$x = x$' must receive the valuation *true*. In **extensional** languages this is true, but it is easy to show that this principle fails when we use destructive operations (figure 7.3). [40]

```
(0-) (define increment
    -> (set *counter* (+ 1 (value *counter*))))
(fn increment )

(1-) (set *counter* 0)
0

(2-) (= (increment) (increment))
false
```

Figure 7.4 Self identity failing de dicto in Shen

Figure 7.4 shows that if destructive operations are used then self-identity *apparently* breaks down. *De re*, this Law cannot fail, but the *de dicto* interpretation of it applied to Shen, based on the simple mathematical reading of a functional program, does break down here.

This failure means that standard logical tools are not fit for the job of reasoning about destructive programs and the programmer who wants to do this has to use something more complicated that appeals to the concept of *state* and *environment*.

---

[39] The distinction between *de re* and *de dicto* comes from mediaeval logic; it literally means 'of things' and 'of speech'.

[40] In fact the principle fails even within the non-destructive subset of Shen. The expression (= (/. X (+ X X)) (/. X (* X 2))) returns false even though the functions are extensionally identical. Shen returns false because it compares the representation of the functions within the machine and not the functions themselves. The example illustrates the limitation of trying to capture the concept of identity within a functional language. To be of service in reasoning in Shen, the Law of Self Identity, *for all x, x = x* has to be qualified so that the variable *x* ranges only over objects of a particular kind; specifically symbols, strings and vectors and lists of such etc and destructive operations excluded.

For functional programmers who prefer to be able to reason cleanly, destructive operations are avoided; and in *purely functional languages* they do not exist.

The last reason for avoiding destructive operations is concerned with *concurrency*; defined as the ability of a computer to sustain multiple simultaneous computational processes. Following the destructive model can create programs whose output is highly unpredictable.

For example, suppose we split a computation into two parallel processes; a process A that takes a global *counter* and destructively subtracts 2 and a process B that takes the same global and destructively doubles it. The final value of *counter* is inherently unpredictable. If *counter* = 4 and process A is applied and then process B; then *counter* is set to 2 by A and to 4 by B. But if B reaches *counter* before A, then *counter* is set to 8 by B and to 6 by A. The final value is therefore 4 or 6 depending on the order in which the processes are applied.

The debate can be argued at length. The advantage of operating in an impure language, of which Shen is one, is that the programmer can decide for himself which side to come down on and whether to use destructive operations or not. In the next chapter we will look at the time properties of destructive operations on *vectors*.

Further Reading

The original assault on the use of assignments, and the procedural programming style, that embodies them was made by Backus (1977) in his ACM Turing award address. "Can Programming be liberated from the von Neumann style? A functional style and its algebra of programs" belaboured procedural assignment based programming as "fat and weak".

Floyd-Hoare logic was an early attempt to come to grips with the challenge of reasoning about programs that required the use of state. A nice account is found in Gordon (1988). Boyer-Moore (1979, 1997) contrasts an approach to reasoning that involves purely functional programming.

A good discussion of the challenges of concurrent programming is found in the early chapters of Reppy (2007).

8 Vectors

8.1 Vectors

A vector is a sequence of items that can be constructed by the operation @v which adds an item to the front of a vector. The simplest vector is the **empty vector** written <>. The @v operation is polyadic, (@v 1 2 3 <>) is treated as (@v 1 (@v 2 (@v 3 <>))).

```
(1-) (@v 0 <>)
<0>

(2-) (@v 1 2 3 <>)
<1 2 3>
```

Figure 8.1 Some small vectors

Vectors are printed within angles < ... > for ease of reading but this is not a readable format (i.e. it cannot be typed in this form). Like @s, @v can be used within pattern-matching functions. For example, the following function receives a vector of numbers and outputs a vector in which each number is incremented by 1.

```
(define add1
  <> -> <>
  (@v N V) -> (@v (+ N 1) (add1 V)))
```

At this point, the similarity between vectors and lists will be so apparent that a reasonable question must arise; why should any language incorporate vectors *and* lists? The answer is that vectors and lists have different computational properties arising from their internal representation within the computer and we need to take time out to understand this.

8.2 Lists and Vectors

A list is held within memory as a chain of **cons cell** pairs which reflect the cons-form representation of a list. [1] in cons form is (cons 1 []) and represented as a cons cell pair in computer memory. One cell points to the location at which the first element may be found, the second to the location where the rest of the list may be found.

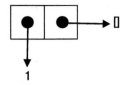

A longer list like [1 2 3] is simply a linked chain of such cons cells.

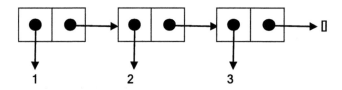

Consing an element to the front of the list (e.g. zero) requires only adding another cons cell pair which is a constant time operation.

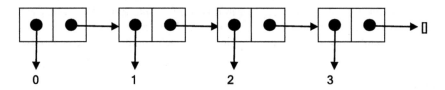

Locating the nth element of a list is *not* a constant time operation but a linear time operation; the third element of the list [1 2 3] can only be located by traversing three pointers.

In contrast to a list a vector is a series of pointers arranged by contiguous address in memory. In figure 8.2 our vector begins at a machine address that we have nominated as #523 which is the start address S of the vector.

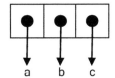

#523 #524 #525

a b c

Figure 8.2 A representation of a vector

Every successive location of memory up to #525 contains a pointer (integer) that points to the address at which the vector element is found. If we want to find what the *n*th element of the vector contains we need only search in the address to find the right pointer. Hence locating the *n*th element of a vector is a constant time operation.

However if we want to add an element to a vector; say to splice an element into the first position of the vector without losing anything that is already in the vector, then we face the problem that the first element is already occupied. Replacing the first element is an option but then information contained in the original is lost. The only real option is to create a new vector and copy the contents of the old one and this is a linear time operation.

In the case of a list this problem is not so acute; given a list

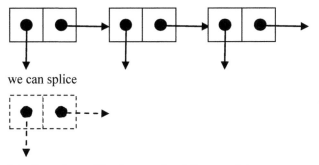

we can splice

into the pole position by merely adding a pointer.

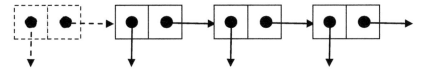

Hence consing to a list is a constant time operation.

It is important to know that vectors and lists have different time complexities in designing our programs. If our programs are intensively constructing and disassembling sequences of objects, then it makes sense to use lists for that purpose. If our sequences are relatively static and we are using them to store information then vectors are a logical choice. For this reason many languages, including Shen, contain both lists and vectors.

Because of the time penalties incurred in adding elements to a vector, @v is an expensive operation because every time it is invoked the vector has to be copied. For instance, the time taken to increment the contents of a vector V using add1 is proportional to the summation $\Sigma(n)$ of the size n of V because each invocation of @v involves copying the vector. In the case of a list it would be linear.

This performance overhead is often reflected in the handling of strings in Shen. In many platforms, strings are held as vectors of characters or unit strings and hence @s is effectively a vector building operation. Hence for the same reasons @s is relatively slow and sometimes unacceptably slow if the string is very large. Downloading a large text file and processing it using @s is not practical, though for strings of a few hundred characters it works fine. In these cases, it makes sense to work with the file as a list of unit strings and in chapter 9 we will explore this more fully.

8.3 Handling Vectors

The @v operator theoretically allows us full control over vectors if we ignore the heavy time costs in using it. Locating the nth element of a vector is easily defined.

```
(define nth-vector
  1 (@v X _) -> X
  N (@v _ Vector) -> (nth-vector (- N 1) Vector))
```

However having followed the discussion so far, you will realise this is a colossally inefficient method of locating the nth element of a vector since we should be able to access the nth element directly. <-vector takes a vector and a number and does exactly that; (<- vector *vector* 56) will return the 56th element of *vector*.

Vectors in Shen are **1-indexed**; that is, the first index in them begins with 1 which is in contrast to vectors in other languages which are **zero indexed**. Because Shen vectors are often built on top of native vectors there is a zeroth element to a Shen vector whose contents Shen reserves for its own management and this cannot be accessed through <-vector. In **standard vectors**, which are the ones we mostly deal with, the zeroth index holds the size of the vector and is retrieved by the function (limit *vector*). Passing a number to <-vector which is larger than the limit of the vector is called an **out of bounds** vector call and will raise an error.

When a vector is created, there is a contiguous portion of memory laid aside for the contents of that vector. Using @v we are very much unaware of this fact since the portion of memory laid aside is exactly determined by the elements supplied to @v. However we can choose to create an **vacant vector** of say 1000 indices *none* of which are occupied by any chosen element. The function call (vector 1000) will create such a vector. The **empty vector**, which we abbreviated as <>, is in fact (vector 0).

The interaction between <-vector and a vacant vector is interesting; when we ask for the 56th element of a vacant vector using <-vector, an error message is returned telling us that there is nothing there. Similarly if we try to pattern-match over a vector with vacancies in it we can get an error telling us there is nothing there.

```
(5-) (define f
       (@v X _) -> X)
(fn f)

(6-) (f (vector 3))
hdv needs a non-empty vector as an argument; not <... ... ....>
```

Figure 8.3 Attempted pattern matching over a vacant vector

In fact there is something there, **the failure object** designated by the 0-place function (fail) and printed as ... . <-vector refuses to return this object for reasons of security that we shall understand in chapter 17. A vacant vector of limit 5 is printed in the form <... ... ...>.

A Shen vector is thus rather like a bank account in that we cannot take anything out unless it has first been put in. Vectors of other languages actually often allow a default element to be retrieved from a vacant vector. In 8.6 we shall see how to do that.

8.4 Timing Operations

In the previous section we remarked that an object could be spliced into a vector in constant time if we were willing to destructively overwrite part of the existing vector. Such a vector operation does exist in Shen.

(vector-> *vector* 56 a) will insert a into the 56th index of *vector* by destructively overwriting the data stored at that index. In computing terms, Shen vectors are **mutable** objects that can changed by the operations applied to them. For reasons explained in our section on assignments, destructive operations are a source of contention in computing because the behaviour of programs that use them is harder to fathom. However being able to destructively change a vector in constant time is extremely useful if we are using the vector to hold global information or we want to ensure our program runs quickly.

In this section we will learn the Shen technology for measuring the performance of programs by an examination of the contrasting performance between destructive and non-destructive vector programs. To get the timings we use the time function. We create a vector of 1000 numbers (rather slowly) using @v.

```
(define build-me-a-vector
  _ 0 -> <>
  X N -> (@v X (build-me-a-vector X (- N 1))))
```

Again we encode a version of add1; but this time the program cycles through the vector destructively changing the elements without using @v and hence without copying.

```
(define destructive-add1
  V -> (destructive-add1-loop V 1 (limit V)))

(define destructive-add1-loop
  V Limit Limit -> (vector-> V Limit (+ 1 (<-vector V Limit)))
  V Count Limit -> (destructive-add1-loop
                      (vector-> V Count (+ 1 (<-vector V Count)))
                      (+ Count 1)  Limit))
```

The program is longer and more abstruse than the pattern-directed version but runs in linear and not polynomial time.

```
 (11-) (set *v* (build-me-a-vector 0 1000))
<0 0 0 0 0 0 0 0 0 0 0 0 0 0 0 0 0 0 0 0... etc>

(12-) (time (add1 (value *v*)))
run time: 0.3739999532699585 secs
<1 1 1 1 1 1 1 1 1 1 1 1 1 1 1 1 1 1 1 1... etc>

(13-) (value *v*)
<0 0 0 0 0 0 0 0 0 0 0 0 0 0 0 0 0 0 0 0... etc>

(13-) (time (destructive-add1 (value *v*)))
run time: 0.0 secs

(14-) (value *v*)
<1 1 1 1 1 1 1 1 1 1 1 1 1 1 1 1 1 1 1 1... etc>
```

Figure 8.4 Destructively and non-destructively processing a vector

The profiler is a more detailed tool for measuring performance; the command (profile f) profiles the function f and the command (unprofile f) unprofiles the function f by removing the profiling code. The command (profile-results f) produces the timing for f, initialising the f counter to zero (figure 8.5). The results are displayed as an **ordered pair** – a structure we will meet again in chapter 17.

```
(2-) (profile add1)
add1

(3-) (profile build-me-a-vector)
build-me-a-vector

(4-) (time (do (add1 (build-me-a-vector 0 1000)) ok))

run time: 0.5460000187158585 secs
ok

(5-) (profile-results add1)
(@p add1 0.37400001287460327)
```

Figure 8.5 Running the profiler on vector operations

As can be seen, the tail recursive destructive version is much faster than the linear recursive non-destructive version. The lesson to be drawn from this is that if we merely want to interrogate the vector or process it without losing the original, then if time is not an issue or the vector is small, the non-destructive @v is useful. If we want to maintain a large global vector which is permanently updated by an operation *f* which is required to be fast, then it makes sense to use the destructive vector-> in defining *f*. In the next section we will apply this approach in earnest.

8.5 Hash Tables

Computers are extremely good at storing large amounts of information and retrieving it very quickly. In order to do this the computer needs to be able to associate a request for information with the location at which the information can be found and retrieve the information quickly.

A *hash function* is one way of doing this; it maps an object called a *key* to a natural number. If the request for information takes the form of a key, then a hash function can be applied to the request to get a natural number. The natural number can then be used to access the location at which the key can be found.

We have already seen that vectors give constant-time access to any item. A *hash table* can be viewed as a combination of a hash function *h* and a vector *V*, where the number produced by *h* is used to index into *V*.

There are cases where the hash function is not bijective; that is, when two different keys are mapped to the same number *n*; this is called a *collision*. In case of a collision, further search within the $h(n)$th entry of *V* may be needed to retrieve the answer.

91

The function hash in Shen allows us to create hash tables very easily. Given an expression *E* and a number *N* (hash *E N*) returns a number between 1 and including *N*. Hence by fixing *N* to be the limit of the vector *V*, we can effectively create a hash table for storing information.

We can use this technology to create a toy database system. We begin by creating a largish vector to serve as a database whose elements are all initially [] (indicating no information is stored there). The following two functions db-> and <-db create the means to insert and retrieve information into that vector. Figure 8.6 gives the code.

```
(set *db* (build-me-a-vector [] 1000))

(define db->
   Key Details -> (let DB (value *db*)
                       Hash (hash Key (limit  DB))
                       Entry (<-vector DB Hash)
                       (vector-> DB Hash [[Key | Details] | Entry])))

(define <-db
   Key -> (let DB (value *db*)
               Hash (hash Key (limit  DB))
               Entry (<-vector DB Hash)
               (find-details Key Entry)))

(define find-details
   Key [[Key | Details] | _] -> [Key | Details]
   Key [_ | Entries] -> (find-details Key Entries)
   _ _ -> void)
```

Figure 8.6 A toy database

Figure 8.6 shows our database in action.

```
(4-) (db-> "Mark Tarver" [[age 64] [nationality "British"]])
<[] [] [] [] [] [] [] [] [] [] [] [] [] [] [] [] [] ... etc>

(5-) (<-db "Mark Tarver")
["Mark Tarver" [age 64] [nationality "British"]]

(6-) (<-db "David Tarver")
void
```

Figure 8.7 Using a toy database

8.6 Property Vectors and Semantic Nets

The definitions of db-> and <-db are given to show the principle of working with hash tables in Shen. The Shen system functions put and get supply high-level access to hash tables in Shen. The function put receives

1. An expression e_1.
2. A pointer p which is used to point to ...
3. ... a value e_2 within ...
4. an (optionally user-specified) vector v.

put effectively does much of what db-> does in our previous program; it hashes e_1 into the property vector v index i and inserts e_2 into the information stored at this index. If no vector v is supplied Shen uses the system property vector built into the Shen installation.

get operates in a manner analogous to <-db; it receives three inputs e_1, p and an optional property vector v and searches i for the information placed by put and returns it. If v is not supplied the system property vector is used. If no information can be found, an error is returned.

```
(1-) (put "Mark Tarver" details [[age 54] [nationality "British"]])
[man]

(2-) (get "Mark Tarver" details)
[[age 54] [nationality "British"]]

(3-) (get "Mark Tarver" sex)
value not found
```

Figure 8.7 Using put and get with the system property vector

Semantic nets are a fun way of illustrating the usefulness of put and get. Semantic nets were introduced into Artificial Intelligence by Quillian (1968) as a model for the way humans hold information about objects and the relations between objects. Semantic nets are usually represented by **labelled directed graphs,** that is, as diagrams consisting of arrows (called **arcs)** with names or **labels** attached to the arrows. These arrows connect points or **vertices** that also have names. A semantic net which records the fact that I (Mark Tarver) am a man might consist of an arc labelled is_a leading from the vertex "Mark Tarver" to a vertex man.

$$\text{"Mark Tarver"} \xrightarrow{\text{is\_a}} \text{man}$$

A statement of the form "All Xs are Ys" can be viewed as stating a relation between concepts; so "All men are human" becomes:-

$$man \xrightarrow{\text{type\_of}} human$$

which states that the concept man is a **subtype** of the type of human, or (same thing) that human is a **supertype** of the type of man.

From "Mark Tarver is a man" and "All men are human" we can derive "Mark Tarver is human". Semantic nets allow for simple inferences like this by means of a search. Such a search starts from the "Mark Tarver" vertex and attempts to reach the vertex human, travelling in the direction of the arrows. If it succeeds it returns yes otherwise it returns no.

Property vectors are very good at representing the links in a semantic net. From "Mark Tarver" we construct a pointer that points to all the concepts $C_1,...,C_n$ which Mark Tarver is an instance. We call this pointer is_a. From each $C_1,..,C_n$ we can (if we want) create pointers in the same way, called type_of to show the supertypes of $C_1,..,C_n$.

Figuratively speaking, to find if Mark Tarver falls under a concept C, we place "Mark Tarver" in a 'box', and then we add to the box all the concepts $C_1, ...,C_n$ under which Mark Tarver falls in virtue of the is_a relation (i.e. all the concepts pointed to from "Mark Tarver" by the pointer is_a). For each of $C_1,...,C_m$, we add to the box every concept C_n which is a supertype of some C_i already in the box. We repeat this process until the box cannot be filled any more; at which point we look in the box to see if C is in the box. If it is, then Mark Tarver falls under the concept C and the answer is yes. If not, the answer is no.

The program that computes this algorithm is given in figure 8.8[41]; our box is a list that initially contains one object ([Object]), which is where our query begins.

```
(set *semantic-net* (vector 1000))

(define query
  [is Object Concept] -> (if (belongs? Object Concept) yes no))

(define belongs?
  Object Concept
  -> (element? Concept (fix42 (fn spread-activation) [Object])))

(define spread-activation
  [ ] -> [ ]
  [Vertex | Vertices]
  -> (union (accessible-from Vertex) (spread-activation Vertices)))
```

---

[41] Our program contains one feature explored in the chapter 11; (trap-error (get ....) (/. E [])) has the effect that if get raises an error because no information is found then the empty list is returned instead of an error message.

[42] fix (short for fixpoint) iteratively applies a function to an input until no change can be produced. See appendix A.

```
(define accessible-from
  Vertex -> [Vertex | (union (is_links Vertex) (type_links Vertex))]])

(define is_links
  Vertex -> (trap-error (get Vertex is_a (value *semantic-net*)) (/. E [])))

(define type_links
  Vertex -> (trap-error (get Vertex type_of (value *semantic-net*)) (/. E [])))

(define assert
  [Object is_a Type]
  -> (put Object is_a (adjoin⁴³ Type (is_links Object)) (value *semantic-net*))
  [Type1 type_of Type2]
  -> (put Type1 type_of (adjoin Type2 (type_links Type1)) (value *semantic-net*)))
```

Figure 8.8 A simple semantic net in Shen

We can test this program.

```
(1-) (assert ["Mark Tarver" is_a man])
[man]

(2-) (assert [man type_of human])
[human]

(3-) (query [is "Mark Tarver" human])
yes
```

Figure 8.9 Using a semantic net to record information and ask questions

8.7 Native Vectors and Print Vectors

The standard vectors which discussed so far are built on top of the native vectors of the platform under which Shen runs. Shen imposes its own discipline on the native vectors in order to ensure that vectors behave uniformly across platforms.

Shen includes native vector functions which are primitive; these functions are address->, <-address, absvector and absvector?. They are the analogues of the functions vector->, <-vector, vector and vector? and behave similarly. Rather than reprise this material, we will just note the differences.

(absvector *n*) creates a native vector of *n* indices. The address-> function will access all the indices of a native vector, including the zeroth index which vector-> does not access. <-address will access even an index which is vacant (i.e. where no object has been inserted) but the nature of the object returned is platform dependent. The function absvector? will return true for all standard vectors but

---

⁴³ adjoin adds an element to a list if it is not already there.

95

also vectors which are not standard. The Shen definitions of the standard vector functions are couched in terms of the native functions.

```
(define vector?
  V -> (and (absvector? V) (integer? (<-address V 0))))

(define vector->
  V N X -> (if (= N 0) (error "index 0 used") (address-> V N X)))

(define <-vector
  _ 0 -> (error "index 0 used")
  V N -> (let X (<-address V N)
           (if (= X (fail)) (error "index is vacant") X)))

(define vector
  N -> (address-> (vector-fill (absvector N) 1 N) 0 N))

(define vector-fill
  V N N -> (address-> V N (fail))
  V M N -> (vector-fill (address-> V M (fail)) (+ M 1) N))
```

In terms of security and uniformity of behaviour, standard vectors are superior to native ones, but there is an advantage of performance in working with native vectors. Native vectors also allow us to define **non-standard vectors** and one important kind is a **print vector.**

A print vector is a non-standard vector where the zeroth element is not taken up by an integer (as with a standard vector) but by a symbol signifying a **print function.** A print function determines how that vector is printed off by mapping the vector to a string which is printed off as the print representation of that vector. This is highly useful if we want to define our own datatypes with special print conventions.

For example, suppose we want to add rational numbers as part of a number tower to Shen. We could choose a representation based on two element lists, but we may want a representation that allows rational numbers to be printed back in mathematical dress. So (rat 1 3) is printed as 1/3 and not [1 3] or <1 3>.

Internally our rational numbers will be held as a non-standard vector, a **print vector**, of two numbers with a tag in the zeroth index indicating that this vector is supposed to represent a rational number.

Since the vector is not a standard vector, we cannot use vector to create it and vector-> to set it up. Instead the print vector is created as a native vector and the address-> used to insert the appropriate elements. Here is the function rat (figure 8.10).

```
(4-) (define rat
  M N -> (let Vector (absvector 3)
              TagVector (address-> Vector 0 rational-number)
              Vector+M (address-> TagVector 1 M)
              Vector+N (address-> Vector+M 2 N)
              Vector+N))
(fn rat)


(5-) (rat 4 5)
<<rational-number 4 5>>
```

Figure 8.10 Creating a rational number as a non-standard vector

The double angles indicate that the vector is a native vector. To turn this vector into a print vector we need to define rational-number as a print function. This function must build a string, given the vector in which it is embedded as an input. The string is built by taking the numerator and denominator and converting them into strings and placing them each side of the division sign (/). Entering (rat 4 5) returns a value printed in the accepted mathematical idiom.

```
(6-) (define rational-number
  Vector -> (@s (str (<-address Vector 1))
              "/"
              (str (<-address Vector 2))))
(fn rational-number)

(7-) (rat 4 5)
4/5
```

Figure 8.11 Creating a rational number as a print vector

Exercise 8

1. Define each of the following functions; where appropriate, write a destructive version (using vector->) and non-destructive version (using v@) and compare timings.

   a. vector-append that appends two vectors together.
   b. vector-reverse that reverses a vector.
   c. vector-subst that substitutes one element for another throughout a vector.
   d. vector->list that maps a vector of elements to a list of the same elements
   e. list->vector that is the inverse of d.
   f. vector-extend that extends the size of a vector allowing more element to be written to it.

2. Define a function retract that allows you to remove assertions from the semantic net, so that stating (retract ["Mark Tarver" is_a man]) removes the corresponding assertion.

97

3. *Rewrite the function assert to include the backpointers instance_of and super_type so that if "Mark Tarver is a man" is stated then a backpointer instance_of then points from man to a list containing Mark Tarver. Similarly if [man type_of human] is asserted then a backpointer super_type points from man to a list containing human. Amend the query program to allow the semantic net to cope with questions like (query [what is human]), so that it returns the list of all the humans of which it knows.

4. Extend the semantic net program to cope with disjunctive and conjunctive queries. For instance, (query [[Joe is_a man] or [Mark_Tarver is_a man]]) should return yes. (query [[Joe is_a man] and [Mark_Tarver is_a man]]) should return no.

5. *Extend the program to cope with conditional queries. For instance, (query [if [Joe is_a man] then [Joe is_a human]]) should return yes. To do this, you might want to assert the antecedent of the query during query time and test for the conclusion, and then retract the antecedent at the end of the computation.

Further Reading

Vectors are a fundamental data structure in computer science and are found in the early computer languages from Fortran onwards. Other data structures are often implemented in terms of vectors. In Common Lisp a string is implemented as a vector of characters; see Steele (1990) on strings and vectors. Matrix arithmetic, which is easily represented by 2 dimensional arrays, has been intensively studied in computing. See Sadler and Thorning (1993) for matrix arithmetic.

There are a number of data structures which attempt to combine the best features of vectors and lists – including binary trees and growable arrays

9 I/O

9.1 Streams

I/O, or input/output, covers all those aspects of a programming language that depend upon reading user input or printing the results of computation. In Shen both inputs and outputs are done through **streams**. A stream that is designed for input to be read from it is a **source** and one designed for output to be written to it is called a **sink**.

The basic stream that receives output for printing is the **standard output stream** (stoutput) which prints the results to the command window. pr receives a string and a sink and prints the string to the sink returning the string as a value. If only the string is supplied, then the sink defaults to the standard output stream.

```
(5-) (pr "hello world")
hello world"hello World"
```

Figure 9.1 Printing a string

When we use pr in this way, simply supplying a string input, Shen understands that the string is to be printed to the standard output i.e. the command window. We can state this explicitly using the zero place function stoutput that returns the standard output stream.

```
(6-) (stoutput)
#<SYNONYM-STREAM :SYMBOL SB-SYS:*STDOUT* {1000345563}>

(7-) (pr "hello world" (stoutput))
hello world"hello World"
```

Figure 9.2 Invoking the standard output

Instead of using the standard output, we can choose to nominate some other form of sink which prints to a file. In order to do that we need to create a stream that acts as this sink. The function that does this is open which receives two arguments.

1. A string that indicates the path to the program or file required.
2. The keyword in or out which indicates whether the stream is a source or a sink.

When a stream is created in this way it is open until it is closed by the function close, which closes the stream and returns the empty list. Generally when we open a stream as a sink or a source we want to carry the stream around as an argument to a function like pr. Here we open a stream as a sink to a file and print hello world to it.[44]

```
(8-) (let Stream  (open "hello world.txt" out)
        Print (pr "hello world" Stream)
        (close Stream))
[]
```

Figure 9.3 Printing a string to a file

The file hello world.txt now contains the message hello world. Any previous content is overwritten. Notice the difference between writing to standard output and writing to some other stream. When we write to standard output the string we output is echoed back to us by being printed in the command window. When we write to a file, the string is not echoed back to us.

9.2 Print Functions

pr is a very basic print operation; the functions print and output are a little more flexible for printing to the standard output stream. print accepts any argument and prints it to standard output, returning that argument.

```
(2-) (print [1 2 3])
[1 2 3][1 2 3]

(3-) (print "hi there")
"hi there""hi there"
```

Figure 9.4 Printing arbitrary objects

print will attempt to print anything, including objects from within the native platform which are entirely foreign to Shen.[45] The polyadic function output is

---

[44] Writing to a sink is not a required feature of Shen. In the Javascript implementation of Shen, Javascript restricts access to the user's personal disk space for reasons of security.

[45] For example, in the Common Lisp platform of Shen, the expression (CODE-CHAR 54) returns an object called a **character** which is not part of the range of datatypes that Shen understands. Shen prints this as funex125 (the number component is computer generated), meaning that a functional object has been returned that Shen does not know how to print.

rather more sophisticated than print; it accepts a string and a series of zero or more following arguments. With zero following arguments it behaves much like pr with a single argument. But the output function shares the same features as make-string, except that it prints the resulting string (figure 9.5).

```
(4-) (output "~A = ~A~%" [1 + 1] 2)
[1 + 1] = 2
"[1 + 1] = 2"
```

Figure 9.5 Using output

The function nl, which returns zero, can be used to print *n* new lines. Without an argument it prints 1 new line.

```
(4-) (do (nl 2) (pr "Two blank lines! What a waste  of space") (nl))


Two blank lines! What a waste of space
0
```

When writing to a file, make-string and pr are used together to print formatted output to a file. In figure 9.6 (1 + 1) = 2 is printed to a file.

```
(12-) (let Stream  (open "simple sum.txt" out)
           String (make-string "~R = ~R~%"  [1 + 1] 2)
           Print (pr String Stream)
           (close Stream))
[]
```

Figure 9.6 Using make-string *and* pr *to print formatted output to a file*

write-to-file is a compact way of writing an object *x* to a file *f* in which a sink stream is opened to *f* and *x* is printed to *f*; the stream is then closed and *x* returned without the user having to go to the bother of creating a stream and then closing it. As with using open, any previous content in *f* is overwritten and if a string is written, the contents of the string appear in *f* without the enclosing quotes. The code in 9.7 creates a file containing (1 + 1) = 2.

```
(11-) (let String  (make-string "~R = ~R~%"  [1 + 1] 2)
             (write-to-file "simple sum.txt" String))

"(1 + 1) = 2"
```

Figure 9.7 Using write-to-file *to output to a file*

All output that is produced by Shen, including error messages is filtered through the print and output functions. It is sometimes useful to be able to silence this output to enable silent loading of files. The assignment (set *hush* true) will silence printing from Shen.

9.3 Reading Input

Shen contains several functions designed to work on the **standard input stream** (stinput) – that is the command window into which code is typed. The most basic is read-byte which reads a single byte off the input stream. The other read functions are defined in terms of read-byte.

The function read takes an input and parses it through the Shen reader *without* evaluating it. lineread works in the same way except several inputs terminated by a new line are read into a single list. input *both* reads in the user input *and* evaluates it (figure 9.8).

```
 (7-) (input)
(* 7 8)
56

(8-) (read)
(+ 7 8)
[+ 7 8]

(9-) (lineread)
1 2 3 4
[1 2 3 4]
```

Figure 9.8 Using input, read *and* lineread

If no arguments are given to these functions then they are defined relative to the standard input. But each of these functions is actually a 1-place function that receives as its second argument a source. If we supply a source using open then source is drawn from a file. Thus if we place the following in a file mytest.shen.

(* 3 7) (+ 7 8) "John" "loves""Mary"

Then the expression

```
(let Stream (open "mytest.shen" in)
     Print1 (input Stream)
     Print2 (read Stream)
     Print3 (lineread Stream)
     Close (close Stream)
     (output "~A ~A ~A" Print1 Print2 Print3))
```

will output the message

21 [+ 7 8] [John loves]

returning the string

"21 [+ 7 8] [John loves]"

Notice that all the read functions are destructive. If we read a source then we are consuming the contents of the source and hence

```
(let Stream (open "mytest.shen" in)
    (= (read Stream) (read Stream)))
```

will generally return false unless the second readable expression in the file is the same as the first.

If we want to simply read in the contents of a file into one large list without evaluating the contents then read-file just takes a file name and reads a file using Shen parsing. read-file may raise an error if it is used to parse files that fail Shen syntax requirements and is only to be used to read files, without evaluating the contents, that contain Shen programs or data. If we want to read *and* evaluate the contents of the file then the command is, of course, load.

The zero place function it is sometimes useful; it records verbatim the last input to the standard input and returns a string containing this input. This function is often useful in retaining a record of what the user actually typed in. Figure 9.9 shows a session where user input is recorded and evaluated and the normal form and the original expression are returned in a list.

```
(25-) (it)
"(it)"

(26-) (let X (input)
         It (it)
         [X It])
(* 3 4)
[12 "(* 3 4)"]
```

Figure 9.9 Using it to capture user input

103

9.4 Reading from a String

The function read-from-string will read input from a string S and invokes the Shen program reader, applying the following rules the following rules.

Rule I.   The outer quotes of S are replaced by [...].
Rule II.   Inner (...)s and | within S are replaced by [...].
Rule III.   Inner [...]s are replaced by expressions in cons form.
Rule IV.   Numbers are parsed by Shen syntax rules.
Rule V.   Macroexpansions and currying are applied.[46]

Figure 9.10 shows some samples.

```
(12-) (read-from-string "* 2 3")
[* 2 3]

(13-) (read-from-string "(* 2 3)")
[[* 2 3]]

(14-) (read-from-string "[12e4]")
[cons 120000 []]

(15-) (read-from-string "(* 1 2 3)")
[[* 1 [* 2 3]]]

(16-) (read-from-string "(f r)")
[[[fn f] r]]

(17-) (read-from-string "(f a b)")
[[[[fn f] a] b]]

(18-) (read-from-string "(fn reverse)")
[[lambda Y1041 [reverse Y1041]]]
```

Figure 9.10 Reading from a string using read-from-string

Let's look at what is happening here. In entry 12, read-as-string returns the result according to rule I. In entry 13, rules I and II are used. In entry 14 rules I, III and IV are used. Rule IV is responsible for converting the e number into an integer.

In all cases, the read-from-string function is acting as an extension of the Shen reader (which it is), converting the input into a canonical form. Observing the activity of this function gives a window on the activity of the Shen reader which is obviously a lot busier than a simple reader. Let's look at the later examples to see what the reader is doing and why.

------

[46] See chapter 10 for more on macros.

In entry 15, the Shen reader is performing a macroexpansion by inserting the brackets into multiplication because in Shen (* 1 2 3) is treated as (* 1 (* 2 3)). In example 16, (f r) is treated as an application, but unlike the multiplication sign, f is not associated with any function in Shen.

The reader therefore wraps an fn call around f which would, if ((fn f) r) were evaluated, cause Shen to seek the lambda definition of f in a lookup table in the hope that it had been defined and apply it to r. In entry 17 the same technique is applied but the expression is curried to receive a lambda abstraction. In entry 18, the fn is compiled out in favour of an abstraction since Shen optimises the code by performing the lookup at compile time.

The read-from-string function is therefore optimised to read Shen code and the output is coloured by the conventions of the Shen reader. This can be a nuisance if a more direct reading of the string is desired.

A sister function read-from-string-unprocessed acts as read-from-string but rule V is suspended.

```
(12-) (read-from-string-unprocessed "* 2 3")
[* 2 3]

(13-) (read-from-string-unprocessed "(* 2 3)")
[[* 2 3]]

(14-) (read-from-string-unprocessed "[12e4]")
[cons 120000 []]

(15-) (read-from-string-unprocessed "(* 1 2 3)")
[[* 1 2 3]]

(16-) (read-from-string-unprocessed "(f r)")
[[f r]]

(17-) (read-from-string-unprocessed "(f a b)")
[[f a b]]

(18-) (read-from-string-unprocessed "(fn reverse)")
[fn reverse]
```

Figure 9.11 Reading from a string using read-from-string-unprocessed

9.5 String Searching Text Files

Shen is designed to read a stream as a series of bytes. Since files are stored as bytes, a consequence of Shen's byte stream oriented architecture is that many files can be read or written into Shen using read-byte and write-byte; not just text files, but graphic and audio files.

In this section we'll see how byte reading can be used to optimise string search. String searching is a basic problem in many applications where we want to quickly find a piece of text within large body of information. Our example involves string search for the first line of a poem beginning "*You are old, Father William*" within a file containing the text for *Alice in Wonderland* by Lewis Carroll. The task is to find the position of the beginning of this text.

We'll look at three solutions of this problem in ascending order of efficiency. Our first attempt (figure 9.12) uses a system function read-file-as-string which reads the contents of a file to a string and then does a search using string pattern-matching.

```
(define whereis-father-william.v1
  File -> (let String (read-file-as-string File)
               (find-father-william.v1 String 1)))

(define find-father-william.v1
  (@s "You are old, Father William" _) N -> N
  (@s _ S) N -> (find-father-william.v1 S (+ N 1)))
```

Figure 9.12 A short but inefficient string search program

The answer (49,831) takes 78.45 seconds in Shen/SBCL on a 1.4GHZ laptop. because the program spends its time building and disassembling strings. Since strings are often kept as vectors of characters, this involves a great deal of vector copying. This vector copying is repeated, albeit implicitly, within read-file-as-string. The program is conveniently short but highly inefficient.

The read-file-as-string function takes 46s to read Carroll's book into a string. Since Shen's reader is based on byte reading, the fastest operation is reading a byte. read-file-as-bytelist reads a file to a list of bytes and reads *Alice in Wonderland* in 0.01s.

Our second attempt to find Father William uses read-file-as-bytelist to store the contents of *Alice in Wonderland* as a list of bytes and n->string to convert the list to a list of unit strings.

```
(define whereis-father-william.v2
  File -> (let Bytes (read-file-as-bytelist File)
               Strings (map (fn n->string) Bytes)
               (find-father-william.v2 Strings 1)))

(define find-father-william.v2
  [ ($ "You are old, Father William") | _] N -> N
  [_ | Y] N -> (find-father-william.v2 Y (+ N 1)))
```

Figure 9.13 A faster way of finding Father William

This version finds Father William in 0.39s; a speedup of 200 times and represents the optimum balance between clarity of code and performance. Beyond version 2 there are further optimisations; but they all involve a certain obfuscation of the code. For example, dispensing with the conversion to strings by n->string and using the bytes directly yields large benefits (figure 9.14).

```
(define whereis-father-william.v3
  File -> (let Bytes (read-file-as-bytelist File)
            (find-father-william.v3 Bytes 1)))

(define find-father-william.v3
  [89 111 117 32 97 114 101 32 111 108 100 44 32 70 97 116 104 101 114 32 87 105
             108 108 105 97 109 | _] N -> N
  [_ | Y] N -> (find-father-william.v3 Y (+ N 1)))
```

Figure 9.14 A byte centred way of finding Father William

This version computes the solution in 0.03s; over 2,000 times faster than our original.

Exercise 9

1. Define a function file-append that receives a string *s* as a name of a file *f* and an input *x* and appends *x* to *f*.

2. Devise a spellchecker; obtain from the internet a file containing list of recognised English words and write a function spellcheck that takes a file as input and raises a spelling error warning whenever it encounters a word not in the word list. Create the system so that the line number of the spelling error is cited as well as the word. Arrange to give the user the option of dumping all these warnings to a file.

3. Devise a program text-file? that tests a file to see if it is a text file. A text file is defined as one which contains only characters which lie within the keyboard range.

4. Devise a function file-exists? that receives a string and tests if the corresponding file exists.

5. Devise a program bytes that estimates the size of a file by returning the number of bytes in it.

6. Devise a program html->text that reads an HTML file and strips the HTML leaving the bare text.

Further Reading

String searching has been subject to several algorithms developed over time. Wikipedia (https://en.wikipedia.org/wiki/String-searching_algorithm) contains a review. The Shendoc 30 file avaialble on the Shen website discusses the implementation of streams in Shen.

10 Macros and Packages

10.1 Macros

A Shen macro is a piece of code that modulates the way in which code is read into the working Shen image. Syntactically, a Shen macro looks like a standard function with three distinct differences.

1. The keyword defmacro is used instead of define.
2. Every macro takes one and only one input; i.e. its **arity** is 1.
3. Every macro has a default case X -> X inserted by Shen as a final rule. Thus the macro always behaves as the identity function if the rules supplied by the programmer fail to apply to an input.

Every Shen program, when loaded, is read in as a list of expressions. For example, the expression (+ 1 2) in a file is read in as a list [+ 1 2]. It is the task of the Shen reader to read in that expression and it is the task of the Shen evaluator to evaluate it. The program is read in as a series of **tokens**. Roughly, the set of tokens within an expression is the set of evaluable subexpressions found within it. For example, in [+ 1 2] the tokens are +, 1, 2 and [+ 1 2]. The application of the list of Shen macros to a token t is called **macroexpansion**. This process works as follows.

Let $f_1,...,f_n$ be macros in reverse order of their introduction; let t be a token. Let the application $(f_1... (f_n t)...) = t'$ represent the composition of all $f_1.., f_n$ on t. Then either

1. $t = t'$ in which case the macroexpansion acts as the identity function and t is unchanged.
2. $t \neq t'$ in which case the macroexpansion of t is identical to the macroexpansion of t'.

To begin with a simple case, suppose we wanted to create an infix +. The following macro does just that.

```
(defmacro +-macro
  [X + Y] -> [+ Y X])
```

+macro edits our infix notation into the acceptable prefix notation. Note if the token is not an infix addition then +-macro behaves as the identity function – hence X -> X is not needed as a default case in a macro.

Macros allow us to create our own programming notation for many different types of problem. Here is a slightly more advanced example; let us suppose we have defined a max function which given two numbers returns the larger (or if the numbers are the same, returns that number). Our max function works for two inputs, but we want max to be polyadic so that we can enter (max 1 2 3 4) and return 4. Figure 10.1 shows to create a macro to make our max function polyadic.

```
(0-) (defmacro max-macro
       [max W X Y | Z] -> [max W [max X Y | Z]])
(fn max-macro)

(1-) (define max
       X Y -> X where (> X Y)
       _ Y -> Y)
(fn max)

(2-) (max 1 2 3 4)
4
```

Figure 10.1 Setting up a polyadic max function using a macro

The definition in 10.1 is deceptively simple and works because macros are repeatedly applied to all tokens of an input until no change can be produced by their application. (max 1 2 3 4) is read in as the list [max 1 2 3 4] and the first pass of the max-macro produces [max 1 [max 2 3 4]]. The macro is then applied to [max 2 3 4] to produce [max 2 [max 3 4]] and the whole expression that exits the reader is read as [max 1 [max 2 [max 3 4]]].

What exits from the reader is a list; it is the task of the evaluator to take that list and evaluate it to produce the appropriate result. Thus if we enter (+ 5 6), the Shen reader produces [+ 5 6] and the evaluator returns 7. What if we enter a list like [+ 5 6] to the reader? This is read as a list expression too; the evaluator translate to cons form returning [cons 5 [cons 6 []]].

Though this sounds a little involved, the process actually allows the programmer a great deal of power and control as we shall see. The power arises from the fact that all Shen programs are read in as lists and Shen is *par excellence*, a list programming language. Therefore by reading in programs as lists and creating the facility to change the way that the reader treats those lists, we can effectively create our own programming environment and our own special notations. We shall see a few examples in this chapter.[47]

---

[47] One of the first languages to introduce macros and indeed the inspiration for Shen macros was Common Lisp. See Steele (1990) for an exposition.

The evaluator that does the job of evaluating the lists produced by the reader is actually available as a function to the Shen programmer; it is called eval-kl.

```
(3-) (eval-kl [+ 7 8])
11

(4-) (eval-kl 16)
16
```

Figure 10.2 eval-kl *in action*

The kl suffix is a nod towards the underlying Kλ out of which Shen is built; eval-kl is one of the fundamental primitive functions out of which all of Shen is constructed.

eval-kl is actually a leaner cousin of a similar more programmer-friendly function eval which does the same job but applies all the macros to its input before applying eval-kl to the result. Since Shen uses a macros a lot in its construction, eval can work where eval-kl fails. The example in 10.3 works for eval but not eval-kl because define needs a macro within Shen to be evaluated.

```
(3-) (eval [define f
              1 -> 2])
(fn f)

(4-) (f 1)
2
```

Figure 10.3 eval *in action*

Is eval useful? Macros are more generally applicable, but sometimes eval and eval-kl can be used to effect as we shall see an example in chapter 15. For example, we can run a Shen program P that *dynamically*[48] generates a list that represents a function definition and by evaluating it, generate a new program P*.

Such a program is called a **metaprogram** (a program that generates programs). Even more intriguingly, the program P* that is generated can be a modification of P, so that the eval function opens the possibility of self-modifying programs. The eval function thus allows certain intriguing and alarming possibilities reminiscent of Skynet in *Terminator*. Self-modifying programs are outside the ambit of this book, but have been investigated within artificial intelligence.

---

[48] The emphasis is on *dynamic* here, because the program P* is created during the execution (evaluation) of P. Actually it is more common for programs to be generated during the *read* part of the read-evaluate-print loop, and in that case macros are the better approach.

10.2 Changing the Order of Evaluation

Macros enable the user to define polyadic functions in Shen which are not definable without their aid. But macros also allow us to create functions in which the usual applicative order of evaluation is suspended in favour of our own chosen version.

Suppose we are working with the task of modelling an electronic circuit which uses NOR gates, where (nor X Y) returns 1 just when both X and Y are 0. The straightforward Shen definition is.

```
(define nor
  0 0 -> 1
  _ _ -> 0)
```

But this function is driven by *strict evaluation*; if we are using it to model a circuit then nor will evaluate both inputs before returning 1 or 0. However if the first input is 1 then the evaluation of the second input need not be made. What is required is something more like the lazy evaluation of the conditional if. At the expense of readability (nor X Y) can be more efficiently rendered as (if (= X 0) (if (= Y 0) 1 0) 0).

Macros enable us to reconcile efficiency with readability. We define a macro in which every expression of the form (nor X Y) is replaced or **inlined** by the expression (if (= X 0) (if (= Y 0) 1 0) 0).

```
(3-) (defmacro nor-macro
        [nor X Y] -> [if [= X 0] [if [= Y 0] 1 0] 0])
(fn nor-macro)

(4-) (nor 0 1)
0
```

10.3 Defining our own Notation

In a calendar program, a 0-place function date generates the current date in the format day, month and year. Part of the calendar program's task is to generate the current date and print it in an acceptable format and for this purpose we have a function now which does exactly that.

```
(define now
  -> (let Date (date)
          Day (nth 1 Date)
          Month (nth 2 Date)
          Year (nth 3 Date)
          (output "~A, ~A, ~A~%" Day Month Year)))
```

111

In order to pass the output of date to the print function, we have to construct four local assignments that create local variables for the date, day, month and year. In other languages[49], local assignments can also be used to pattern-match on the input in the same way that patterns are used in Shen functions. i.e.

```
(define now
  -> (let* [Day Month Year] (date)
          (output "~A, ~A, ~A~%" Day Month Year)))
```

Such a construction will not compile in Shen, but with macros it can be made to work. Here is the code.

```
(defmacro let*-macro
  [let* [X | Y] FCall Result] -> (let F (gensym (protect F))
                                  [let F FCall
                                       (recursive-let 1 [X | Y] F Result)]))

(define recursive-let
  _ [] _ Result -> Result
  N [cons V Vs] F Result
  -> [let V [nth N F] (recursive-let (+ N 1) Vs F Result)])
```

Figure 10.4 Setting up a pattern-matching local assignment

The macro accepts a pattern-matching let and expands it to a series of local assignments as in our original legal program. The pattern-matching let has the form [let [X | Y] FCall Result]. The FCall will be matched to some function call (like (date)) and we begin by storing the result of this call

```
(let F (gensym (protect F))
  [let F FCall ...
```

To a local variable in order not to repeat this computation. This local variable must be fresh to avoid clashes with any variables in the expression, so we use gensym to generate a new symbol for us. The recursive-let function then works through the list making the code for the appropriate local assignments.

10.4 Packages

Our examples show how macros can be used to create polyadic functions, change the order of evaluation or create our own special notation. Metaprogramming really begins when we generate, not single functions, but whole programs from our chosen notation. In order to do this we need to look first at **packages**.

Packages are essentially a simple device to package up programs in order to minimise **name collisions**. A name collision occurs when we have two programs

---

[49] O'Caml being an example.

that accidentally choose the same identifier for a function or a global variable. In that case, loading both these programs will cause an error in one of the programs since one function or global will overwrite the other.

The accepted solution to this problem is to create a separate **name space** for each program so that these identifiers live in their separate name spaces. To do this in Shen, we place the two programs in different packages by creating an expression of the form (package *<package name> <external> <program>*). *<package name>* is a lowercase symbol, *<external>* evaluates to a list of symbols and *<program>* is Shen code.

When a package P is loaded, Shen **unpackages** the code by renaming every function *f* defined in P by prefixing *<package name>* followed by a dot (.) to *f*. The resulting name *<package name>.f is the* fully qualified name or **FQN** of the function.

Hence as long as the package name is unique, we do not have to consider the possibility of name collisions when loading it. Given (package *P E x1...xn*), the Shen reader evaluates *E* to *E** and prepends *P*. before all the symbols in $x_1, .., x_n$ apart from those symbols which are

1. Symbols listed as belonging to the system (such as ->, define, cons, append, =, == etc).
2. Symbols which are variables.
3. Symbols which are listed by the user to be exempted from renaming by being present in *E**.
4. Symbols already prefaced by *P*.
5. Symbols which are prefaced by shen..[50]

Figure 10.5 shows an example where a package is entered to the top level.

```
(0-) (package foo [(intern "howdy")]
         X foo hello howdy 5 "xyz" cons)

X              \\ a variable is not renamed.
foo            \\ foo is not  renamed
foo.hello      \\ hello is renamed
howdy          \\ howdy is an element of the normal form of [(intern "howdy")]
5              \\ 5 is not a symbol
"xyz"          \\ "xyz" is not a symbol
cons           \\ cons is a system function

(1) (external foo)
[howdy]
```

Figure 10.5 Unpackaging according to package conventions

---

[50] All the code for Shen, which is written in Shen, is contained in the package 'shen'..

The process of replacing a package by explicitly renaming the contents of the package is **unpackaging**. Symbols which are renamed are **internal** (to the package). Symbols which are not are **external**. The function external takes a package name and returns the list of all those symbols which have been declared external to that package at the point the function is called.

We can package the square root program of chapter 6 within our own maths package called my-maths-stuff. We may decide that some of the functions in the maths package should be accessible without having to type my-maths-stuff. The functions that stand out as generally useful to a user are sqrt average and abs.

```
(package my-maths-stuff [sqrt average abs]

(define sqrt
  N -> (let Guess (/ N 2.0)
       (run-newtons-method N  (average Guess (/  N Guess)) Guess)))

(define run-newtons-method
  _ Better_Guess Guess -> Better_Guess
                  where (close-enough? Better_Guess Guess)
  N Better_Guess _
  -> (run-newtons-method  N
     (average Better_Guess  (/  N Better_Guess)) Better_Guess))

(define average
  M N -> (/ (+ M N) 2.0))

(define close-enough?
  Better_Guess Guess -> (< (abs (-  Better_Guess Guess)) .001))

(define abs
  N -> (if (> 0 N) (- 0 N) N)) )
```

Now the list of functions printed off shows that sqrt, average and abs are all functions directly accessible to the user; only the auxiliary functions are hidden in the package. The expression (external maths-stuff) will retrieve all the external functions of that package.

```
(4-) (external maths-stuff)
[sqrt average abs]

(5-) (external whatsthis)
package whatsthis has not been used

(6-) (external shen)
[! } { --> <-- && : ; :- := _ *language* *implementation* *stinput*
*home-directory* *version* *maximum-print-sequence-size* *macros* *os*
*release* *property-vector*... etc]
```

Since Shen is written in Shen it also inhabits a package called (unsurprisingly) shen. Typing (external shen) returns the list of keywords and symbols used in Shen that are accessible to the user. This list is quite long and is truncated by ... in printing. The system functions of Shen are all external to the Shen package and are found in this long list.

These external symbols have a special status in that function definitions attached to them cannot be overwritten and they are accessible to every package. It is open to you to give your function symbols the same status by applying systemf to them.

```
(4-) (define append X Y -> X)
append is not a legitimate function name.

(5-) (systemf sqrt)
sqrt

(6-) (define sqrt  X -> X)
sqrt is not a legitimate function name.
```

systemf monopolises the use of your naming conventions to the global namespace. It effectively locks out any other programmer from redefining that function.

10.5 Packages that Use Packages

Milo wishes to devise an engineering package that uses my-maths-stuff package. Within the engineering package the sqrt, abs and average functions are used. Since these are cited in the engineering package they will be prefixed by engineering which is not what he wants. To escape that Milo exempts them by typing (package engineering [sqrt abs average] ...)

However we are working continuously on the maths package and adding more and more functions that are external to that package. What Milo wants to do is to be able to freely access our latest work without having to continuously add to the list of maths functions that are exempt from renaming in the engineering package.

Milo can avoid having to look up these functions by making *all* the external maths functions accessible within the engineering package.

(package engineering (append (external my-maths-stuff) *engineering functions*)

The external function allows Milo to spread his engineering package over several files. For example if Milo has his engineering package spread out in files A and B, to be loaded in that order, he can write in A.

115

```
(package engineering (append (external my-maths-stuff) engineering functions)
```

Code for file A)

In file B Milo writes

```
(package engineering (external engineering)
```

Code for file B)

The invocation of external means that the symbols external in file A will be inherited by the program in file B.

10.6 The Null Package and Macros

One very special package is the **null package**, signified by writing the word null in place of the package name. The effect of incorporating a program within this package is precisely zero. No symbols are changed within the package and the program is read in as it is written. It looks, at first sight, that the null package is entirely useless. In fact, the null package is extremely useful and is the key to metaprogramming in Shen and liberating the full power of macros.

In order to be able to do metaprogramming, we need freedom to develop our own notation, and if necessary, generate significant programs from this notation. Macros allow this to a limited degree. The limitation arises from the fact that macros are essentially 1-1 functions; as taught so far they can at best replace one token by another token. What is missing is a way of replacing a token by an entire series of expressions which constitutes a program. However if we have a means of parcelling up *n* arbitrary expressions into one package, then effectively we also have a means of using macros to generate programs. The null package provides exactly that means.

A simple example uses macros and packages to add **anonymous functions** to Shen. An anonymous function is a function defined in the usual manner, but which lacks an identifier. For example in the following program, there are two functions enter-choice and process-choice which receive an input and process it.

```
(define enter-choice
  -> (do (output "Choose: ") (process-choice (input))))

(define process-choice
  1 -> (print hi)
  2 -> (print why)
  3 -> (print die))
```

Figure 10.7 A basic program for processing user input

116

In a language with anonymous functions, we can choose not to name the second function but instead use it anonymously thus;

```
(define enter-choice
  -> (do (output "Choose: ")
         ((anon 1 -> (print hi)
                2 -> (print why)
                3 -> (print die))  (input)))))
```

Figure 10.8 The same program recoded using an anonymous function

Here (anon .....) is an anonymous function which effectively works a little like an abstraction except its internal structure mirrors a Shen defined function. To achieve the effect of anonymous functions, we use packages and macros. Given the expression of 10.8, we generate a packaged expression (figure 10.9) in which the anonymous function is extracted and given a machine-generated name.

```
(package null []

  (define enter-choice
    -> (do (output "Choose: ") (f479  (input)))))

  (define f479
    1 -> (print hi)
    2 -> (print why)
    3 -> (print die))  )
```

Figure 10.9 The generated code

The program for compiling an anonymous function is shown in figure 10.10.

```
(define find-anon-funcs
  [anon | X] -> [[anon | X]]
  [X | Y] -> (append (find-anon-funcs X) (find-anon-funcs Y))
  _ -> [])

(define process-anon-macros
  Def [] -> Def
  Def Anons -> [package null [] | (replace-anon-calls Def Anons)])

(define replace-anon-calls
  Def [] -> [Def]
  Def [[anon | Rules] | Anons] -> (let F (gensym f)
                                       FDef [define F | Rules]
                                       NewDef (subst F [anon | Rules] Def)
                                       [FDef | (replace-anon-calls NewDef Anons)]))

(defmacro anon-macro
  [define F | X] -> (process-anon-macros [define F | X]
                       (find-anon-funcs [define F | X])))
```

Figure 10.10 Using a macro and the null package for anonymous functions

117

The working program is shown below.

```
(5-) (define enter-choice
   -> (do (output "Choose: ")
          ((anon 1 -> (print hi)
                 2 -> (print why)
                 3 -> (print die)) (input)))))
(fn f479)
(fn enter-choice)

(9-) (enter-choice)
Choose: 1
hihi
```

10.7 DSLs, Macros and Packages

A DSL is a *domain specific language*; that is, a formal language that is specifically designed to represent computations about a specific doman. DSLs have been designed for writing web pages (HTML), designing circuits (Verilog), mathematics (Mathematica), statistical inference (Stan) and many more.

It is very easy to design DSLs in Shen using macros and packages. Macros effectively operate one-one, replacing one s-expr by another. To achieve many-one, we wrap the many in a container. To achieve one-many, we wrap the many into one using the null package which parcels up the contents. These devices allow you to splice DSLs into Shen code subject to the Shen reader reserving certain reserved characters for its own use such as those for comments, [,] | and so forth.

If we wanted a DSL which could be spliced into Shen code *and* which used reserved characters , then it is best to embed the DSL code in a string.

(dsl "*<domain specific code goes here>*")

But even better is to parameterise the dsl function to allow different DSLs to coexist. For example, SML or Standard ML is well known functional language from Edinburgh. If we wished to be able to splice SML code into Shen we could write:

(dsl ml "*<ML code goes here>*")

The dsl function then switches the Shen reserved characters for something more innocuous , before reading the contents to a list and passing the result to compile-ML.

```
(define dsl
  ml Code -> (compile-ML
                (read-from-string-unprocessed
                   (read-reserved-chars Code))))

(define read-reserved-chars
  "" -> ""
  (@s "|" Code) -> (@s " alt! " (read-reserved-chars Code))
  (@s "," Code) -> (@s " " (read-reserved-chars Code))
  (@s F "(" Code) -> (@s "(" F (read-reserved-chars Code))
  (@s S Code) -> (@s S (read-reserved-chars Code)))

(define compile-ML
  ML -> ML)
```

Here is a trial run.

```
(4-) (dsl ml "fun factorial 0 = 1
              | factorial n = n * factorial (n - 1);")
[fun factorial 0 = 1 alt! factorial n = n * factorial [n - 1] ;]
```

Obviously we would want to put some meat into compile-ML to make it produce executable Shen code in list form. Once we're happy that we are outputting legal Shen then we can incorporate our code into the Shen reader by using a macro.

```
(defmacro dslmacro
  [dsl Language Code] -> [package null [] | (dsl Language Code)])
```

Now if we splice (dsl ml "<*ML code goes here*>") into a Shen file and load it, the ML code will be compiled into Shen.

10.8 Macro Management

Are macros a good thing? Having followed the chapter so far, you will probably consider the answer must be 'yes'. A friend Dr Gyorgy Lajos once said 'You can have sharp tools with which you can also cut yourself, or you can have blunt tools which do not cut well but protect you from harm.' Macros are a razor sharp tool.

For this reason software managers do not always welcome macros precisely because they are so powerful. The ability to define your own personal notation is a delight for experimental programmers, but is not welcome in commercial settings where third-party readability is at a premium. Shen macros are particularly open to abuse; for example, a lethal specimen rewrites 3 as 2.

```
(7-) (defmacro def3
        3 -> 2)
(fn def3)

(8-) (+ 3 3)
4
```

Apart from being an April Fool's joke on unsuspecting Shen programmers, a macro of this sort is of little use. It is in fact an example of a **red macro**, that is, a macro that changes the global run-time environment of the Shen system by changing the semantics of Shen itself.

A red macro is not necessarily a toxic macro, nevertheless red macros are far-reaching in their effects. (undefmacro def3) removes this macro.

A macro that is not red is a **green macro**. Can this categorisation be calculated by computer? Substantially - assuming the code is packaged - yes. If the external symbols on the left-hand side of the macro are a subset of the external symbols of Shen then the macro is red. In the case of def3 the set of symbols involved is the empty set which is obviously a subset of the external symbols of the Shen. If a macro is internal to a package and contains symbols on the left-hand side which are internal to that package then the macro is green and the effects are local to the package. Thus it is possible to effectively compute the existence of red macros.

10.9 Macroexpansion and Unpackaging

There are two possible regimes for macroexpansion and unpackaging.

1. Expressions are macroexpanded before they are unpackaged; this is a **macro first** regime.
2. Expressions are unpackaged before they are macroexpanded; this is a **package first** regime.

Let us consider the consequences of a macro first regime. We define a simple macro.

```
(defmacro a->b
  a -> b)
```

If we enter

```
(package foo [] a)
```

Then under a macro first regime, a is rewritten to b and unpackaging produces foo.b. Under a package first regime, a is unpackaged to foo.a and the macro does not apply, foo.a being returned.

The consequence of a macro first regime is that any macro can interact with the internal symbols of any package and this is not desirable for obvious reasons. So the regime in Shen is package first.

10.10 Working Inside a Package

in-package allows the user to place the REPL *inside* a package with a package without having to prefix function names by the package name. When working inside a package, all function symbols *heading* applications or as arguments to fn are renamed according to the conventions of that package. That is to say, given an application $(f x_1 ... x_n)$, where f is a symbol, f may be renamed according to the conventions of the package. However *within* an application there is no renaming (figure 10.11).

```
(0-) (package foo []
          (define double
              X -> (+ X X)) )
(fn foo.double)

 (1-) (double 5)
fn: double is undefined

(2-) (in-package foo)
foo

(3-) f  \\ not in an application
f

(4-) (double 5)
10

(5-) (define triple
          X -> (* 3 X))
(fn triple)   \\ the name is not packaged

(6-) (triple 3)
The function COMMON-LISP-USER::foo.triple is undefined.

(7-) (in-package null)
null

(8-) (double 5)
fn: double is undefined

(9-) (triple 3)
9
```

Figure 10.11 Working inside a package

The purpose of this arrangement is to exempt from renaming, symbols which are not acting as functions. For example, if we choose to work within a package nlp devoted to natural language processing, then the expression (parse [John kicked the ball]) typed to the REPL should be rendered as (nlp.parse [John kicked the ball]) and not (nlp.parse [John nlp.kicked nlp.the nlp.ball]).

The principle holds that, when placing the REPL inside a package, idle symbols should not be packaged. This is not true when we statically place code within package in a *file* where any suitable symbol will be packaged unless we direct otherwise. The difference in convention arises because in the case of a file the contents are in plain view and we have complete control over what is packaged and what is not. In the case of the REPL, because symbols are dynamically generated by user interaction with the REPL, convenience of use (which is why we choose to work inside a package) is more important. Figure 10.7 shows a session within a package

Notice that the function triple defined when working inside the package is not renamed. Hence hacking packaged code using in-package in the REPL would still require the FQN. However hacking code inside the REPL is not good practice, files and editors exist for that purpose. The purpose of in-package is to allow the user interact with existing code without having to type in FQNs.

A consequence of in-package is that Shen can support large libraries where many programmers compete in using the same identifier f for different functions. Promoting f to the global namespace is not an option and rendering f internal to programmer packages and using the FQN is tedious. Placing the user inside the package allows each programmer to rule his own kingdom.

Exercise 10

1. Devise a macro that makes > polyadic so that (> 3 2 1) returns true.

2. Write a macro that allows you to use standard 2 digit hex notation \xNN for characters in strings. Thus "\x12" should print out in the same way as "c#18;".

3. Devise a version of /. that uses pattern matching; (/. [Y Z] Z) receives a 2 element list and returns the second element and if the input is not a 2 element list returns an error.

5. Extend the dsl function to the following languages and design compilers into Shen.
   a. SML into Shen.
   b. Prolog in Edinburgh syntax into Shen Prolog.
   c. SQL into Shen.

Further Reading

Metaprogramming was a feature of the first functional programming language Lisp. Macros are part of the Lisp tradition and are well explained in Seibel (2005) which also includes a chapter on Lisp packages.

11 Exceptions and Continuations

The two topics covered in this chapter deal with the control flow of a program, that is, the order in which instructions are executed. Exceptions allow us to break the execution of a program and return the control to an earlier point or to surface to the top level with an error message. Continuations allow us to carry computations as actual objects which can be activated at our will. Both of these are powerful tools in the hands of experienced programmers. We begin with looking at exceptions.

11.1 Exceptions

A basic feature of any programming language is the ability to stop the flow of computation when an anomalous condition is realised and signal an error. The simple-error function is one of the primitive functions in which Shen is written and its role is to raise an error whenever such a condition is encountered. simple-error receives a string and maps it to an **exception**; a computational object that, unless trapped, surfaces to the top level in which the contents of the string are printed as an error message.

For example, suppose we maintain a vector of employee names in which every employee is uniquely identified by a number which indexes into the vector. If we supply a number which lies outside the range of the vector then the system signals an out of bounds error message vector call is out of range. This is not precisely informative to a naive user of our system who may know nothing of vectors. One solution is substitute our own error message by first testing to see if the index lies outside the limit of the vector

```
(define get-employee
  N Vector -> (if (> N (limit Vector))
                  (simple-error "this number is larger than our database!")
                  (<-vector Vector N)))
```

This works fine except that in cases where we try to access a number within the limit, but one which has not been assigned any employee, the system crashes with an error message because nothing has been stored at the vector index. One way round this is to plug all the vector spaces with void as we did in 8.3. But a more elegant solution is to trap the error and substitute one of our own error messages. This has the advantage that we can also trap out of bounds error messages too.

123

For this purpose we use a higher-order function trap-error that receives two inputs; an expression *x* and a function *f*. If the evaluation of *x* raises an exception *e*, then this exception is passed to *f* and (*f e*) is returned. If *x* does not raise an exception, then the normal form of *x* is returned. In figure 11.1, we use an abstraction that receives the system exception as an argument E and then discards it, replacing it by our own error message.

```
(define get-employee
  N Vector -> (trap-error (<-vector Vector N)
                (/. E (simple-error "this number does not occur our database!"))))
```

Figure 11.1 Trapping an error

Since an error can be raised for one of two reasons; either an out of range call or a call to an unassigned index, it would be useful if we could determine which error is involved and tailor our response accordingly.

The function error-to-string allows us to map an exception to the string from which it was generated. Using this function we can arrange our response.

```
(define get-employee
  N Vector -> (trap-error (<-vector Vector N)
                (/. E (simple-error (error-response (error-to-string E))))))

(define error-response
  "vector element not found" -> "this number is not in our database"
  _ -> "this number is larger than our database!")
```

A slightly more sophisticated function than simple-error is error which does what simple-error does but includes all the formatting facilities of output. The program below now prints (e.g.) #123 is not in our database.

```
(define get-employee
  N Vector -> (trap-error (<-vector Vector N)
                (/. E (let ErrorString (error-response (error-to-string E))
                        (error "#~A ~A ~%" N ErrorString)))))
```

Error trapping can be useful if we want to incorporate a global into our program but only initialise it if and when it is called. The function push allows us to push values onto a variable without having to initialise it. push uses trap-error to initialise the variable to [Value] when push is first invoked avoiding the need to initialise the variable in the program or the top level.

```
(define push
  Value Variable -> (set Variable (trap-error [Value | (value Variable)]
                                    (/. E [Value]))))
```

Hence we can write (push 0 *stack*) without having to consider whether *stack* has been initialised.

124

11.2 Continuations

Lazy evaluation is the technique of delaying a computation until such time as the result of the computation is known to be needed. Examples of lazy evaluation appeared in chapter 2 with the introduction of if, and and or. All these functions selectively evaluate their arguments only when these evaluations need to be made. An elegant way of performing lazy evaluation in Shen is to use the services of freeze and thaw.

freeze receives an expression *x* and instead of evaluating *x*, returns a promise called a **continuation** to evaluate *x* if asked. This promise will be honoured if it is **thawed**. thaw will receive the frozen expression and thaw it to produce the normal form of *x*. Figure 11.2 shows a simple example.

```
(3-) (freeze (+ 1 2))
#<CLOSURE :LAMBDA NIL [+ 1 2]>

(4-) (thaw (freeze (+ 1 2)))
3
```

Figure 11.2 Using freeze and thaw

freeze and thaw allows us to explore interesting computational paradigms. For instance, nearly forty years ago, in a paper *Cons Should not Evaluate its Arguments,* Friedman and Wise argued that cons should not be strict in its evaluation but should hold suspended evaluations. The result is a **lazy list** used in languages like Haskell. To do this in Shen we construct a lazy cons that allows us to build lazy lists.

```
(defmacro @c-macro
  [@c X Y] -> [cons [freeze X] [freeze Y]])
```

The lazy list composed of 1 and 2 is written (@c 1 (@c 2 [])). For convenience we also define the equivalent of a polyadic list operator which allows the lazy list composed of 1 and 2 to be written (@l 1 2).

```
(defmacro @l-macro
  [@l] -> (freeze [])
  [@l X | Y] -> [@c X [@l | Y]])
```

The lazy equivalent of hd and tl is @hd and @tl.

```
(define @hd
  X -> (thaw (hd X)))

(define @tl
  X -> (thaw (tl X)))
```

```
(6-) (@l 1 2 3)
#<FUNCTION (LAMBDA ()) {1006839DDB}> | #<FUNCTION (LAMBDA ())
{100687CB5B}>]

(7-) (@hd (@l 1 2 3))
1

(8-) (@tl (@l 1 2 3))
[#<FUNCTION (LAMBDA ()) {1006A8E3EB}> | #<FUNCTION (LAMBDA ())
{1006A8E25B}>]
```

Lazy lists allow the possibility of constructing data structures that mimic the effect of computing with infinitely large lists such as the list of all prime numbers. Let's define the set of all primes as a lazy list.

```
(define primes
  -> (primes-from 2))
```

(primes-from 2) will construct a lazy list of all the primes from 2 onwards.

```
(define primes-from
  N -> (@c N (primes-from (next-prime (+ N 1)))))
```

```
(define next-prime
  X -> X                          where (prime? X)
  X -> (next-prime (+ 1 X)))
```

The task of finding the first prime divisor of a number can be defined as an operation on the lazy list of all primes.

```
(define first-prime-divisor
  N -> (first-prime-divisor-help N (primes)))
```

```
(define first-prime-divisor-help
  N Primes -> (let D (@hd Primes)
                (if (divisor? D N) D (first-prime-divisor-help N (@tl Primes)))))
```

```
(define divisor?
  D N -> (integer? (/ N D)))
```

Figure 11.3 shows a test.

```
(38-) (first-prime-divisor 1257)
3

(40-) (first-prime-divisor 1246681)
29
```

Figure 11.3 A prime divisor using lazy lists

For efficiency and convenience, freeze is one of the primitive functions, but actually we can define freeze and thaw in terms of abstractions using macros.

```
(defmacro freeze-macro
  [freeze X] -> [/. (gensym⁵¹ (protect Y)) X])
```

```
(defmacro thaw-macro
  [thaw X] -> [X 0])
```

Exercise 11

1. Implement a database system that uses of a linked series of files. A query can be directed at a single file or distributed over any number of files. When a query is directed at a single file and the data is missing then an error is raised. When the query is directed at a number of files and the data is missing from a file, the error is trapped and the search directed to the next file in the series.

2. Implement a program with an error stream. When the program raises an error it is trapped and sent to a file to be recorded before being raised at the top level.

3. Improve your answer to 2. by creating a function errstream with two arguments; the first is an expression to be evaluated. The second is an expression which is returned if the first argument raises an error. Arrange that the suppressed error message is written to the same file as in 2.

4. Represent the Cartesian product program of chapter 4 as a lazy list.

5. Represent the powerset program of chapter 4 as a lazy list.

6. Represent the Goldbach's conjecture program as a lazy list; if the user enters RETURN, the program returns a new instance of the conjecture.

7. Devise a simulation of a UNIX operating system that allows the user to place a job in background by typing bg *command*. Your job will be held as a continuation and bg will return a job number *n*. Typing fg *n* will execute the job.

8. In object-oriented (OO) programming, objects are not just data but data with 'intelligence'; that is, an object can respond to commands sent to it. Implement an OO version of a database program where the database is held as an abstraction that receives user input and can modify itself accordingly.

---

⁵¹ (gensym (protect Y)) generates a new symbol such as Y4567. The purpose is to protect from accidental variable capture if the symbol Y occurs in the expression denoted by X.

Further Reading

Scheme (Abelson and Sussman, 1984) was famous for introducing many ideas which became standard including continuations. The idea of a continuation was present in operating systems in the form of a **thread**; a computational process that could be passed around or activated. Such technology has become more common with the development of concurrent programming.

Websites

See http://www.sbcl.org/manual/Threading.html for an exposition of threads for SBCL which are held a continuations.

12 Non-Determinism

It's choice - not chance - that determines your destiny.

Jean Nidetch

12.1 Non-deterministic Algorithms

An important class of algorithms is grouped under the heading of **non-deterministic algorithms**. In a deterministic algorithm, every step is determined and there is no possibility of choice. Non-deterministic algorithms present a series of steps in which, at some point, there is an undetermined choice as to what step to take out of a set of possibilities, and the algorithm leaves it to us to determine how the right choice is made. The stage of a non-deterministic algorithm where such a choice arises is called a **choice point**.

The problem in programming a non-deterministic algorithm into a computer is that computers do not *choose* anything; they only do what they are told to do. One way of representing non-determinism to a computer is to get it to order the choices available and to try each one in turn. If a choice turns out to be unsuccessful, then the computer **backtracks** to the choice point and tries the next choice in the ordering.

12.2 Depth First Search

Non-deterministic algorithms are common in **search** where the solution may not be obvious and computations may have to be undone when initial choices turn out to be wrong.

A search problem is a triple $<s, f, g>$ composed of a start state s, a state function f that maps a state to a set of states and a goal function g that maps a state to a boolean and recognises when the search problem has been solved. If $(g\ s)$ = true then s is a **goal state**.

An example of a search problem is the problem of finding, from a given set s of natural numbers, a series of numbers whose summation is equal to some given natural number n. For instance, if s = {2, 7, 9} and n = 27, then a solution is [2 7 9 9]. Our start state s is composed of the empty list and the state function f

129

generates from any state s_i, a list of states $[[2 \mid s_i]\ [7 \mid s_i]\ [9 \mid s_i]]$. The goal function g returns true just when S' totals 27 and false otherwise.

The challenge of search is to conduct the generation of new states efficiently so that a goal state is reached with the minimum computation. This may not be easy because the further into the seach we go, the greater the number of possible paths of computation. In our example, every application of f to a state generates three new states and iterating f over those states generates three more from every state. Hence every level l of search raises the number of possible paths to 3^l. For this reason search programs can get bogged down in possibilities; a phenomenon known as the **combinatorial explosion**.

There are ways of coping with this explosion; a popular method, **depth–first search**, is good at constraining the memory requirements of search because, instead of generating every layer of search, depth-first search chooses only one possible solution and runs with it. This is a choice point of course. The immediate problem that the choice might be wrong and the possible solution may turn out to be a dead end. At this point the computer will have to return to the last choice point and choose again.

One nasty possibility is that the wrong choice is taken and the computer never gets to recognise it. Depth–first search may fail to find a solution, preferring to beaver away endlessly on the wrong path. A useful adjunct is a **failure function** which recognises if a state can never lead to a solution. In our problem, if the summation (sum) of the numbers in a state exceeds 27, we know that the state is a failure state and we need not persevere with it. Such a function can be built into f to filter out useless states. The various pieces of our search problem can be easily coded.

```
(define goal?
  S -> (= (sum S) 27))

(define f
  S -> (remove-if-no-good  [[2 | S] [7 | S] [9 | S]]))

(define remove-if-no-good
  Ss -> (remove-if (/. X (> (sum X) 27)) Ss))

(define remove-if
  _ [] -> []
  F [X | Y] -> (remove-if F Y)        where (F X)
  F [X | Y] -> [X | (remove-if F Y)])
```

The challenge is to join these bricks of code together to form a coherent program. The mortar in this case is a **search strategy** and the one we have chosen to implement is depth-first search. Since two of the elements of search are functions, it follows that depth-first search will be implemented as a higher-order function. Implementing depth-first search is a 7 line program in Shen, but to achieve this economy we need to look at the resources Shen supplies for computing with choice points.

In Shen, rules that mark choice points are signalled by the use of <- instead of -> within a function definition. The effect of this change is that the expression R to the right of <- is returned only provided R does *not* evaluate to the **failure object**. The failure object is returned by the 0-place function (fail) and is printed out as three dots ... . If R *does* evaluate to the failure object, then the rule is skipped and Shen **backtracks** to this point the next rule is tried. For instance the function

```
(define return-n
   10 <- (fail)
   10 -> 9
   N -> N)
```

returns 9 for 10 and n for any other number n. The input 10 on the first line causes (fail) to be evaluated. However the result of (fail) is not returned because the back arrow <- is used. The rule is thus skipped and the second line returns 9. The following equivalence is convenient way of grasping the use of <- in Shen.

The rule $P_1,...,P_n$ <- R is equivalent to $P_1,...,P_n$ -> R where (not (= R (fail)))[52]

Another means of forcing backtracking is through the higher-order fail-if function which takes two arguments; a function f and an object x and triggers failure if $(f x)$ is true. fail-if is a powerful means of controlling backtracking which allows the elements of an infinitely large class to count as failure objects. In figure 12.1 return-n acts as the identity function for numbers less than or equal to 45 but triggers failure if the number is greater. Shen skips to the next rule in this case, but since there is no next rule an error is triggered.

```
(5-) (define return-n
        N <- (fail-if (/. X (> X 45)) N))
(fn return-n)

(6-) (return-n 45)
45

(7-) (return-n 46)
error: partial function return n
```

Figure 12.1 Invoking backtracking

A convenient way of grasping the use of fail-if in Shen is to remember the following equivalence

---

[52] The rule is declaratively accurate but inefficient, because the result R returned from the rewrite rule is evaluated twice in the right-hand side of the equivalence, but only once in the left hand side. In chapter 15 we shall see how continuations are used to compile these constructions efficiently.

$P_1,...,P_n$ <- (fail-if F R)   is equivalent to $P_1,...,P_n$ -> R where (not (F R))

Preliminaries over, the depth-first program can be encoded (figure 12.2).

```
(5-) (define depth
        State F G? -> (depth-help [State] F G?))
(fn depth)

(6-) (define depth-help
        [State | _] _ G? -> State                where (G? State)
        [State | _] F G? <- (depth-help (F State) F G?)
        [_ | States] F G? -> (depth-help States F G? )
        _ _ _ -> (fail))
(fn depth-first)

(7-) (depth [] (fn f) (fn goal?))
[7 2 2 2 2 2 2 2 2 2 2 2]
```

Figure 12.2 Depth first search in Shen

Certain beautiful programs, and this is one of them, are best left to contemplation.

12.3 Recursive Descent Parsing

Languages, whether natural like English or French, or artificial, like Pascal or Shen, possess a syntax whereby certain series of symbols are grammatically acceptable and others are not. To take English as an example, "John kicks the ball" is an acceptable English sentence but "the kicks ball John" is not. One basic facility that every competent programmer needs is that of being able to design, upon request, programs that recognise whether a certain series of symbols is grammatically acceptable according to the syntax rules of a given language. Such programs are called **recognisors** for the sentences of the language in question.

A recognisor for a language may only return two values; indicating either that its input is grammatical or that it is not. Rather more useful is a *parser* which returns either the verdict that the input is not grammatical or else, if the input is grammatical, returns a description of the **grammatical structure** of the input. [53]

For example, a linguist would say that "John kicks the ball" is a grammatical sentence composed of two parts - a *noun phrase* comprising the *name* "John" and a *verb phrase* "kicks the ball". The verb phrase is composed of two parts, a *transitive verb* "kicks" and another *noun phrase* "the ball". Finally the concluding noun phrase is built out of a *determiner* "the" and a *noun* "ball". This

---

[53] Such programs can be a big challenge to write because of the size of the grammars for English. For instance, realistic grammars will contain several thousand rules, which pose a severe computational challenge for any parser. Happily most programmers do not set themselves such an ambitious task and the techniques taught in this chapter will suffice to solve simple parsing problems.

analysis is sometimes represented as a tree structure in which *sent* stands for *sentence, np* stands for *noun phrase, vp* stands for *verb phrase, vtrans* stands for *transitive verb, det* stands for *determiner* and *n* stands for *noun.* Such a tree is called a **parse tree** (figure 12.3).

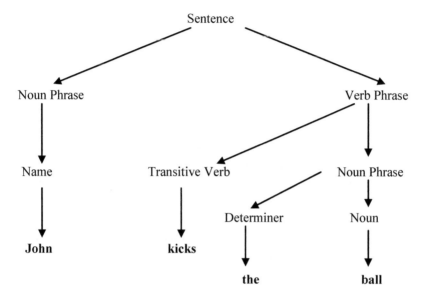

Figure 12.3 A parse tree representing the syntax of "John kicks the ball"

The choice of representation is conventional; the same information can be given as a list.

[[sent --> np vp] [np --> name] [name --> "John"] [vp --> vtrans np] [vtrans ---> "kicks"] [np --> det n] [det --> "the"] [n --> "ball"]]

Grammar rules are rules that attempt to define what counts as grammatical in the language studied. The shape and form of these grammar rules vary according to the system used, but by far the commonest form is the **context-free grammar** (also called a **type 2 grammar**). A context-free grammar consists of a series of context-free grammar rules. Each such rule consists of a left-hand side and a right-hand side separated by some agreed symbol (generally →, but also sometimes ::=). The left-hand side has but one symbol and the right-hand side one or more symbols. For example, here is a simple grammar which parses our specimen sentence.

133

1.	*sent* → *np vp*	9.	*det* → "this"
2.	*np* → *name*	10.	*n* → "ball"
3.	*np* → *det n*	11.	*n* → "girl"
4.	*name* → "John"	12.	*vp* → *vtrans np*
5.	*name* → "Bill"	13.	*vp* → *vintrans*
6.	*det* → "the"	14.	*vtrans* → "kicks"
7.	*det* → "a"	15.	*vtrans* → "likes"
8.	*det* → "that"	16.	*vintrans* → "jumps"

Figure 12.4 A grammar for a simple fragment of English

One symbol, called **the distinguished symbol**, occurs to the left of the arrow but never to the right; in our example this is *sent*. A series of expressions $e_1,...e_n$ are **expansions** of an expression e if there is a rule $e \rightarrow e_1,...e_n$ in the grammar. The expressions that occur in the grammar but never on the left of → are called **terminals**. A **lexical category** is a non-terminal whose expansions are always terminals. In order to prove a sentence S is grammatical according to the grammar rules we can follow a non-deterministic procedure the **naive top down parsing procedure**.

Naive Top Down Parsing Procedure.

Let i = the list containing only the distinguished symbol, let S be the sentence to be parsed.

Repeat.

    If i consists of only terminals and i = S, then halt. S is grammatical. Print the proof.[54]

    If i consists of only terminals and $i \neq$ S, then halt. The proof has failed.

    Otherwise choose a non-terminal i_n in i. Choose an expansion of i_n and set the new value of i to the result of replacing i_n in the old value of i by the chosen expansion.

To illustrate, we wish to prove ["John" "kicks" "the" "ball"] is grammatical according to *G*. The symbol →*n* indicates that a symbol may be expanded according to the *n*th rule in *G*. The following chain of expansions constitutes a proof that ["John" "kicks" "the" "ball"] is grammatical.

---

[54] Most usually, this proof is presented as a parse tree, but there is no necessity to do so. The parse tree is only significant in rendering graphically the history of the expansions that were used to prove the sentence grammatical. The difference between a parser and a recognisor is not that the parser produces a parse tree and the recogniser does not, but that the parser produces a proof of its verdict whereas the recognisor does not.

[*sent*] →₁ [*np vp*] →₂ [*name vp*] →₄ ["John" *vp*] →₁₂ ["John" *vtrans np*] →₁₄ ["John" "kicks" *np*] →₃ ["John" "kicks" *det n*] →₆ ["John" "kicks" "the" *n*] →₁₀ ["John" "kicks" "the" "ball"]

Though the basic top down parsing procedure is perfectly sound it requires modification for three reasons.

1. It cannot show a sentence is ungrammatical. A negative result from this procedure could be due to a faulty choice of expansions earlier in the proof. For instance if [*np vp*] →₃ [*det n vp*] had been chosen instead of [*np vp*] →₂ [*name vp*], then the parse would have failed.

2. The basic top down parsing procedure provides no clue as to which expansions to use.

3. The basic top down parsing procedure provides no clue as to which non-terminals to expand.

The solution to the second problem is also a solution to the first. We mimic the non-determinism in the basic top down parsing procedure by arranging to backtrack if the procedure has led to a dead end. Since by this method all available expansions will be tried, if a negative result is still returned then this must be because the input sentence is ungrammatical and so our improved procedure can return a message to this effect. The solution to the final problem is to adopt a convention as to which non-terminal will be expanded first and the most convenient choice is to work on the leftmost or leading non-terminal in *i*.

In this revised form, the top down parsing procedure is still inefficient because it has to convert all non-terminals to terminals before comparing the result with the input sentence to see if they are identical. But it is often possible to spot dead-ends before this stage. For instance, if the chain [*np vp*] →₃ [*det n vp*] →₆ ["the" *n vp*] had been followed, then the failure of "the" to match the input "John" would signify straight away that further expansion of ["the" *n vp*] was a waste of time.

A much improved performance arises when we arrange that whenever the leading expression i_l of i is a terminal, that further expansion proceeds only if $i_l = S_1$ (where S_1 is the first element of S). Computationally it is then convenient to remove i_l from i and S_1 from S so that the parse finally succeeds when every word in S has been accounted for; i.e. S has been reduced to an empty list.   This adaptation of the basic top down parsing procedure is called **recursive descent parsing**.

12.4 A Recursive Descent Parser in Shen

Building a recursive descent parser for G in Shen is not too difficult. Each non-terminal N in G is represented by a function in Shen. The nature of this representation varies according to whether N is a lexical category or not. Let us deal with the case where N is a lexical category using an example. These are the rules dealing with the lexical category n (Noun).

$$n \rightarrow \text{"ball"}$$
$$n \rightarrow \text{"girl"}$$

An initial attempt to construct a function for n would simply receive the input list and check to see if the head of the list was "girl" or "ball". If so, following recursive descent parsing, the head of the list is removed. If not, then (fail) is returned showing the function has failed to find a noun.

```
(define n
  ["ball" | Words]  -> Words
  ["girl" | Words] -> Words
   _ -> (fail))
```

This is almost adequate except that if the head of the list is a noun, then the fact that the relevant expansion has been used must be recorded so that it can be returned at the end of the parse. A solution is to make the input a pair composed of (a) the sentence being parsed (a list of strings) and (b) a list of the rules used to parse it so far. This second list will be returned at the end of the parse as a proof that the sentence is grammatical. The revised version now reads.

```
(define n
  [["girl" | Words] Proof]  -> [Words [[n --> "girl"] | Proof]]
  [["ball" | Words] Proof]  -> [Words [[n --> "ball"] | Proof]]
   _ -> (fail))
```

Now consider the construction of a function for a non-lexical category; for example *vp*. *vp* has two expansions *vp* $\rightarrow$ *vtrans np* and *vp* $\rightarrow$ *vintrans*. If the first expansion is used then (a) the front of the sentence will be scanned for a transitive verb and (b) if there is one, the remainder of the sentence will be scanned for a noun phrase. However either of these procedures might fail in which case the failure object will be found. In such an event we will want to try the second expansion. So the outline form of the function vp will be

```
(define vp
  Sentence
    <- (<parse-noun-phrase> (parse-transitive-verb> Sentence)))
  Sentence -> (<parse-intransitive-verb> Sentence))
```

The gaps *<parse-transitive-verb>*, *<parse-noun-phrase>* and *<parse-intransitive-verb>* will be taken up by the functions that encode *vtrans*, *np* and *vintrans* respectively so the function will look like this.

```
(define vp
  Sentence <- (np (vtrans Sentence))
  Sentence <- (vintrans Sentence)
  _ -> (fall))
```

But since the input is a pair, we need again to record the expansion used. So the final form is:-

```
(define vp
  [Sentence Proof]
    <- (np (vtrans [Sentence [[vp --> vtrans np] | Proof]]))
  [Sentence Proof] -> (vintrans [Sentence [[vp --> vintrans] | Proof]])
  _ -> (fail))
```

Dealing with all the other expansions in the same way generates the program in figure 12.5.

```
(define sent
  [Input Proof] <- (vp (np [Input [[sent --> np vp] | Proof]]))
  _ -> (fail))

(define np
  [Input Proof] <- (n (det [Input [[np --> det n] | Proof]]))
  [Input Proof] <- (name [Input [[np --> name] | Proof]])
  _ -> (fail))

(define name
  [["John" | Input] Proof] -> [Input [[name --> "John"] | Proof]]
  [["Bill" | Input] Proof] -> [Input [[name --> "Bill"] | Proof]]
  _ -> (fail))

(define det
  [["the" | Input] Proof] -> [Input [[det --> "the"] | Proof]]
  [["a" | Input] Proof] -> [Input [[det --> "a"] | Proof]]
  [["that" | Input] Proof] -> [Input [[det --> "that"] | Proof]]
  [["this" | Input] Proof] -> [Input [[det --> "this"] | Proof]]
  _ -> (fail))

(define n
  [["ball" | Input] Proof] -> [Input [[n --> "ball"] | Proof]]
  [["girl" | Input] Proof] -> [Input [[n --> "girl"] | Proof]]
  _ -> (fail))

(define vp
  [Input Proof] <- (np (vtrans [Input [[vp --> vtrans np] | Proof]]))
  [Input Proof] <- (vp [Input [[vp --> vintrans] | Proof]])
  _ -> (fail))
```

```
(define vtrans
  [["kicks" | Input] Proof] -> [Input [[vtrans --> "kicks"] | Proof]]
  [["likes" | Input] Proof] -> [Input [[vtrans --> "likes"] | Proof]]
  _ -> (fail))

(define vintrans
  [["jumps" | Input] Proof]
  -> [Input [[vintrans --> "jumps"] | Proof]]
  _ -> (fail))
```

Figure 12.5 A parser for our simple fragment of English

All that is needed to complete the program is the driver function that builds the input and applies the function representing the distinguished function and tests to see if the parse is successful (figure 12.6).

```
(define parse
  Sentence -> (let Parse (sent [Sentence []])
                (if (parsed? Parse)
                    (output_parse Parse)
                    ungrammatical)))

(define parsed?
  [[] _] -> true
  _ -> false)

(define output_parse
  [_ Parse_Rules] -> (reverse Parse_Rules))
```

Figure 12.6 The top level of the parser

The program can now be used to parse sentences according to the grammar rules (figure 12.7).

```
(22-) (parse ["the" "girl" "likes" "the" "ball"])
[[sent --> np vp] [np --> det n] [det --> "the"] [n --> "girl"] [vp --> vtrans np]
[vtrans --> "likes"] [np --> det n] [det --> "the"] [n --> "ball"]]

(23-) (parse ["the" "cat" "likes" "the" "girl"])
ungrammatical
```

Figure 12.7 The parser in action

The extraction of a program like the above from a grammar is actually a mechanical process, so it is more sensible to program the computer to generate the parser than to code it by hand. Such a program is a **parser-generator** – a metaprogram that receives a grammar as input and generates a parsing program as an output. We will examine the use of such a program in the next chapter.

Exercise 12

1. Bratko (1990) "A **non-deterministic finite state machine** (NDFSM) is a machine that reads a series of symbols and decides whether to accept or reject that series. A NDFSM has a number of states and upon receipt of a symbol will change from being in one state to being in another. There is a privileged set of states called **final states** and if the automaton is in one of these states when it finishes reading a series then it accepts that series, otherwise it rejects it. If there is one state that has to be chosen in order for the whole list to be accepted, then the NDFSM will choose that state and not one that will cause the list to be rejected." The operation of a NDFSM can be represented by a labelled directed graph in which the nodes of the graph represent the states of the NDFSM, and the labels on the arcs are the inputs required to get the NDFSM to jump from one state to the next. The figure below shows a NDFSM as a labelled directed graph.

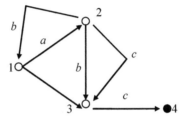

There is one final state in this NDFSM, state 4. Initially the NDFSM is in state 1. This automaton accepts the input *a b a b a c* in the following way. The input *a* causes the automaton to go to state 2, the *b* to state 1, the *a* to state 2, the b to state 1, the *a* to state 3 and the *c* to state 4. Write a program to simulate this NDFSM.

The next problems are all taken from Werner Hett's web site of *Ninety-Nine Prolog Problems*.

3. **The eight queens problem.** This is a classical problem in computer science. The objective is to place eight queens on a chessboard so that no two queens are attacking each other; i.e., no two queens are in the same row, the same column, or on the same diagonal. Write a program that computes all the solutions for this problem. Your program will systematically place queens and force a backtrack when a queen cannot be added to the board without attacking another queen already on it.

4. **The knight's tour.** Another famous problem is this one: how can a knight jump on a chessboard in such a way that it visits every square exactly once?

5. ***Graceful labelling problem.** This problem is taken from Werner Hett who records.

> "Several years ago I met a mathematician who was intrigued by a problem for which he didn't know a solution. His name was Von Koch, and I don't know whether the problem has been solved since.

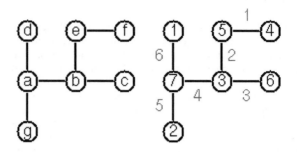

Anyway the puzzle goes like this: Given a tree with N nodes (and hence N-1 edges). Find a way to enumerate the nodes from 1 to N and, accordingly, the edges from 1 to N-1 in such a way, that for each edge K the difference of its node numbers (labels) equals to K. The conjecture is that this is always possible. [The diagram above shows a solution for one tree].

For small trees the problem is easy to solve by hand. However, for larger trees, (and 14 is already very large), it is difficult to find a solution. And remember, we don't know for sure whether there is always a solution!"

Write a program that calculates a labeling scheme for a given tree.

6. *Again from Werner Hett.

"Given a list of integer numbers, find a correct way of inserting arithmetic signs (operators) such that the result is a correct equation. Example: With the list of numbers [2,3,5,7,11] we can form the equations 2-3+5+7 = 11 or 2 = (3*5+7)/11 (and ten others!)."

Write a program that finds the list of all possible solutions to this problem.

7. Write a function path to find an acyclic path P from node A to node B in the graph G. The function should return all paths via backtracking.

8. Write a function cycles to find a closed path (cycle) P starting at a given node A in the graph G. The function should return all cycles from A via backtracking.

9. Two graphs G_1 and G_2 are *isomorphic* if there is a 1-1 function from the set of nodes of G_1 onto the set of nodes of G_2 such that for any nodes X,Y of G_1, X and Y are adjacent in G_1 if and only if f(X) and f(Y) are adjacent in G_2. Write a function that determines whether two graphs are isomorphic.

Further Reading

The use of backtracking in programming dates at least as far back as Hewitt's (1969) PLANNER and became widely used when Prolog (Kowalski (1979)) made its appearance. A more restrictive version of the backtracking used in Shen appeared in the MetaLisp programming language (Lajos (1990)) and in Wright (1991). Liu and Staples (1993) introduce a backtracking extension into C. Haynes (1987) and more recently Sitaram (1993) experimented with backtracking in Scheme, a functional language that is a dialect of Lisp. Charniak and McDermott (1985), discuss improvements to our implementation of basic backward chaining which involve applying rules that generate the fewest subgoals. Chapter 6 of that book contains a very readable exposition of the issues involved in using backward chaining in implementing reasoning systems. Chronological backtracking is not the only form of backtracking; **dependency-directed backtracking** aims to intelligently analyse the reasons for why a search ends in a failure node and tries to undo those decisions that are directly responsible for the failure. This area is also studied within **constraint programming**, which studies the **constraint satisfaction problem** of assigning values to each element of a set of variables in such a way that a set of constraints is satisfied. Problems which fall under this category range from DNA sequencing to scheduling.

13 Shen YACC

13.1 A Short History of Shen YACC

Programs which generate parsers in the manner of the last chapter are very much a commodity now in computing and most major languages field such programs, although the parsing strategies vary. A more useful tool than a parser-generator is a **compiler-compiler**, which generates a compiler - that is to say, a program that not only parses the input but transforms it into some representation in another formal language. The study of compilers spans not only computer languages, but also natural language processing (NLP). NLP involves encoding assertions in languages like English and German into artificial or formal languages used for information storage.

The compiler-compiler studied in this chapter is Shen YACC[55] which was built to service the requirements of parsing Shen into Kλ. The genealogy of the system goes back to the Ph.D. work described in Lajos (1990) which in turn was derived from the **TDPL** (top down parsing language) formalism of Alexander Birman, documented in Aho and Ullman (1973). Shen YACC uses the recursive descent parsing strategy described in the last chapter, but augments this strategy by adding **semantic actions** that translate the input to an output, instead of simply producing a parse tree. Shen YACC incorporates certain familiar constructions such as guards, and the less familiar constructions, <e>, <!> which we will come to grips with in this chapter.

The structure of Shen YACC is more complex than the parser-generator of the last chapter, but nevertheless it shares the general anatomy. Parsing (and compilation) proceed by analysing an *input-output pair*. The input is the object to be parsed and the output is the response of the compiler. In chapter 22 we'll look more closely at the anatomy of the compiler-compiler.

---

[55] The terminology YACC means 'yet another compiler-compiler'; a now generic title for compiler-compilers derived from Steve Johnson's YACC (Johnson, 1970); a compiler-compiler developed at AT&T for the language B – a predecessor of C.

13.2 Programming in Shen YACC

A computable relation exists between the grammar rules of the last chapter and the parse that represented them. Rather than hand code a parser, it is easier to use Shen YACC to generate the parser (figure 13.1).

```
(defcc <sent>
  <np> <vp>;)

(defcc <np>
  <name>;  <det> <n>;)

(defcc <name>
  "John";  "Bill";)

(defcc <det>
  "a"; "that"; "the";)

(defcc <n>
  "ball"; "girl";)

(defcc <vp>
  <vtrans> <np>;  <vintrans>;)

(defcc <vtrans>
  "kicks"; "likes";)

(defcc <vintrans>
  "jumps";)
```

Figure 13.1 A Shen YACC program acting as a recognisor

In Shen YACC, non-terminals are identified by angles <...>. Every rule within a Shen YACC definition is terminated by a semi-colon and there can be several rules relating to one non-terminal, as in this example. Warnings are generated when this program is loaded e.g.

```
(defcc <np>
  <name>;  <det> <n>;)
warning: <name> has no semantics.
warning: <det> <n> has no semantics.
```

because no **semantic actions** have been issued as to what to do with the input when it is parsed. By default, if no semantic action is given for a rule *r*, then Shen YACC practises a technique called **semantic completion**. Semantic completion allots to *r* an action that collects the list of those terminals that fall under *r*. The semantic action is separated from the syntactic component by :=. Thus the rule <np> <vp>; is completed by the Shen compiler to <np> <vp> := (append <np> <vp>) and "ball" is completed to "ball" := ["ball"].

The higher-order function compile invokes a Shen YACC non-terminal on an input (figure 13.2). Since semantic completion has been used in every rule, if the input is grammatical, it is returned as an output. If it is not grammatical, a parse error is raised.

```
(10-) (compile (fn <sent>) ["the" "girl" "likes" "the" "ball"])
["the" "girl" "likes" "the" "ball"]

(11-) (compile (fn <sent>) ["the" "girl" "likes" "the" "cat"])
parse failure
```

Figure 13.2 Invoking compile

The program that Shen YACC has generated is a recognisor for the sentences of the grammar which produces only two outputs; one output for grammatical sentences and another for non-grammatical ones.

By overriding the semantic completion and inserting our own actions, we can arrange for Shen YACC, not only to parse an input, but also to generate some significant output. To start gently, here is a Shen YACC program that returns true if the numbers of as and bs are the same. Figure 13.4 shows it in action.

```
(defcc <asbs>
    <as> <bs> := (= (length <as>) (length <bs>));)

(defcc <as>
    a <as>;
    a;)

(defcc <bs>
    b <bs>;
    b;)
```

```
(3-) (compile (fn <asbs>) [a a a b b b])
true

(4-) (compile (fn <asbs>) [a a a b b b b])
false

(5-) (compile (fn <asbs>) [a a a c b b b b])
parse failure
```

Figure 13.3 A simple Shen YACC program that counts tokens of two kinds

The program incorporates a semantic action in the definition of the top level non-terminal; the as and the bs are collected into two lists and the lists are compared.

Since no semantic actions are given for <as> and <bs>; these non-terminals simply collect all the tokens that fall under them, returning a list in each case. The compiler can give three verdicts, true, false or an error if the list contains other than as followed by bs. An alternative encoding (13.4) avoids lists and counts the tokens on the fly.

```
(6-) (defcc <asbs>
        <as> <bs> := (= <as> <bs>);)
<asbs>

(7-) (defcc <as>
        a <as> := (+ 1 <as>);
        a := 1;)
<as>

(8-) (defcc <bs>
        b <bs> := (+ 1 <bs>);
        b := 1;)
<bs>

(9-) (compile (fn <asbs>) [a a a a a b b b b b])
true

(10-) (compile (fn <asbs>) [a a a a a b b b b b])
false

(11-) (compile (fn <asbs>) [a a a a a b b b b b c])
parse failure
```

Figure 13.4 Optimising our counting program

13.3 The Empty Expansion and Guards

A more advanced case allows 'dead characters' between the as and the bs, so that in [a a a c c % b b b] the c c % is ignored (figure 13.5).

```
(10-) (defcc <asXbs>
        <as> <dead> <bs> := (= <as> <bs>);)
<asXbs>

(11-) (defcc <dead>
        X <dead> := skip   where (not (= X b));
        <e>;)
<dead>

(12-) (compile (fn <asXbs>) [a a a a a c c % b b b b b])
true
```

Figure 13.5 Using the empty expansion and a guard

The first line of <dead> says that dead characters can consist of an element X followed by dead characters on the condition that X is not b. Here, like Shen, a guard places an extra condition on the rule. The second line introduces a special non-terminal <e>, the **empty expansion** which consumes no input and always succeeds (by default in a semantic action <e> returns []). This line allows <dead> to be called without consuming any characters and hence allows there to be no dead characters.

Guards allow Shen YACC to compute languages which are not expressable in context-free grammars. An example is the language $a^n b^n c^n$ for $n \geq 1$ composed of equal numbers of as, bs and cs, which is not characterised by any CF grammar.

```
(defcc <asbscs>
    <as> <bs> <cs> := true  where (and (= <as> <bs>) (= <bs> <cs>));)
<asbs>

(defcc <as>
    a <as> := (+ 1 <as>);
    a := 1;)
<as>

(defcc <bs>
    b <bs> := (+ 1 <bs>);
    b := 1;)
<bs>

(defcc <cs>
    c <cs> := (+ 1 <cs>);
    c := 1;)
<bs>
```

Figure 13.6 A non-CF grammar in Shen YACC

13.4 Non-Terminals and Semantic Actions

Consider the following grammar for a language L

```
(defcc <asbas>
  <as> b <as>;)

(defcc <as>
    a <as>;   a;)
```

Figure 13.7 A language L characterised by repeating a non-terminal

The set of L sentences defined by this grammar is the set a_m b a_n where m and n are greater than zero. If we submit an input to the parser generated from this grammar we get an interesting result.

```
(12-) (compile (fn <asbas>) [a b a a a a a])
[a a a a a b a a a a a]
```

The output is not the same as the input. The semantic completion that Shen YACC uses is

```
(defcc <asbas>
  <as> b <as> := (append <as> [b | <as>]);)
```

The problem here is that the grammar uses <as> for both the as preceding the b and the as following it. Since there is no way of disambiguating from the description, which <as> is invoked in the semantics, Shen follows the course of associating the output with the last occurrence of the repeated non-terminal. In this case, this is the <as> that is bound to the list of as following b. Hence the output consists of five as followed by a b followed by five more as. To make our intentions unambiguously clear, we need to rename one of the repeated <as>.

```
(defcc <asbas>
  <as> b <as+>;)

(defcc <as>
    a <as>;    a;)

(defcc <as+>
  <as>;)
```

Figure 13.8 Disambiguating the characterisation of L

The renamed <as+> has the same properties as <as>. But renaming means that the semantic completion uses two styles of non-terminal; one for the as preceding the b and one for the as after it. Using this grammar, the compiler acts as the identity function on all L sentences.

The example illustrates the importance of understanding semantic completions in Shen YACC. The method of semantic completion follows three rules.

1. The output from a non-terminal is *appended* to the output.
2. A terminal is *consed* to the output unless it is a wild card which is ignored.
3. In cases of ambiguity where a non-terminal is repeated, the output of the non-terminal is the output associated with its final occurrence.

Though these rules are not hard to follow, it is useful, when mastering Shen YACC, not to rely on semantic completion but to program in the actions oneself – especially if there is doubt on the result of the compilation. For example the language L can be characterised by this grammar.

147

```
(defcc <asbas>
   <as> <b> <as+>;)

(defcc <as>
     a <as>;
     a;)

(defcc <b>
   b;)

(defcc <as+>
   <as>;)
```

Figure 13.9 Another characterisation of L

The program works as before; however if we change the definition of <b> to include a semantic action of returning b, the program crashes.

```
(defcc <b>
   b := b;)
(fn <b>)

(compile (fn <asbas>) [a a a b a a a a a])
The value b is not of type LIST.
```

The reason this happens is that Shen YACC constructs the semantic completion

```
(defcc <asbas>
   <as> <b> <as+> := (append <as> <b> <as+>);)
```

Since <b> is returning a symbol and not a list, the attempt at appending fails. Since we want to override the default completion we would add

```
(defcc <asbas>
   <as> <b> <as+> := (append <as> [<b> | <as+>]);)
```

13.5 Handling Lists in Shen YACC

Shen YACC accepts lists and wildcards except | is not recognised to the left of :=. The following compiler recognises all inputs, and outputs the input stripped of all lists of as.

```
(defcc <remove>
   [<as>] <remove> := <remove>;
   X <remove>;
   <e>;)

(defcc <as>
   a <as>;
   a;)
```

A common confusion is to forget that the input to compile is *always* a list itself in which the sentence is read. Thus

```
(defcc <xs>
  [x x];)
```

fails in (compile (fn <xs>) [x x]) which fits the definition

```
(defcc <xs>
  x x;)
```

and the correct input is (compile (fn <xs>) [[x x]])

13.6 Efficient Parsing

A common parsing problem is removing structured 'noise' from a file where 'noise' is defined as unwanted data and 'structured' denotes that the beginning and end of the noise is well defined. Examples of structured noise are program comments in relation to a compiler. Let's suppose we are writing a compiler for a language in which % is used to open a multiline comment and % is used to close it. The task is to strip the comments from the code. We read in the program as a list of unit strings.

```
(defcc <strip>
  <comment> <strip> := <strip>;
  X <strip>;
  <e> := [];)

(defcc <comment>
 "%" <stuff>  "%" := skip;)

(defcc <stuff>
  X <stuff> := skip           where   (not (= X "%"));
  <e> := skip;)
```

Figure 13.10 An (inefficient) comment stripper

However guards are invoked only *after* expansions are tried and not *before*. The reason is that frequently a guard cannot be evaluated until the expansion has been made (this is the case with the program in 13.6). So the line

X <stuff> := skip   where   (not (= X "%"));

is not efficient because it is only invoked by <stuff> has been applied. In this case it is better to apply the guard immediately (figure 13.11).

149

```
(defcc <strip>
  <comment> <strip> := <strip>;
  X <strip>;
  <e> := [];)

(defcc <comment>
 "%" <stuff> "%" := skip;)

(defcc <stuff>
  <token> <stuff> := skip ;
  <e>;)

(defcc <token>
  X := skip  where (not (= X "%"));)
```

Figure 13.11 An (efficient) comment stripper

13.7 Consuming the Input

Shen YACC requires that any parse consume all the input and failure to 'clean one's plate' will cause parse failures. A simple example containing this mistake is a program <look> that tests to see if a sentence occurs embedded in the input. A naive encoding is

```
(defcc <look>
  <sent> := true;
  _ <look>;)
```

But this only works if the sentence is at the end of the input. If it is not then the unconsumed input will cause a parse failure. We can easily write an auxiliary which simply recursively consumes the remaining input.

```
(defcc <look>
  <sent> <skip> := true;
  X <look>;)

(defcc <skip>
  _ <skip> := skip;
  <e>;)
```

But this is unnecessary and computationally inefficient because <!> will immediately consume the remaining input and return it as the result. Thus

```
(defcc <look>
  <sent> <!> := <!>;
  _ <look>;)
```

returns all of the input after the first sentence encountered. <!> can be used within a list to consume the contents of a list.

```
(45 -) (defcc <asbs>
        [a <!>] b := <!>;)
<asbs>

(46-) (compile (fn <asbs>) [[a 1 2 3] b])
[1 2 3]
```

Figure 13.12 Using <!>to consume input

The issue of consuming the input arises in several contexts. For example the recursive definition of <as> as

```
(defcc <as>
  a;
  a <as>;)
```

will fail on the following input.

```
(compile (fn <as>) [a a])
parse error here: ...a
```

The message indicates that part of the input has not been consumed in the parse and that unconsumed input is returned in the error message. The reason for this is that <as> is called with the base case first, which succeeds, returning control to the top level with the second a unconsumed. The common solution, given overlapping rules of this kind, is to place the longest expansion first.

The non-terminal <end> will fail if the entire input has not been consumed; if it succeeds the input and output are unchanged. It is sometimes useful to use this non-terminal in a toplevel concept to ensure that all input has been consumed.

13.8 Limited Backtracking

Shen YACC practices backtracking between expansions of a non-terminal. If one expansion fails, then the next is tried. However backtracking takes place *between* expansions and not *within* expansions and this limited backtracking affects the declarative reading of Shen YACC. Here is an example that defines a language L.

```
(defcc <?bscs>
  <?s> <bs> <cs>;)

(defcc <?s>
  a <?s>;
  a;
  b <?s>;
  b;)

(defcc <bs>
  b <bs>;
  b;)

(defcc <cs>
  c <cs>;
  c;)
```

Figure 13.13 An example of limited backtracking

Declaratively the above rules admit the sentence [a a a b b b c c c] as a sentence of L. But (compile (fn <?bscs>) [a a a b b b c c c]) generates a parse error, because Shen YACC does not backtrack *within* the expansion <?bscs> ::= <?s> <bs> <cs> to consider the possibility that <?s> may be expanded ambiguously with respect to the input. Instead the rule <?bscs> ::= <?s> <bs> <cs> is interpreted to make <?s> a *greedy* consumer of the input. In this case it consumes [a a a b b] leaving no bs left for <bs>.

The limited backtracking model can pose problems if the behaviour interacts with the 'longest expansion first' requirement. We'll see an example of this in the next section.

13.9 Left Recursion

Direct left-recursion is fairly common in grammars. A definition is directly left recursive if it has the form

```
(defcc v
  .......
  v ...
  ......)
```

A simple example is an NLP program that expresses the idea that a sentence can be a conjunction of sentences, a natural expression is:

```
(defcc <sent>
  <sent> "and" <sent>;
  <np> <vp>; )
```

However this function will causes a memory stack overflow if asked to parse a conjunction, since in the first rule, the non-terminal <sent> directly calls itself without consuming any of the input.[56] The solution is to rephrase the definition to eliminate the left-recursion.

```
(defcc <sent>
  <np> <vp> "and" <sent> := [<np> <vp> & <sent>];
  <np> <vp>;)
```

Figure 13.12 Eliminating left recursion

Another common example involving left-recursion is the specification of the language of arithmetic expressions of which 1 + x - 3, 6 * (y / z) are examples. Suppose we want to convert such expressions to fully parenthesised prefix. This is most naturally encoded as a left-recursive grammar.

```
(defcc <expr>
  <expr> <op> <expr+> := [<op> <expr> <expr+>];
  [<expr> <op> <expr+>] := [<op> <expr> <expr+>];
  <number> := <number>;)

(defcc <expr+>
  <expr>;)

(defcc <number>
  N := N          where (number? N);)

(defcc <op>
  X := X          where (element? X [+ - * /]);)
```

This fails because the first expansion of <expr> is left-recursive. Arriving at a non-left recursive definition is an interesting exercise in understanding Shen YACC. To begin we try

```
(defcc <expr>
  <number> <op> <expr> := [<op> <number> <expr>];
  [<expr> <op> <expr+>] := [<op> <expr> <expr+>];
  <number> := <number>;)
```

---

[56] **Indirect left recursion** is more insidious and occurs when there is a mutual recursion between non-terminals. Here <sent> calls <sent*> which calls <sent>.

```
(defcc <sent>
  <sent*> "and" <sent> := [<sent*> & <sent>];
  <np> <vp>; )

(defcc <sent*>
  <sent>;)
```

This works on inputs that are entirely unparenthesised, but fails to work on inputs that are parenthesised– even inputs that we think should parse!

```
(125-) (compile (fn <expr>) [1])
1

(126-) (compile (fn <expr>) [1 + 2 + 3])
[+ 1 [+ 2 3]]

(127-) (compile (fn <expr>) [[1 + 2]])
parse error
```

The failure of the last case is interesting because it looks at first as if it should succeed. The parse is the victim of the dual strategy of placing the longest expansion first together with the limited backtracking model used in Shen YACC.

Given the input [1 + 2], the second expansion [<expr> <op> <expr+>] is used. So far, so good. But the <expr> function then uses the expansion <number> <op> <expr> to consume *all* the input, leaving nothing for <op> and <expr+> to process. We could fix this by abandoning the 'longest expansion first' rule and writing

```
(defcc <expr>
  <number> := <number>;
  <number> <op> <expr> := [<op> <number> <expr>];
  [<expr> <op> <expr+>] := [<op> <expr> <expr+>]; )
```

This does solve the errant case, but now (compile (fn <expr>) [1 + 2 + 3]) does not work since the short expansion is used which does not consume all the input. Hence however we order these definitions, the result is not a working model.

In this case, the simplest method is to define a class of *terms*. An arithmetic expression is just a series of terms linked by operations or a term on its own.

```
(defcc <expr>
  <term> <op> <expr> := [<op> <term> <expr>];
  <term> := <term>;)
```

A term is then defined as either a number or something which can be parsed as an expression. The second alternative is covered by an invocation to the compiler.

```
(defcc <term>
  N := N  where (number? N);
  E := (parse-term E);)

(define parse-term
  E -> (compile (fn <expr>) E))
```

And this works.

```
(140-) (compile (fn <expr>) [[1 - 0 * 8] + [5 + 8] * 7])
[+ [- 1 [* 0 8]] [* [+ 5 8] 7]]

(141-) (compile (fn <expr>) [[1 - 0 * 8] + [5 + 8] * a7])
parse error
```

Figure 13.14 Parsing arithmetic

Exercise 13

1. Devise a Shen YACC program that

    a. Reverses a list.
    b. Divides an even numbered list into two lists. If the list is not even numbered then a parse error is returned.
    c. Removes all numbers from a list and returns them as a output.
    d. Gives the length of a list.
    e. Sums a list of numbers to a total.
    f. Recognises if a list is sorted high to low.

2. Devise a YACC program for a fragment of English and show that it can recognise sentences. Include adjectives, prepositions and sentence connectives in your grammar.

3. *Build a natural language front-end to a database system that enables database queries to be conducted in your native language and answered by the computer.

4. Write an HTML stripper in YACC that extracts raw text from HTML pages.

5. *Find a procedural language that you know, such as C or Java and write a YACC program that parses programs in it.

6. *Write a compiler for the language ML that compiles ML into Shen.

Further Reading

Meta II was a very early compiler-compiler introduced by D. V Schorre (1964). The original YACC was developed at AT&T by Steve Johnson and the technology was ported to various languages including ML. Aho and Ullman (1973) gives an overview of YACC. Lajos (1990) introduced MetaLisp which was the foundation of Shen YACC.

Websites

http://www.techworld.com.au/article/252319/a-z_programming_languages_yacc gives an interview with Johnson on YACC.

14* Lambda Calculus

In this chapter, we are going to delve more deeply into some of the theory behind Shen. The lambda calculus, invented by **Alonzo Church** (1940), provides a notation for talking and reasoning about functions. Understanding lambda calculus is important to understanding of Shen for two reasons. First because the lambda calculus is the basis of the notation Kλ into which Shen is compiled. Second, because the type theory of the lambda calculus forms part of the underlying type theory of Shen (studied in part II of this book) and of every typed functional language since ML.

14.1 The Notation of the Lambda Calculus

The syntax of the pure lambda calculus is very simple.

Syntax Rules for the Pure Lambda Calculus

1. $x, y, z, x', y', z',....$ are all variables.
2. Any variable on its own is an expression of the lambda calculus.
3. If e_1 and e_2 are lambda expressions then the **application** $(e_1\ e_2)$ of e_1 to e_2 is an expression of the lambda calculus.
4. If e is an expression of the lambda calculus and v is a variable then $(\lambda\ v\ e)$ (called an **abstraction**) is an expression of the lambda calculus.
5. Nothing else is an expression of the lambda calculus.

Just as in Shen, when we wish to apply a function f to an input i, the lambda calculus requires us to write $(f\ i)$. The function *square* is said to be **applied** to 3, and the whole expression (square 3) is called an **application**.

Strictly speaking, the syntax of the pure lambda calculus makes no explicit allowance for referring to numbers, so (square 3) is not an expression of the pure lambda calculus. Many authors allow the pure lambda calculus to be enriched by a set of constants (Hindley and Seldin (1986) call this an **applied lambda calculus**), and they allow these constants to count as lambda calculus expressions. We will follow this example, and for the moment admit numbers and names of functions into the lambda calculus. Later in this chapter, we shall see how they can be reduced to expressions of the pure lambda calculus.

156

Abstractions are used within the lambda calculus to reveal the internal structure of a function. An abstraction has the form (λ *v* *e*), where *v* is a variable and *e* is an expression of lambda calculus. "(λ *v* *e*)" signifies a function that given some input *v*, returns the output *e*. The simplest example is the abstraction (λ *x* *x*), which denotes the **identity function** that receives any input *x* and returns *x*. Here are some more examples.

Abstraction	Interpretation
(λ *x* 3)	receives any input *x* and returns 3.
(λ *x* *y*)	receives any input *x* and returns *y*.
(λ *x* (*x* 5))	receives any input *x* and returns the result of applying *x* to 5.
(λ *x* (*x* *x*))	receives any input *x* and returns the result of applying *x* to *x*.
(λ *x* (λ *y* (*x* *y*)))	receives any input *x* and returns a function (λ *y* (*x* *y*)) which receives any input *y* and applies *x* to *y*.

Figure 14.1 Some abstractions and their interpretations

An occurrence of a variable *v* is **bound** in an abstraction if *v* occurs within an expression of the form (λ *v* *e*), and if it is not bound it is **free**. It is important to distinguish between *occurrences* of variables and variables themselves. The same type of variable may occur several times in one lambda expression and, in relation to that expression, some of the occurrences can be free and some can be bound. For example, in the application ((λ *x* (*y* *x*)) *x*) there are three occurrences of the variable *x*. Reading from left to right, the first two are bound and the last is free. A lambda expression where all variables are bound is said to be a **closed lambda expression** or **combinator**.

We perform a **substitution for the free variable occurrences** within a lambda expression when we uniformly replace all free occurrences of that variable throughout the lambda expression. For example, substituting *z* for free occurrences of *x* in ((λ *x* (*y* *x*)) *x*) gives ((λ *x* (*y* *x*)) *z*)); the first two occurrences of *x* are not replaced because they are bound. A substitution of an expression *y* for the free occurrences of a variable *x* in a lambda expression *e* is written $[e]_{y/x}$. Here are some more examples.

Expression	Result
$[(λ \, x \, x)]_{y/x}$	(λ *x* *x*)
$[(λ \, y \, x)]_{z/x}$	(λ *y* *z*)
$[(λ \, x \, (x \, y))]_{y/z}$	(λ *x* (*x* *y*))
$[(λ \, x \, (y \, (λ \, y \, (x \, y))))]_{z/y}$	(λ *x* (*z* (λ *y* (*x* *y*))))

Figure 14.2 Performing substitutions

14.2 Reasoning with the Lambda Calculus

The lambda calculus was originally designed as a formal system for proving the equality of functions expressed in lambda calculus notation. We write $e_1 = e_2$, where e_1 and e_2 are lambda calculus expressions, to state that e_1 and e_2 denote the same function. Obviously if e_1 and e_2 are syntactically identical then $e_1 = e_2$ holds. This is the first rule of the lambda calculus.

$e = e$

The next rules deal with the obvious properties of $=$; symmetry and transitivity.

From $e_1 = e_2$ derive $e_2 = e_1$.
From $e_1 = e_2$ and $e_2 = e_3$ derive $e_1 = e_3$.

The next three rules state the principle that equals may be substituted for each other.

From $e_1 = e_2$ derive $(e_3\ e_1) = (e_3\ e_2)$
From $e_1 = e_2$ derive $(e_1\ e_3) = (e_2\ e_3)$
From $e_1 = e_2$ derive $(\lambda\ v\ e_1) = (\lambda\ v\ e_2)$

In addition, there are three more rules for proving lambda expressions equal; the rules of **α conversion, β reduction** and **η conversion**.

$(\lambda x\ x)$, $(\lambda y\ y)$ and $(\lambda z\ z)$ are all ways of referring to the identity function. Consequently the equations $(\lambda x\ x) = (\lambda y\ y)$ and $(\lambda y\ y) = (\lambda z\ z)$ are both true, and should be provable in the lambda calculus. α conversion allows this proof by legitimising the uniform replacement of a bound variable within an abstraction by some other variable. We write $(\lambda x\ x) \to_\alpha (\lambda y\ y)$ to show that $(\lambda x\ x)$ is convertible to $(\lambda y\ y)$ by α conversion. It does not matter what replacement variable is used, provided that the replacement is performed uniformly and there is no **variable capture**.

A variable capture occurs when the effect of inserting the replacement variable is to bind a free variable. For instance the function $(\lambda x\ (x\ y))$ can be α converted to $(\lambda z\ (z\ y))$, but it cannot be α converted to $(\lambda y\ (y\ y))$ without capturing or binding the previously free y. We formulate the rule for α conversion so that variable captures are not allowed.

The Rule of α Conversion

Any expression $(\lambda v\ e)$ may be α converted to $(\lambda v'.[e]v_{/}v)$ provided v' does not occur free in e.

If e_1 and e_2 can be made identical by α conversions alone then they are **congruent** to each other and this is written $e_1 \approx e_2$.

The application of the function $(\lambda x \, (square \, x))$ to 3 produces $(square \, 3)$. We can write this as $(square \, 3)$ or $((\lambda x \, (square \, x)) \, 3)$. In any event, the following equation must be true.

$$((\lambda x \, (square \, x)) \, 3) = (square \, 3)$$

Deriving $(square \, 3)$ from $((\lambda x \, (square \, x)) \, 3)$ requires replacing each free occurrence of x within $(square \, x)$ by 3 and eliminating the λx; an operation called β **reduction**. This operation is written $((\lambda x \, (square \, x)) \, 3) \rightarrow_\beta (square \, 3)$. Here is an example where β reduction is applied twice.

$$((\lambda x \, ((\lambda y \, (x \, y)) \, z)) \, z) \rightarrow_\beta ((\lambda x \, (x \, z)) \, z) \rightarrow_\beta (z \, z)$$

As with α conversion, there is a proviso to β reduction. We must take care with expressions where a variable has both free and bound occurrences. Thus suppose we attempt to β reduce $((\lambda x \, (\lambda y \, (x \, y))) \, y)$ without regard to the fact that y occurs both free and bound in different occurrences; we derive

$$((\lambda x \, (\lambda y \, (x \, y))) \, y) \rightarrow_\beta (\lambda y \, (y \, y)) \quad ???$$

However if we should first do α conversion on $((\lambda x \, (\lambda y \, (x \, y))) \, y)$ to get $((\lambda x \, (\lambda z \, (x \, z))) \, y)$, and then perform β reduction we derive $(\lambda z \, (y \, z))$; but plainly $(\lambda z \, (y \, z)) \neq (\lambda y \, (y \, y))$.[57]

The reduction of $((\lambda x \, (\lambda y \, (x \, y))) \, y)$ to $(\lambda y \, (y \, y))$ is wrong because the second occurrence of y in $((\lambda x \, (\lambda y \, (x \, y))) \, y)$ (which is free) becomes bound if placed in the scope of λy. In this case, to perform β reduction, it is first necessary to rename the bound occurrences of y using α conversion, and only then can β reduction be performed. The rule of β reduction, like the rule for α conversion, has a clause within it stipulating that variables may not be captured.

The Rule of β Reduction

$((\lambda v \, e_1) \, e_2)$ may be transformed by β reduction to $[e_1]e_2/v$ provided no free occurrence of a variable in e_2 becomes bound.

In some cases, the result of performing all possible β reductions is an expression free of λs. This need not always be so. The expression $((\lambda x \, ((\lambda y \, ((z \, x) \, y))) \, 3)$ β

---

[57] In case there is doubt on this issue, reflect that $(\lambda z \, (y \, z))$ designates a function that receives an input and applies y to it, and $(\lambda y \, (y \, y))$ designates a function that receives an input and applies it to itself.

reduces to $(\lambda\, y\, ((z\ 3)\ y))$ and the λ is retained after the β reduction. If the result of a β reduction is an abstraction, then the operation of β reduction is said to be a **partial application**.

The η conversion rule is the least intuitive of the lambda calculus rules.

The Rule of η Conversion

Any abstraction $(\lambda\, v\, (e\ v))$ may be transformed by η conversion to e if v does not occur free in e.

An example of η conversion is $(\lambda\, x\, ((y\ z)\ x)) \rightarrow_\eta (y\ z)$. The principle of **Functional Extensionality** justifies η conversion. This principle says that two functions are identical if they produce the same outputs given the same inputs. That is:-

$$\text{If for all } x,\ (f\, x) = (g\, x) \text{ then } f = g.$$

The argument in defence of η conversion is as follows. η conversion is justified if we can show that, if e is any lambda calculus expression and v is a variable is not free in e, $(\lambda\, v\, (e\ v)) = e$. By the Principle of Functional Extensionality, the proof is secured if it can be proved that, for any a, $((\lambda\, v\, (e\ v))\ a) = (e\ a)$. β reduction on $((\lambda\, v\, (e\ v))\ a)$ gives $(e\ a)$ (since e contains no free occurrences of v, β reduction leaves e unchanged), so the equation is proved.

A **redex** is an expression that can be reduced by any of the rules of the lambda calculus; a β-redex is a redex that can be reduced by the β rule.

14.3 The Church-Rosser Theorems

When working with the lambda calculus, the goal is often to reduce a lambda expression to its simplest form. For example, the simplest form of $(((\lambda\, x\, (\lambda\, y\, ((+\ x)\ y)))\ 3)\ 5)$ is $((+\ 5)\ 3)$ (or 8 if the rules of arithmetic are added to the lambda calculus). The expression $((+\ 5)\ 3)$ is a **normal form** of $(((\lambda\, x\, (\lambda\, y\, ((+\ x)\ y)))\ 3)\ 5)$. We say that e is **lambda convertible** to e' when e can be converted to e' by α, β or η conversion rules. In the context of the lambda calculus, a normal form of an expression e is any expression e' where

(a) e is lambda convertible to e' and
(b) at most only α conversion can be applied to change e'.

An important theorem called the **first Church-Rosser theorem** has a bearing on the search for normal forms. Let $e_1 \geq e_2$ obtain when e_1 is reducible to e_2 by zero or more α conversions and/or β reductions. The first Church-Rosser theorem states that if $e_1 \geq e_2$ and $e_1 \geq e_3$ and e_2 and e_3 are not syntactically identical, then there is an e_4 such that $e_2 \geq e_4$ and $e_3 \geq e_4$.

An immediate corollary of the first Church-Rosser theorem is that all normal forms are congruent to each other.

Proof: suppose e_1 reduces to two non-identical normal forms e_2 and e_3, then by the first Church-Rosser theorem there exists an expression e_4 to which e_2 and e_3 are reducible. However, since e_2 and e_3 are normal forms, e_2 and e_3 are convertible to e_4 by α conversion alone. Since $e_2 \approx e_4$ and $e_3 \approx e_4$, then $e_2 \approx e_3$.

This theorem is a basis for the lambda calculus as a foundation for functional programming. If the theorem did not obtain, then two equally acceptable computations of the same lambda expression could terminate with significantly different results. This would make computation with lambda calculus quite hopeless.

A **reduction strategy** for the lambda calculus is a strategy that determines how reductions are performed. Two reduction strategies are **normal order** and **applicative order evaluation**.

The rule of normal order evaluation is that β-redexes must always be reduced from the outside inwards, and where there is a choice, working from the leftmost such redex. The rule of applicative order evaluation is that the leftmost most deeply embedded β-redex must always be reduced first. Another way of expressing this is to say that, given an expression (e_1 e_2) to evaluate, applicative order evaluation first performs β reduction on e_1 and then $e2$ before attempting β reduction on the whole expression.

For example, reducing ((λx (x x)) ((λy y) z)) to a normal form by normal order evaluation involves three steps; the β-redexes are bolded.

$$(\mathbf{(\lambda x\ (x\ x))\ ((\lambda y\ y)\ z)}) \rightarrow_\beta (\mathbf{((\lambda y\ y)\ z)}\ ((\lambda y\ y)\ z)) \rightarrow_\beta (z\ \mathbf{((\lambda y\ y)\ z)}) \rightarrow_\beta (z\ z)$$

Applicative order evaluation derives the same result in two steps.

$$(\mathbf{(\lambda x\ (x\ x))\ ((\lambda y\ y)\ z)}) \rightarrow_\beta (\mathbf{(\lambda x\ (x\ x))\ z}) \rightarrow_\beta (z\ z)$$

When bound variables are repeated, applicative order evaluation is often more efficient than normal order evaluation. However, sometimes, normal order evaluation will find a normal form where applicative order evaluation fails.

For instance ((λx z) ((λx (x x)) (λx (x x)))) has the normal form z, but using applicative order evaluation, this normal form is not computed since ((λx (x x)) (λx (x x))) $\rightarrow_\beta$ ((λx (x x)) (λx (x x)))! Applicative order evaluation repeats this step endlessly. The **second Church-Rosser theorem** states if a lambda expression has a normal form, then normal order evaluation will find it.

The expression $((\lambda x \ (x \ x)) \ (\lambda x \ (x \ x)))$ itself has no normal form. An important theorem of the lambda calculus is that there is no mechanical procedure for accurately determining, in all cases, whether a lambda expression has a normal form. This theorem is a corollary of another important theorem about the lambda calculus that was proved by Church, namely, that it is **Turing-equivalent**. This means that the lambda calculus is powerful enough to serve as a programming language. If there was an algorithm $\mathscr{H}$ that could determine if the normal order evaluation of any lambda expression terminated, we would also have a decision procedure for finding if *any* program terminated (i.e. translate it into lambda calculus and then apply $\mathscr{H}$). However, Turing's proof of the **Unsolvability of the Halting Problem**, states that there is no such procedure to be found.[58]

14.4 Conditionals

It is surprising that a formal system as basic as the pure lambda calculus should have the expressive power of a programming language. The usual control features of conventional programming languages are not in evidence; there are no commands like **if.... then ....else** or **and**. There are no commands like **do ... while** or **for ... next**. There are not even integers or booleans in the lambda calculus.

The basic technique for dealing with this problem is to identify a set of equations that describe the behaviour of the wanted features and then to choose representations in the lambda calculus which reflect those equations. Thus in the case of if ...then ...else, true and false, we have two essential equations.

(if true then X else Y) = X
(if false then X else Y) = Y

The boolean true can be identified with the lambda expression $(\lambda x \ (\lambda y \ x))$ and the boolean false with $(\lambda x \ (\lambda y \ y))$. The conditional **if...then...else** is identified with $(\lambda z \ (\lambda x \ (\lambda y \ ((z \ x) \ y))))$. If these identifications are correct, then the lambda equivalent of (if true then a else b) should evaluate to a.

Calculating this identity by hand is tedious and error prone – and unnecessary, because the task is computational and an interpreter for an applicative order evaluator for lambda calculus is a short program in Shen (figure 14.3).

---

[58] Turing's result shows that there is no algorithm which can determine for any arbitrary computer program (Turing machine) whether it will halt for any arbitrary input. This is one of the most famous proofs in computer science and is intimately related to the proof of the undecidability of first-order logic. See Boolos and Jefferies (1977) for more on this.

```
(define aor
  [lambda V [E V]] -> E        where (not (free? V E))
  [lambda X Y] -> [lambda X (aor Y)]
  [[lambda X Y] Z] -> (let Alpha (alpha [lambda X Y])
                           (aor (beta Alpha (aor Z))))
  [X Y] -> (let AOR [(aor X) (aor Y)]
               (if (= AOR [X Y])
                   AOR
                   (aor AOR)))
  X -> X)

(define free?
  V V -> true
  V [lambda V _] -> false
  V [lambda _ Y] -> (free? V Y)
  V [X Y] -> (or (free? V X) (free? V Y))
  _ _ -> false)

(define alpha
  [lambda X Y] -> (let V (gensym x)
                      [lambda V (replace X (alpha Y) V)])
  [X Y] -> [(alpha X) (alpha Y)]
  X -> X)

(define beta
  [lambda X Y] Z -> (replace X Y Z))

(define replace
  X [lambda X Y] _ -> [lambda X Y]
  X X Z -> Z
  X [Y Y*] Z -> [(replace X Y Z) (replace X Y* Z)]
  X [lambda Y Y*] Z -> [lambda Y (replace X Y* Z)]
  _ Y _ -> Y)
```

Figure 14.3 An applicative order evaluator for pure lambda calculus

The most awkward rule to program is the alpha rule and here we use it to prevent capture by renaming *all* the bound variables in an abstraction before performing beta reduction.[59]

Armed with this program we can test our conjecture; we define (t) to mean the lambda abstraction standing for true and (f) for false and if* for the lambda expression for if.

---

[59] In chapter 22 on logic programming we will see that a similar process called 'standardisation apart' is used in Prolog.

```
(2-) (define t
      -> [lambda x [lambda y x]])
(fn t)

(3-) (define f
       -> [lambda x [lambda y y]])
(fn f)

(4-) (define if*
       -> [lambda z [lambda x [lambda y [[z x] y]]]])
(fn if*)

(5-) (aor [[[(if*) (t)] a] b])
a

(6-) (aor [[[(if*) (f)] a] b])
b
```

Figure 14.4 Proving that (((if true) a) b) = a in lambda calculus

The equations work, but working with our evaluator is still laborious; both at the human end, because the expressions are deeply bracketed, and at the computing end, because the enforced α conversion makes computation very expensive. We can begin to approach some of the functionality of a programming language by arranging for the reader to curry expressions for us.

```
(define curry
  [lambda X Y] -> [lambda X (curry Y)]
  [W X Y | Z] -> (curry [[W X] Y | Z])
  [X Y] -> [(curry X) (curry Y)]
  X -> X)
```

We define aor+ as;

```
(define aor+
  X -> (aor (curry X)))
```

Now (aor+ [(if*) (f) a b]) evaluates as (aor [[[(if*) (f)] a] b]).

14.5 Weak Head Normal Form

Our evaluator delves into abstractions to evaluate them. The abstraction [lambda x [[lambda y y] a]] is evaluated to [lambda x a]. But functional languages do not carry evaluation to that length; the internals of an abstraction are not evaluated. If we type (/. X (+ 1 "a")) to Shen the evaluator compiles it without raising an error message, showing the body of the abstraction remains unevaluated.

Blocking the evaluation of a body of an abstraction means that the evaluator does not return, in all cases, a normal form, but returns an expression in **weak head**

164

normal form (WHNF). Generally returning an expression in WHNF is sufficient for computational purposes.

Formally an expression is in WHNF if one of the following hold.

1. It is an abstraction $(\lambda\, x\, y)$ for *any y*.
2. It is a constant. In an applied lambda calculus, this might include strings, numbers and booleans and function symbols.
3. It is a partial application of some *n*-place function *f* in an applied lambda calculus to a series of arguments $x_1...x_m$ where $n > m$.

If we insist that the objects of computation must be closed lambda expressions then η reduction (which depends on free variables) becomes unnecessary *and* in addition, if we agree to reduce only to WHNF, then α conversion becomes unnecessary because the variable capture problem disappears too.

The expression $(\lambda\ x\ ((\lambda\ y\ (\lambda\ x\ (+\ x\ y)))\ x))$ is in WHNF because it is an abstraction; it contains a constant, the addition symbol '+'. It contains a redex which is bolded which if applied naively (without α conversion) results in a variable capture of *x*. However since the expression is in WHNF, no reduction is applied and no α conversion is needed.

If this expression is applied to, say, the number 8, then the whole expression is a redex which reduces to $((\lambda\ y\ (\lambda\ x\ (+\ x\ y)))\ 8)$ and then to $(\lambda\ x\ (+\ x\ 8))$. However note that if we allow the free variable *x* to replace 8 in $((\lambda\ y\ (\lambda\ x\ (+\ x\ y)))\ 8)$ we get $((\lambda\ y\ (\lambda\ x\ (+\ x\ y)))\ x)$ in which variable capture is again possible unless the bound *x* is renamed. However by blocking the use of free variables, this case is prevented. Bringing these changes into a model means that the code for the evaluator becomes much simpler (figure 14.5) and the model is easier to operate and faster to execute.

```
(define aor
  [[lambda X Y] Z] -> (aor (replace X Y Z))
  [X Y] -> (let AOR [(aor X) (aor Y)]
             (if (= AOR [X Y]) AOR  (aor AOR)))
  X -> X)

(define replace
  X [lambda X Y] _ -> [lambda X Y]
  X X Z -> Z
  X [Y Y'] Z -> [(replace X Y Z) (replace X Y* Z)]
  X [lambda Y Y*] Z -> [lambda Y (replace X Y* Z)]
  _ Y _ -> Y)
```

Figure 14.5 An evaluator for closed WHNF

14.6 Tuples

Continuing with the reconstruction of programming concepts in lambda calculus, the operation of forming the pair $<x, y>$ of two elements x and y gives us a **tuple**. Tuples can be treated as the analogue of lists because the three element list $[x\ y\ z]$ can be represented as the tuple $<x, <y, z>>$.

We represent the tupling operation by the curried expression $((tuple\ x)\ y)$. Together with this pairing operation are two operations first and second that take first and second elements of a pair. These operations must satisfy the equations.

$$(first\ ((tuple\ X)\ Y)) = X$$
$$(second\ ((tuple\ X)\ Y)) = Y$$

We define these concepts as follows. Our $=_{df}$ notation means "is defined as".

$$tuple =_{df} (\lambda\ x\ (\lambda\ y\ (\lambda\ z\ ((z\ x)\ y))))$$
$$first =_{df} (\lambda\ x\ (x\ true))$$
$$second =_{df} (\lambda\ x\ (x\ false))$$

Figure 14.6 gives the Shen equivalents.

```
(7-) (define tuple
        -> [lambda x [lambda y [lambda z [[z x] y]]]])
(fn tuple)

(8-) (define first
        -> [lambda x [x (t)]])
(fn first)

(9-) (define second
        -> [lambda x [x (f)]])
(fn second)

(10-) (aor+ [(first) [(tuple) a b]])
a

(11-) (aor+ [(second) [(tuple) a b]])
b
```

Figure 14.6 Lambda calculus tuples in Shen

14.7 Numbers

Lambda calculus lacks any natural numbers, but there are many ways of representing them. Each representation treats natural numbers as built up by compositions of the successor function to 0.

i.e. 1 = (succ 0), 2 = (succ (succ 0)),.... etc.

The differences lie in how succ and 0 are defined. We use a definition from **Barendregt** (1984) that defines the natural numbers in terms of the progression.

$0 = (\lambda\, x\, x)$
$1 = ((\text{tuple false})\ 0)$
$2 = ((\text{tuple false})\ 1)\ .....$

We introduce succ as a function that adds 1 to a natural number, a zero test function zero? which, when applied to 0, evaluates to the lambda calculus representation of true. We also introduce the predecessor function pred that subtracts 1 and $\perp$ as a constant indicating the error condition of attempting to find the predecessor of 0. The following definitions meet those constraints.

$\text{succ} =_{df} (\lambda\, x\ ((\text{tuple false})\ x))$
$\text{zero?} =_{df} (\lambda\, x\ (x\ \text{true}))$
$\text{pred} =_{df} (\lambda\, x\ (((\text{if (zero?}\ x))\ \perp)\ (\text{second}\ x)))\ (\lambda\, x\ (x\ \text{false}))$

```
(8-) (define zero
        -> [lambda x x])
(fn zero)

(9-) (define succ
        -> [lambda x [(tuple) (f) x]])
(fn succ)

(10-) (define zero?
        -> [lambda x [x (t)]]])
(fn zero?)

(11-) (define pred
        -> [lambda x [(if') [(zero?) x] error! [(second) x]]])
(fn pred)

(12-) (aor+ [(zero?) (zero)])
[lambda x [lambda y x]]

(13-) (aor+ [(pred) [(succ) (zero)]]])
[lambda x x]
```

Figure 14.7 Arithmetic in lambda calculus

167

14.8 Recursion and the Y combinator

The lambda calculus is rich enough to provide surrogates for conditionals, booleans, tuples, natural numbers and the basic arithmetical operations of adding and subtracting 1 from a number.   What is still missing is some construction that will do the job of a **do … while** or **repeat .. until** of a conventional procedural programming language.   To illustrate how lambda calculus copes with this challenge, we will consider the definition of addition in lambda calculus. Two equations give the properties of addition.

$$0 + Y = Y$$
$$X + Y = (\text{succ} ((\text{pred } X) + Y))$$

To represent these equations in lambda calculus, we use an expression called the **fixpoint combinator Y** or **Y combinator** whose behaviour is described by the following equation.

$$(\mathbf{Y} f) = (f (\mathbf{Y} f))$$

It is possible to define **Y** in pure lambda calculus, and there are several ways of doing so; we leave it as an exercise to show that the following definition satisfies $(\mathbf{Y} f) = (f (\mathbf{Y} f))$.

$$\mathbf{Y} = (\lambda f (V\, V)) \text{ where } V = (\lambda x (f (x\, x)))$$

We can use the **Y** combinator to represent addition (here written *add*) over the natural numbers. We first transcribe the equations for addition into lambda calculus. For clarity we omit currying and use the usual if … then .. else notation.

$$add =_{df} (\lambda x (\lambda y (\text{if (zero? } x) \text{ then } y \text{ else } (\text{succ } (add (\text{pred } x)\, y)))))$$

add mentions itself within its own definition; from our studies we know that this is a recursive definition of *add*. We could compute additions with this definition if we added a rule that said that we were allowed to replace any occurrence of '*add*' in a lambda expression by the right-hand side of this definition.   In doing so, we would be enriching the rules of the lambda calculus by allowing replacement according to a definition as an extra rule in the lambda calculus. This is precisely the step taken in the next chapter, but in this section we want to show that, in principle, the pure lambda calculus can represent addition without needing this extra rule.

In our next step, we replace the occurrence of "*add*" by a new bound variable. We abbreviate this expression as ADD.

$$\text{ADD} =_{df} (\lambda f (\lambda x (\lambda y (\text{if (zero? } x) \text{ then } y \text{ else } (\text{succ } (f (\text{pred } x)\, y))))))$$

Now we define + as **(Y ADD)**. This new definition of + will add numbers. Figure 14.8 shows the evaluation of ((+ 1) 2).

Expression	Justification
((+ 1) 2)	
(((**Y** ADD) 1) 2)	definition of +
(((ADD (**Y** ADD)) 1) 2)	definition of **Y**
(((λf (λx (λy (if (zero? *x*) then *y* else (succ (f (pred *x*) *y*))) (**Y** ADD))))) 1) 2)	definition of ADD
((λx (λy (if (zero? *x*) then *y* else (succ ((**Y** ADD) (pred *x*) *y*)))))) 1) 2)	β reduction
((λy (if (zero? 1) then *y* else (succ ((**Y** ADD) (pred 1) *y*))) 2)	β reduction
(if (zero? 1) then 2 else (succ ((**Y** ADD) (pred 1) 2)))	β reduction
(succ (((**Y** ADD) 0) 2))	(zero? 1) is false
(succ (((ADD (**Y** ADD)) 0) 2))	definition of **Y**
(succ (((λf (λx (λy (if (zero? *x*) then *y* else (succ (*f* (pred *x*) *y*))) (**Y** ADD)))))) 0) 2))	definition of ADD
(succ ((λx (λy (if (zero? *x*) then *y* else (succ ((**Y** ADD) (pred *x*) *y*))))))) 0) 2))	β reduction
(succ ((λy (if (zero? 0) then *y* else (succ ((**Y** ADD) (pred 0) *y*))) 2))	β reduction
(succ (if (zero? 0) then 2 else (succ ((**Y** ADD) (pred 0) 2))))	β reduction
(succ 2)	(zero? 0) is true

Figure 14.8 Evaluation using Y-combinators

If we try to reproduce this behaviour using our evaluator, the program crashes with a memory error. This arises from the feature of applicative order evaluation; that *all* the arguments to a function are always evaluated before the function is applied; and this applies to *if* as well. This leads to the rather disastrous result in the penultimate line of figure 14.8 that the recursive call is evaluated even though (zero? 0) is true. For normal order evaluation, the correct result is returned.

One solution is to replace applicative order evaluation by normal order evaluation. Alternatively we retain applicative order, but introduce the evaluation of the conditional as a special case to be treated in a non-strict manner. The addition of special rules for *if*, + etc. to a lambda calculus L are δ **rules** of L. In our study of the SECD machine we will pick up this story again.

169

Exercise 14

1. Which variable occurrences are free and which are bound in the following expressions?

    a. $((y\,x)\,y)$,
    b. $((\lambda\,y\,(y\,x))\,y)$,
    c. $(x\,x)$,
    d. $(y\,(\lambda\,y\,(x\,(y\,z))))$

2. Perform the necessary substitutions on the following.

    a. $[(y\,x)\,y]_{z/y}$,
    b. $[(y\,x)\,y]_{z/x}$,
    c. $[(\lambda\,y\,((y\,x)\,y))]_{z/y}$,
    d. $[(y\,(\lambda\,y\,(x\,(y\,z))))]_{z/y}$
    e. $[(x\,x)]_{z/x}$,

3. Reduce the following to a normal form using α, β and η conversion.

    a. $((y\,x)\,y)$,
    b. $((\lambda\,x\,(\lambda\,y\,(x\,x)))\,y)$,
    c. $((\lambda\,x\,(\lambda\,y\,(x\,y)))\,(\lambda\,x\,(x\,y)))$

4. *Implement an interpreter for the pure lambda calculus that reduces lambda expressions to a normal form using normal order evaluation.

Further Reading

Gordon (1988) (chapters 4-7) gives a nice introduction to the lambda calculus. For the encyclopaedic accounts, Barendregt (1984) and Hindley and Seldin (1986), but Barendregt (1992) (pp 118-147) for a quick look.

Web Sites

(http://www.santafe.edu/~walter/AlChemy/software.html) provides a standalone lambda calculus interpreter written in C. Colin Taylor provides a version (http://drcjt.freeyellow.com), including source code) which will run on a Palm Pilot. http://worrydream.com/AlligatorEggs/ is a delightful explanation of lambda calculus based on alligators.

15 * Kλ

15.1 From Lambda Calculus to Kλ

Chapter 14 showed that it is possible to program in the pure lambda calculus but programming at this level of detail is not attractive. For example the number 2 in our pure lambda calculus is:-

$$(((\lambda x \, (\lambda y \, (\lambda z \, ((z \, x) \, y)))) \, (\lambda x \, (\lambda y \, y)))$$
$$(((\lambda x \, (\lambda y \, (\lambda z \, ((z \, x) \, y)))) \, (\lambda x \, (\lambda y \, y))) \, (\lambda x \, x)))$$

Practical programming requires a barrier of abstraction between the programmer and the complexity of these expressions. We answered this problem in our evaluator by *naming* lambda calculus expressions, so that instead of writing [lambda x [lambda y x]] we wrote (t).

But the result is still not a practical functional programming language. Functional programming languages do not rely on Y-combinators for recursion or represent numbers as lambda expressions, but make use of δ rules that come with the instruction set in the resident hardware, treating numbers as primitive objects. Like Shen, functional programming languages also facilitate the definition of functions by not requiring function applications to be curried. If we introduce these changes, and add facilities for I/O and recursion, we end up with an enriched lambda calculus that is suitable for the purposes of programming.

Hidden inside of Shen is a miniature functional language of just this capability called **Kλ**. Though it is not much used in applications, it has a vital role within the internals of Shen because all Shen function definitions are ultimately compiled and defined within this tiny language. If we contrast Kλ with pure lambda calculus; then we find these differences.

1. Kλ allows expressions to be named within definitions; so a function can call itself in its definition without having to use a Y-combinator.
2. Applications do not have to be curried.
3. Numbers can be written as decimal numbers, and not as lambda expressions. The same applies to booleans.
4. There are 50 primitive functions built in for the manipulation of lists, vectors, numbers, strings and symbols plus 4 optional internal primitives.

171

The syntax of Kλ is very simple. The basic concept is a **symbolic expression** or s-expr which is defined as follows

An **atom** is either a boolean, a Shen number (but excluding e-numbers which are not assumed by Kλ), a symbol, a string or the empty list (). All atoms are symbolic expressions.

An **abstraction** is of the form (lambda *symbol s-expr*) and corresponds to an abstraction of the lambda calculus. This too is a symbolic expression.

An **application** is a series of *n* (*n* ≥ 0) symbolic expressions encased in parentheses (....) (other than an **abstraction** or a **definition** below). An application can be curried but Kλ does not require it. An application is a symbolic expression.

A Kλ **definition** is of the form (defun *symbol* (*parameters*) *s-expr*) where *symbol* is a symbol, *parameters* is a series of *n* (*n* ≥ 0) non-identical symbols and *s-expr* is a symbolic expression.

Since the Shen compiler compiles Shen into Kλ, Kλ is in a sense the *lingua franca* of the implementation and we can converse with Shen in the notation of Kλ. Generally this is not useful for programming purposes, because Kλ is much more prolix than Shen, but it is educational in understanding how Kλ works. Another good reason for understanding Kλ is that Kλ is a **Lisp**; one of a family of languages of which the oldest was Lisp 1.5 and the progenitor of all other functional languages.

Applications in Kλ and Shen have much the same form; a function is applied to arguments in prefix form. Abstractions are written with lambda rather than /. and Kλ follows strictly the notation of the lambda calculus (/. X Y Y) must be written (lambda X (lambda Y Y)). Currying and partial applications are allowed; (+ 5 8) and ((+ 5) 8) are equivalent.

A function definition in Kλ can be treated as effectively giving a name to an abstraction. The definition of the successor function in Kλ can be written (defun succ () (lambda x (+ x 1))). Typing this into Shen shows this to work.

```
(0-) (defun succ () (lambda x (+ x 1)))
(fn succ)

(1-) ((succ) 5)
6
```

Kλ contains 50 primitive functions, most of which we have met in the preceding pages (figure 15.1).

Boolean operations:	if, and, or, cond.
Symbol operations:	intern
String operations:	pos, tlstr, cn, str, string?, n->string, string->n
Global operations:	set, value
Exception handling:	simple-error, trap-error, error-to-string
List operations:	cons, hd, tl, cons?
Vector operations	absvector, address->, <-address, absvector?
Stream operations	write-byte, read-byte, pr, open, close
Numeric operations:	+, -, *, /, >, <, >=, <=, number?
Function definitions	defun
Abstraction builders	lambda
Local assignments	let
Equality	=
Evaluation	eval-kl
Continuations	freeze
Type declarations	type
Time	get-time
Global variables	*standard-input* *standard-output*
Internal functions	shen.char-stinput? shen.char-stoutput?
	shen.write-string shen.read-unit-string

Figure 15.1 The primitive instructions of Kλ

Apart from the internal functions, which we will cover in the next section, we've met most of these functions in the preceding pages. Any Shen function can be constructed out of these primitives. Here is a function that totals the numbers in a list. () is the empty list in Kλ.

```
(0-) (defun total ()
   (lambda x (if (= () x)  0
                 (+ (hd x) ((total) (tl x))))))
total

(1-) ((total) (cons 3 (cons 7 ()))))
10
```

This function tests two lists to see if the first is a prefix of the second

```
(2-) (defun prefix ()
   (lambda x (lambda y (if (= () x) true
                       (if (= y ())  false
                       (if (= (hd x) (hd y))
                           ((prefix) (tl x) (tl y))
                           false))))))
prefix

(3-) ((prefix) [1] [1 2])
true
```

We have chosen our coding to emphasise the continuity of Kλ with the lambda calculus of the last chapter. However it is not usual to write Kλ functions in the form above; it is more natural to place the lambda bound variables in the list of formal parameters after the name of the function. This style allows functions to be applied without extensive parenthesising.

Lastly Kλ, like nearly all members of the Lisp family, contains a construction cond for avoiding heavily nested conditionals which does very much the same job that cases does in Shen.

```
(4-)  (defun prefix (x y)
          (cond ((= () x)  true)
                ((= y ())  false)
                ((= (hd x) (hd y)) (prefix (tl x) (tl y)))
                (true  false)))
prefix

(5-) (prefix [1 2] [1 2 3])
true
```

Figure 15.2 Using cond *in Kλ*

Kλ is a very simple functional language; pattern-matching and the use of @s, @p, |, [...] are all missing from Kλ. A list of three numbers 12 45 67 has to be written in cons form in Kλ as (cons 12 (cons 45 (cons 67 ()))). This makes Kλ a very cumbersome language to program in, but it was not designed to be such but to serve as a sort of functional assembly language for porting Shen. For this reason there are no comment conventions for Kλ programs.

However one side-effect of embedding Kλ into the Shen environment is that many of the Shen idioms can be embedded into Kλ. This arises because the Shen reader actually translates these conventions into the language of Kλ. The result is a sort of pidgin language which allows Kλ to compete in brevity and clarity with established Lisps used for programming. For example the following computes in Shen because the reader translates the list notation into cons form.

```
(defun cons-10 (x)
 [0 1 2 3 4 5 6 7 8 9 | x])
```

The technique is interesting but not so important because the purpose of Kλ is to serve as a target language into which Shen is compiled.

174

15.2 Character Streams and Byte Streams

In chapter 9 we represented a stream in an intuitive way as one way street that allows information to flow down it. Just as there are streets which allow only certain kinds of vehicles to go down them, so there are streams which allow only certain kinds of information to flow down them. The most basic division is between **byte streams** and **character streams**.

A byte stream accepts only bytes as traffic and the word 'byte' defaults to indicate 8 bits unless otherwise specified. A more precise term now used is **octet**. Shen streams are byte (usually 8 bit) streams and the fundamental operations are read-byte and write-byte which read and write bytes from and to streams. Since Shen reads and writes bytes by their decimal representations, for an 8 bit byte, the legitimate values for these functions are in the range 0 to 255.

The relation between the bytes traded and the characters represented is called an **encoding**. Extended ASCII (256 characters) is the encoding of one byte to a character. ASCII (128 characters) is the character set representable in 7 bits. ASCII encompasses the keyboard character set shown in figure 5.2 and represents the minimum range of characters that any Shen platform must support.

Ultimately all streams traffic in bytes, because this is the *lingua franca* of the computer, and some implementations (SBCL being one) allow the programmer to read a stream with both character and byte operations, but this cannot be assumed. In many languages (e.g. C, Java, Python, CLisp) the standard input and standard output streams are character streams; that is, the programmer may direct only characters or strings to be read from or sent to them and not bytes. Since Shen works in bytes, for these character-oriented platforms some adaption is needed to glue the Shen reader and writer to the standard input and output. Prior to 2021, this was achieved by *ad hoc* adjustments to the kernel code.

In 2021, a more structured approach to dealing with this problem was introduced involving the introduction of four primitives directed towards languages which support character based standard streams. These primitives are internal to the Shen package (they are not designed for the user) and are prefaced by shen. They are used in the kernel code to glue byte-oriented operations to character streams. They are as follows.

1. A 1-place primitive function shen.char-stinput? which takes a stream as an argument and returns true if it is a character based standard input.
2. An equivalent function shen.char-stoutput? which takes a stream as an argument and returns true if it is a character based standard output.
3. A 1-place function shen.write-string which prints a string to the standard output.
4. A 1-place function shen.read-unit-string that reads a unit string from the standard input.

These functions operate to define pr and read-byte as follows (figure 15.3).

procedure pr (*String, Stream*)

1. If *Stream* is a character based standard output stream
    a. write *String* to *Stream* using shen.write-string.
2. Else
    a. convert *String* to a list *L* of unit strings.
    b. map each element of *L* to a list of bytes *B* based on extended ASCII encoding and
    c. write each element of *B* to *Stream* using write-byte
3. Return *String*.

procedure read-byte (*Stream*)

1. If *Stream* is a character based standard input stream
    a. read one unit string off the *Stream* using shen.read-unit-string and map it to a byte.
2. Else just read the byte.

Figure 15.3 The operation of the internal primitives of Kλ

Since reading a byte is a very low level operation which is used intensively in reading files, repeatedly testing for every byte read to see if the input stream is character based is unacceptably slow. Therefore the kernel code tests the stream *once* to determine if it is character based and uses procedure 1a. if it is and 2. if it is not.

In Shen implementations which run purely off byte streams, these four intermediary functions are trivially definable or redundant. The functions shen.char-stinput? and shen.char-stoutput? need to be defined for byte stream platforms unless the kernel code is adjusted to remove them, but their definition is trivial.

(define shen.char-stinput?
  _ -> false)

(define shen.char-stoutput?
  _ -> false)

For purely byte stream oriented implementations shen.write-string and shen.read-unit-string need not be defined since the control paths containing calls to these functions can never be activated. Thus not all implementations of Shen will support the internal functions described in this section, since their utility is *internal to the configuration of the platform.*

15.3 Foreign Functions

Shen treats any application of an undefined function f by wrapping an fn call around the function andusing currying. Shen consults a table to determine what to do when f is called. If f is used without being defined in Shen it will have no listed arity and an error is returned fn: f is undefined.

If f is defined outside Shen then the lambda table containing the information about the arity of f needs to be updated prior by the user. The expression (update-lambda-table f n) (where $n \geq 1$) will update the table by citing the arity of f.

If f is defined outside Shen but has no specific arity then (specialise f 1) entered prior will cause all applications to be uncurried. (specialise f 0) restores the default.

15.4 Manipulating Kλ

Every Shen function f is compiled into Kλ and the Kλ source can be read by the command (ps f) (print source) which prints the Kλ source as a list. This source can be itself manipulated and the result can be evaluated to result in a new definition. This feature is useful in the manipulation of Kλ because the source can be evaluated to produce a new program.

Our case example is production of a trace stack, whereby the list of functions called in a program is stored. The usefulness of the trace stack is that, if our program crashes, the stack will show the last function f to be called, which is generally the source of the error.

To construct such a facility in Shen, we need to construct a **wrapper function** f_w for any function f which acts exactly as f does but places a record of every call on the trace stack. In order to do this f_w will assume the same name as f in order that programs that calls f will be intercepted by f_w from wherever they originate. The call will be recorded on the stack and the arguments will be sent to a function f' whose coding will be exactly that of f. In other words, our trace program will do two things.

1. The Kλ source for f will be called up and a copy f' will be created and evaluated.
2. The body of f will be changed to point to f', but in addition a piece of code recording the call to f will be inserted.

These operations will not affect the results returned by (ps f) which records the Kλ source generated from the Shen definition. Hence we use this original code to restore the system once we decide not to trace the stack of calls any more. The program is very short (figure 15.4).

```
(define trace
  F -> (trace-h (gensym f') (ps F)))

(define trace-h
  F* [defun F Params Body]
  -> (do (eval-kl [defun F* Params Body])
         (eval-kl [defun F Params [do [record F] [F* | Params]]])))

(define record
  F -> (set *callstack* [F | (trap-error (value *callstack*) (/. E []))]))

(define untrace
  F -> (eval-kl (ps F)))
```

Figure 15.4 A trace program for Kλ

15.5 From Shen to Kλ via an Extended λ Calculus

In this section we will look at how Shen can be compiled to Kλ via an extended lambda calculus $\mathcal{L}$. This approach is found in Peyton-Jones (1988) and was the original method for compiling Shen until the simpler 'triple stack' method discussed in the next section was introduced in Shen 24. $\mathcal{L}$ will play a significant part in proving the credentials of the Shen type checker and we shall examine it in more detail in chapter 28. It is important to see that any Shen program can be expressed in this enriched notation.

$\mathcal{L}$ contains one significant addition to lambda calculus, which is the appearance of pattern-matching abstractions. A conventional abstraction is part of lambda calculus, but pattern-matching abstractions are not part of lambda calculus; they are, however, part of $\mathcal{L}$ The syntactic difference between a conventional abstraction and a pattern-matching abstraction is that a conventional abstraction may contain only a variable after the λ, whereas a pattern-matching abstraction may have a pattern.

For our purposes, a pattern is either a base expression (i.e. a symbol, string, number or boolean) or the empty list, or an expression built out of patterns by the use of cons, @s, @p and @v. Thus the expression, (λ X X) is a conventional lambda abstraction, but the expression (λ (cons 1 [ ]) 2) is a pattern-matching abstraction. Here are some more examples with their attendant interpretations.

Expression	Interpretation
(λ (cons 1 [ ]) 2)	a function that receives (cons 1 [ ]) and returns 2.
(λ 1 2)	A function that if it receives an 1 and returns 2.
(λ (cons X [ ]) X)	receives a unit list and returns the first element.

What happens if (λ (cons 1 [ ]) 2) is applied to, say, the number 3? Intuitively the input 3 does not match the pattern (cons 1 [ ]) and so the application fails. In such a case we designate the object ⊗ as being the result of this application - indicating a match failure.

We shall explain how Shen is compiled to $\mathcal{L}$ by reference to the compilation of the member function. Here is the initial function.

```
(define member
  _ [ ] -> false
  X [X | _] -> true
  X [_ | Y] -> (member X Y))
```

1. All lists are translated to cons form, and all wildcards are replaced by unique variables. We emphasise the process by bolding the parts that change.

```
(define member
  V [] -> false
  X (cons X W) -> true
  X (cons Z Y) -> (member X Y))
```

2. Ensure that each rule is **left linear**, where a left linear rule is one that does not contain the same variable twice to the left of the arrow. This entails renaming repeated variables and adding a guard.

```
(define member
  V [] -> false
  X (cons U W) -> true      where (= U X)
  X (cons Z Y) -> (member X Y))
```

3. Determine the arity n of the function f by counting the number n of patterns to the left of each arrow in each rule $r_1,...,r_m$. If there is a different number in any two rules, then an error is raised. Let $v_1,...,v_n$ be a list of fresh variables. From a function (define f $r_1,..,r_m$) generate $f =_{df} (\lambda v_1 .. (\lambda v_n\ r_1,..,r_m))$.

member $=_{df}$ (λ A (λ B (V [ ] -> false
                X (cons U W) -> true   where (= U X)
                X (cons Z Y) -> (member X Y))))

4. Replace each rule

$p_a ...p_n$ -> q where g

by

$p_a ...p_n$ -> (where g q)

member $=_{df}$ (λ A (λ B (V [ ] -> false
                X (cons U W) -> (where (= U X) true)
                X (cons Z Y) -> (member X Y))))

179

5. Change the definition from $f =_{df} (\lambda v_1 \, .. \, (\lambda v_n \, r_1,..,r_m))$ to $f =_{df} (\lambda v_1 \, .. \, (\lambda v_n$ (cases $r_1,..,r_m)$).

    member $=_{df}$ (λ A (λ B **(cases** V [ ] -> false
                                     X (cons U W) -> (where (= U X) true)
                                     X (cons Z Y) -> (member X Y))))

6. Given $f =df (\lambda v_1 \, .. \, (\lambda v_n$ (cases $r_1,..,r_m)$))) replace each $r_i = p_a \, ...p_n \, -> q$ by a **rule application** of the abstraction $(\lambda p_a \, ... \, (\lambda p_n \, q))$ to the arguments $v_1,...,v_n$

    member $=_{df}$ (λ A (λ B
                (cases (((λ V (λ [ ] false)) A) B)
                    (((λ X (λ (cons U W) (where (= U X) true))) A) B)
                    (((λ X (λ (cons Z Y) (member X Y)) A) B))))

This completes the transformation of Shen to $\mathcal{L}$. The generation of $\mathcal{L}$ expressions is an intermediate step in the compilation of Shen. The target is to generate expressions in Kλ. This involves eliminating the rule applications.

7. For each rule application $r = ((\lambda p \, q) \, v)$ apply the following recursively throughout r.

    a.   If p is a variable apply β reduction to r.
    b.   If p is a constant, (i.e. a non-variable symbol, string, boolean, number etc) then substitute $((\lambda \, v_f \, (\text{if } (= v_f \, p) \, q \, \otimes)) \, v)$ for r, where v_f is a fresh variable and $\otimes$ is a symbol indicating match failure
    c.   If $p = (\text{cons } p_1 \, p_2)$ substitute $((\lambda \, p_1 \, (\lambda \, p_2 \, (\text{if } (\text{cons? } v) \, \otimes) \, (\text{tl } v) \, (\text{hd } v))$ for r.
    d.   If $p = (@p \, p_1 \, p_2)$ substitute $((\lambda \, p_1 \, (\lambda \, p_2 \, (\text{if } (\text{tuple? } v) \, \otimes) \, (\text{snd } v) \, (\text{fst } v))$ for r.
    e.   If $p = (@v \, p_1 \, p_2)$ substitute $((\lambda \, p_1 \, (\lambda \, p_2 \, (\text{if } (\text{vector? } v) \, \otimes) \, (\text{tlv } v) \, (\text{hdv } v))$ for r.
    f.   If $p = (@s \, p_1 \, p_2)$ substitute $((\lambda \, p_1 \, (\lambda \, p_2 \, (\text{if } (\text{string+? } v) \, \otimes) \, (\text{tlv } v) \, (\text{hdv } v))$ for r.[60]

Step 7 is the most complex transformation, let's see how this works out in the case of the member expression from step 6. The first line is

    (((λ V (λ [ ] false)) A) B)

which by 7a. using β reduction gives $((\lambda \, [\,] \text{ false}) \, B)$. Applying 7b to this expression gives

    (if (= B []) false $\otimes$)

The second rule was

---

[60] string+? is an internal function in the Shen package that tests for a non-empty string.

(((λ X (λ (cons U W) (where (= U X) true))) A) B)

The outermost application is covered by 7a., β reduction gives

((λ (cons U W) (where (= U A) true)) B)

This expression is covered by 7c. and the result is

((λ U (λ W (if (cons? B) (where (= U A) true) ⊗)) (tl B)) (hd B))
Two steps of β reduction gives

((λ W (if (cons? B) (where (= (hd B) A) true) ⊗)) (tl B))
    (if (cons? B) (where (= (hd B) A) true) ⊗)

The final rule was

(((λ X (λ (cons Z Y) (member X Y)) A) B))

By 7a. and β reduction

((λ (cons Z Y) (member A Y)) B)

By 7c.

((λ Z ((λ Y (if (cons? B) (member A Y) ⊗)) (tl B)) (hd B))

Two steps of β reduction gives

((λ Y (if (cons? B) (member A Y) ⊗)) (tl B))
(if (cons? B) (member A (tl B)) ⊗)

So in total the function appears after step 7 as follows.

    member =_{df} (λ A (λ B
        (cases (if (= B []) false ⊗)
            (if (cons? B) (where (= (hd B) A) true) ⊗)
            (if (cons? B) (member A (tl B)) ⊗))))

8.   Replace (where *p q*) by (if *p q* ⊗).

    member =_{df} (λ A (λ B
        (cases (if (= B []) false ⊗)
            (if (cons? B) **(if (= (hd B) A) true ⊗) ⊗)**
            (if (cons? B) (member A (tl B)) ⊗))))

9.   Replace (if *p* (if *q r* ⊗) ⊗) by (if (and *p q*) *r* ⊗).

```
member =_df (λ A (λ B
            (cases (if (= B []) false ⊗)
                   (if (and (cons? B) (= (hd B) A)) true ⊗)
                   (if (cons? B) (member A (tl B)) ⊗))))
```

10. Replace cases by cond. To adapt the syntax to the use of cond, apply the following transformation τ recursively to $f =_{df} (\lambda v \ldots \lambda v_n (\text{cond } c_1 \ldots c_n))$ to generate $f =_{df} (\lambda v \ldots \lambda v_n (\text{cond } \tau(c_1 \ldots c_n)))$ where τ is defined as

$\tau((\text{if } p\ q\ \otimes)\ c_i \ldots) = (p\ q)\ \tau(c_i \ldots)$
$\tau((\text{if } p\ q\ \otimes)) = (\text{true (error "partial function } f\text{"}))$

```
member =_df (λ A (λ B
            (cond ((= B []) false)
                  ((and (cons? B) (= (hd B) A)) true)
                  ((cons? B) (member A (tl B)))
                  (true (error "partial function member)))))
```

11. Replace $f =_{df} (\lambda v \ldots \lambda v_n\ p)$ by $(\text{defun } f\ (v \ldots v_n)\ p)$.

```
(defun member (A B)
    (cond ((= B []) false)
          ((and (cons? B) (= (hd B) A)) true)
          ((cons? B) (member A (tl B)))
          (true (error "partial function member)))))
```

Step 11 completes the transformation into Kλ.

15.6 Compiling Out Choicepoints

We have not explained how to compile backtracking constructions that use <-. There is a missing step 1.5.

1.5 Replace every rule $p_a \ldots p_n <- q$ by $p_a \ldots p_n -> (© q)$

© is the choice point flag and remains in the code to indicate a choice point to be compiled out. A function which contains such a choice point will generally be of the form $(\text{defun } f\ (v_1 \ldots v_n)\ (\text{cond } c_1 \ldots c_k\ (p\ (©\ q))\ c_{k+2} \ldots c_{k+m}))$ where $(p\ (©\ q))$ contains the first occurrence of the choice point flag in the function definition. The trick is to isolate the code after the choice point and turn it into a continuation and assign it to a local variable, thus delaying the computation. This continuation is then thawed if needed. The local assignment avoids repeating code. The process is repeated throughout $c_{n+2} \ldots c_{n+m}$ to eliminate the choice point operators.

```
(defun f (v₁ ... vₙ)
  (cond c₁ ... cₖ
      (true  (let Freeze (freeze (cond cₖ₊₂ .... cₖ₊ₘ))
              (if p   (let Result q
                      (if (= Result (fail))
                          (thaw Freeze)
                          Result))
                      (thaw Freeze))))))))
```

Figure 15.5 Compiling out a choice point in Kλ

15.7 The Triple Stack Method

The triple stack method was used in all versions of Shen after 2019 and is much easier to follow and gives a faster compilation. We'll use the member function as before to illustrate the approach.

```
(define member
   _ [] -> false
   X [X | _] -> true
   X [_ | Y] -> (member X Y))
```

The initial steps are the same as before; lists are translated to cons form, and all wildcards are replaced by unique variables and the rules are left-linearised.

```
(define member
   V [] -> false
   X (cons U W) -> true      where (= U X)
   X (cons Z Y) -> (member X Y))
```

Again we construct a list of formal parameters [A B], but they are not used to build an abstraction in $\mathcal{L}$. Rather they are placed in a stack and the corresponding patterns are compared to them. The first step is to construct the three stacks.

1. The first stack U is initially empty. It will contain the list of tests needed to be made on the input to satisfy the patterns.
2. The second stack S will contain the list of the n patterns.
3. The third stack T will contain the n formal parameters.
4. The final input to the procedure is the result R returned from the function if the patterns fire.

We'll take the final rule in this function as our case example. Thus the corresponding elements are:

$$U = [], S = [X \text{ [cons Z Y]}], T = [A \text{ B}], R = [\text{member X Y}]$$

The triple stack method steps through stacks S and T in tandem comparing the ith element of each. Each comparison forces the following actions:

183

1. If the ith element S_i of S is a variable then
    i. S_i is popped off S,
    ii. T_i is popped off T
    iii. and every free instance of S_i in R is replaced by T_i.
2. If the ith element S_i of S is an atom then
    i. S_i is popped off S,
    ii. T_i is popped off T
    iii. and the test $[= S_i\ T_i]$ is pushed onto U.
3. If the ith element S_i of S is a constructor of the form $[Op\ S_a\ S_b]$ then
    i. S_i is popped off S
    ii. Ti is popped off T.
    iii. A lookup table is used to find appropriate recognisor Op_R for Op (e.g. for cons it would be cons?).
    iv. Similarly lookup tables are used to find the selectors Op_{SelA} and Op_{SelB} for this operation (for cons it would be hd and tl).
    v. The test $[Op_R\ T_i]$ is pushed onto U.
    vi. S_a and S_b are pushed onto S
    vii. $[Op_{SelA}\ T_i]$ and $[Op_{SelB}\ T_i]$ are pushed onto T.
4. If $S = T = []$ then
    i. if $R = [\text{where } P\ Q]$, then set R to Q and push P onto U and halt.
    ii. otherwise halt.

At the end of this process, when $S = T = []$, the stack U and the amended result R are returned. Since the stack discipline means that the tests in U are returned in reverse order, U needs to be reversed and the components 'anded' together to form an s-expr in Kλ. The result is a line of Kλ code.

In our case example, we begin with

$$U = []$$
$$S = [X\ [\text{cons Z Y}]]$$
$$T = [A\ B]$$
$$R = [\text{member X Y}]$$

The first iteration matches the X to A producing

$$U = []$$
$$S = [[\text{cons Z Y}]]$$
$$T = [B]$$
$$R = [\text{member A Y}]$$

The second iteration finds the cons constructor, so the output is

$$U = [[\text{cons? B}]]$$
$$S = [Z\ Y]$$
$$T = [[\text{hd B}]\ [\text{tl B}]]$$
$$R = [\text{member A Y}]$$

184

The third iteration eliminates the Z.

U = [[cons? B]]
S = [Y]
T = [[tl B]]
R = [member A Y]

The final iteration eliminates the Y.

U = [[cons? B]]
S = []
T = []
R = [member A [tl B]]

The resulting Kλ code is ((cons? B) (member A (tl B)) which is inserted into the Kλ function.

Two methods have been provided to compile Shen to Kλ. The initial steps of left-linearisation and the replacement of wildcards is the same. Thereafter they seem to differ greatly in approach. However they issue in the same object code. To see why this is, remember the rule used for converting an $\mathcal{I}$ function to to Kλ. For each application $r = ((\lambda\ p\ q)\ v)$ apply the following recursively throughout r.

a.   If p is a variable apply β reduction to r.
b.   If p is a constant, then substitute $((\lambda\ v_f\ (\text{if}\ (=\ v_f\ p)\ q\ \otimes))\ v)$ for r, where v_f is a fresh variable and $\otimes$ is a symbol indicating match failure
c.   If $p = (\text{cons}\ p_1\ p_2)$ substitute $((\lambda\ p_1\ (\lambda\ p_2\ (\text{if}\ (\text{cons?}\ v)\ \otimes)\ (\text{tl}\ v)\ (\text{hd}\ v))$ for r.
d.   If $p = (@p\ p_1\ p_2)$ substitute $((\lambda\ p_1\ (\lambda\ p_2\ (\text{if}\ (\text{tuple?}\ v)\ \otimes)\ (\text{snd}\ v)\ (\text{fst}\ v))$ for r.
e.   If $p = (@v\ p_1\ p_2)$ substitute $((\lambda\ p_1\ (\lambda\ p_2\ (\text{if}\ (\text{vector?}\ v)\ \otimes)\ (\text{tlv}\ v)\ (\text{hdv}\ v))$ for r.
f.   If $p = (@s\ p_1\ p_2)$ substitute $((\lambda\ p_1\ (\lambda\ p_2\ (\text{if}\ (\text{string+?}\ v)\ \otimes)\ (\text{tlv}\ v)\ (\text{hdv}\ v))$ for r.

These rules for compiling $\mathcal{I}$ are systematically comparing a pattern p with an input v. The difference in the triple stack method is that, rather than working inside an application of an extended λ abstraction, these comparisons are driven by placing p and v on the S and T stacks and pushing the generated tests onto the U stack. The generated code is the same in both cases because the tests generated are identical and the decomposition of v into its components by the appropriate selectors is also identical.

The triple stack method is thus an efficient procedural abstraction of function application in $\mathcal{I}$. The reason why we need to retain $\mathcal{I}$ is that it will form an intermediate representation language for proving important properties of Shen programs in the later chapters.

15.8 Factorising Kλ

Consider the Shen definition and the generated Kλ in figure 15.6. The Kλ code is not optimal; (cons? V4) is potentially repeated in the course of evaluation. The expression (tl V4) can be evaluated more than once in the course of executing this function.

```
(define f
   [a] -> a
   [b] -> b)

(defun f (V4)
   (cond ((and (cons? V4) (and  (= a (hd V4)) (= () (tl V4)))) a)
         ((and (cons? V4) (and (= b (hd V4)) (= () (tl V4)))) b)
         (true (shen.f-error f))))
```

Figure 15.6 A Shen definition with the corresponding Kλ

There are two classes of inefficiency in this code which we can call *horizontal* and *vertical* inefficiencies. The vertical inefficiencies come from *between* successive rules where common *recognisors* on the input are repeated because the patterns overlap. The horizontal inefficiencies occur *within* a rule because the repeated variables in the result require the same *selections* are repeated. **Factorisation** involves removing these repeated tests by remembering the results of past computations if needed and storing them; a process referred to as **memoisation**.

We'll first outline the factorisation algorithm in Shen *without* the use of code and then fill in the finer details by including the relevant kernel code. The factorisation algorithm is driven by *vertical optimisations*; that is, the elimination of vertical inefficiencies in the code by factoring out repeated recognitions. The nature of these recognitions drives the *horizontal optimisations*. For example, the vertical optimisation of a cons? test suggests that one should look for horizontal optimisations wrt hd and tl.

The input to the factorisation algorithm is a Kλ definition (defun f (cond *Cases*)) where *Cases* will be a series of expressions each of the form (*Test Result*). If the definition has any other form (cond is absent) then factorisation leaves it unchanged.

Main Loop:

where *Cases* = ((*Test Result*) ...)

1. if *Test* has the form (and P Q) then partition the *Cases* into those whose tests lead with P, *Cases*$^{+P}$, and those which do not, *Cases*$^{-P}$. If *Test* is not a conjunction then factorise ... in (if *Test Result* ...).

2. Form the conditional (if P *Before* *After*) where *Before* is the code derived from $Cases^{+P}$ and *After* is the code derived from $Cases^{-P}$.

This is simple enough; the main question is how *Before* and *After* are generated. A sketch looks like this.

Before Code:

1. Given P is of the form $(R? \; X)$ where $R?$ is a recognisor (eg. cons?) compute the relevant selections $(S_1 \; X)$ and $(S_2 \; X)$ (e.g. (hd X) and (tl X)). If these selections are repeated in $Cases^{+P}$ then locally bind them in $Cases^{+P}$ to give horizontally optimised code.
2. Feed the horizontally optimised code back into the main loop.

The after code is simpler.

After Code:

1. Feed $Cases^{-P}$ into the main loop.

This is a sketch. Now to explore the complexities and missing elements.

An important missing element is that if P is true and the *Before* code fails to return a normal form then control has to go back to the *After* code. For example if the *Before* code optimises P in ((and P Q) R) but Q returns false in execution, then R cannot be returned, but still the computation must have somewhere to go. 'Somewhere to go' in this case means invoking the *After* code.

This means that the *After* code may be invoked several times within the body of the Before code. We then have a choice of how the *After* code is invoked. We may either **inline** that code or create a procedure through **procedural abstraction**.

A procedure call is inlined by replacing it by the actual body of code contained in the procedure. In functional programming, we inline a function call $(f \, x_1 ... \, x_n)$ by substituting the result of replacing the formal parameters in the definition of f by $x_1 ... \, x_n$. Inlining buys some speed, since a function call to f is no longer needed, at the expense of memory, since the inlined code is generally bulkier than the original procedure call.

The converse of inlining is **procedural abstraction.** We replace the inlined code by a procedure call and define the *After* code under a procedure. There two different ways of doing this.

1. We can create a local variable and bind it to a lambda function which represents the *After* code.
2. We can create a help function h which contains the *After* code and use call to h in the *Before* code.

187

These are both legitimate, but in practice the latter results in faster code since it is not necessary to dynamically create an association between a variable and a body of code. Some procedural abstraction is essential wrt Shen functions with many rules if exponential code is to be avoided. The choice between inlining and abstracting is something we will pick up later. This is the outline of our approach. Now let's see in detail how this is written in Shen.

```
(define factorise-code
  [defun F Params [cond | Cases]]
  -> [defun F Params (vertical Params Cases [f-error F])]  where (value *factorise?*)
  Code -> Code)
```

The input to the factorise-code is a Kλ definition. A flag determines if factorisation is performed. If the definition has no cases then factorisation does not apply. If it does and the flag is set to true then factorisation is performed by first looking for the vertical inefficiencies. The vertical function is passed the list of function parameters, the list of cases and an exit condition which by default is to return an error. The vertical optimisation function is next (figure 15.6).

```
(define vertical
  _ [[true Result] | _] _ -> Result
  Params [] Exit -> Exit
  Params [[[and P Q] Result] | Cases] Exit
  -> (let Before+After (split-cases P [[[and P Q] Result] | Cases] [])
       (branch P Params Before+After Exit))
  Params [[Test Result] | Cases] Exit
    -> [if Test Result (vertical Params Cases Exit)])
```

Figure 15.6 Vertical optimisation

The vertical function takes three inputs and has two base cases. The inputs are a list of variables which are potential parameters; the second is the code to be factorised and the third is an exit condition to be inserted if the factorised code does not return a solution when executed. The first base case is; if the leading case says that a result is to be returned unconditionally, then the optimisation is to return that result. The second base case is that if all cases have been exhausted then the exit condition is returned.

The other cases are that that the leading test is a conjunction or it is not. If a conjunction then code is divided into before and after components using the leading test P and these components used to construct a conditional – a branch in the code. If not, then a branch is constructed in a straightforward way. Figure 15.7 shows how cases are split around a test P.

```
(define split-cases
  P [[[and P Ps] Result] | Cases] Before -> (split-cases P Cases [[Ps Result] | Before])
  P [[P Result] | Cases] Before -> (split-cases P Cases [[true Result] | Before])
  _ After Before -> [(reverse Before) After])
```

Figure 15.7 Splitting cases around a test P

The branch function constructs an *if ... then ... else* statement.

```
(define branch
  P Params [Before After] Exit
  -> (let Else (else Params After Exit)
         Then (then P Params Before Else)
      [if P Then Else]))
```

The else component deals with the *After* code. The function recurses using vertical to construct the code and then queries whether the resulting code should be inlined. If the answer is positive, then the code is returned as is. If the answer is negative then a procedure call is made.

```
(define else
  Params After Exit -> (let Else (vertical Params After Exit)
                         (if (inline? Else) Else
                            (procedure-call Params Else))))
```

If Else is a flat application of a function to a series of atomic terms then there is no value in forming a procedure and the code should be inlined.

```
(define inline?
  [X | Y] -> (and (atom? X) (inline? Y))
  X -> (atom? X))
```

If the code should not be inlined then a procedure call is returned and the relevant procedure (function) compiled into Shen.

```
(define procedure-call
  Params Code -> (let F (gensym else)
                     Used (remove-if-unused Params Code)
                     KL [defun F Used Code]
                     EvalKL (eval-kl KL)
                     Record (record-kl F KL)
                     [F | Used]))
```

remove-if-unused checks the code to see if any of the variables are not used in the body of the procedure. If so they are removed.

```
(define remove-if-unused
  [] _ -> []
  [V | Vs] Code -> (if (occurs? V Code) [V | (remove-if-unused Vs Code)]
                      (remove-if-unused Vs Code)))
```

The then function computes the horizontal optimisations using the P test.

```
(define then
  P Params Before Else -> (horizontal (selectors P Before) Params Before Else))
```

The selectors are those expressions which merit optimisation. The selectors function (figure 15.8) assembles these expressions.

189

```
(define selectors
  [R? X] Before -> (let Hd [(selector1 R?) X]
                        Tl  [(selector2 R) X]
                        RptedHd? (rpted? Hd Before)
                        RptedTl? (rpted? Tl Before)
                        (cases (and RptedHd? RptedTl?) [Hd Tl]
                               RptedHd? [Hd]
                               RptedTl? [Tl]
                               true [])) where (recognisor? R?)
  _ _ -> [])
```

Figure 15.8 Selecting expressions to optimise

The test P must be of the form [R? X] where R? is a recognisor used in pattern matching (cons?, tuple? etc). The functions selector1 and selector2 map the recognisor R? to the relevant selectors.   The function then tests to see if these selectors have been applied more than once to the argument X in the code.   This gives a case statement of four possible cases. The output of these cases is a list of candidate expressions for horizontal optimisation.

```
(define recognisor?
  R? -> (element? R [cons? tuple? +string? +vector?]))

(define selector1
  cons? -> hd
  tuple? -> fst
  +string? -> hdstr
  +vector? -> hdv)
(define selector2
  cons? -> tl
  tuple? -> snd
  +string? -> tlstr
  +vector? -> tlv)

(define rpted?
  X Y -> (> (occurrences X Y) 1))
```

Finally the horizontal function performs horizontal optimisation (figure 15.9).

```
(define horizontal
  [] Params Before Else -> (vertical Params Before Else)
  [S | Ss] Params Before Else
  -> (let V (gensym (protect V))
          [let V S (horizontal Ss [V | Params] (subst V S Before) Else)]))
```

Figure 15.9 Horizontal optimisation

The horizontal optimisation recurses down the list of optimised selections.   As local bindings are introduced they are added to the list Params which is eventually passed as an argument to vertical optimisation.   The local variables generated by horizontal can now become new parameters to procedure calls generated from factorisation.

15.9 Factorisation at Work

Factored code is hard to read; figure 15.10 compares the factorised and unfactorised code from the Shen program in figure 15.5. The factorised code has removed the repeated tests and selections.

Shen	Factorised	Unfactorised
(define f [a] -> a [b] -> b)	(defun f (V4) (if (cons? V4) (let V5 (hd V4) (let V6 (tl V4) (if (= a V5) (if (= () V6) a (shen.else7 V6 V5)) (shen.else7 V6 V5)))) (shen.f-error f))) (defun shen.else7 (V6 V5) (if (= b V5) (if (= () V6) b (shen.f-error f)) (shen.f-error f)))	(defun f (V4) (cond ((and (cons? V4) (and (= a (hd V4)) (= () (tl V4)))) a) ((and (cons? V4) (and (= b (hd V4)) (= () (tl V4)))) b) (true (shen.f-error f))))

Figure 15.10 Factorised and unfactorised code side by side

What kind of performance improvement does factorisation afford? This is question of the 'how long is a piece of string' kind. It is of course depends on the case. Here are four benchmarks to consider.

Benchmark 1 uses the bubble sort program of chapter 6

```
(define bubble-sort
  X -> (fix (fn bubble) X))

(define bubble
  [] -> []
  [X] -> [X]
  [X Y | Z] -> [Y | (bubble [X | Z])]  where  (> Y X)
  [X Y | Z] -> [X | (bubble [Y | Z])])
```

to sort [0 1 2 3 4 5 6 7 8 9] 10^6 times.

Benchmark 2 is to compute (bruno [2 3] 3) 10^6 times (an example from Bruno Deferarri).

```
(define bruno
  [1 X | Xs] 1 -> X
  [1 X | Xs] 2 -> Xs
  [2 X | Xs] _ -> X)
```

Benchmark 3 is to compute (h "string?") 10^6 times given

```
(define h
  (@s "s" "t" "r" "i" "n" "g") -> 0
  (@s "s" "t" "r" "i" "n" "g" "?") -> 1)
```

Benchmark 4 is to compute (balance [black a x [red b y [red c z d]]]) 10^6 times (an example from a tree balancer written by Justin Grant)

```
(define balance
  [black [red [red A X B] Y C] Z D] -> [red [black A X B] Y [black C Z D]]
  [black [red A X [red B Y C]] Z D] -> [red [black A X B] Y [black C Z D]]
  [black A  X [red [red B Y C] Z D]] -> [red [black A X B] Y [black C Z D]]
  [black A  X [red B Y [red C Z D]]] -> [red [black A X B] Y [black C Z D]]
  S -> S)
```

Figure 15.11 shows the results.

	bubble sort	bruno	string	balance
Iterations	1e6	1e7	1e6	1e6
Factorised	7.30s	0.83s	2.4s	2.4s
Unfactorised	7.52s	0.97s	13.15s	13.33s
Speedup	3%	17%	548%	560%

Figure 15.11 Factorised and unfactorised code performance on four benchmarks

The benchmarks show that factorisation benefits jump spectacularly for string handling and for overlapping list patterns which are deeply nested. The reason for the big gain in the string program is that string matching is subject to vector copying. In Lisp and many languages, strings are held as vectors of characters and vector copying is expensive.

List operations are the most heavily optimised operations in almost any functional language. The time saved by memoising a computation C can be insignificant if C takes very little time and is not repeated more than once.   The latter condition is absent from deeply nested list patterns.

One disadvantage of factorisation is that tail recursive functions can cease to be so and generally become mutually recursive with the attendant problems of memory consumption.   For this reason factorisation is not a default setting in Shen.

Further Reading

Kλ is throughly dscribed in the Shendoc document on the Shen site that first appeared in September 2011 as Shendoc 1.7. Compilers for Kλ now exist in C, CLR, Common Lisp, Emacs Lisp, Erlang, Go, Haskell, Java, JavaScript, Ruby, Scheme, Truffle and Wasp Lisp.

An earlier version of Shen, Qi, was specific to Common Lisp. The Qi Merlin compiler factorised using the Common Lisp GO (a version of the notorious GOTO) instead of procedure calls.

The resulting code was highly unreadable, but so efficient than faster code could only be written by a Lisp programmer with considerable effort. In a shoot-off to encode a symbolic simpifier between Qi/Merlin and three programmers writing Common Lisp, the times for the hand-coded Lisp programs were 4x and 2x worse than the Qi-generated Lisp. The only Lisp program to achieve parity did so by painfully hand-coding exactly the same optimisation techniques that the Merlin compiler used. Details can be found in http://www.lambdassociates.org/Studies/study10.htm (use the Wayback machine).

Bruno Deferrari created a port specific version of factorisation for Shen based on the Merlin compiler; this works for Scheme and Common Lisp. Details can be found at https://github.com/Shen-Language/shen-sources/blob/master/doc/extensions/factorise-defun.md#example

The compilation of pattern-matching code is described in Peyton-Jones (1988) and in Field and Harrison (1988). Modern functional languages run lists of patterns through a finite state machine to factorise the object code. Crochemore and Hancart (1997) describe the procedure.

16 Writing Good Programs

The previous chapter covered the last elements of what may be called the *core* Shen language. Core Shen is a very powerful programming language and it is possible to write a great number of good and useful programs in it. Many textbooks say little about how to write good programs, preferring to teach by example, rather than through precept. But because we have now covered enough to know how powerful and elegant functional programming can be, it is worth pausing to try and distil what we have learnt about how to write functional programs.

First it must be said that functional programming is a *craft*. Like any craft, it takes practice and practice is the best teacher. The more exercises you do, the better you become, and hopefully you should outgrow the exercises in this book, and go on to pursue ideas of your own. In course of working on programs, you will develop an intuitive appreciation of how to tackle problems and, with luck, you will become a craftsman. Here are 11 precepts, designed to help you improve your technique, which tell you what to aim at and what to avoid.

1. *Employ top down programming methodology to tackle difficult problems.*

Most significant programming tasks are too difficult for you to know exactly how they are to be solved. Functional programmers respond by a top down methodology, whereby the top level functions of the program are coded first, then the functions immediately below the top level, and so on down to the system functions. At each step they postpone the consideration of exactly how the given functions they cite in a definition are themselves implemented until they come to define them. Use the same technique and don't be afraid of being banal. For example, suppose you are given the task of getting a computer to make a move in chess and you have decided to employ some method whereby the computer generates a list of likely moves and analyses them. However you are still a little hazy about how the best moves are selected. No matter; you can make an appropriate beginning by writing.

```
(define play-move
  Position -> (select-best-move (generate-likely-moves Position)))
```

2. Make a program clear before you try to make it efficient.

Inexperienced programmers are sometimes tempted into trying to optimise before they have fully understood what they are doing. Even if the program then works, the programmer is not quite sure what is going on, and debugging the program becomes very difficult. Aim to be clear initially and forget about being clever until later. Often clear programs tend to be efficient anyway.

3. Get used to throwing away code.

Declarative programmers talk about **throwaway designs** - programs that are written in order to help the understanding, but which are thrown away and replaced by something better once that understanding has been achieved. Don't be afraid to throw things away instead of patching them up.

4. Use significant variable and function names.

If a variable is supposed to stand for a list of towns, then use Towns rather than X. Similarly if a function is supposed to sort towns by population call it sort-by-population rather than sbp. You may think you know what sbp means now, but returning after 3 weeks holiday it may mean nothing to you (or your co-workers). Suitable variable and function names remove the need to attach copious comments.

5. Look for a common pattern in different processes, and try to capture it with higher-order functions.

We covered this in the chapter on higher-order programming. Acquire the habit of looking for common patterns in diverse processes and of using higher-order functions to capture these patterns. Apart from being an excellent mental training, forming this habit will lead you to simpler and often faster programs.

6. If a procedure is used more than once, then it should be defined within its own function.

If there is a procedure, which is called again and again within your program, hive it off into a separate function and give it a name. Not only does this lead to a shorter program, since you can just invoke the procedure through the name of the function instead of typing in the whole procedure, but also the program becomes easier to maintain.   If the procedure has to be changed, then only its definition need be altered, rather than everywhere it is called.

7. Avoid writing large function definitions.

Students who have attained some experience in functional programming, but are not yet expert, often write large unwieldy functions into which a large amount of activity is squeezed. Keep functions small. In terms of clarity, it is better to have a lot of short simple functions than a few large complex ones.

8. Avoid heavily parenthesised expressions.

This maxim is best bracketed with 7. Creating expressions with deep parentheses is visually confusing. Compare this function from the text.

```
(define <-db
  Key -> (let DB (value *db*)
            Hash (hash Key (limit  DB))
            Entry (trap-error (<-vector DB Hash) (/. E []))
            Details (assoc Key Entry)
            (if (empty? Details)
              (error "information not found~%")
              Details)))
```

with the equivalent function stripped of the elucidating local assignments.

```
(define <-db
  Key -> (let Details (assoc Key (trap-error (<-vector (value *db*)
                          (hash Key (limit (value *db*)))) (/. E [])))
            (if (empty? Details)
              (error "information not found~%")
              Details)))
```

The first version breaks up the logical stages of querying a DB and uses local assignments to annotate these stages. The second saves two lines, but requires a bracket balancing editor to write it, and cannot be comprehended without spending as much time as was needed to code it.

9. Try to avoid using assignments to hold information unless the information is of a permanent non-changing kind.

A source of "spaghetti code", where the thread of control is lost, is due to assignments over-playing their role. Ideally global values should be used to represent information which remains almost unchanged throughout the execution of program. In this role, they reduce the need to create extra inputs to functions, since a function can consult the global value if it needs to access this information. However, if a global value changes throughout a program, then the program is in danger of being a "spaghetti program". It is very difficult to correct mistakes in the program since the source of the error involving the global value cannot be easily localised.

10 . Tackle complex problems by successive approximation.

Some problems are too complex to be solved in the first pass. A good technique is to use *successive approximation*. Begin by simplifying the problem to something manageable and add the complexities in each approximation until you achieve the desired solution.

11 . If you find yourself feeling discouraged, tired or annoyed then don't continue to hack away at your program. Give it up and do something else and return to it later.

Writers of computer science texts often neglect the truism that programming is a human activity and that human beings get upset. Being upset and writing good code just do not go together. Anything you do while you tired or unsettled is liable at best to be worthless and at worst to be counterproductive. Most experienced programmers can recall making mistakes when feeling like this (a favourite is deleting some vital file). Save your work, log off, and walk away.

Part II

Working with Types

17 Types

Socrates: *Well then, since we have agreed that kinds of things can similarly mix with each other, is there not some sort of knowledge that one needs to take one's progress through the realm of statements, if one is going to point correctly which kinds will harmonise with which, and which are mutually discordant?*

Theaetetus: *Of course one needs knowledge, and possibly the greatest there is.*

Plato *Theaetetus*

17.1 Types and Type Security

The observations that Plato made over 2,300 years ago also hold true in computing. Programmers manipulate objects of many types, and for each type there is a set of specific legitimate operations that can be performed on the objects which belong to or **inhabit** that type. It is sensible to multiply two numbers or to take the head of a list. It is not sensible to try to take the head of a number or multiply two lists. The ability to recognise and avoid discordant **type errors** of this kind is one important form of knowledge that the programmer needs to possess if his programs are to work.

Since type errors must be avoided in order to have a properly working program, computer languages provide varying degrees of support to ensure that programs written in them are free from type errors, or **type secure**. In languages like Lisp and Python, type errors are often found when programs crash. Both these languages support **dynamic type checking;** only when programs are run, are the type errors in them detected.

In statically typed languages, type errors are detected in programs without having to run them. Statically typed languages are almost invariably **strongly typed languages** - i.e. every object of computation and every function must belong to a type, and the set of recognised types is rigorously laid down. This is a condition of being able to analyse programs to determine their type-security. The **type discipline** of the language is given by the rules, which determine how objects and types are associated. When functional programmers talk of typed programming languages, they mean languages that are statically and strongly typed.

17.2 Modifying the Read-Evaluate-Print Loop

In statically typed functional programming languages, the read-evaluate-print loop is modified to become a read-check-evaluate-print loop. The extra steps in the loop are italicised.

The Read-Check-Evaluate-Print Loop

Do until the user exits.

1. Read in the user's input.
2. *Type check it.*
3. *If there is a type error, output an error message and go to 1.*
4. If there is no type error, evaluate it to give the normal form.
5. Print the normal form together with its type.

If (tc +) is typed to the Shen top level, the Shen switches over to this loop.[61] After evaluation, the normal form and its type are printed separated by a colon, so 6 : number means 6 belongs to the type number. '6 : number' is an example of a typing (i.e. a functional expression together with a type). Typings can be entered to the evaluator. If a typing $e : t$ is typed to the top level, the Shen interpreter performs two operations.

1. If $e : t$ is not provable, then a type error is signalled.
2. Else e is evaluated to a normal form $e\Downarrow$, and $e\Downarrow : t$ is printed.

Figure 17.1 shows a session with the typechecker.

```
(0-) (tc +)
true

(1+) (* 7 8)
56 : number

(2+) (* 7 a)
type error

(3+) howdy
howdy : symbol

(4+) true
true : boolean
```

Figure 17.1 Base types in Shen

---

[61] (tc -) switches back to dynamic type checking.

Every typed functional language has a set of predefined types called **base types**, and operators called **type operators** for creating new types out of old ones. Shen has five base types.

1. symbol; e.g. a21, computer_studies, myname.
2. string; e.g. "my name is".
3. boolean; true, false.
4. number; e.g. ..., -3, -2, -1, 0, 1, 2, 3,... , 3.1462.
5. unit

A **type operator** is a means of building new types out of old.   Shen has six inbuilt type operators:

1. list
2. vector,
3. *
4. lazy
5. stream
6. $\rightarrow$

We will explain the semantics of many of these operators by giving the conditions under which objects inhabit the types constructed by them.

17.3 Lists, Vectors and Tuples

Lists, vectors and tuples are ways of grouping objects together; they each have their own type rule.

Rule for the Type Operator list

Where A is any type, list L : (list A) just when for each x in L, x : A.

Figure 17.2 shows a session with lists in typed Shen.

(6+) [3 4]
[3 4] : (list number)

(7+) ["a" "b" "c"]
["a" "b" "c"] : (list string)

(8+) [["a"]]
[["a"]] : (list (list string))

Figure 17.2 Typed lists in Shen

201

[3 4] inhabits the type (list number) which is the type of all lists whose elements are all number; a list of strings inhabits the type (list string); a list of lists of strings inhabits the type (list (list string)). What if we submit a list of symbols and integers to Shen?

```
(9+) [76 trombones]
type error
```

There is no type to which each element of the list belongs, the list does not inhabit a list type and consequently is treated as badly typed by Shen. Strongly typed functional languages do not naturally tolerate lists containing objects of different types.

Tuples restore some of the flexibility that is lost by imposing type homogeneity on lists. A tuple in Shen is strictly a **pair**, written in set theory as $<x, y>$ and in Shen as (@p x y). A tuple is a nested series of pairs in formal set theory where $<x, y, z>$ is shorthand for $<x, <y, z>>$. Similarly in Shen, @p is a polyadic function so that (@p 1 2 3) is parsed and printed as (@p 1 (@p 2 3)).

@p builds a tuple from x and y of types A and B respectively; the resulting tuple inhabits the **product type** (A * B) .

Rule for the Product Type *

(@p x y) : (A * B) just when x : A and y : B.

The function fst isolates the first element of a tuple and the function snd isolates the second element (figure 17.3). Pattern matching with tuples is part of Shen.

```
(1+) (@p 76 trombones)
(@p 76 trombones) : (number * symbol)

(2+)  (fst (@p 1 a))
1 : number

(3+) (snd (@p 1 a))
a : symbol

(4+) (define foo
        {(number * symbol) --> number}
        (@p 76 trombones) -> 76)
(fn foo) : ((number * symbol) --> number)
```

Figure 17.3 Tuples in typed Shen

202

The rule of the vector type is similar to the rule for lists; vector contents must belong to the same type.

Rule for the Type Operator vector

Where A is any type, vector v : (vector A) just for any $i > 0$ within the limit of v, $i(v)$: A.

The type rule for vectors only applies to standard vectors. A native vector that contains unassigned indices will have those indices filled with some platform-dependent object. Hence in general it is not possible to guarantee that a native vector will contain objects of a uniform type because a retrieval from it can yield an arbitrary object. For standard vectors, since nothing can be retrieved unless it is first entered, this problem does not arise.

```
(8+) (@v 76 0 <>)
<76 0> : (vector number)

(9+) (@v 76 trombones <>)
type error
```

Figure 17.4 Vectors in typed Shen

17.4 Lazy Types

Objects which inhabit lazy types are generated by the freeze function; the rule is straightforward.

Rule for the Type Operator lazy

Where A is any type, (freeze x) : (lazy A) just for x : A.

---

freeze generates objects which belong to lazy types and thaw removes the laziness.

```
(8+) (freeze (* 7 8))
#<CLOSURE LAMBDA NIL (shen.multiply 7 8)> : (lazy number)

(9+) (thaw (freeze (* 7 8)))
56 : number
```

Figure 17.5 Lazy types

17.5 The Small Arrow Type

The next rule relates to the types of functions and gives the conditions under which a function inhabits a type constructed by the infix **small arrow operator** $\rightarrow$.

Rule for the Small Arrow Type $\rightarrow$

For any types A and B, $f : (A \rightarrow B)$ just when for all x, if $x : A$ then $(f x) : B$.

Here is an example entered to Shen. The symbol --> is used for the type operator $\rightarrow$.

```
(10+) (define double
      {number --> number}
      X -> (* X 2))
(fn double) : (number --> number)
```

Figure 17.6 Type checking a function in Shen

(fn double) has the type number $\rightarrow$ number, because if x is a number then (double x) is a number.

Unlike the previous cases, in typed mode Shen will not verify the type of any function unless this type is specified in the function definition. This marks Shen out as an **explicitly typed** language in the manner of Hope (Burstall et al. 1980) rather than one of the group of **implicitly typed** languages like ML or Haskell which do not require this information.[62] The type or **signature** of the function is entered in curly brackets immediately after the name of the function.

The rule for $\rightarrow$ applies only to 1-place functions; but from chapter 6 we recall that this is no limitation on the expressive power of a functional notation because currying allows us express n-place functions in terms of 1-place ones. We consider the function + as being a 1-place function that when applied to an number m returns a function that adds m to whatever number n is supplied to it.

If we apply + to 1, we return an expression that adds 1 to an object. If we apply that expression to another number, we derive the successor of that number (figure 17.7)

---

[62] There is a very good reason why this information is required in Shen which has to do with the issue of the combinatorial explosion; a phenomenon we touched on in chapter 12 but did not actually witness. We will return to this theme in chapter 26.

```
(1+) (+ 1)
#<CLOSURE :LAMBDA [Z1414] [+ 1 Z1414]> : (number --> number)

(2+) ((+ 1) 2)
3 : number
```

Figure 17.7 Type checking and using a partial application

By the rule for the type operator →, the function + has the type number → (number → number). If + is defined in the manner of chapter 2, this is the type that Shen allocates to the function.

```
(3+) (define plus
        {number --> (number --> number)}
        0 X -> X
        X Y -> (+ 1 (plus (- X 1) Y)))
(fn plus) : (number --> (number --> number))
```

In many textbooks the internal parentheses for the type operator → are omitted, so that number → (number → number) is written as number → number → number. Shen permits this shorthand and automatically inserts the missing parentheses, as in this example.

```
(8+) (define average
        {number --> number --> number}
        M N -> (/ (+ M N) 2))
(fn average) : (number --> (number --> number))
```

This notational shorthand is used throughout this book. Figure 17.8 shows two functions from previous chapters together with their types.

```
(define add1
  {(vector number) --> (vector number)}
  <> -> <>
  (@v N V) -> (@v (+ N 1) (add1 V)))

(define whitespace?
  {string --> boolean}
  S -> (let N (string->n S) (element? N [9 10 13  32])))
```

Figure 17.8 Some functions from the previous chapters with types

The arrow operator is polyadic in Shen; it may be used as a monadic operator for zero place functions. Thus the following is legitimate.

```
(define pi
  {--> number}
  -> 3.142)
```

205

17.6 Polymorphic Types

A **polymorphic function** is a function that can be applied to arguments of different types. For example the append function can be used to append lists of numbers or list of symbols or lists of strings. We could say that append has the type (list string) → (list string) → (list string), but with equal reason we could also say that it has the type (list symbol) → (list symbol) → (list symbol).

In fact there is an infinite set Σ of variable-free types to which append belongs and there is no reason to single out one element of Σ as *the* type of append. Instead we say append inhabits the type (list A) → (list A) → (list A) for any type A that one cares to mention.[63]

The type (list A) → (list A) → (list A) is the **most general type** with respect to the types in Σ; because every member of Σ is a substitution instance of it. The presence of a variable in the type of append shows that the type of this function is a **parametric polytype**.[64] The inhabitation rule for a polytypes is as follows:-

---

Rule for Polytypes

If A is a polytype, x : A just when, for any type B which results from the uniform substitution of types for variables in A, x : B .

Figure 17.9 reproduces the Cartesian product program of chapter 4 with the appropriate polytypes.

```
(define cartesian-product
  {(list A) --> (list A) --> (list (list A))}
  [] _ -> []
  [X | Y] Z -> (append (pair X Z) (cartesian-product Y Z)))

(define pair
  {A --> (list A) --> (list (list A))}
  _ [] -> []
  X [Y | Z] -> [[X Y] | (pair X Z)])
```

Figure 17.9 A type secure version of the Cartesian product program

---

[63] Most of the standard list handling functions in Shen are polymorphic, **reverse** : (list A) → (list A) and **element?** : A → (list A) → boolean; these functions and their types can be seen in appendix A. In contrast the functions of the previous section were **monomorphic** and their variable-free types are **monotypes**.

[64] The qualifier 'parametric' implies that there are non-parametric polytypes; indeed there are. An object x displays non-parametric polytyping or **ad hoc polymorphism** when it belongs to two types a and b such that $a \neq b$ and there is no type c of which a and b are instances where x : c. We will see an example in the next chapter. The terms 'parametric polymorphism' and '*ad hoc* polymorphism' were coined by Strachey. ML was the first language to introduce parametric polytyping.

The old program computed the Cartesian product of a list of symbols and a list of numbers forming a list of lists containing symbols and numbers. The type checked version is more restrictive; both input lists must contain elements of the same type. A way of recapturing some of the functionality of the old program is to generate tuples rather than two element lists. Figure 17.10 shows the revised program that uses @p in place of the previous list constructor.

```
(define cartesian-product
  {(list A) --> (list B) --> (list (A * B))}
  [] _ -> []
  [X | Y] Z -> (append (pair X Z) (cartesian-product Y Z)))

(define pair
  {A --> (list B) --> (list (A * B))}
  _ [] -> []
  X [Y | Z] -> [(@p X Y) | (pair X Z)])
```

Figure 17.10 A revised version using tuples instead of lists

Since lists are built by consing to the empty list, the empty list must be capable of accepting an arbitrary object of any type. The empty list is a polymorphic object; of type (list A).[65] For similar reasons, the empty vector is also polymorphic.

```
(11+) []
[] : (list A)

(12+) <>
<> : (vector A)
```

Higher order functions are generally polymorphic and their nature means that arrow types are found embedded in their signatures. The converge program of chapter 6 is typed as follows.

```
(define converge
  {(A --> A) --> A --> (A --> A --> boolean) --> A}
  F X R -> (converge-help F (F X) X R))

(define converge-help
  {(A --> A) --> A --> A --> (A --> A --> boolean) --> A}
  _ New Old R -> New                    where (R Old New)
  F New _ R -> (converge-help F (F New) New R))
```

F has the type $A \rightarrow A$ (since it is recursively applied to X to its own output, it must have the same type as its input). X has to have the type A if F has the type $A \rightarrow A$. Since R compares X and (F X), $R : A \rightarrow A \rightarrow$ boolean.

---

[65] For those who know first-order logic and prefer a formal explanation, this follows from our rule R for list types. Let L be a list and let $x \, \varepsilon \, L$ be the relation between x and L when x is an element of L. R states that $\forall A \, L : (list \, A)$ iff $\forall x \, x \, \varepsilon \, L \rightarrow x : A$. Since $\sim \exists x \, x \, \varepsilon \, []$, then it follows that $\forall A \, [] : (list \, A)$.

17.7 Equality Types

The equality function = is polymorphic. Objects can be compared using = only when they are of the same type. [66]

(13+) (= 6 6)
true : boolean

(14+) (= a 6)
type error

(15+) (= (/. X (* X 2)) (/. X (+ X X)))
false : boolean

The equality function has the type A → A → boolean. Theoretically one can compare objects of any kind with = as long as they have the same type. In practice only objects which belong to **equality types** can be reliably compared for equality. In Shen these equality types include

1. The base types symbol, string, number, boolean.
2. Types created by applying the operators list, *, vector to equality types.
3. Types created by defining new types in terms of equality types.

Examples of objects that do not belong to equality types are functions. In mathematical terms the functions (λx (* x 2)) and (λx (+ x x)) are one and the same. However within Shen, (= (/. X (* X 2)) (/. X (+ X X))) yields the answer false. The reason being that Shen looks at the machine representation of these two expressions and finds them non-identical. The general problem of judging the equality of two functions is not a decidable matter.[67]

---

[66] Shen also provides a more inclusive equality function == which operates exactly as does =, but allows comparison of objects of different types. The type of == is A → B → boolean. In most statically typed languages, == is not supported. The reasoning is that since objects of different types can never be equal, there is no point comparing objects of different types to see if they are the same. We can think of an analogy in a world where every person is the citizen of only one country. In such a world the question "Is Mr Jules, French citizen of Paris, one and the same as Mr Jules, resident of London and British citizen" must always be answered in the negative. In the real world, where dual citizenship abounds, such questions are sensible and are sometimes answered positively. The world of programming is closer to the real world in allowing objects to have "dual citizenship" and so Shen caters for this. We shall see a real application in chapter 19.

[67] Other functional languages, such as ML, treat attempts to compare the identity of terms belonging to non-equality types by outputting an error. After SML '97, the type real was removed from the list of equality types; so 3.0 = 3.0; now forces an error in SML. The justification is that floating point numbers cannot be compared for equality because rounding errors and the limits of storage mean that floats cannot be represented with complete accuracy. Instead modern SML requires that an attempt to test for the equality of reals is replaced by a test to see if they differ by less than a designated quantity.

17.8 Stream Types

A stream in Shen is either of the type (stream in) or (stream out) depending on whether it is a source or a sink. (open <filename> in) creates a stream of the type (stream in) and (open <filename> out) of type (stream out).

The function read-byte has the type (stream in) → number and pr has the type string → (stream out) → string. stinput and stoutput will return objects of the form (stream in) and (stream out) respectively. The function open does not have a type that can be directly expressed as an arrow type.

input+ is the typed correlate of input. Unlike input, input+ receives two arguments; a type A and a stream. If the stream is omitted, then the standard input is used. The expression entered is then type checked and if it inhabits the type A, then it is evaluated. If not an error is returned. Here is an example.

```
(7+) (input+ number)
(* 5 6)
30 : number

(8+) (input+ symbol)
(* 5 6)
type error: (* 5 6) is not of type symbol
```

Since input+ can be used to read any stream, we can use it to read a file item by item and return just those items which belong to a desired type. In figure 17.11 we use it to filter a file of junk for expressions which evaluate to numbers. The higher-order function chomp takes a reader and applies it to the input stream, terminating when the stream is empty.

```
(define filter-numbers
 {string --> (list number)}
  File -> (chomp (/. S (input+ number S)) (open File in)))

(define chomp
 {((stream in) --> A) --> (stream in) --> (list A)}
  Reader Stream -> (trap-error [(Reader Stream) | (chomp Reader Stream)]
                  (/. E (if (eos? (error-to-string E))
                            (close Stream)
                            (chomp Reader Stream)))))

(define eos?
 {string --> boolean}
  "error: empty stream" -> true
  _ -> false)
```

Figure 17.11 Filtering a file using input+

Here is a test case - a readable file junk.txt

```
------------------------------------------------
      1 2 a gg
      "3455"
      456
      7890
      (* 7 8 9)

      true            isk;k;vk;vk
------------------------------------------------
```

Filtering the numbers using our program yields a list of numbers.

```
(14+) (filter-numbers "junk.txt")
[1 2 456 7890 504] : (list number)
```

The unit type is a special type that is used by a few system functions; one of them being read-file which has the type string → (list unit). When an object is assigned the type unit, it means that it is simply an object of some kind to which no type information is attached. Hence there is no inhabitation rule for the unit type. 'read-file : string → (list unit)' asserts that read-file accepts a string and returns a list of objects about which no type information can be assumed.

The main utility of the unit type is that units are still susceptible to polymorphic functions; that is to say, we can use functions like print and output on the output of read-file and maintain type security.

17.9 Types and Optimisation

When a function is type checked, the type information gleaned from this process can be attached to the Kλ in the form of type declarations. Entering (optimise +) allows this to happen. (figure 17.13).

```
(11+) (optimise +)
true

(12+) (define identical?
      {string --> string --> boolean}
      X X -> true
      _ _ -> false)
(fn identical?) : (string --> (string --> boolean))

(13+) (ps identical?)
[defun identical? [V547 V548]
    [cond [[= [type V548 string] [type V547 string]] [type true boolean]]
        [[type true boolean] [type false boolean]]]] : (list unit)
```

Figure 19.13 Automatically generating type annotations

The degree to which Shen makes use of these type annotations when compiling Kλ depends on the platform. It is legal and feasible to ignore them completely, but some compilers may choose to act on them in order to optimise the resultant code. Hence the function identical? above may actually be optimised to work only with strings. Whether this occurs or not, a basic principle to which Shen adheres is that all purely declarative type secure programs must behave in the same way when given type secure inputs. This condition is called the **weak portability requirement** which all platforms for Shen must respect. **Strong portability** requires that all programs must behave in the same way irrespective of whether the program or the input is type secure. Strong portability is not a condition in Shen and indeed several ports do not obey it.[68]

17.10 Changing the Type of a Function

It is unsound practice to change the code for a function f after it has been successfully type checked and compiled if that change engenders changing the type. Such a change, while itself type secure with respect to f, may render the entire program type insecure unless appropriate changes are made everywhere f is called.

During development it s quite common to change the types of functions and even their arity. Shen permits this as an alternative to exiting the image and starting again but issues a warning that the change may make the program type insecure. After such changes it is sound practice to load the program again. Any code issued for distribution should pass a clean load.

17.11 The Limits of Inbuilt Types

The set of types whose members can be constructed by means of the type operations and base types built into Shen constitutes the set Σ^S of inbuilt types that Shen can compute. Σ^S is infinitely large and incorporates the types of many of the functions of the previous chapters, but not all. The lambda calculus evaluator aor in chapter 14 cannot be given a type within Σ^S because it manipulates λ expressions. λ expressions are not uniform lists in the ordinary sense, nor are λ expressions necessarily lists at all since they can be symbols.

Practically speaking, for static typing to be useful in a language there has to be a way for the user to extend the set of recognisable types beyond the limits of the inbuilt types of the system. Such a facility exist within Shen in the form of the **sequent calculus** studied in the next chapter.

---

[68] E.g the Javascript port of Shen in which + will append two strings as well as adding two numbers.

Exercise 17

1. Define the following functions with types (problems inspired by Werner Hett).

    a. a function last that returns the last element of a list;
    b. a function mirror which tests to see if a list is of even length and if its first half is a mirror image of its second; thus [a b c c b a] would pass this test;
    c. a function remdup that removes duplicates of a list;
    d. a function partition that takes an equivalence relation and a list and partitions the list by the relation. Thus (partition (fn ==) [1 1 3 4 2 7 8 5 8 9]) = [[1 1] [3] [4] [2] [7] [8 8] [5] [9]]. The order of the elements does not matter.
    e. run-length; which takes a list as an input and returns a list of pairs giving the frequency of each element. Thus (run-length [1 1 3 4 2 7 8 5 8]) = [(@p 1 2) (@p 3 1) (@p 4 1) (@p 2 1) (@p 7 1) (@p 8 2) (@p 5 1) (@p 9 1)].
    f. duplicate; which duplicates the elements of a list; (duplicate [a b c] 3) = [a a a b b b c c c].
    g. drop; which drops every nth element from a list. (drop [a b c d e f g h i k] 3) = [a b d e g h k]

2. Provide correct types to all the functions contained in the following programs.
    a. the prime program of chapter 3;
    b. the change counting program of chapter 3;
    c. the powerset program in figure 4;
    d. the Goldbach conjecture program of chapter 4;

3. Attach to each of the following functions, its most general type.

        (define prim
          0 X F -> X
          N X F -> (F (- N 1) (prim (- N 1) X F)))

        (define mapf
          _ _ [] -> []
          C F [X | Y] -> (C (F X) (mapf C F Y)))

        (define prependX
          X -> (append X))

        (define has?
          Test [ ] -> false
          Test [X | Y] -> (or (Test X) (has? Test Y)))

        (define s*
          _ [] -> []
          _ [X] -> [X]
          R [X Y | Z] -> [Y | (s* R [X | Z])]   where (R Y X)
          R [X Y | Z] -> [X | (s* R [Y | Z])])

        (define s
          R X -> (fix (/. Y (s* R Y)) X))

        (define a
          F -> (/. X (/. Y (F X Y))))

212

4. Reimplement the semantic net program in figure 8.8 so that a semantic net appears as a list of pairs; each pair being composed of a symbol, and another pair composed of a pointer (is_a or type_of) and a list of properties. Thus asserting that Mark Tarver is both male and a teacher would be represented by the nested pair (@p Mark_Tarver (@p is_a [male teacher])). Since you will not be using a property list, your program will contain a top level function that maintains the semantic net as bound to a formal parameter. This same top level function will query the user as to whether she wishes to assert or query the system. Your program must pass the type checker.

Further Reading

Types that are not polytypes are **monotypes**, and languages that allow polytypes are **polymorphic languages**. Languages, which are strongly typed but do not admit polytypes are called **monomorphic languages**. An example of a monomorphic procedural language is Niklaus Wirth's **Pascal** to which Holmes (1993) provides a good introduction. Edinburgh ML (Gordon, Milner and Wadsworth (1979)) was the first statically typed polymorphic functional programming language. Discussions of the relative advantages of typed languages (like SML) and untyped languages (like Lisp) have appeared in user groups. The introduction to Abelson and Sussman (1996) contains some interesting observations on this topic as does Backhouse (1990).

213

18 Sequent Calculus

18.1 Sequent Calculus and Computer Science

Sequent calculus was developed by a German mathematician and logician Gerhard Gentzen during the unpromising conditions of World War II as an alternative to the **axiomatic** or **Hilbert systems** of logic that had existed up to his time. Gentzen's groundbreaking development was to offer two alternative presentations of logic – **natural deduction** and **sequent calculus**.

Gentzen's work originally arose within the framework of first-order logic, but was quickly taken up to present deductive systems of many different kinds including type theory. In 1984 Cardelli represented the type theory of a simple functional language using sequent notation and so it has been known for more than 30 years both that type checking within computer languages is a deductive process and that deductive processes can be represented in sequent calculus notation.

It would seem that building in sequent calculus into a programming language would offer the quickest route to providing type security. In fact this did not happen and instead developers produced special purpose algorithms like Milner's 𝒲 algorithm to drive type checking, even though they often wrote their theory papers with the help of sequent calculus. Most modern functional languages are derived from the Hindley-Milner approach including ML and Haskell.

There are at least two reasons why computer science took this direction. First during the 70s and early 80s there was little understanding of how to compile sequent calculus rules into efficient code. As we shall see in chapter 26, an essential intermediate step in effecting this compilation is to compile sequent calculus into Horn clause logic.

Horn clause logic is the basis of **logic programming**, studied in chapter 25. But logic programming entered computing relatively late in 1973 and only received a generally portable high-performance encoding 10 years later with the development of the Warren Abstract Machine and 5 years after Milner had introduced and worked out the theory for ML.

Torkel Franzen (1988) wrote a report explicitly noting the close connection between intuitionistic (single-conclusion) sequent calculus and logic programming. But the practical fusion of sequent calculus with functional programming had to wait until machine performance and the diffusion of logic programming technology allowed the author to make the first experiments in 1992 in using sequent calculus to drive type checking.

The second reason for not specifying types in sequent calculus is that the sequent calculus in its undiluted form is enormously powerful; in fact it is a programming language in its own right. In 2007, J. T. Gleason proved the Turing equivalence of the Shen type notation by writing an SKI combinator machine in it (a kind of λ calculus evaluator). Designers of SML and Haskell to a degree consciously or unconsciously shunned giving the user this power. We will look at the issues here in section 22.4.

The sequent calculus introduced here is a notational restriction of the original sequent calculus introduced by Gentzen. In particular, the multiple conclusion format of Gentzen is not used and what we study is single conclusion sequent calculus, generally a more natural idiom for reasoning and one with close connections to Prolog. Readers interested in comparing the classical approach of Gentzen, and in particular natural deduction, are referred to the further reading.

18.2 Introducing Sequent Calculus

The primordial material for any argument is a list of assumptions and a proposition which is to be proved. A sequent is an ordered pair $<\Delta, \chi>$ of just such a list of assumptions Δ and a proposition χ. From the point of view of mathematical and logical reasoning, the important question is whether the proposition χ follows from the assumptions Δ. If it does then the sequent $<\Delta, \chi>$ is said to be **valid**. If the assumptions are true and the sequent is valid then the sequent is said to be **sound**. Plainly the conclusion of any sound sequent is true.

In logic and mathematics, the focus is on the question of validity which is supposed to be a matter of pure thought. That is to say, no empirical investigation is required to establish validity of a sequent, although empirical investigation may be required to demonstrate the truth of the assumptions. The sequent

<[mercury boils at 356.73 °C], mercury's boiling point > 100 °C>

is undoubtedly valid and can be established by reflection, but the soundness of the argument requires an empirical investigation in chemistry.

In logic and mathematics, the announcement of a sequent as valid is presented in the form of a proof. Nothing that is non-obvious should be stated unless it is accompanied by some form of proof. The revolution in logic that took place in the late 19th and early 20th centuries was concerned with the formalisation of this concept of proof. The notation that became preeminent was **first-order logic**.

215

Though this revolution predated the computer revolution by more than half a century, what the logicians achieved was the reduction of the process of proof recognition to something that required no understanding of meaning, and only a recognition of the proper relations between the symbols involved. That is to say, the correctness of a fully formalised proof became a computable matter.[69]

The formalisation of proof requires that the steps of any proof be broken down to a level where each step is the product of a mechanical procedure. In functional terms, each step represents the application of a computable function to the previous steps of the proof. Such a computable function is an **inference rule**.

The structure of such a formal proof suggests that the form of an inference rule ρ must be

ρ: 'Any sequent of the form $S = \langle\Delta, \chi\rangle$ is provable if ... are provable.'

In cases where ... and Δ are empty, the inference rule is stating that S is unconditionally provable. Such an inference rule is called an **axiom**. Some more terminology. The elements of ... are the **premises** of ρ, S is the **conclusion** of ρ, Δ is the **context** of the S, the elements of Δ are **hypotheses** and χ is the **succeedent** of S.[70]

Generally sequent calculus inference rules are presented with the premises placed above a line with the conclusion placed below it. 'S is valid if $S_1, ..., S_n$ are all valid' is written as

$$\frac{S_1, ..., S_n}{S}$$

In certain textbooks, whitespace is used to separate premises which is slightly inconvenient in computing. Shen notation, which we will come to in the next chapter, uses semi-colons to separate premises and commas to separate items within a context. Also it is common to write the sequent not as $\langle\Delta, \chi\rangle$ but as $\Delta \gg \chi$ or sometimes $\Delta \vdash \chi$ - the $\gg$ or $\vdash$ symbol being read as 'therefore'. From now on we will follow these conventions.

---

[69] For some years it was an open question as to whether it was also possible to not only computably check proofs in first-order logic, but also to computably check validity. It fell to Turing and Church independently in the '30s and '40s to demonstrate that, as far as first-order logic was concerned, there was no algorithm for demonstrating the validity in first-order logic. This did not hamper the subsequent attempts by scientists to develop reasoning engines which would compete with human beings. This endeavour marks the beginning of **automated deduction**, a fascinating field which abuts on some of the topics in this book, including logic programming.

[70] The terminology is confusing. Logic is the unfortunate victim of naming conventions whereby 'sound' has at least three meanings and 'premise' has two. In logic, 'premise' is sometimes applied to the assumptions of an argument, what here we call hypotheses.

18.3 Propositional Calculus

Courses of elementary logic generally begin with **propositional calculus** (PC) and here we use it here to illustrate the application of sequent notation because we suppose some familiarity with this system. PC is a proof system which captures some basic patterns of inference involving & (and), v (or), ~ (not), → (if ... then ...) and ↔ (if and only if).

As well as these symbols there is an unlimited supply of propositional variables p, q, r,... p', q', r', ... These propositional variables can be made to stand for sentences.

The syntax of our propositional calculus can be stated quite simply.

1. A propositional variable on its own is a formula of PC. Such a formula is a **PC atom**.
2. The special atom *falsum* (explained later) is a formula of PC.
3. If P and Q are formulae of PC so is each of the following:
   $(\sim P), (P \& Q), (P \to Q), (P \text{ v } Q), (P \leftrightarrow Q)$.

Identifying p with the sentence 'Logic is easy' and q with the sentence 'Students like logic' determines the meaning of all propositional wffs containing only p and q as variables (figure 18.1).

Wff	Interpretation
$(p \to q)$	If logic is easy then students like logic.
$(p \text{ v } q)$	Either logic is easy or students like logic.
$((\sim p) \text{ v } q)$	Either logic is not easy or students like logic.
$((\sim p) \& (\sim q))$	Logic is not easy and students do not like logic.
$(p \leftrightarrow q)$	Logic is easy if and only if students like logic.

Figure 18.1 A reading of some propositional calculus wffs

In logical parlance, $(\sim p)$ is the **negation** of p. $(p \& q)$ is the **conjunction** of p and q, $(p \text{ v } q)$ is the **disjunction** of p and q.

In terms of sequent calculus, the proof theory of PC can be explained by giving the inference rules associated with &, v, ~, → and ↔. These symbols are the **logical constants** of PC in contrast to p, q, r,... p', q', r', which are the **logical variables**.

The logical constant & has two derivation rules. Here is the first. The first rule defines how to deal with a conjunction that forms the succeedent which is to the right of the >>. For this reason it is called the **right rule** for &.

$\Delta \gg P$;
$\underline{\Delta \gg Q};$
$\Delta \gg (P \& Q)$;

The rule states effectively that (P & Q) is provable from a context Δ if P is provable from Δ and so is Q. Generally when the nature of the context is irrelevant, then it is omitted and the rule is written as

&-*right*
P;
$\underline{Q;}$
(P & Q);

The variables Δ, P and Q are **metavariables**; that is variables used in the rule to mark places where the nature of the input is not important. The term 'metavariable' arises from the fact that sequent calculus is essentially a metalanguage evolved for the purpose of describing other languages like PC. In Shen uppercase is used to mark variables and again we follow suit.

The left rule for & says a conjunction that forms a hypothesis is split into its components

&-*left*

$\underline{\Delta, P, Q \gg R};$
$\Delta, (P \& Q) \gg R$;

Again Δ is read as given and the whole is written as

$\underline{P, Q \gg R};$
(P & Q) $\gg$ R;

The &-*left* rule can be applied to any hypothesis and the nature of the rule does not determine, if there is a choice to be made, which hypothesis is to be unpacked. Hence this rule is non-deterministic in application.

The left (L) and right (R) rules for & are symmetrical; they both involve splitting a conjunction into its parts. In Reeves and Clarke (1990) a useful shorthand is introduced whereby these two rules are expressed in a shorthand as an **LR rule** using the double underline

P;
Q;
$\overline{\overline{}}$
(P & Q);

This shorthand is optional but is used later in Shen. When using this notation it is important to always remember that it is only a shorthand for writing two rules in longhand.

The rules for v are *asymmetrical* – there two right rules and one left rule.

v-*right1*
$$\frac{\text{P;}}{\text{(P v Q);}}$$

v-*right2*
$$\frac{\text{Q;}}{\text{(P v Q);}}$$

A disjunction is provable if *either* of its components is provable. The left rule for v is sometimes called a **proof by cases** in mathematics.

v-*left*

$$\frac{\text{P} \gg \text{R;}}{\text{Q} \gg \text{R;}}$$
$$\frac{}{\text{(P v Q)} \gg \text{R;}}$$

R is provable from (P v Q) if R is provable from P and R is provable from Q. The rules for → are also asymmetrical.

→-*right*

$$\frac{\text{P} \gg \text{Q;}}{\text{(P} \rightarrow \text{Q);}}$$

→-*left*

$$\frac{\text{(P} \rightarrow \text{Q)} \gg \text{P;}}{\text{(P} \rightarrow \text{Q)} \gg \text{Q;}}$$

The →-*left* is a restriction of a more general rule called *modus ponens*.

$$\frac{\text{(P} \rightarrow \text{Q); P;}}{\text{Q}}$$

The difference in formulation may appear to be slight but they are significantly different. The →-*left* rule requires that the implication occur in the context whereas *modus ponens* makes no such restriction. The modus ponens rule is an example of a **synthetic** inference rule, because the set of metavariables in the premises is not a subset of those in the conclusion. Inference rules that are not synthetic are said to be **analytic**. Synthetic rules are less common in type checking than analytic ones and in the next chapter we will look at some of the dangers of using them carelessly.

The rules for ~ and ↔ are simple and symmetrical. (~ P) is shorthand for (P → falsum) where falsum is placeholder for any absurd proposition. (P ↔ Q) is defined as ((P → Q) & (Q → P)).

def~
(P → falsum);
═══════════
(~ P);

def↔
((P → Q) & (Q → P));
═══════════════════
(P ↔ Q);

The definition of negation has its origins in the idea that one way of denying a proposition P is to assert that if P is true then some absurdity follows. (e.g. 'If Nixon was innocent then my aunt is my uncle').

The next rule *lemma* allows us to introduce a new succeedent and, having proved it, to incorporate this into the new context.

lemma
P;
P >> Q;
─────────
Q;

In mathematics this is called **introducing a lemma**. If we are proving Q, then we can break or cut into the proof to prove P and then add P to the context and return to proving Q. In logic this is a form of the **cut rule**. The cut rule is an example of a **structural rule** since no logical constant is involved here. Two other structural rules are *swap* – that allows us to change the order of hypotheses and *thin*, that allows us to remove hypotheses.

swap
Q, P >> R;
──────────
P, Q >> R;

thin
Q;
────────
P >> Q;

Finally there needs to be an axiom to ensure that proofs terminate; *hyp* states that a sequent is valid if the succeedent is also an hypothesis.

hyp

P >> P;

These rules collectively define a system called **minimal logic** that is somewhat weaker than PC. To construct full PC, two more rules are needed. First, a rule for deriving a proposition from a proof of an absurdity. If falsum is provable then anything follows. This is sometimes called the *principle of explosion*.

explosion
falsum;
P;

This rule set now defines a weaker version of PC called **intuitionistic propositional calculus**. Adding the *law of the excluded middle* gives full classical PC.

lem

(P v (~ P));

18.4 First Order Logic (FOL)

In propositional calculus, atomic sentences are simple symbols. If we take the two sentences "Tarver likes the *Guardian*" and "Tarver likes the *Independent*", and represent them in PC we derive two sentences p (representing "Tarver likes the *Guardian*") and q (representing "Tarver likes the *Independent*"). Neither of these representations gives any clue that these two sentences share anything - that they both concern me and what I like.

First-order logic (FOL) captures these similarities by allowing atomic sentences, unlike those of PC, to have an internal structure. In FOL, an atomic sentence is composed of a **predicate** followed by zero or more **terms**. The predicate ascribes properties to the objects denoted by the terms. So in FOL, "Tarver likes the *Guardian*" is represented as "likes(Tarver, *Guardian*)" and "Tarver likes the *Independent*" as "likes(Tarver, *Independent*)".

A term in FOL can be structured, "likes((father-of Tarver), *Guardian*) represents the proposition that the father of Tarver likes the *Guardian*.

If we replace "Tarver" in "likes(Tarver, *Guardian*)" by a variable "*x*", we derive the **open sentence** "likes(*x*, *Guardian*)" in which the *x* is **free**.

Though both "Tarver likes the *Guardian*" and "Tarver likes the *Independent*" are true, an open sentence such as "likes(*x*, *Guardian*)" is neither true nor false because variables do not denote objects. One way to turn open sentences into sentences that are true or false is to replace the variables by denoting terms (like "Tarver", or "the man next door to me in #28"). Another way is to **bind** the variables by the **quantifiers** $\forall$ or $\exists$. Here is an example.

for every substitution for x, "likes(x, *Guardian*)" is true.

which in FOL is written "$\forall x$ likes(x, *Guardian*)", which is plainly false. Another way is to assert

for some substitution for x, "likes(x, *Guardian*)" is true.

which is itself true, and which in FOL is written "$\exists x$ likes(x, *Guardian*)". Since FOL includes all of the logical constants of PC, as well as quantifiers and structured atomic sentences, its expressive capacity is much greater than PC. Correspondingly, the syntax of FOL is more complex than PC.

Syntax Rules for First Order Logic

1. A variable is any of x, y, z, x', y', z'...
2. A predicate is any non-variable symbol other than $\sim$, &, $\rightarrow$, v, $\leftrightarrow$, $\exists$, $\forall$.
3. A name is any non-variable symbol/string/number/boolean other than $\sim$, &, $\rightarrow$, v, $\leftrightarrow$, $\exists$, $\forall$.
4. A functor is non-variable symbol other than $\sim$, &, $\rightarrow$, v, $\leftrightarrow$, $\exists$, $\forall$.
5. A term is either
   a. a name or ...
   b. a variable or ...
   c. an expression $(f\,t_1,...,t_n)$ made of a functor f followed by n ($n \geq 0$) terms.
6. $\sigma(t_1,..t_n)$ is a formula of FOL if σ is a predicate and $t_1,..,t_n$ ($n \geq 0$) are terms. $\sigma(t_1,..t_n)$ is a **first-order atom**.
7. If A and B are formulae of FOL so are ($\sim$ A), (A & B), (A $\rightarrow$ B), (A v B), (A $\leftrightarrow$ B).
8. If A is a formula of FOL and v is a variable then ($\exists v$ A) and ($\forall v$ A) are formulae of FOL .

Our syntax for FOL allows for 0-place predicates, but these are, in effect identical to the propositional variables of PC. Hence we will borrow on the syntax of PC and write (p v q) rather than ($p(\ )$ v $q(\ )$). All the inference rules of PC are also inference rules of FOL. In addition, there are left and right rules for the quantifiers.

$\forall$–*right*
$A_{t/v}$ is the result of replacing all free instances of v by a fresh name t.
$\underline{A_{t/v;}}$
($\forall v$ A);

The ∀–*right* rule contains a novelty; a **side condition**, '$A_{t/v}$ *is the result of replacing all* ....' when placed on the inference rule, both explicates and restricts its application.

This side condition calls for a **fresh** or arbitrary name. The meaning of 'arbitrary' is a little subtle. In conventional usage to select something arbitrarily is to select it at random. This is not the sense of 'arbitrary' needed here. For instance, one could 'prove' that all numbers are odd by arbitrarily selecting 3 and stating that since 3 is odd and selected arbitrarily, all numbers are odd. This is obviously wrong.

The problem thus arises of how we show that our choice of name is genuinely arbitrary, or arbitrary in sense that allows us to claim that the name chosen stands proxy for all cases. The philosopher's answer is that the object chosen must have no special conditions attached to it. This is correct, but changes the problem into - how are we supposed to recognise that no special assumptions are attached?

The logician supplies a syntactic criterion; the object supplied should be given a unique name, which does not occur anywhere else in the proof or in any rule; such a name is **fresh**. This shows up immediately what is wrong with the 'proof' that all numbers are odd. We begin with the sequent

$$odd(3) \gg \forall x \ odd(x)$$

We select our so-called arbitrary case, 3.

$$odd(3) \gg odd(3)$$

However, here the proof fails, since "3" is not a fresh name and so is not arbitrary in the required sense.

The ∀–*left* rule allows the instantiation of a universally quantified formula. Given the assumption '$\forall x \ physical(x)$' (everything is physical), then the assumption '$physical(5)$' (the number 5 is physical) can be added.

∀–*left*
$A_{t/v}$ is the result of replacing all free instances of v by any term t.
$\underline{A_{t/v}, (\forall v \ A) \gg P;}$
$(\forall v \ A) \gg P;$

The ∃-*right* rule states that an existentially quantified succeedent can be proved if some instance of can be proved. '$\exists x \ prime(x)$' can be proved if some instance e.g. '$prime(5)$' can be proved.

∃–*right*
$A_{t/v}$ is the result of replacing all free instances of v by any term t.
$\underline{A_{t/v};}$
$(\exists v \ A);$

The ∃-*left* rule states that an existentially quantified hypothesis can be replaced by some arbitrary instance.

∃–*left*
$A_{t/v}$ is the result of replacing all free instances of v by a fresh name t.
$\underline{A_{t/v_2} >> P;}$
$(\exists v\, A) >> P;$

In justification, consider the proposition; '$\exists x\ man(x)$'. As one of a list of assumptions, this statement may be replaced by '$man(c)$' as long as 'c' is fresh. The validity of this move can be justified by pointing out that if we know that something is a man, then there is no harm in stating 'and let c be the man in question', provided that no assumptions are smuggled in about c.

18.5 Proof Trees and Goal Stacks

Framed in terms of sequents, each inference rule maps a sequent S to a series of sequents $S_1,...,S_n$ where S is valid if $S_1,...,S_n$ are all valid. Such a process can be represented in the form of a **tree**, a familiar computing data structure, whereby S is a node and $S_1,...,S_n$ are daughter nodes. In automated deduction, S is sometimes called the **goal** and $S_1,...,S_n$ are **subgoals**. In order to avoid an infinite regress, it must be supposed that some sequents can be treated as valid without generating daughter nodes.

A **proof tree** is a labelled tree which at the root contains the sequent that is to be solved, sometimes called the **proof obligation**. The labels on the tree are the inference rules to be invoked in the proof. When a sequent is solved then that path on the tree is sealed with ◻. Figure 18.2 shows a sequent proof from our version of PC.

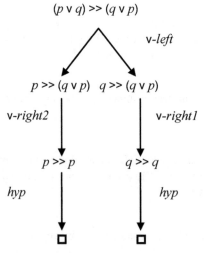

Figure 18.2 A tree proof of $(p \lor q) >> (q \lor p)$

224

In producing a proof with the aid of a computer, at any stage in a the proof, the computer will be trying to prove one of the nodes on the proof tree. A simple way of keeping track of them is to place them all in a list and work from the front. Such a list is a **stack**; i.e. a series of elements in which elements are always added (pushed) or removed (popped) from the front. A stack to keep track of goals in a proof is a **goal stack**. Every proof begins with the proof obligation as the only goal on the goal stack. At any stage in the proof, the only available goal is the goal at the front of the stack.

It is important to see the difference between a proof tree and a goal stack. A proof tree keeps the entire history of the proof process, including the proof obligation that started the proof off. The goal stack only keeps those goals that remain to be solved. At the end of the proof, the proof tree is a record of the way the proof was done. At the end of proof, the goal stack is merely an empty stack. A proof tree does not correspond to a single stack, but rather a series of stacks, where each stack results from its predecessor by some act of inference. A goal stack is thus a snapshot of the leaves of a growing proof tree. This is illustrated in figure 18.3, which shows how a proof tree changes and grows in relation to the goal stack.

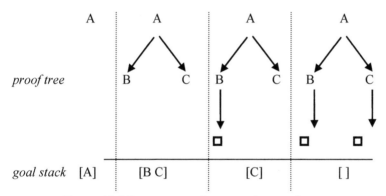

Figure 18.3 Representing the state of a proof tree using a stack

The computational advantages of a goal stack are that it is simple to represent as a list, and efficient in terms of memory usage, since it does not retain those parts of the proof tree which are irrelevant to the completion of the proof. Shen maintains such a stack in the implementation of type checking.

18.6 Implementing a Stack Based System: Proplog

We'll now look at the implementation of a very simple stack based reasoning program based on a very simple logic called **Proplog** (Maier and Warren (1988)). Proplog is a subset of PC suitable for automated reasoning on the computer. In fact Proplog is precisely the propositional subset of **Horn clause logic,** (studied in chapter 25), an important subset of first-order logic and significant for forming the basis of logic programming and type checking in Shen.

We introduce Proplog here as a way of both preparing the ground for the examination of Horn clause logic in chapter 25 and to illustrate the implementation of a stack-based sequent theorem prover. The syntax of Proplog is simple.

1. A propositional variable on its own is a formula of Proplog. This is generally referred to as an **atom** or a **fact** in logic programming
2. A conjunction of Proplog atoms is a Proplog formula
3. If A is either a conjunction of Proplog atoms or an atom and B is an atom then (A → B) is a Proplog formula. This is referred to as a **rule** in logic programming.

If we allow first-order atoms to supplant Proplog atoms then what we derive is precisely Horn clause logic.

There are three sequent rules for Proplog

hyp

$$\overline{P >> P;}$$

→-left
$$\frac{(P \rightarrow Q) >> P;}{(P \rightarrow Q) >> Q;}$$

&-right
$$\frac{P;\ Q;}{(P \& Q);}$$

A Proplog context consists of a set of rules and facts and a Proplog succeedent is an atom or a conjunction of atoms. In order to automate Proplog inferencing on the computer, a **control strategy** had to be developed for applying these inference rules. The simplest strategy is to place the proof obligation $\Delta >> Q$ on a stack **S** and perform **backward chaining** (figure 18.4).

A Backward Chaining Proof Procedure for Proplog

Do until success or failure

1. If S = [] signal success and halt.
2. If S = [S_1 | S_n] and S_1 = Δ >> Q then
    a. If Q $\in$ Δ set S to S_n. (*hyp*)
    b. If Q = (Q_1 & Q_2), set S to [Δ >> Q_1; Δ >> Q_2; | S_n] (*&-right*).
    c. If (P $\rightarrow$ Q) $\in$ Δ, set S to [Δ >> P; | S_n] (*$\rightarrow$-left*).
    d. Else signal failure and halt.

Figure 18.4 The Proplog proof procedure

Here is a simple schematic problem to illustrate the approach. The assumptions are

$(p \rightarrow q)$, $(r \rightarrow q)$, $((s \& t) \rightarrow r)$, $(u \rightarrow r)$, $((s \& v) \rightarrow r)$, v, s.

We can prove q by backward chaining as follows:-

Begin with *q*.
  Prove *q* by proving *r*.
   Prove *r* by proving (*s* & *v*).
    Prove *s*.
    Prove *v*.
    Signal success and halt.

As a proof tree this is shown in figure 18.5.

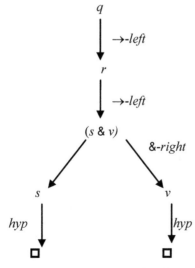

Figure 18.5 A completed proof tree

The snag comes in programming the computer to do proofs like this, because in the above proof we unconsciously avoided the obvious dead ends (like trying to prove q by using $(p \rightarrow q)$). These dead-ends are called **failure nodes** and are sometimes marked by a single daughter node ■. A failure node is a node of the proof tree which cannot be closed with a □, nor can it be extended to produce subgoals. A proof tree cannot count as a completed proof if it contains a failure node.

Since the computer has no intelligence of its own, we need to program some technique into it to avoid being stuck in failure nodes. The problem is that our proof procedure is non-deterministic; it assumes that the right choice of rule is always made without providing any means of finding it.

The solution we will follow is to order all the choices open to the computer and try each one in the ordering, backtracking if needed to try a new choice. The backtracking we will use is chronological backtracking to the last point at which a goal was solved.

Implementing a backward chaining inference engine of the kind needed is an eleven line program in Shen (figure 18.6). To make things even easier for us, we arrange to maintain the context as a separate argument because the nature of the proof process in Proplog means that the context never changes.

```
(define backchain
  Context Succeedent  -> (backchain* Succeedent Context Context))
```

```
(define backchain*
  P [P |_] _ -> true \\ hyp
  [P & Q] _ Context
  -> (and (backchain* P Context Context)
          (backchain* Q Context Context)) \\ &-right
  Q [[P => Q] | Hypotheses] Context
  -> (or (backchain* P Context Context) \\ →-left
          (backchain* Q Hypotheses Context)) \\ choice point!
  Q [_ | Hypotheses] Context -> (backchain* Q Hypotheses Context)
  _ _ _ -> false)
```

Figure 18.6 Backward chaining for Proplog implemented in Shen

18.7 Soundness and Completeness

Our little program is an example of an **inference engine** or **theorem-prover** for Proplog. A theorem-prover is a program that is designed to automate the process of formal proof. Let us write $\Delta \gg_{Proplog} P$ to mean that from a context Δ, the conclusion P can be derived by the rules of inference for Proplog. Let us write $\Delta \gg_{program} P$ when P can be derived from Δ using our program. What is the relation between $\gg_{Proplog}$ and $\gg_{program}$? One desirable relation is

228

If $\Delta \gg_{program} P$ then $\Delta \gg_{Proplog} P$

This should certainly be true for any Δ and P; if our program says that P follows from Δ, then, according to the rules of inference for Proplog, we should be able to derive P from Δ. A theorem-prover which has this property is said to be **sound**. The converse relation is

If $\Delta \gg_{Proplog} P$ then $\Delta \gg_{program} P$

A theorem-prover with this property is said to be **complete**. If a theorem-prover is both sound and complete and guaranteed to terminate then it constitutes a decision procedure for the formal system in question. If no such theorem-prover exists then the system is said to **undecidable**.

Backward chaining with chronological backtracking is complete as a proof procedure provided that:-

1. there is no proof tree which has a branch which can be grown to infinity and
   …
2. … at any stage in a proof there are only a finite number of ways that the proof tree can be grown.

Our theorem-prover for Proplog is sound but incomplete because condition 1. is not met. For example, the problem

$$(backchain\ [[p => q]\ [r => q]\ [q => r]\ [[s\ \&\ v] => r]\ v\ s]\ r)$$

causes an infinite loop, even though the conclusion is derivable from the assumptions according to the rules of inference of Proplog. The reason why is that assumptions [r => q] [q => r] are used by our theorem-prover to backward chain from r to form a branch which can be infinitely extended.

$$r \longrightarrow q \longrightarrow r \longrightarrow q \longrightarrow r \longrightarrow \ \ldots\ldots$$

The construction of a complete and terminating theorem-prover for Proplog requires detecting and trapping these loops; a not too difficult problem that is left as an exercise to this chapter.

Exercise 18

1. Give proof trees for the following

    a. $\forall x\ (F(x) \rightarrow \sim G(x))$, $\forall x(H(x) \rightarrow G(x)) \gg \forall x\ F(x) \rightarrow \sim(H(x))$
    b. $\forall x\ (F(x) \vee G(x)) \rightarrow H(x)$, $\forall x \sim(H(x)) \gg \forall x \sim F(x)$
    c. $\forall x(G(x) \rightarrow \sim H(x))$, $\exists x(F(x)\ \&\ G(x)) \gg \exists x\ F(x)\ \&\ \sim(H\ (x))$
    d. $\forall x(F(x) \vee G(x)) \rightarrow H(x)$, $\exists x \sim(H(x)) \gg \exists x \sim(F\ (x))$
    e. $\forall x \forall y \forall z\ F(x,y,z) \gg \forall z \forall y \forall x\ F(x,y,z)$
    f. $\forall x \exists y \forall z F(x,y,z) \gg \forall x \forall z \exists y F(x,y,z)$
    g. $\exists x \exists y \forall z\ F(x,y,z) \gg \forall z \exists y \exists x\ F(x,y,z)$
    h. $\gg \exists y \exists x(F(x)) \rightarrow (F(y)))$
    i. $\gg \forall x \exists y(R(x,y) \rightarrow \exists x \exists y R(x,y))$
    j. $R(x,x)$, $\forall x \forall y \forall z((R(x,y)\ \&\ R(y,z)) \rightarrow R(x,z))$
        $\gg \forall x \forall y(R(x,y) \rightarrow \sim(R(y,x)))$
    k. $\gg \exists y(\exists x(F(x)) \rightarrow (F(y)))$

2. Write a proof assistant for FOL based on the rules given here.

3. *Can you to some degree automate your proof assistant so that it gives advice on what to do or even does it for you?

Further Reading

The best introduction to the material in this chapter is Tarver (2014).

The sequent based notation used to define types in Shen was introduced by Gentzen (1934), and Diller (1990) and Duffy (1991) provide good introductions to the use of this notation in modern logic.

There are many introductions on FOL including Hodges (1977) which is based on (non-automated) tableau. For a natural deduction treatment see Lemmon (1978); and Mendelson (1987) for a Hilbert (or axiomatic) approach. Smullyan (1968) and Fitting (1990) deals with tableau; Fitting provides Prolog code for implementing it. Beckert and Posegga (1997) implement a high-performance Prolog version.

Tarver (1992) described a machine learning algorithm to get the computer to learn to use sequent calculus. The experiment was conducted on a theorem-prover for PC and uses genetic programming techniques. Lopes (1998) developed this algorithm for a range of systems including modal, intuitionistic and second-order logics and showed that in certain cases, the computer-generated programs were superior to the humanly created ATPs for the same logic.

Proof assistants based on sequent calculus include, Gordon, Milner and Wadsworth (1979)., Constable et al (2012) and Paulson (1990). Milner was responsible for introducing the idea of tactics for proof assistants that automated proof steps in a type secure way.

19 Concrete Types

19.1 Enumeration Types

In the previous chapter, we covered the elements of sequent calculus. In this chapter, we begin to use sequent calculus to define types within programs beginning with the simplest type - an **enumeration type.** There are a finite number of inhabitants of an enumeration type which are given by stating each one. For example the days of the week can be stated as an enumeration type.

if $x \in \{$"Monday", "Tuesday", "Wednesday", "Thursday", "Friday", "Saturday", "Sunday"$\}$
    then x : day

Written in sequent calculus, this statement emerges as seven axioms

---
"Monday" : day;

"Tuesday" : day;

"Wednesday" : day;

"Thursday" : day;

"Friday" : day;

"Saturday" : day;

"Sunday" : day;

In Shen derivation rules are entered in the form (datatype *<name>* *<derivation rules>*), where the *<name>* is a symbol and the *<derivation rules>* are written in sequent notation. Conventionally the name of the datatype is generally used as *<name>*. A notational convenience is that Shen does not require typings (i.e. expressions of the form X : A) to be entered with the outer brackets in datatype definitions. The underlines in are represented in Shen by 3 or more underscores

---.

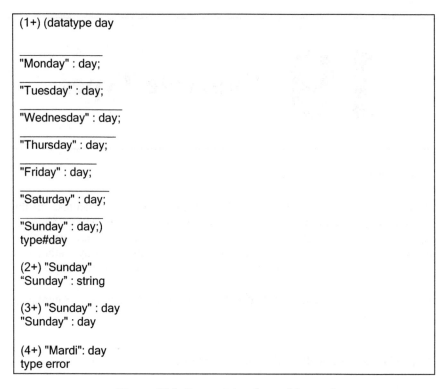

```
(1+) (datatype day

  _____
  "Monday" : day;
  _____
  "Tuesday" : day;
  _____
  "Wednesday" : day;
  _____
  "Thursday" : day;
  _____
  "Friday" : day;
  _____
  "Saturday" : day;
  _____
  "Sunday" : day;)
type#day

(2+) "Sunday"
"Sunday" : string

(3+) "Sunday" : day
"Sunday" : day

(4+) "Mardi": day
type error
```

Figure 19.1 Recognising days of the week

The effect of this datatype definition is to allow these strings to be of more than one type: "Sunday" is both of type string and of type day. This string now exhibits overloading or what Strachey called *ad hoc polymorphism* mentioned in chapter 17. It belongs to two types which are not instances of any type less general than the universal type A which is the type of all objects that have some type or other.

Entering "Sunday" to the Shen top level returns the verdict that "Sunday" : string. Given that "Sunday" is overloaded, Shen always defaults to the base type if possible. To get Shen to agree that "Sunday" is now also of type day, a typing must be entered (figure 19.1).

The definition works, but 7 axioms occupy a deal of space which was not reflected in our set theory notation. Side conditions enable derivation rules to be condensed. There are two forms of side condition in Shen – **tests** and **local assignments**; we deal with the use of local assignments in 19.7 but by far the most common side conditions are tests.

A test side condition uses the if keyword which, placed before the derivation rule and followed by some boolean expression *E* creates a side condition. If *E* evaluates to false when the derivation rule is applied, then the derivation rule fails in its application. Figure 19.2 shows the use of a test to shorten the definition of the datatype day.

```
(datatype day

if (element? Day ["Monday" "Tuesday" "Wednesday"
                  "Thursday" "Friday" "Saturday" "Sunday"])
_____
Day : day;)
```

Figure 19.2 Using a side condition to simplify a definition

Once we have defined day, we can define month.

```
(datatype month

if (element? Month ["January" "February" "March"  "April"
                    "May" "June" "July" "August" "September"
                    "October" "November" "December"])
_____
Month : month;)
```

And we can easily write a function that maps a number from 1-12 to a month.

```
(define decode-month
  {number --> month}
  1 -> "January"
  2 -> "February"
  3 -> "March"
  4 -> "April"
  5 -> "May"
  6 -> "June"
  7 -> "July"
  8 -> "August"
  9 -> "September"
  10 -> "October"
  11 -> "November"
  12 -> "December")
```

Side conditions permit us to define types where itemising each inhabitant by name is unacceptable for practical purposes. For example, we might have a list of 50,000 employees in a file and wish to define an employee as a member of this list.

```
(datatype employee

        if (element? E (read-file "employees.txt"))
        _____
        E : employee;)
```

233

It is also common to find that **intervals** are commonly used in programming because it often transpires that an entry must fall within a certain interval to be admitted for computation. For example, we may insist that employees must be aged between 18 and 64.

```
(datatype age

if (number? Age)
if (>= Age 18)
if (<= Age 64)
_____
Age : age;)
```

Figure 19.3 Age as an interval type

These formulations have in common with enumeration types the feature that their specification can be done using only axioms; we can call them **axiomatic types** of which enumeration types are a special case.

19.2 Left and Right Rules

Enumeration types are the simplest examples of defined types and employ only axioms in their formulation. More complex types require derivation rules that are not axioms. We consider as a case in point a database system for a company which holds employee details, including the department in which they work.

The list of acceptable departments is [wages recruitment sales advertising]. We add this as an enumeration type to the previous types

```
(datatype department

if (element? D [wages recruitment sales advertising])
_____
D : department;)
```

An employee record is a list composed of a name (a string), an age (a number) and a department (a symbol) in which the person works. Our database is a list of such records. We want a database retrieval function get-age which given a person's name and our database extracts the person's age from it.

A record is a list, but it is not a homogeneous list, being composed of three different types. We need to define it and we wish to assert proposition Φ

Φ: [N A D] : record if and only if N : string and A : age and D : department

Such an assertion cannot be made within an axiom but requires premises. In sequent notation we write (datatype record

  N : string; A : age; D : department;
  [N A D] : record;)

Now equipped we write our get-age function

(define get-age
  {string --> (list record) --> age}
  _ [] -> (error "no details for this name~%")
  N [[N A D] | _] -> A
  N [_ | Records] -> (get-age N Records))

When we enter this function to Shen we get the result

type error in rule 2 of get-age

Why has this happened? The answer is that our derivation rule is too weak to capture the 'if and only if' in Φ. What we have asserted is Φ_R.

    Φ_R: if N : string and A : age and D : department then [N A D] : record

To validate our function we need more information. Line 2 states

N [[N A D] | _] -> A

But by knowing [N A D] : record we cannot deduce A : age according to what we have entered. To complete the formalisation we have to add that from [N A D] : record as an hypothesis we can derive N : name and A : age and D : department. We want to capture

    Φ_L: if [N A D] : record then N : string and A : age and D : department

The second rule captures the other side of the equivalence

(datatype record

  N : string; A : age; D : department;
  [N A D] : record;

  N : string, A : age, D : department >> P;
  [N A D] : record >> P;)

Now the function checks and compiles. Note that commas separate the hypotheses in the premise.

Looking at what we have done, we have in fact treated records in the same manner in which logical constants were treated in the previous chapter. To complete the definition of a record we have had to construct a right rule and a left rule. The original rule was a R rule, dealing with decomposing record types in the consequent. The rule above is a L rule, dealing with the decomposition of the record type as a hypothesis. Both are needed to make the program work.

Symmetrical right-left pairs like this are very common and Shen uses the Clarke-Reeves shorthand introduced in chapter 18 to combine such rules into an LR rule. Because of keyboard restrictions the double underlines are replaced by three or more equals signs.

(datatype record

N : string; A : age; D : department;
===========================
[N A D] : record;)

There is an alternative way of doing all this; represent records as tuples. A record is then an object of type (string * age * department) and get-age becomes.

(define get-age
  {string --> (list (string * age * department)) --> age}
  _ [] -> (error "no details for this name~%")
  N [(@p N A D) | _] -> A
  N [_ | Records] -> (get-age N Records))

This works fine, although typing '(string * age * department)' is rather a bore compared to typing 'record'. Shen permits us to define our own shorthand for types. (synonyms $t_1,...,t_n$) where n is even defines a shorthand for types so that every t_i, where i is odd, is a symbol and every t_{i+1} is the type which defines it. Hence we can avoid always typing '(string * age * department)' by entering at the top of any file containing our program.

(synonyms record (string * age * department))

After this Shen will **demodulate** (replace) record within every type entered or loaded by (string * age * department). The two techniques seem almost equivalent in effect and for most cases they are, however there are subtle differences between using an LR rule to define a type and using synonyms. The latter is rather stronger as we shall see in the next section.

19.3 Handling Global Variables

Global variables need to be declared with respect to their type. To declare a global variable *test* to be of type (list number), the type of the value of *test* has to be declared of type (list number).

(datatype some-globals

(value *test*) : (list number);)

236

An interesting example provided by Aditya Siram shows how using synonyms differs from using the corresponding LR rule. Siram defined *test* as

(datatype some-globals

_____

(value *test*) : numbers;)

Where numbers was taken as a synonym for (list number). However the expression (head (value *test*)) did not return a number as expected but a type error.

The source of the error was the definition of numbers which was defined as

X : (list number);
=============
X : numbers;

This definition is equivalent to

X : (list number) >> P;
X : numbers >> P;

X : (list number);
X : numbers;

Here the first (L) rule is no use to the proof of (head (value *test*)) : number. Let us try to prove (head (value *test*)) : number from (value *test*) : numbers, the R rule above and the type for head. Applying the rule for head first derives (value *test*) : (list number) which cannot be proved by the R rule. However if the ordering of the LR rule was reversed to

X : numbers;
============
X : (list number);

then (head (value *test*)) would typecheck. But far better is to declare numbers and (list number) to be synonyms.

(synonyms numbers (list number))

The example shows two important things. First that LR rules are not indifferent with respect to ordering;   these two forms are not equivalent

$$\frac{\alpha}{\beta} \quad \text{and} \quad \frac{\beta}{\alpha}$$

Second an LR rule is not logically equivalent to the corresponding synonyms declaration; these two forms are not equivalent.

(synonyms α β)   and   α
                                    ===
                                    β

19.4 Recursive Types (I): the Lambda Calculus

The user-defined types studied so far are non-recursive; they consist either of atoms or finite or homogeneous sequences of non-recursive objects. But some of the data objects manipulated in the previous chapters are not like that. We shall look at two cases from the previous chapters.

1. The lambda calculus interpreter of chapter 14.
2. The Proplog theorem prover of chapter 18.

The lambda calculus interpreter was designed to evaluate lambda expressions represented as nested lists. To type check such a program we need to manipulate recursive types.

The simplest lambda expression is a symbol which is not lambda. An application is a two element list [*x y*] where *x* and *y* are lambda expressions and an abstraction is a three element list [lambda *x y*] where *x* is a symbol which is not lambda and *y* is a lambda expression. Figure 19.4 lays this out in Shen. The fact that lambda-expr occurs both in the premises and the conclusion of the last two rules defining it marks out lambda-expr as recursive.

(datatype lambda-expr

        if (not (= X lambda))
        X : symbol;
        _____
        X : lambda-expr;

        X : lambda-expr; Y : lambda-expr;
        =========================
        [X Y] : lambda-expr;

        if (not (= X lambda))
        X : symbol; Y : lambda-expr;
        =====================
        [lambda X Y] : lambda-expr;)

Given this type we can annotate the lambda calculus evaluator of chapter 14 with the right types (19.4).

238

```
(define aor
  {lambda-expr --> lambda-expr}
  [lambda V [E V]] -> E        where (not (free? V E))
  [lambda X Y] -> [lambda X (aor Y)]
  [[lambda X Y] Z] -> (let Alpha (alpha [lambda X Y])
                        (aor (beta Alpha (aor Z))))
  [X Y] -> (let AOR (type [(aor X) (aor Y)] lambda-expr)
             (if (= AOR [X Y])
                 AOR
                 (aor AOR)))
  X -> X)

(define free?
  {lambda-expr --> lambda-expr --> boolean}
  V V -> true
  V [lambda V _] -> false
  V [lambda _ Y] -> (free? V Y)
  V [X Y] -> (or (free? V X) (free? V Y))
  _ _ -> false)

(define alpha
  {lambda-expr --> lambda-expr}
  [lambda X Y] -> (let V (gensym x)
                    [lambda V (replace X (alpha Y) V)])
  [X Y] -> [(alpha X) (alpha Y)]
  X -> X)

(define beta
  {lambda-expr --> lambda-expr --> lambda-expr}
  [lambda X Y] Z -> (replace X Y Z))

(define replace
  {lambda-expr --> lambda-expr --> lambda-expr --> lambda-expr}
  X [lambda X Y] _ -> [lambda X Y]
  X X Z -> Z
  X [Y Y*] Z -> [(replace X Y Z) (replace X Y* Z)]
  X [lambda Y Y*] Z -> [lambda Y (replace X Y* Z)]
  _ Y _ -> Y)
```

Figure 19.4 A type secure lambda calculus evaluator

A demonstration.

```
(5+) (aor [[lambda x x] a])
a : lambda-expr

(6+) (aor [[lambda x [x x]] a])
[a a] : lambda-expr

(7+) (aor [[lambda x [lambda y x]] y])
[lambda x1220 y] : lambda-expr
```

239

19.5 Recursive Types (II): Proplog

This example is a little more complex than the lambda calculus case; mainly because there is an asymmetry between Proplog succeedents and the hypotheses used to process them. Succeedents are essentially conjunctions or atoms, but hypotheses are either atoms or implications.

Let's begin by tackling atoms and conjunctions. A Proplog atom is a symbol other than & or =>.

```
if (not (element? P [& =>]))
P : symbol;
P : atom;
```

We make atoms a limiting case of conjunctions – a conjunction with only one proposition in it.

```
P : atom;
P : conjunction;
```

In all other cases a conjunction is defined recursively

```
P : conjunction; Q : conjunction;
========================
[P & Q] : conjunction;
```

An implication is one form of hypothesis; being composed of an conjunction, an implication sign and an atom.

```
P : conjunction; Q : atom;
==================
[P => Q] : hypothesis;
```

An hypothesis can be an atom.

```
P : atom;
P : hypothesis;
```

Putting all this into a datatype definition and entering it allows the program of chapter 18 to be type checked. Notice that == is used in this program to test the equality of objects under different types.

```
(define backchain
  {(list hypothesis) --> conjunction --> boolean}
  Context Succeedent -> (backchain* Succeedent Context Context))

(define backchain*
  {conjunction --> (list hypothesis) --> (list hypothesis) --> boolean}
  P [Q | _] _ -> true          where (== P Q) \\ hyp
  [P & Q] _ Context
  -> (and (backchain* P Context Context)
          (backchain* Q Context Context))  \\ &-right
  Q [[P => Q] | Hypotheses] Context
  -> (or (backchain* P Context Context)  \\ &-left
         (backchain* Q Hypotheses Context))  \\ choice point!
  Q [_ | Hypotheses] Context -> (backchain* Q Hypotheses Context)
  _ _ _ -> false)
```

Figure 19.5 Proplog as a type secure program

A short demonstration.

```
(5+) (backchain [p q [[p & q] => r]] r)
true : boolean

(6+) (backchain [[s => r] p [p => q] [q => r]] r)
true : boolean

(7+) (backchain [[s => r] [p => q] [q => r]] r)
false : boolean
```

19.6 Dynamic Type Checking

We now consider the simulation of a simple calculator. Our calculator program takes numbers or lists and evaluates them to a number result (figure 19.6). Having loaded the program and set it running, we can calculate the answers to problems like [88.9 + 8.7] and [56.8 * [45.3 - 21.7]].

```
(define do-calculation
  [X + Y] -> (+ (do-calculation X) (do-calculation Y))
  [X - Y] -> (- (do-calculation X) (do-calculation Y))
  [X * Y] -> (* (do-calculation X) (do-calculation Y))
  [X / Y] -> (/ (do-calculation X) (do-calculation Y))
  X -> X)
```

Figure 19.6 A calculator function

However, as soon as type checking is switched on, entering the program produces a type error, because do-calculation is designed to deal with mixed lists and strong typing does not allow such lists. Recursive types provide a way of tackling this problem (figure 19.7).

```
(datatype arith-expr

    X : number;
    X : arith-expr;

    if (element? Op [+ - * /])
    X : arith-expr; Y : arith-expr;
    =========================
    [X Op Y] : arith-expr;)
```

Figure 19.7 An attempt at defining a datatype of arithmetic expressions

Armed with these datatype rules, we define our calculator (figure 19.8).

```
(2+) (define do-calculation
    {arith-expr --> arith-expr}
    [X + Y] -> (+ (do-calculation X) (do-calculation Y))
    [X - Y] -> (- (do-calculation X) (do-calculation Y))
    [X * Y] -> (* (do-calculation X) (do-calculation Y))
    [X / Y] -> (/ (do-calculation X) (do-calculation Y))
    X -> X)
type error: rule 1 of do-calculation
```

Figure 19.8 An erroneous attempt to produce a type secure calculator

do-calculation fails to type check because + produces numbers and not arith-exprs as required by our type assignment. Suppose we change the type of do-calculation to arith-expr → number.

```
(3+) (define do-calculation
    {arith-expr --> number}
    [X + Y] -> (+ (do-calculation X) (do-calculation Y))
    [X - Y] -> (- (do-calculation X) (do-calculation Y))
    [X * Y] -> (* (do-calculation X) (do-calculation Y))
    [X / Y] -> (/ (do-calculation X) (do-calculation Y))
    X -> X)
type error: rule 5 of do-calculation
```

Figure 19.9 Another erroneous attempt to produce a type secure calculator

Now the final rewrite rule fails to typecheck because Shen finds that it cannot prove that the input X is a number from the assumption that X is an arith-expr (remember that our rules say that all numbers are arith-exprs; not that all arith-exprs are numbers).

Our solution is to use a **tag** to mark out the numbers within an arith-expr. Figure 19.10 introduces the tag num as a way of marking out numbers.

242

```
(datatype  arith-expr

        X : number >> Y : A;
        [num X] : arith-expr >> Y : A;

        X : number;
        [num X] : arith-expr;

        if (element? Op [+ - * /])
        X : arith-expr; Y : arith-expr;
        =====================
        [X Op Y] : arith-expr;)
```

Figure 19.10 Using tags

This solution works with the following definition of do-calculation.

```
(define do-calculation
    {arith-expr --> number}
    [X + Y] -> (+ (do-calculation X) (do-calculation Y))
    [X - Y] -> (- (do-calculation X) (do-calculation Y))
    [X * Y] -> (* (do-calculation X) (do-calculation Y))
    [X / Y] -> (/ (do-calculation X) (do-calculation Y))
    [num X] -> X)
```

The use of tags makes for confusing reading - typing in [[num 2] + [num 3]] is a counterintuitive way of adding 2 and 3. **Verified objects** make life easier.   A verified object is an object that inhabits the type verified.   The inhabitation rule for this type is: X : verified just when the normal form of X is true. No self-evaluating object of Shen is recognised as belonging to this type - not even true! At this point you will wonder what the point of such a type is.

Actually, this type is very useful.   When Shen dynamically type checks definitions that include guards, it assumes that if the rule fires, then the guard must evaluate to true and hence Shen assumes that, in that circumstance, the guard is of the type verified. For instance, we can assume that if an input X passes the guard (number? X) (which tests for numberhood) that X is a number so, we can write:

$$\overline{\text{(number? X) : verified} >> \text{X : number;}}$$

If we insert this rule in the datatype rules for arith-expr, and place a guard in the do-calculation function, then the whole thing typechecks.

```
(datatype arith-expr

_____
(number? X) : verified >> X : number;

X : number;
X : arith-expr;

if (element? Op [+ - * /])
X : arith-expr; Y : arith-expr;
=====================
[X Op Y] : arith-expr;)

(define do-calculation
  {arith-expr --> number}
  [X + Y] -> (+ (do-calculation X) (do-calculation Y))
  [X - Y] -> (- (do-calculation X) (do-calculation Y))
  [X * Y] -> (* (do-calculation X) (do-calculation Y))
  [X / Y] -> (/ (do-calculation X) (do-calculation Y))
  X -> X                    where (number? X))
```

Figure 19.11 A type secure version of do-calculation using verified objects

19.7 Analytic and Synthetic Rules

A sequent rule is **analytic** just when every variable that occurs above the line in the rule either occurs below the line or is bound in a local assignment using let. When a variable occurs above the line which neither occurs below the line nor is bound in a local assignment within a side condition then that variable is said to be **free**. An analytic rule is thus a rule that contains no free variables. Most datatype rules used in sequent rules are analytic, and in fact all the examples used so far are analytic rules.

A **synthetic** rule is a rule that is not analytic and thus does contain free variables. A simple example of such a rule is the rule defining couples which are two element lists of possibly diverse types.

```
X : A; Y : B;
[X Y] : couple;
```

In this definition A and B are free variables standing for any given type. Shen programmers working with advanced types will eventually encounter synthetic rules and should be aware of the pitfalls of dealing with them. There is nothing specifically toxic about such rules if they are properly understood, but one mistake is common with such rules.

In defining a synthetic rule, it is important to grasp the interplay between the free variables and their position in the sequent. For example it seems intuitive that

244

the proper definition of the type couple of two element list of different objects should be

```
X : A; Y : B;
=========
[X Y] : couple;
```

Recall that the double underline is really only a conventional shorthand and that the above rule is really asserting two inference rules.

```
X : A; Y : B;
[X Y] : couple;

X : A , Y : B >> P;
[X Y] : couple >> P;
```

However the second rule is wrong; it asserts that from the assumption that [X Y] : couple that X : A and Y : B for *any* A and for *any* B can be inferred. Essentially the free variables A and B now stand proxy for any type. The correct rule asserts that from the assumption that [X Y] : couple that X : A and Y : B for *some* A and for *some* B can be inferred.

Shen allows the use of local assignments within side conditions. Since the nature of A and B is not fixed; the correct rendition uses fresh to generate arbitrary placeholders for these types.

```
let A (fresh)
let B (fresh)
X : A , Y : B >> P;
[X Y] : couple >> P;
```

The new version uses local assignments to bind the free variables to arbitrary values indicating that the identity of A and B are not known. The new rule is now analytic.

19.8 Defining Polyadic Types

The square bracket notation in sequent calculus is syntactic sugar for a cons expression and the rules for expanding that notation into cons form were discussed in section 4.2. When we write

(datatype record

```
N : string; A : Age; D : department;
===========================
  [N A D] : record;)
```

we really mean

(datatype record

N : string; A : Age; D : department;
============================
(cons N (cons A (cons D []))) : record;)

Now there is a fact we must point out here which seem fairly obvious, but it is important. This fact is that these conses are not actually executed during the course of the proof. To put this in the parlance of logic, the function cons here is being *mentioned* and *not used*. But there are occasions in working with sequent calculus where we actually want to *use* cons during the construction of a proof.

A nice example of this was provided by the construction of a database program in Shen.[71] Part of this program involved the manipulation of records. A record is an entry in a database file; for example.

Name: Mark Tarver
Occupation: scholar
Age: 61
Nationality: British

or as a list structure

[" Mark Tarver" "scholar" 61 "British"]

In this system the type record represents the types of the contents of the record. The type of ["Mark Tarver" "scholar" 61 "British"] is (record string string number string). In order to formalise this, we have to create record as a polyadic type operator which takes as many types as there are elements in the record. This is where we need to actually *use* pattern directed list processing within the sequent calculus. To do this we use | within *round* brackets - a device not allowed elsewhere in Shen. When we do that we indicate that we are list processing inside the formalisation to express our meaning (figure 19.12).

(datatype rec

X : A;
===========
[X] : (record A);

X : A;
[Y | Z] : (record | As);
===================
[X Y | Z] : (record A | As);)

Figure 19.12 Using | to create a polyadic parametric type for records

---

[71] This example comes from work by Neal Alexander. For pedagogic reasons I have simplified his treatment which gained efficiency over lists by using vectors for records.

246

The significance of the rules in 19.12 is this. The first rule says that a record composed of a single element or **field** X has the type (record A) if X has the type A. The second rule says that [X Y | Z] has the type (record A | As) if X has the type A and [Y | Z] has the type (record | As). Here we are *using* | to divide up the list of types. (record A | As) does not mean what [rec A | As] does. Using [record A | As] would create a very strange type with conses in it - not what we need.

A test shows our definition works.

```
(2+)  [1 a v]
[1 a v] : (record number symbol symbol)
```

We can now go on to define selector functions that isolate fields from records in our database.

```
(define name
  {(record string string number string) --> string}
    [Name _ _ _] -> Name)

(define occupation
  {(record string string number string) --> string}
    [_ Occupation _ _] -> Occupation)

(define age
  {(record string string number string) --> number}
    [_ _ Age _] -> Age)

(define nationality
  {(record string string number string) --> string}
    [_ _ _ Nationality] -> Nationality)
```

Figure 19.13 Selector functions for a polyadic record type

Exercise 19

1. Define the enumeration type coin for British coinage and type check the next-denomination function in chapter 3 using this type (count 0 as of type coin for this question).

2. Define a type wff for propositional calculus based on the rules for PC given in chapter 18.

3. Using your rules in 1 define a *sequent* as a pair ((list wff) * wff) composed of a list of *hypotheses* and a *conclusion*. A *problem* is a list of sequents. An inference rule for PC takes a problem and outputs a problem. For example &R takes a problem where the sequent heading it has the form (@p Hyp [P & Q]) and replaces this sequent by two sequents (@p Hyp P) and (@p Hyp Q). Code the rules for PC and show that your functions have the type problem --> problem.

4. Extend your definition in 2 to incorporate first-order logic as described in chapter 18.

5. Code the quantifier rules and show that they have the type problem --> problem.

6. [a [b c d] [e] [f]] describes a tree

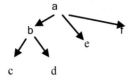

Define tree as a polymorphic type operator which can take a type argument; the type of the above is (tree symbol).

7. From your answer to 6 define

   a. A function leaves that takes an object of type (tree A) and returns a list of leaves of type (list A).
   b. A function size of type (tree A) --> number that returns the number of nodes in the tree.
   c. A function paths of type (tree A) --> (list (list A)) that returns all the paths from the root node.
   d. A function nodes of type (tree A) --> (list A) that returns the list of nodes in the tree.
   e. A function subtree? of type (tree A) --> (tree A) --> boolean that tests to see if the first argument is a subtree of the second. Here [b c d] is a subtree.
   f. A function prune of type (tree A) --> (tree A) --> (tree A) that removes the first argument as a subtree from the second.
   g. A function graft of type (A --> A --> boolean) --> (tree A) --> (tree A) that orders the daughters of every node by an ordering relation R so that if x precedes y as a daughter then Rxy.

8. Devise a database which takes employee records of the form Id (number), Name (string) Age (a number from 18 to 100), Position (worker, manager, tycoon), Wages (fixed as 10,000 for workers, 30,000 for managers and 1000,000 for tycoons). Create the following functions.

   h. A function find of type number --> database --> record that takes an id and the database and returns the record that holds the person's details.
   i. A function payroll of type database --> number that totals the wages for the company.
   j. A function level of type position --> (list string) that returns the list of all those people in that position in alphabetical order.
   k. A function year of type age --> (list string) that returns the list of all those people of that age in alphabetical order.

9. How would you recode 3. to make record a parametric type?

Further Reading

Enumeration types are found in all the main statically typed functional languages including ML (Wikstrom, 1988) and Haskell (Thompson, 1999). The use of sequent calculus to define types is not a feature of those languages and the algebraic approach (discussed in chapter 21) is used instead.

Web Sites

http://homepages.inf.ed.ac.uk/stg/NOTES/node79.html gives a good account of abstract datatypes in ML. http://www.haskell.org/haskellwiki/Abstract_data_type provides the equivalent for Haskell.

20 Proof and Control

Type checking is computationally expensive, sometimes involving hundreds of thousands of inferences for a single program. The Shen type checker executes at the rate of many thousands of such inferences per second, but even so there can be instances where the type checker spends a longer time than necessary validating the program. In some cases, type checking may be subject to timeout. This almost always occurs at the site of a type error; hence localising and fixing these errors is often the key to avoiding timeouts.

This chapter deals with techniques for controlling the search space in Shen type theories and improving the performance of type checking. Specifically we will

1. See how to adjust the timeout feature.
2. See how to use cuts to control the search space.
3. See how to use type annotations to guide the type checker and to improve the performance of our code.
4. How to use mode declarations to control potential infinite loops.
5. How to use the Shen spy tool for tracing the type checker at work.
6. How to order type rules to get the maximum performance.
7. The use of preclude and include to marshal type theories.

20.1 Controlling Timeout

By default Shen includes a timeout feature that cuts off the type checker when it has expended more than a million inferences in solving a problem. When this occurs, the process is aborted and the error

maximum inferences exceeded

is raised. In 9 out of 10 of cases, when this message arises then the type checker has encountered a type error and is backtracking furiously in an attempt to find some non-existent solution.

It is possible to reset the timout limit by the maxinferences function that receives a number *n* and sets the limit at *n*. However, generally, increasing *n* will have little effect other than to delay the return of a negative response. It is better at this point, to roll up one's sleeves and seek the source of the error.

20.2 Using spy to Trace Type Checking

When Shen raises a type error or experiences timeout then the messages it raises give a strong indication as to the location of the error.   If a type error is raised then the message

type error in rule n of f

is often raised. If you have experienced timeout, then the timeout message will be preceded by a series of messages about the functions that have been successfully type checked.   Hence your error will be certainly located immediately after the last expression that has been successfully type checked.

If you have examined the offending expression and cannot determine the source of the problem, then it is best to turn on the spy feature.

The spy feature is enabled by (spy +) and disabled by (spy -). When enabled, the spy feature will print off interactively the steps of reasoning that the type checker is making. At each step, spy will display the problem it is working on and pause the process.[72] Each step is printed as a sequent; that is, as a consequent to be proved and a list of hypotheses from which it is to be proven.

Starting with a simple example; we want to type check a list of two numbers [1 2]; the list is converted to cons form and printed out as a consequent (cons 1 (cons 2 ())) : Var2.   There are no hypotheses. The variable Var2 is a place holder for a type; the proof obligation is

Prove there exists a value for Var2 *such that* (cons 1 (cons 2 ())) : Var2

With spying enabled Shen prints out this problem.

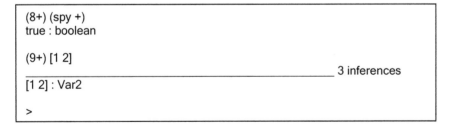

Figure 20.1 Tracing the type checker

---

[72] Typing ^ will abort type checking.

The proof will be a **constructive existence proof**; that is, we not only want to demonstrate that there is such a value, we want to do so by finding a specific value that does the job.[73] Hitting RETURN to the > prompt moves the proof on.

```
_____ 12 inferences
?- 1 : Var5
```

The proof now focuses on the first item; effectively Shen has applied the rule

X : A; Y : (list A);
_____
(cons X Y) : (list A);

Hitting RETURN moves the proof on again.

```
_____ 16 inferences
?- [2] : (list number)
```

The transition from the previous step to this one is important. The variable has disappeared and the type checker is hunting for a list of numbers. How did this happen? Effectively the type checker is armed with the following rule.

if (number? N)
_____
N : number;

The conclusion N : number is compared to the consequent of the previous problem which is 1 : Var5. The variable Var5 is bound to number and the binding is transmitted to the rest of the proof.

Once the type checker has grasped the right direction, the proof runs smoothly. The inference counter does not go up in increments of one, because Shen makes several low level inference steps which are not displayed here.

```
_____ 21 inferences
?- 2 : number

>
_____ 25 inferences
?- [] : (list number)

>
[1 2] : (list number)
```

---

[73] The difference can be thought of in these terms; if we are investigating a suspicious death we may prove that it was a murder and hence somebody was the murderer without knowing who. A constructive existence proof of the murder would produce the actual murderer.

252

Here is another example involving a simple numerical function

```
(4+) (define double
        {number --> number}
        N -> (* 2 N))
```
_____ 3 inferences
?- (define double {number --> number} N -> (* 2 N)) : Var2

>
_____ 23 inferences
?- &&N : number

1. &&N : Var9

>

We assume &NN is of type number and prove ((* 2) &&N) (the curried form) is of
type number. &&N is a placeholder for an arbitrary object.

_____ 33 inferences
?- ((* 2) &&N) : number

1. &&N : number

>
_____ 43 inferences
?- (* 2) : (Var15 --> number)

1. &&N : number

>
_____ 52 inferences
?- * : (Var17 --> (Var15 --> number))

1. &&N : number

>
_____ 55 inferences
?- 2 : number

1. &&N : number

>
_____ 59 inferences
?- &&N : number

1. &&N : number

(fn double : (number --> number)

Generally it is useful to place (spy +) into your file immediately before the expression that triggers the type failure. In that way spy is invoked only at the point of failure and not throughout the entire program.

20.3 Using Cuts

Suppose we have defined a type constant to mean any boolean, string, symbol or number. We can write this as follows.

(datatype constant

V : boolean;
_____
V : constant;

V : string;
_____
V : constant;

V : number;
_____
V : constant;

V : symbol;
_____
V : constant;)

constant is effectively a sum of a series of **subtypes** boolean, string etc. Moreover all these subtypes are disjoint because nothing can be an inhabitant of two different subtypes of constant. However if we track a proof involving constant, we find that in cases of type failure, the type checker will backtrack through all these cases even though success in one of these cases means that the remainder are not worth considering.

The **cut,** written !, controls the unrestricted backtracking so that these unnecessary cases are not considered. Syntactically, the cut will fit anywhere a premise will fit.

(datatype constant

V : boolean; !;
_____
V : constant;

V : string; !;
_____
V : constant;

V : number; !;
_____
V : constant;

V : symbol; !;
_____
V : constant;)

Figure 20.2 Using cuts in a datatype definition

254

Proof theoretically any goal which is a cut succeeds. However if the control backtracks to the point at which the cut was called, then all rules which are subsequent to the cut in the datatype in which the cut was invoked will not be considered as alternatives for that choice point.[74] Effectively the cut commits the type checker to the choice in which it occurs (figure 21.2).

The above cuts are **green** because they makes the process of proof more efficient but do not change what is derivable. A **red cut** changes what is derivable and is often the result of a mistake in the placing of !. Here is an example

(datatype constant

$$\frac{!; V : boolean;}{V : constant;}$$

$$\frac{!; V : string;}{V : constant;}$$

$$\frac{!; V : number;}{V : constant;}$$

$$\frac{!; V : symbol;}{V : constant;)}$$

Here as soon as the type checker encounters the first rule, the cut causes the proof to be committed to that choice *before* it is established that V is a boolean. Hence effectively the cut has eliminated all the other rules apart from the first one from the definition of constant.

Cuts can be placed before or after a premise and before or after the assumptions below the line in a sequent rule. For instance

$$\frac{}{(f \: X \: Y), !, (f \: Y \: Z) >> (f \: X \: Z);}$$

would commit the proof to looking for (f Y Z) when (f X Y) is encountered. This would fail the problem (f a b), (f a c), (f c d) >> (f a d) since (f a b) would be found and the search would commit to looking for (f b d).

20.4 Type Annotations

The 'function' type is one of the primitives in Kλ. type receives two arguments; first an expression e of some kind and secondly a type t. The result returned is the normal form of e, but if type checking is enabled, then the typechecker will

---

[74] Students of Prolog will recognise the similarity to the Prolog cut. In fact, the cut here is compiled into a Prolog cut. See chapters 25 and 27 for details.

typecheck *e* : *t*. Used within a function definition type places the constraint that *e* has to be proved to be of type *t* (figure 21.3).

```
(11 +) (type (+ 8 9) number)
17 : number

(12+) (type (+ 6 7) symbol)
type error

(13+) (define paren
        {A --> (list A)}
          X -> [(type X number)]])
type error in rule 2 of paren
```

Figure 20.3 Using type

In cases where the user wants to disambiguate his intention, it can be occasionally useful to annotate the program with this function. The scare quotes in the opening sentence to this section are an indication that type is not a function in the sense that append or cons are, but is a construction that is handled in a special way by the compiler – rather as define is.

20.5 preclude **and** include

The next method is a means for controlling large search spaces when there are a great many types in use. Generally in large Shen programs, the program is generally the product of more than one hand. In such a case, the programmer working on one part of the system might actually use only a fragment of the type discipline of the whole system. Nevertheless, the type checker, unless instructed, will slog through the program armed with the entire type system.

The commands preclude, include, preclude-all-but and include-all-but allow the programmer to optimise the type checker to the program at hand. Thus it is possible to have a massive type system in Shen and programs of many thousands of lines, and yet type check them in reasonable speed by configuring the type checker to ignore those types whose rules are not needed.

The command preclude accepts a list of symbols which are names of datatypes or synonyms and sets them aside from use in type checking. Placing the command (preclude [lazylist]) at the head of a file will cause the type checker to ignore the rules for the lazylist datatype. The command (include [lazylist]) works the opposite way, placing the rules back into the type environment. The command (preclude-all-but [lazylist]) will preclude all user defined datatypes apart from lazy lists, whereas (include-all-but [lazylist]) will include all user defined datatypes apart from lazy lists. Reasonably enough, (preclude-all-but [ ]) will set aside all user defined datatypes and (include-all-but [ ]) will include all of them.

20.6 Ordering Rules: Subtypes

A is a **subtype** of B when every *x* that inhabits A, inhabits B. We can say that integers are a subtype of numbers.

(datatype integer

if (integer? N)
_____
N : integer;

N : integer;
_____
N : number;)

This does the trick; but a more general method is to define subtype as a type operator

(datatype subtype

(subtype A B); X : A;
_____
 X : B;)

Figure 20.4 Defining subtype as a type operator

We can then simply write as an axiom

_____
(subtype integer number);

And then treat integers just like other numbers.

(8+) (+ (input+ integer) (input+ integer))
5
6
11 : number

The power and simplicity of this approach is beguiling; it does conceal one pitfall. It seems manifest to us that a list of integers is a list of numbers. But the following function does not typecheck.

(define listint->listnum
  {(list integer) --> (list number)}
  L -> L)

We get a type error; which *prima facie* we should not, since integers are simply a type of number. If we track this proof then we get the resulf in figure 20.5.

257

```
(3+) (define listint->listnum
       {(list integer) --> (list number)}
       L -> L)

_____ 21 inferences
?- &&L : (list integer)

1. &&L : Var15

>

_____ 27 inferences
?- &&L : (list number)

1. &&L : (list integer)

>

_____ 41 inferences
?- (subtype Var16 (list number))

1. &&L : (list integer)

>
type error in rule 1 of listint->listnum
```

Figure 20.5 A failure involving the subtype operator

In fact given that *A* is a subtype of *B* and *x* : (*f A*), the conclusion *x* : (*f B*) is not formally derivable from our subtype definition. We can define listint->listnum as a function that recursively coerces a list of integers to a list of numbers.

```
(define listint->numlist
  {(list integer) --> (list number)}
  [] -> []
  [N | Ns] -> [N | (listint->numlist Ns)])
```

Here since the list of integers is explicitly deconstructed item by item, the subtype rule applies to N.

Subtypes, whether explicitly defined using a subtype operator as in this example, or simply by listing the special cases are computationally expensive. The subtype rule given in figure 20.4 can be invoked at every stage of a proof. Even if we avoid explicitly using the subtype operator, injudicious ordering of the rules can cause inferences to stack up; as in the following example.

258

```
(datatype expr

      E : symbol;
      E : expr;

      E : number;
      E : expr;

      E : boolean;
      E : expr;

      E : string;
      E : expr;

      E : expr; Es : (list expr);
      ===================
      [E | Es] : expr;)
```

Given any problem of the form (cons *x* ... *y*) : expr, Shen will first attempt to prove that (cons *x* ... *y*) is a symbol, a number ... etc. before using the final LR rule to decompose the expression. In such cases significant improvement can be found by simply placing the LR rule first in these list of rules.

20.7 Controlling Infinite Loops: Mode Declarations

In section 20.3 we defined a type constant as composed of several subtypes. Melvin has a better idea; define a type operator union so that X : (union string symbol boolean number) states in one rule what took four separate rules to do previously. But what are the rules for union? Having learnt macros, Melvin decides to make union a 2-place type operator and rely on macros to insert the missing elements.

```
(defmacro union-macro
  [union W X Y | Z] -> [union W [union X Y | Z]])
```

So far, so good. Now the rules for union; Melvin knows that there should be a left and a right rule for union. Melvin's right rule states that you can prove X : (union A B) if you can prove X : A.

Rule a

```
X : A;
X : (union A B);
```

Spurred on, Melvin adds the other right rule

Rule b

```
X : B;
X : (union A B);
```

The left rule follows the familiar pattern for disjunction

Rule c

X : A >> P;
X : B >> P;
‾‾‾‾‾‾‾‾‾‾‾‾‾‾‾‾‾‾‾‾‾
X : (union A B) >> P;

Placing these all into a datatype definition; Melvin tries it out. At first it works beautifully.

```
(5+) [1 a]
[1 a] : (list (union number symbol))

(6+) (@v 1 a 2 b <>)
<1 a 2 b> : (vector (union number symbol))
```

But then when Melvin types an expression in that should produce an error, the type checker goes into an infinite loop and the top level topples over.

```
(7+) (* 1 a)

*** - Program stack overflow. RESET
*** - Program stack overflow. RESET
```

Now let's see, courtesy of spy, what happens when Shen is supplied with the rule for union and (* 1 a) is checked. The initial stages are routine, the expression is curried and checked as ((* 1) a).

```
(4+) (* 1 a)
‾‾‾‾‾‾‾‾‾‾‾‾‾‾‾‾‾‾‾‾‾‾‾‾‾‾‾‾‾‾‾‾‾‾‾‾‾‾‾  3 inferences
?- ((* 1) a) : Var2

>
‾‾‾‾‾‾‾‾‾‾‾‾‾‾‾‾‾‾‾‾‾‾‾‾‾‾‾‾‾‾‾‾‾‾‾‾‾‾‾  12 inferences
?- (* 1) : (Var5 --> Var2)

>
‾‾‾‾‾‾‾‾‾‾‾‾‾‾‾‾‾‾‾‾‾‾‾‾‾‾‾‾‾‾‾‾‾‾‾‾‾‾‾  17 inferences
?- * : (Var7 --> (Var5 --> Var2))

>
‾‾‾‾‾‾‾‾‾‾‾‾‾‾‾‾‾‾‾‾‾‾‾‾‾‾‾‾‾‾‾‾‾‾‾‾‾‾‾  20 inferences
?- 1 : number

>
‾‾‾‾‾‾‾‾‾‾‾‾‾‾‾‾‾‾‾‾‾‾‾‾‾‾‾‾‾‾‾‾‾‾‾‾‾‾‾  24 inferences
?- a : number
```

This proof obligation cannot be discharged, and after this point, the computer becomes involved in futile attempts to discharge the proof. None of these work and lead to an infinite regress. The reasons are clear in the structure of Melvin's rules. Let *x* be any expression which is not type secure (like ((* 1) a)). We begin by trying to constructively prove that *x* : V for some V. Since V is a variable we can invoke the conclusion of *rule a* on it; i.e.

X : (union A B);

and the new target is X : A – which when instantiated is just ((* 1) a) : A. But this conclusion is essentially just what we started with, except with a change of variable. Hence the computer repeats this move *ad infinitem*.

One way of stopping this is to constrain the inferences the computer is allowed to make using **mode declarations**.[75]

(datatype union

    <u>X : A;   </u>
    X : (- (union A B));

    <u>X : B;   </u>
    X : (- (union A B));

    X : A >> P;
    <u>X : B >> P;   </u>
    X : (- (union A B)) >> P;)

Figure 21.4 Using mode declarations

The mode declaration (- ...) enforces an exact match between the expression in its scope and what it is matched to. In effect, (union A B) cannot be matched to a variable. The consequence is that the bizarre loop goes away. The declaration (+ ...) restores the default and the innermost mode has priority. Thus (- (f (+ c) b)) would use the default over c but restricted matching over the rest of the formula.

This actually works quite nicely for functions that use Melvin's union types because the explicit typing attached to these functions means that union types appear explicitly in the type and unification is rarely needed. But [1 a] no longer typechecks as (union number symbol), since there is not an exact match. This problem can be circumvented by entering the expression as a typing [1 a] : (list (union A B)) which will trigger the appropriate search.

---

[75] Post 2020, Shen allows mode declarations of the form (- (union A B)) instead of (mode (union A B) -). The latter still works however.

20.8 Dependent Types

In the cases we have studied so far we have had typings in which terms and types are disjoint from each other. Types like boolean are found to the right of the colon, but not to the left. Terms like 1, 2, 3 are found to the left of the colon but not to the right. Terms may be built of smaller terms (terms depending on terms) and types may be built out of smaller types (parametric types). But the division of terms and types means that we do not have terms depending on types or types depending on terms.

In *dependent types*, these restrictions do not hold. We can have terms depending on types and types depending on terms. Let's have a look at the latter.

We'll construct a simple dependent parametric type (we'll see shortly our 'simple' type gets us into deep waters) called seq which takes two types. The first represents some numeric value within the natural numbers and the second is a type. seq functions rather like list except it contains a numeric value that indicates the length of the list. Here are the rules.

(datatype seq

$$\frac{}{[] : (seq\ 0\ A);}$$

$$\frac{X : A;\ Y : (seq\ N\ A);}{[X\ |\ Y] : (seq\ (+\ 1\ N)\ A);)}$$

seq is a dependent type since it uses terms (+ 0, 1) in its vocabulary. A quick test to shows it works.

```
(4+)  [a b c] : (seq N A)
[a b c] : (seq (+ 1 (+ 1 (+ 1 0))) symbol)

(5+) (define tlseq
        {(seq (+ 1 N) A) --> (seq N A)}
        [_ | Y] -> Y)
(fn tlseq) : ((seq (+ 1 N) A) --> (seq N A))
```

seq uses successor notation to represent numbers - (seq (+ 1 (+ 1 (+ 1 0)) symbol) rather than (seq 3 symbol). The reason for this is that performing an actual subtraction or addition on N is not possible, since the proof begins with N as a variable.

As soon as we get past these shallow waters and engage in significant problems with seq we run into problems. For example, we recognise that appending two sequences together gives a sequence whose size is the sum of the inputs. But if we ask the type checker to prove this, it cannot.

```
(define app
  {(seq M A) --> (seq N A) --> (seq (+ M N) A)}
  [] X -> X
  [X | Y] Z -> [X | (app Y Z)])
type error in rule 1 of app
```

In fact this problem requires an inductive proof over the natural numbers to be completed.

These problems arise from the limits of Shen's procedural interpretation of sequent calculus which was designed for fully automatic type inferencing. The sequent calculus in Shen allows you to *state* any type discipline you like; in fact, we know that Shen sequent calculus is a Turing equivalent notation in its own right. However being able to *state* whatever you like does not mean you can *prove* anything you like even if what you are trying to prove is theoretically provable from the rules given.

Shen *can* formalise dependent types in sequent calculus and engage in proofs of programs that use them. In fact, in the construction of a type theory for a graphical version of Shen, dependent types are part of the background type theory for the graphics. The widget command in that system has the type:

W : symbol; Options : (options Widget);
(widget W Widget Options) : Widget;

The asymmetry between what can be stated and what can be proved in Shen is reflected in what signatures attached to functions. Shen makes the simplifying assumptions that the types of the functions it has to prove are, syntactically, the kind that are found in ML. These signatures are then stored in a table.

But dependent types often require complex signatures that defy this restriction. For example the following function receives a type and returns a freely chosen object of that type.

(define enter
  Type -> (input+ Type))

Here a type occupies the term position. But we cannot formulate the type of this function in arrow notation. We can however, *state* it in sequent calculus as a dependent type.

(enter A) : A;

263

With dependent types we reach the limits of what can be proved without user interaction. In terms of power, Shen occupies a position somewhat beyond that held by ML and Haskell, but below that of *formal verification* systems like Coq or NQTHM which are designed for interaction and can cope with inductive theorem proving.

But such proofs can only be automated to a limited degree; even after 40 years of research in the field, these proofs require extensive and expert human interaction to prove significant results (or in some cases even trivial ones). For this reason, these systems are still very much rooted in the research labs that are developing them and there has been very little actual user pull from Shen users to develop this facility for Shen.

20.9 Creating a Tabula Rasa

A feature rarely used but useful for those experimenting with exotic versions of Shen, is the ability to create a *tabula rasa* by eliminating the type theory underlying Shen. What is left is the sequent calculus shell (with user defined datatypes) which can be used to create new type disciplines. The function enable-type-theory does this trick. (enable-type-theory -) sets aside the inbuilt Shen type theory, (enable-type-theory +) restores it. In figure 21.5 we create an integer type and then disable Shen type theory. The system now responds only to our integer type definition and ignores the Shen type theory.

```
(1+) (datatype int

    if (integer? N)
    _____
    N : int;)
type#int : symbol

(2+) 1
1 : number

(3+) (enable-type-theory -)
false : boolean

(4+) 1
1 : int
```

Figure 20.5 Imposing a type theory for integers on Shen

Further Reading

The use of cut derives from logic programming and is explained in Sterling and Shapiro and Bratko. Mode declarations derive from DEC-10 Prolog, see http://www.cs.cmu.edu/afs/cs/project/ai-repository/ai/lang/prolog/doc/intro/prolog.doc although the mode declarations in DEC-10 Prolog were slightly different. preclude and include relate to the assert and retract predicates of Prolog.

Bove and Djyber (2008) give a nice introduction to dependent types in the context of the Agda system. Thompson (1991) explains program synthesis in a dependent type theory TT_0; Boyer and Moore (1997) explain the principles of automated inductive theorem proving. Tarver (2014) in lecture 16 summarises some of the salient ideas of Boyer and Moore.

21 Abstract and Algebraic Datatypes

21.1 Concrete and Abstract Datatypes

Our exposition of types has so far ranged only over what are generally referred to as **concrete datatypes**. A concrete datatype is fixed by identifying inhabitants of that type as constructable from a finite number of operations over generally recognised data structures. If we define a database as a concrete datatype, say as an association list, then we identify a database with a specific list structure.

However when we do this we are in fact making a contingent choice about how to represent databases because there are several alternative ways organising data e.g. hash tables and binary trees. It is often useful to be able to build our database program without having to pre-emptively decide on one representation. That is to say, we can construct our database program by building a **barrier of abstraction** between the basic operations needed to drive our database program and how we choose to implement them.

A good example is a **stack**. A stack is a structure into which objects are placed or **pushed** one by one. Objects can also be removed or **popped** one by one. The basic rule governing stacks is that the object popped is the last object that was pushed onto the stack. A concrete example is the magazine of a rifle, in which the last bullet pushed into the magazine is the first to be fired.

First lets see what we know about stacks. We assume that we have a function empty-stack for making the empty stack.

(datatype stack

```
(empty-stack) : (stack A);
```

We also assume that there is an operation push that pushes objects on a stack.

```
push : (A --> (stack A) --> (stack A));
```

266

and finally operations top and pop that return the object on the top of the stack and pop the stack respectively.

---

top : ((stack A) --> A);

---

pop : ((stack A) --> (stack A));

We assume the following equations

(pop (push x s)) = s
(top (push x s)) = x
(pop e) = (top e) = $\bot$ where e is the empty stack

$\bot$ signifies the undefined value, generally an error condition, created when we try to pop an empty stack.

We have defined a stack as an **abstract datatype**; that is, as a datatype defined by the types of the functions used to manipulate it and by the equations that describe the behaviour of those functions. The abstract specification is separated from the **concrete implementation** that represents our contingent choice of a particular datatype to play the role of a stack.

For instance one possible concrete representation is to use [] for the empty stack, cons for push and head and tail for top and pop respectively. This is not an inevitable choice; figure 21.1 shows another encoding in which a stack is a lambda expression.

```
(define empty-stack
    -> (/.  X (if (or (= X pop) (= X top))
                  (error "~this stack is empty~%")
                  (error "~A is not an operation on stacks.~%"))))

(define push
   X S -> (/. Y (if (= Y pop) S
                (if (= Y top) X
                   (error "~A is not an operation on stacks.~%")))))

(define top
   S -> (S top))
```

Figure 21.1 Encoding a stack as an abstract datatype

Lets try it.

267

```
(3+) (empty-stack)
#<COMPILED-CLOSURE empty-stack-1> : (stack A)

(4+) (push 0 (empty-stack))
#<COMPILED-CLOSURE push-1> : (stack number)

(5+) (push a (push 0 (empty-stack)))
type error

(6+) (top (push 0 (empty-stack)))
0 : number
```

By hiding inessential information on how the abstract datatype is implemented and allowing access to the data structure only through the accessor functions, abstract datatypes build a barrier of abstraction between the essential properties of the datatype and the accidental properties of how we choose to implement it. This in turn, reduces information load and allows flexibility in making changes to the representation without having to rewrite large stretches of code.

21.2 Abstract Datatypes in Sequent Calculus

If we contrast the type theory for stacks in the previous section with the type theory for concrete recursive types like lambda expressions in chapter 19, we see that there are significant differences. The type rules for a concrete datatype are of the form

$$\frac{\varphi_1;...;\varphi_m;}{(C \; x_1 \,...x_n) : \; t_0;} \qquad \text{or} \qquad \frac{\varphi_1,...,\varphi_n >> P;}{(C \; x_1 \,...x_n) : \; t_0 >> P;}$$

where C is a recognised constructor function for building structures e.g. cons, @p, @s, @v and $\varphi_1;...;\varphi_m$ is some series of typings. Alternatively they are of the form

$$\frac{x : t_1;}{x : t_0;} \qquad \text{or} \qquad \frac{if \, (h \, x)}{x : t_0;}$$

stating that an atomic expression has the given type t_0 if it can be proved to belong to some given subtype t_1 or it satisfies some computable test h. The process of typechecking proceeds by recursively decomposing $(C \; x_1 \,...x_n)$ into its components. In the abstract datatype definition nothing like that is presented; only the types of the functions needed to construct, deconstruct and recognise the objects of the type.

Midway between these two cases are cases which involve **semi-abstract** datatypes; where the formalisation of the type theory may make use of both forms of rule. We shall look at two case examples: the formalisation of Hilbert proof systems and the formalisation of algebra.

268

21.3 Proofs in a Hilbert System

A **Hilbert proof system** or Hilbert-Ackermann proof system is characterised by proofs which consist of a series of *steps*, each step being either the instantiation of an axiom scheme or derived from previous steps by some rule of inference. Formally a Hilbert proof system is a triple $<F, A, R>$; where F is a set of formation rules for the wffs of the system, A is a set $\{A_1,...,A_n\}$ of *axiom schemes* such that any uniform substitution for the metavariables in A_i results in a wff called an *axiom* and R is a set of inference rules or functions of the type *wff* ... $\rightarrow$ *wff*.

Typically R is a singleton set composed of a single rule *modus ponens* or *mp* which maps p and $p \rightarrow q$ to q. Before the work of Gentzen, Hilbert systems were the basis of much formal work in logic, including Russell and Whitehead's *Principia Mathematica*.

The particular Hilbert system that is studied in this section found in Mendelson's (1997, p.35) formalisation of propositional calculus where it is referred to as system L. System L takes as primitive the connectives $\sim$ and $\rightarrow$.. The rules of formation are simple.

1. An atom is any one of p, q, r, p', q', r' ....
2. If A is an atom then A is a wff.
3. If A and B are wffs, then $(\sim A)$, $(A \rightarrow B)$ are wffs.

In our formalisation we will use => for $\rightarrow$ and allow an atom to be any symbol other than $\sim$ or =>.

```
(define pc-atom?
 {A --> boolean}
 P -> (and (symbol? P) (not (== P =>)) (not (== P ~))))
```

The concrete datatype for wffs in this system is:

```
(datatype wff

 if (pc-atom? P)
 _____
 P : atom;

 P : atom;
 _____
 P : wff;

 P : wff;
 ========
 [~ P] : wff;

 P : wff; Q : wff;
 ============
 [P => Q] : wff;)
```

269

There are three axiom schemes and a rule of detachment for system L (figure 22.2). Each axiom scheme α asserts an infinite set of axioms S_α where $x \in S_\alpha$ just when x is a wff that results from the uniform substitution of all the metavariables in α by wffs.

Axiom Schemes

A1. $(B \to (A \to B))$,
A2. $((A \to (B \to C)) \to ((A \to B) \to (A \to C)))$
A3. $(((\sim A) \to (\sim B)) \to (((\sim A) \to B) \to A))$

Rule of Detachment (*mp*): from A and $(A \to B)$, derive B.

Figure 22.2 The axiom schemes and rules of system L

Here is a proof.

$\vdash (p \to p)$

1. $((p \to ((p \to p) \to p)) \to ((p \to (p \to p)) \to (p \to p)))$
   by A2 p/A, $(p \to p)/B$, p/C
2. $(p \to ((p \to p) \to p))$ by A1 $(p \to p)/A$, p/B
3. $((p \to (p \to p)) \to (p \to p))$ by *mp* 2 1
4. $(p \to (p \to p))$ by A1 p/A, p/B
5. $(p \to p)$ by *mp* 4 3

The natural formalisation of these schemes is to consider that they are functions which fill in the slots in a template when supplied by wffs. Accordingly each axiom scheme is represented by a function of type $wff \to \dots wff$.

```
(define scheme1
  {wff --> wff --> wff}
   P Q -> [Q => [P => Q]])
```

```
(define scheme2
  {wff --> wff --> wff --> wff}
   P Q R -> [[P => [Q => R]] => [[P => Q] => [P => R]]])
```

```
(define scheme3
  {wff --> wff --> wff}
   P Q -> [[[~ P] => [~ Q]] => [[[~ P] => Q] => P]])
```

Likewise, the rule of detachment is also a function of type $wff \to wff \to wff$.

```
(define mp*
  {wff --> wff --> wff}
   P [P => Q] -> Q)
```

270

The crucial aspect of these schemes is that they are involved in the recursive definition of a Hilbert proof. A proof is defined as a series of steps in which each step is either an axiom (i.e. an instance of axiom scheme) or derived from previous steps by *mp*. In order to capture this recursive structure we need to characterise a proof as a list structure built up by certain permitted operations. The operations are not those defined by the familiar constructor functions of cons, @p, @s and @v; they are instead defined using the scheme functions given above. A Hilbert proof therefore shares some of the characteristics of an abstract datatype though in part the specification is concrete i.e. we can see that a Hilbert proof must be a list. Such a type can be called **semi-abstract**.

First an axiom is defined as a substititution instance of an axiom scheme i.e. the result of supplying wffs to the scheme functions. In our terms axioms constitute an abstract datatype.

(datatype axiom

P : wff; Q : wff;
(scheme1 P Q) : axiom;

P : wff; Q : wff; R : wff;
(scheme2 P Q R) : axiom;

P : wff; Q : wff;
(scheme3 P Q) : axiom;)

A proof is a list structure; the base case is that the proof is empty.

(datatype proof

[] : proof; .....

Secondly we can add an axiom to the end of the proof and the result is a proof.

Step : axiom; Proof : proof;
(append Proof [Step]) : proof;

Third, applying *modus ponens* to two elements of a proof and adding the result to the end of the proof is also a proof.

M : number; N : number; Proof : proof;
(append Proof [(mp* (nth M Proof) (nth N Proof))]) : proof;

Last, if we are given to assume something is a proof, we can also assume it is a list of wffs.

Proof : (list wff) >> P;
Proof : proof >> P;)

271

We can now define and typecheck a function mp that performs *modus ponens* on a proof. If *modus ponens* is misapplied, this function returns the proof unchanged.

```
(define mp
  {number --> number --> proof --> proof}
  M N Proof -> (trap-error (append Proof [(mp* (nth M Proof) (nth N Proof))])
                (/. E (do (output "mp failure~%") Proof))))
```

Similarly these three functions, which involve the axiom scheme functions, generate proofs.

```
(define a1
  {wff --> wff --> proof --> proof}
  P Q Proof -> (append Proof [(scheme1 P Q)]))

(define a2
  {wff --> wff --> wff --> proof --> proof}
  P Q R Proof -> (append Proof [(scheme2 P Q R)]))

(define a3
  {wff --> wff --> proof --> proof}
  P Q Proof -> (append Proof [(scheme3 P Q)]))
```

Our top level function is hilbert which receives a wff to be proved and outputs an annotated proof; that is, a proof together with a list of strings which shows the rules and axioms invoked to justify the step.

```
(synonyms ann string)
```

```
(define hilbert
  {wff --> (proof * (list ann))}
  P -> (hilbert-loop P [] []))
```

This passes control to a function hilbert-loop which first tests to see if the proof is complete and if so returns it together with the annotation. If not, then the proof is printed and the user is asked to supply a rule or axiom which is then used to drive the proof forward. Note the use of (it) to record the user input as a string to be used in the annotation. If the user types stop then the proof is aborted.

```
(define hilbert-loop
  {wff --> proof --> (list ann) --> (proof * (list ann))}
  P Proof Ann -> (@p Proof Ann)            where (end-proof? Proof P)
  P Proof Ann -> (let NL (nl)
                      Show (print-proof 1 Proof Ann)
                      Ask (ask)
                      It (it)
                        (if (= It "stop") (error "exit~%")
                          (hilbert-loop P (Ask Proof) (append Ann [It]))))))
```

272

```
(define stop
  {proof --> proof}
  X -> X)
```

A proof ends when the final wff is identical to what is to be proved.

```
(define end-proof?
  {(list wff) --> wff --> boolean}
  [P] P -> true
  [_ P | Ps] Q -> (end-proof? [P | Ps] Q)
  _ _ -> false)
```

print-proof prints the proof as a series of annotated steps.

```
(define print-proof
  {number --> (list wff) --> (list ann) --> symbol}
  _ [] [] -> skip
  N [Step | Proof] [Ann | Anns] -> (do (output "~A. ~R   ~A~%" N Step Ann)
                                        (print-proof (+ N 1) Proof Anns)))
```

ask asks for a function that will produce a step; no error is accepted.

```
(define ask
  {--> (proof --> proof)}
  -> (let Prompt (output "~%> ")
       (trap-error (input+ (proof --> proof))
                   (/. E (do (output (error-to-string E))
                             (nl)
                             (ask))))))
```

Here is 'hilbert' in action.

(4+) (hilbert [p => p])

> (a2 p [p => p] p)

1. ((p => ((p => p) => p)) => ((p => (p => p)) => (p => p)))   (a2 p [p => p] p)

Since a2 has the type *wff → wff → wff → proof → proof*; (a2 p [p => p] p) constitutes a partial application of type *proof → proof*.   The rest of the proof follows the expected pattern.

> (a1 [p => p] p)

1. ((p => ((p => p) => p)) => ((p => (p => p)) => (p => p)))   (a2 p [p => p] p)
2. (p => ((p => p) => p))   (a1 [p => p] p)

273

> (mp 2 1)

1. ((p => ((p => p) => p)) => ((p => (p => p)) => (p => p)))   (a2 p [p => p] p)
2. (p => ((p => p) => p))   (a1 [p => p] p)
3. ((p => (p => p)) => (p => p))   (mp 2 1)

> (a1 p p)

1. ((p => ((p => p) => p)) => ((p => (p => p)) => (p => p)))   (a2 p [p => p] p)
2. (p => ((p => p) => p))   (a1 [p => p] p)
3. ((p => (p => p)) => (p => p))   (mp 2 1)
4. (p => (p => p))   (a1 p p)

> (mp 4 3)

(@p [[[p => [[p => p] => p]] => [[p => [p => p]] => [p => p]]] [p => [[p => p] => p]] [[p
=> [p => p]] => [p => p]] [p => [p => p]] [p => p]] ["(a2 p [p => p] p)" "(a1 [p => p] p)"
 "(mp 2 1)" "(a1 p p)" "(mp 4 3)"]) : (proof * (list string))

21.4 Algebraic Simplification

Simplification is a high school algebra technique for reducing the complexity of
algebraic expressions and is a basic technique of equational reasoning in more
advanced algebra. Examples are the simplification of $x + 5 - 3$ to $x + 2$ and x^2/x to
x. Computer algebra programs, of which there are many, need to perform these
simplifications with accuracy.

What does 'accuracy' mean here?   There are two requirements; a weak syntactic
requirement and a stronger semantic requirement.   The weak syntactic
requirement is that the algebra program output only syntactically legal algebraic
expressions. The semantic requirement is that the simplifications should preserve
the meaning of the expressions reduced.   By 'preserve the meaning of the
expressions' we mean that if x is reduced to y, that $x = y$ should be
mathematically provable.

These two requirement naturally issue in an approach based on semi-abstract
datatypes. The syntactic approach is best realised in a concrete datatype, whereas
the semantic requirement involves building an abstract datatype which operates
over a concrete one.

Our example here is restricted to level 6 algebra to fit within the confines of this
section.   There is however no barrier to taking these ideas into more advanced
algebra and the exercises at the end of this chapter invite you to expand on this
program.

To begin with the concrete syntax, we suppose that algebraic expressions (**exprs**)
are regimented into fully parenthesised form.   Here are the type rules.

```
(datatype expr

_____
(number? X) : verified >> X : number;

P : verified, Q : verified >> R;
(and P Q) : verified >> R;

X : number;
X : expr;

if (not (element? X [- * / +]))
X : symbol;
X : expr;

(fn Op) : (number --> number --> number);
X : expr; Y : expr;
=============
[X Op Y] : expr;)
```

Examples of exprs are [56 + [x - 7]] and [[-245 * 67] - [x * y]]. exprs are a concrete type with respect to our algebra program. Let us say that a algebraic operation is **syntactically valid** when it maps an expr to an expr.

Let us say that a algebraic operation is **semantically valid** when it is meaning preserving. We can say that expressions x and y 'mean the same' if $x = y$ is mathematically provable. A (semantically) valid function produces an expression which is (semantically) ok when that the output is identical in meaning to the input. So we identify a (semantically) valid function as one that takes an expression and produces a (semantically) ok expression.

```
(synonyms valid (expr --> ok-expr))
```

We also assert that if an expression is an ok expression then it is an expression.

```
X : ok-expr;
X : expr;)
```

The next step is to accumulate a series of meaning preserving operations for performing algebraic simplification. One valid operation is to arithmetically simplify (arith); so that [9 - 8] becomes 1. Our goal is to capture this idea of semantic validity.

Any semantically valid operation should also be syntactically valid, so the first step is to prove arithmetic simplification is a syntactically valid operation which is done very simply by defining arith in Shen.

```
(define arith
  {expr --> expr}
  [X Op Y] -> ((fn Op) X Y)      where (and (number? X) (number? Y))
  X -> X)
```

We continue by declaring arith to be (semantically) valid.

```
(fn arith) : valid;
```

A useful algebraic system would include many more operations than arith taking advantage of properties of arithmetic operations like the commutativity and associativity of addition and multiplication and the use of factorisation. However again in the interests of length, these developments are left to the exercises attached to this chapter.

Semantically valid algebraic operations are the bricks of the algebra system, but bricks do not a house make; cement is needed. Our cement is a series of higher-order validity preserving function generators that build bigger and better validity preserving functions. We'll pick out two useful ones: thrash and walk.

walk simply walks through all the subexpressions of an expression applying the function throughout. In programming circles a function like this is called a **tree walker**. We'll appropriate this little function because expression walking is very useful in this application. Walking a valid function over an expression produces an expression that is ok.

```
(define walk
  {valid --> expr --> ok-expr}
  F [X Op Y] -> (F [(walk F X) Op (walk F Y)])
  F X -> (F X))
```

In the context of algebraic simplification, applying a valid operation until you cannot reduce the input further will produce an expression that is ok. thrash does exactly that.

```
(define thrash
  {expr --> valid --> ok-expr}
  X F -> (let Y (F X)
              (if (== X Y) Y (thrash Y F))))
```

We now incorporate this information about valid algebraic operations into the type checker so that when we build our algebra system, the typechecker can not only tell us 'Yes, that function outputs syntactically legal algebra' but also it can tell us 'And also the heuristics you are using are valid'. So syntax AND semantics are secured.

Having defined the class of ok expressions in relation to validity preserving operations we can now deploy powerful functions to drive our algebra program; here's one called **simplifynum** that simplifies pure arithmetic.

```
(define simplify
  {valid --> expr --> ok-expr}
  F X -> (thrash X (walk F)))
```

Here is a test.

```
(10+) (simplify (fn arith) [x + [12 * [5 - 3]]])
[x + 24] : ok-expr
```

What benefits are there in building an algebra program this way? First, by defining the type of expressions as a concrete type we ensure that we can never output syntactic gibberish. But second, by rising above concrete types to define ok expressions as the result of applying meaning preserving operations we can also verify that our algebra program will perform only semantically legal transformations.

Before closing this section we should note one important wrinkle. We have used sequent calculus to overload the **arith** function and used the **fn** symbol to do so. Remembering the rules for the compilation of **fn** in 6.3., **fn** is inlined to a lambda expression when its argument has been defined and if not then it is retained. It is important in this program that **arith** be defined first before it is cited using **fn** in the type theory. Failing to do this can result in a type theory where **fn** is retained in the type theory but inlined in the REPL which will result in unexpected type errors.

21.5 Shen and ML

A reader with experience of other statically typed functional programming like ML may wonder how the type theory in Shen relates to that in ML. The characterising notation for most other functional languages, including ML, is based on the so-called **algebraic datatype** notation. This notation might be more accurately described as a form of limited BNF.

In ML, a type is described by expressing the formation rules for that type in terms of simple objects and constructors over types. Thus the suits of a playing deck are described in ML as

datatype suit = hearts | clubs | diamonds| spades;

which corresponds to the enumeration type

(datatype suit

  if (element? suit [hearts clubs diamonds spades])

  Suit : suit;)

A recursive type, such as the type of natural numbers, would be expressed in ML as

$$\text{datatype natnum = zero | succ of natnum;}$$

and in Shen

(datatype natnum

---

  zero : natnum;

  Natmum : natnum;
  ==================
  [succ Natnum] : natnum;)

The answer then, to the question of the relations of ML type notation to Shen sequent calculus notation *is that the ML type notation maps into a proper subset of sequent calculus.* Let t be the type that is defined algebraically; then this subset is characterised by the following restrictions. Then either t is an inbuilt type of Shen or it is defined in a sequent calculus such that:

  1. Side conditions are not used.
  2. t does not contain a pre-existing type.
  3. Every R rule has the form

  $s : t;)$

     where s is a symbol which is not a variable.
  4. Every LR rule for t has the form

  $x_1 : t_1;...,x_n : t_n;$
  =============
  $[c\, x_1 ... x_n] : t;$

     where $t_1;...,x_n : t_n$ are algebraic types.

We can call this fragment the **algebraic sequent calculus.**

We can introduce ML notation into Shen and arrange for this mapping into algebraic sequent calculus to be done by a macro. For convenience, we change the notation slightly; datatype suit = hearts | clubs | diamonds | spades; becomes

(ml-datatype suit = hearts, diamonds, clubs, spades) and datatype natnum = zero |
succ of natnum; becomes (ml-datatype natnum = zero, succ of natnum). The code
is given in 21.4.

```
(package ml [ml-datatype of]

(define parse-ml
  ML-Rules -> (compile (fn <ml-rules>) ML-Rules))

(defcc <ml-rules>
  <ml-rule> , <ml-rules> := [<ml-rule> | <ml-rules>];
  <ml-rule> := [<ml-rule>];)

(defcc <ml-rule>
  Constructor of <datatypes> := [Constructor | <datatypes>];
  <datatype> := <datatype>;)

(defcc <datatypes>
  <datatype> , <datatypes> := [<datatype> | <datatypes>];
  <datatype> := [<datatype>];)

(defcc <datatype>
  Datatype := Datatype where (not (= Datatype ,));)

(define ml->shen
  Datatype [Constructor | Datatypes] -> (let Vars (map (fn newvar) Datatypes)
                        Conclusion (conclusion Constructor Datatype Vars)
                        Premises (premises Vars Datatypes)
                        (append Premises [============] Conclusion))
  Datatype Instance -> [_____
                        Instance : Datatype;])

(define conclusion
  Constructor Datatype Vars -> [(cons-form [Constructor | Vars]) : Datatype;] )

(define premises
  [] [] -> []
  [V | Vs] [D | Ds] -> [V : D ; | (premises Vs Ds)])

(define cons-form
  [X | Y] -> [cons (cons-form X) (cons-form Y)]
  X -> X)

(define newvar
  _ -> (gensym (protect X)))

(defmacro ml-macro
  [ml-datatype Datatype = | ML-Rules] -> [datatype Datatype
                        | (mapcan (/. ML-Rule (ml->shen Datatype ML-Rule))
                            (parse-ml ML-Rules))]) )
```

Figure 21.4 Embedding ML datatypes into Shen

We can demonstrate the effectiveness of our transcription by comparing the ML version with Shen.

Standard ML of New Jersey v110.74 [built: Tue Jan 31 16:19:10 2012]

```
- datatype natnum = zero | succ of natnum;
datatype natnum = succ of natnum | zero
- succ(succ zero);
val it = succ (succ zero) : natnum
- fun add zero n = n
= |    add (succ m) n = (succ(add m n));
val add = fn : natnum -> natnum -> natnum
- add (succ zero) zero;
val it = succ zero : natnum
```

```
 (9+) (ml-datatype natnum = zero, succ of natnum)
type#natnum : symbol

(10+) [succ [succ zero]]
[succ [succ zero]] : natnum

(11+) (define add
      {natnum --> natnum --> natnum}
      zero N -> N
      [succ M] N  -> [succ (add M N)])
(fn add) : (natnum --> (natnum --> natnum))

(12+) (add [succ zero] zero)
[succ zero] : natnum
```

When we compare the expressive power of Shen and ML, it is obvious that the elimination of side conditions and the restrictions placed on the structure of sequent calculus makes ML a less expressive language than Shen. The type of all natural numbers can be expressed in Shen using side conditions, but cannot be so expressed in ML. The direct and elegant treatment of Hilbert proofs uses a fragment of sequent calculus outside that allowed by ML.

However there is another aspect of working with algebraic sequent calculus; which is that absurd and non-terminating rules cannot be added to the type system. We've already seen examples of non-terminating rules. We can also identify derivation rules which allow us to formulate types which collapse the Shen type system; one such is the universe type $ to which supposedly everything belongs.

(datatype universal

$$\overline{X : \$;)}$$

This type rule causes (* 3 a) to be evaluated because the expression is taken to inhabit the universe type. This rule is not part of the algebraic sequent calculus because X is a variable. Similarly

(datatype string

---

3 : string;)

is admissible in Shen, but not in ML or algebraic sequent calculus because string is a pre-existing type. We can also entirely eliminate the type system by declaring everything to be provable.

(datatype anything-goes

P;)

All these rules fall outside the algebraic sequent calculus. To put the matter succinctly, there is a space of things that can be done in a programming language; some are which are useful, progressive and interesting and some of which are foolhardy and dangerous. What we now know, and see clearly in the gap between Shen and ML, is that these spaces are not *linearly separable.* There is no straight line that leaves the useful and interesting on one side and the foolhardy on the other.[76]

Exercise 21

1. Design a database system using the abstract datatype approach. Show how you can use two different approaches to storing and retrieving data using the same type theory.

2. Upgrade the Hilbert program so that a theorem that has been demonstrated in a past proof can be introduced in a new proof by loading it from a file.

3. Milo receives a wff in a file that his friend Ben says is a theorem, but Milo is not convinced and wants the proof. Instead of simply storing a theorem as a wff in a file, arrange to store it as a wff plus the steps needed to prove it as a theorem. When the theorem is loaded, the computer re-enacts those steps to ensure that the result is a proof.

4. Design a proof assistant for the sequent calculus system described in chapter 18.

---

[76] This fact is still not understood in programming circles, and much discussion of Shen was marred by the inability to recognise that a value judgement was being played out under a scientific guise. There is no *scientific* reason to prefer ML to Shen or Shen to ML in this matter.

5. Can you generalise the answer to 3. So that your proof assistant works with any logic framed in sequent calculus notation?

6. Create a program that allows you to enter sequent calculus rules and generates typed Shen. Show it works by encoding your answer to 3. in your program.

7. In algebra, the expression $2a$ is short for $(2 * a)$. In Shen $2a$ would be parsed as two separate tokens – 2 and a which is not what we want. Design a parser that reads in algebraic expressions and parses them into longhand.

8. Design a printer that takes the long hand of 7. and prints it in shorthand.

9. Add more simplifying operations to the algebra program. Show it works by simplifying the following expressions.

    $2a - 4b +3ab -5a +2b$
    $4(2x+1) - 3x$
    $4(p - 5) +3(p +1)$
    $6(p +3q) - (7 +4q)$
    $4rs -2s - 3(rs +1) - 2s$

The answers are

    $-3a - 2b + 3ab$
    $5x + 4$
    $7p - 17$
    $6p + 14q - 7$
    $rs - 4s - 3$

10. Expand the algebra program so that it includes a type for equations. Prove the following.

    $(a + b)^2 = a^2 + 2ab + b^2$
    $(a - b)^2 = a^2 - 2ab + b^2$
    $(x + a) (x + b) = x^2 + (a + b)x + ab$
    $(a + b)^3 = a^3 + 3a2b + 3ab^2 + b^3$
    $(a + b)^3 = a^3 + 3ab(a + b) + b^3$

11. Integrate your system from 5. and 6. so that you can prove equalities from other equalities

Further Reading

Helma and Veroff (2005) explore abstract datatypes and the importance of barriers of abstraction is explained in Abelson and Sussman (1996). Mendelson explores system L. Wikstrom (1987) and Paulson (1996) both cover concrete and abstract datatypes in ML.

The approach to computer algebra discussed here was first aired by me in the functional programming news group https://groups.google.com/g/comp.lang.functional/c/OQYttMDOhMg/m/X1nCYteXyKsJ).

There is a long history of computer algebra systems. Wikipedia (https://en.wikipedia.org/wiki/List_of_computer_algebra_systems) lists more than a score of them.

22 Typed Shen YACC

22.1 The Big Arrow Type

In 2018, the Shen kernel was upgraded to allow Shen YACC to generate type secure code using the **big arrow notation** ==>. The following informal rule[77] captures the essence of ==>.

Informal Rule for the Big Arrow Operator ==>

For any A and B, (fn f) : (A ==> B) just when if S : A then (compile (fn f) S) : B

In other words a YACC definition of f has the type (A ==> B) if when applied by compile to an input of type A it produces an output of type B. Shen YACC expects that the value of A in A ==> B should be the type of a homogenous list Figure 22.1 gives an example.

```
(2+) (defcc <total>
        {(list number) ==> number}
        X <total> := (+ X <total>);
        X := X;)
(fn <total>) : ((list number) ==> number)

(3+) (compile (fn <total>) [1 2 3 4])
10 : number
```

Figure 22.1 Using YACC with types

We'll illustrate the practical application of typed YACC by looking at how bytes are parsed to numbers in the Shen reader before moving to a more advanced example involving Montague grammers.

---

[77] The big arrow notation is internally expanded by Shen so that the resulting types are in little arrow notation for the purpose of type checking, but for appearance the big arrow notation is printed off in the REPL. The mechanics of this definition are explored in later sections of this chapter.

22.2 Parsing Bytes to Numbers

The Shen reader takes a stream of bytes and parses it into legal Shen. A proper subset of these bytes are the code points dealing with the decimal numbers 0-9 which are represented as follows.

0	48
1	49
2	50
3	51
4	52
5	53
6	54
7	55
8	56
9	57

A series of such bytes, such as 50 54 55 would be parsed into the integer 267. Because Shen supports positive and negative numbers as well as floats and E numbers, four other code points are relevant

+	43
-	45
.	46
e	101

We'll now look at the YACC kernel code that compiles bytes into numbers using types to annotate the code. The input is a list of bytes (numbers) and the output is a number. A number can be fronted by a plus or minus sign. Numbers are either E numbers, floats or integers.

```
(defcc <number>
  {(list number) ==> number}
  <minus> <number> := (- 0 <number>);
  <plus> <number> := <number>;
  <e-number>;
  <float>;
  <integer>;)

(defcc <minus>
  {(list number) ==> symbol}
  45 := skip;)

(defcc <plus>
  {(list number) ==> symbol}
  43 := skip;)
```

The integer case is the simplest and we'll look at that first.

1. Integers

An integer is a series of bytes representing digits and the semantic action is to compute the integer from the digits.

```
(defcc <integer>
  {(list number) ==> number}
  <digits> := (compute-integer  <digits>); )
```

```
(defcc <digits>
  {(list number) ==> (list number)}
  <digit> <digits> := [<digit> | <digits>];
  <digit> := [<digit>];)
```

The semantic action of a <digit> is to generate the number associated with the byte which is obtained by subtracting 48.

```
(defcc <digit>
  {(list number) ==> number}
  Byte := (byte->digit Byte)  where (digit? Byte);)
```

```
(define digit?
  {number --> boolean}
  Byte -> (and (>= Byte 48) (<= Byte 57)))
```

```
(define byte->digit
  {number --> number}
  Byte -> (- Byte 48))
```

An integer (e.g. 12) is computed as 10^1 x 1 + 10^0 x 2.

```
(define compute-integer
  {(list number) --> number}
  Digits -> (compute-integer-h (reverse Digits) 0))
```

```
(define compute-integer-h
  {(list number) --> number --> number}
  [] _ -> 0
  [Digit | Digits] Expt -> (+ (* (expt 10 Expt) Digit)
                              (compute-integer-h Digits (+ Expt 1))))
```

expt computes m^n for all integer values of m and n.

```
(define expt
  {number --> number --> number}
  _ 0     -> 1
  Base Expt -> (* Base (expt Base (- Expt 1)))  where (> Expt 0)
  Base Expt -> (/ (expt Base (+ Expt 1)) Base))
```

2. Floats

A float has an integer component and a fractional component separated by a full stop. The semantic action is to compute the float using these components. The float is computed by summing the integer and fractional components.

```
(defcc <float>
  {(list number) ==> number}
  <integer> <stop> <fraction> := (+ <integer> <fraction>);)

(defcc <stop>
  {(list number) ==> symbol}
  46 := skip;)

(defcc <fraction>
  {(list number) ==> number}
  <digits> := (compute-fraction <digits>);)
```

The fractional component is computed as the sum of a series of products (e.g. .12) is computed as $10^{-1} \times 1 + 10^{-2} \times 2$.

```
(define compute-fraction
  {(list number) --> number}
  Digits -> (compute-fraction-h Digits -1))

(define compute-fraction-h
  {(list number) --> number --> number}
  [] _ -> 0
  [Digit | Digits] Expt -> (+ (* (expt 10 Expt) Digit)
                              (compute-fraction-h Digits (- Expt 1))))
```

3. E numbers

An E number is a float or an integer followed by a byte denoting the lowercase e and a positive or negative integer expressing a log of 10.

```
(defcc <e-number>
  {(list number) ==> number}
  <float> <lowE> <log10>     := (compute-E <float> <log10>);
  <integer> <lowE> <log10>   := (compute-E <integer> <log10>);)

(defcc <log10>
  {(list number) ==> number}
  <plus> <log10> := <log10>;
  <minus> <log10> := (- 0 <log10>);
  <integer>;)

(defcc <lowE>
  {(list number) ==> symbol}
  101 := skip;)
```

```
(define compute-E
  {number --> number --> number}
  N  Log10 -> (* N (expt 10 Log10)))
```

Figure 22.2 gives some sample inputs.

(8+) (compile (fn <number>) [50 54 55])
267 : number

(9+) (compile (fn <number>) [50 54 55 46 53 53])
267.55 : number

(10+) (compile (fn <number>) [50 54 55 46 53 53 101 45 49])
26.755000000000003 : number   \\ 267.55e-1

Figure 22.2 Parsing bytes to numbers.

22.3 Montague Grammars

Montague grammars were developed for English in a series of three important papers by the logician Richard Montague. They are in form, context free grammars of the type commonly met but they are distinguished by their treatment of semantics. Montague believed that English was not importantly different from the formal languages of logic and that it was possible to parse English into logic without loss of important meaning.

There is in my opinion no important theoretical difference between natural languages and the artificial languages of logicians; indeed, I consider it possible to comprehend the syntax and semantics of both kinds of language within a single natural and mathematically precise theory. On this point I differ from a number of philosophers, but agree, I believe, with Chomsky and his associates.

Montague 1970

Montague's 'natural and mathematically precise' notation was an extension of first-order logic which incorporated modal concepts like possible worlds and also moments of time. Unusually for his period, Montague's papers also used lambda abstractions.

Montague's work is a very nice illustration of working with typed Shen YACC because the underlying type theory is simple but the ramifications are profound. We begin with the type theory before going on to the construction of grammars themselves. Our focus is a proper subset of English and for this subset the resources of function-free first-order logic without equality (FOL-) are sufficient.

288

This will be the object language into which compilation from English will proceed.

The most fundamental concept of the type theory is a *term* and the type of all terms is t. For us a term is a symbol that is not an element of [~ v & => <=> e! a!]. This latter list is the list of logical constants of FOL-.

(datatype t

  if (not (element? t [~ v & => <=> e! a!]))
  T : symbol;

  ‾‾‾‾‾‾‾‾‾
  T : t;

We also have occasion later to want to generate fresh terms at will so we add this axiom.

  ‾‾‾‾‾‾‾‾‾‾‾
  (gensym v) : t;)

The other fundamental concept is that of a formula of FOL-. This is encapsulated in the rules for a type f.

(datatype f

  F : t; T : (list t);

  ‾‾‾‾‾‾‾‾‾‾
  [F | T] : f;

The first R rule says that a formula is a non-empty list of terms. This corresponds to an atomic fomula; [likes Bill Mary] would be an example.

The L rules are more complex because of the restrictions on what can count as a term. We cannot assert

  F : t; T : (list t);
  ==========
  [F | T] : f;

which entails

  F : t, T : (list t) >> P;

  ‾‾‾‾‾‾‾‾‾‾‾‾‾
  [F | T] : f >> P;

This is false, since [e! x [p x]] (e! is our ASCII version of ∃) is of type f but e! is not of type t. Hence the L rules are broken into cases. If it is given that [F T] is a two element list of type f and it is verified that F is not the logical constant ~ , then this assumption can be decomposed into the assumptions that F: t and T : t.

(not (= F ~)) : verified;
 F : t, T : t >> P;
_____
[F T] : f >> P;

Second if we have a three element list of the form [F T1 T2] and it is given that
[F T1 T2] : f, then this assumption can be broken into F : t and T1 : t and T2 : t
provided it is verified that T1 is not a logical connective and F is not a quantifier.

(not (element? T1 [v & => <=>])) : verified;
(not (element? F [e! a!])) : verified;
 F : t, T1 : t, T2 : t >> P;
_____
[F T1 T2] : f >> P;

This actually suffices for our purposes since all predicates in our system are either
monadic or dyadic. But for completeness we round off with a third L rule which
extends FOL- to encompass predicates of any arity.

F : t, T1 : t, T2 : t, T3 : t, T : (list t) >> P;
_____
[F T1 T2 T3 | T] : f >> P;

The next two LR rules encompass propositional logic.

P : f;
======
[~ P] : f;

if (element? C [v & => <=>])
P : f; Q : f;
========
[P C Q] : f;

The remaining rules encompass quantifiers.

 X : t; P : f;
========
[e! X P] : f;

 X : t; P : f;
========
[a! X P] : f;)

The next step is to establish a set of recognisors for some of the lexical categories
of English. We will be working with words as terms which means symbols. A
name is a symbol beginning in uppercase, a variable in Shen terms.

```
(define name?
  {t --> boolean}
  Name -> (variable? Name))
```

In our toy grammar, there is a small set of common nouns which can be easily expanded.

```
(define common-noun?
  {t --> boolean}
  CN -> (element? CN [girl boy dog cat]))
```

There are also transitive and intransitive verbs.

```
(define intrans?
  {t --> boolean}
  Intrans -> (element? Intrans [runs jumps walks]))

(define trans?
  {t --> boolean}
  Trans -> (element? Trans [likes greets admires]))
```

This completes the list of categories which are coded outside Shen YACC. What remains is the Montague grammar itself. The easiest course is to explore this grammar top down, beginning with the distinguished symbol.

The top level says that a sentence is a list of terms composed of a noun phrase and a verb phrase and the action of the compiler is to produce a formula. The formula is produced by the application of the output from the noun phrase on the output of the verb phrase.

```
(defcc <sent>
  {(list t) ==> f}
  <np> <vp> := (<np> <vp>);)
```

A noun phrase is either a name or a determiner followed by a common noun or a determiner followed by a relative common noun.

```
(defcc <np>
  {(list t) ==> ((t --> f) --> f)}
  Name := (/. P (P Name))   where (name? Name);
  <det> <rcn> := (<det> <rcn>);
  <det> <cn> := (<det> <cn>);)
```

Obviously <np> has to produce a function given its role in <sent>. The signature says the result is of the type $(t \rightarrow f) \rightarrow f$ which makes this function higher order. In the case where the noun phrase is a name, the semantics says the associated object is a lambda function which constructs a formula by applying its parameter P to the Name. Since P is applied then it must be a function. (/. P (P Name)) will perform as a higher-order function and P will take the term Name and construct a formula with it.

This is less obvious than the more natural method of parsing the name by simply returning it. But in order to allow the uniform treatment of noun phrases in more complex examples, the treatment has to be upped to create a consistent type for all cases of the <np> function.

Another feature of our treatment here is that we are *using* lambda expressions rather than mentioning them. If we were mentioning them then lambda expressions would be part of the resulting output and the type theory of f would have to allow for them and it would be a deal more complex. In Montague's original system, this was indeed the case but here lambda expressions are part of the metalanguage of the system i.e. Shen.

Determiners are either some, every or no.

```
(defcc <det>
  {(list t) ==> ((t --> f) --> (t --> f) --> f)}
  some := (let V (gensym v) (/. P Q [e! V [(P V) & (Q V)]]));
  every := (let V (gensym v) (/. P Q [a! V [(P V) => (Q V)]]));
  no    := (let V (gensym v) (/. P Q [a! x [(P V) => [~ (Q V)]]]));)
```

The action of a determiner is to construct a higher-order two place function that produces a quantified formula for its inputs P and Q. We need gensym here to encourage uniqueness of variables. The parameters P and Q of this function apply to the bound variable x and therefore have the same type as in the name example. The type of the two place function is $(t \rightarrow f) \rightarrow (t \rightarrow f) \rightarrow f$.

A common noun produces a function that takes a term and outputs a function that constructs an atomic formula using that noun.

```
(defcc <cn>
  {(list t) ==> (t --> f)}
  CN := (/. X [CN X])    where (common-noun? CN);)
```

A relative common noun is involved in phrases like '*every girl that*'. Given a preceding determiner, a relative common noun is constrained to produce an object of the same type as a determiner followed by a common noun.

```
(defcc <rcn>
  {(list t) ==> (t --> f)}
  <cn> that <vp> := (/. X [(<cn> X) & (<vp> X)]);
  <cn> that <np> <trans> := (/. X [(<cn> X) & (<np> (/. Y (<trans> X Y)))]);)
```

Given that the output of a verb phrase is the argument to the output of the noun phrase and the type of the output of noun phrase is $(t \rightarrow f) \rightarrow f$ it follows that the type of the output of verb phrase is $t \rightarrow f$.

```
(defcc <vp>
  {(list t) ==> (t --> f)}
  <intrans>;
  <trans> <np> := (/. X (<np> (/. Y (<trans> X Y))));)
```

The intransitive and transitive cases produce 1 and 2 place functions respectively taking terms and returning a formula.

```
(defcc <intrans>
  {(list t) ==> (t --> f)}
  Intrans := (/. X [Intrans X])    where (intrans? Intrans);)
```

```
(defcc <trans>
  {(list t) ==> (t --> t --> f)}
  Trans := (/. X Y [Trans X Y])   where (trans? Trans);)
```

Here are some sample inputs.

```
(1+) (compile (fn <sent>) [Mary likes John])
[likes Mary John] : f

(2+) (compile (fn <sent>) [every girl likes John])
[a! v1 [[girl v1] => [likes v1 John]]] : f

(3+) (compile (fn <sent>) [every girl likes every boy])
[a! v2 [[girl v2] => [a! v3 [[boy v3] => [likes v2 v3]]]]]: f

(4+) (compile (fn <sent>) [every girl likes some boy])
[a! v4 [[girl v4] => [e! v5 [[boy v5] & [likes v4 v5]]]]] : f

(5+) (compile (fn <sent>) [some girl likes every boy])
[e! v6 [[girl v6] & [a! x [[boy v7] => [likes v6 v7]]]]] : f

(6+) (compile (fn <sent>) [every girl that jumps likes Bill])
[a! v8 [[[girl v8] & [jumps v8]] => [likes v8 Bill]]] : f
```

Figure 22.3 Parsing English to FOL-.

22.4* YACC Structures

We now turn to the deeper details of how Shen YACC is implemented. The type theory for Shen YACC is built on a foundation of abstract datatypes and these abstract datatypes are in turn based on the recursive descent model of parsing discussed in chapter 12. Recall from that chapter that the input to our model parser was a structure composed on an input or source code component *I* and an output or object code component *O*. The task of the compiler is to consume the source *I* and produce the output *O*. Let's call this composite of *I* and *O* a **YACC**

structure and assign it the type (str *A B*) where *A* is the type of *I* and *B* is the type of *O*.

A simplifying assumption, which is characteristic of Shen YACC computations, is that the input is a homogenous list of some form (eg. strings or bytes). In that case we can without loss of useful generality consider the case where the YACC structure is of type (str (list *A*) *B*) for any given *A* and *B*.

The action of a Shen YACC program on an input is this: a series of functions f_1 ... f_n representing non-terminals are applied to the source *I*. This source is progressively consumed until it is empty. Each function f_i returns a YACC structure and the output components of all the structures returned by f_1 ... f_n are used to construct the final output *O*.

No f_i consults the output component of any YACC structure it receives as an input and consumes only the input component. Hence the type of f_i is an instantiation of the variables *A* and *B* in (str (list *A*) *C*) → (str (list *A*) *B*). The free *C* indicates the 'don't care' attitude of f_i to the nature of the output component of its argument.

For reasons of appearance, it is more attractive to write the type of f_i in big arrow notation according to the following rule.

Formal Rule for the Big Arrow Operator ==>

where *C* is free

For any *A* and *B*, f : ((list *A*) ==> *B*) iff f : (str (list *A*) *C*) → (str (list *A*) *B*)

22.5* Abstract Operations

We now detail the types and operations in the YACC abstract datatype.

1. =hd?

Action: The input component *I* of a YACC structure is checked to see if

      a.   *I* is non-empty
      b.   The first element *h* of *I* is such that *h* = *t*.

If these tests succeed then true is returned; if not then false is returned.

Type: (str (list *A*) *B*) → *A* → boolean
Comment: this operation is the standard operation when a top down parser must consult the input to see if a terminal is present.

2. comb

Action: a 2-place function that combines its arguments to produce a YACC structure.

Type: (list A) $\rightarrow B \rightarrow$ (str (list A) B)

3. in->

Action: a 1-place function that takes a YACC structure and returns the input component.

Type: (str (list A) B) $\rightarrow$ (list A)

4. <-out

Action: a 1-place function that takes a YACC structure and returns the output component.

Type: (str (list A) B) $\rightarrow B$

5. parse-failure

Action: a zero-place function that returns an object signifying a parse failure.

Type: (str (list A) B)

Comment: whenever a parse fails at any point, this object is returned. The parse-failure function returns an object ϕ that matches the type of every YACC structure. For the purpose of type checking this type is required if the compiler is to be free to raise ϕ at any point in the parse. ϕ cannot be decomposed into components and the in-> and <-out functions are not defined for ϕ.

These five functions are the basic primitives; the remainder are definable in terms of these five.

6. parse-failure?

Action: a one-place function that returns true if supplied with the parse-failure object ϕ and false otherwise.

Type: (str (list A) B) $\rightarrow$ boolean

Comment: this test is carried out whever the input is subject to a parsing action. Definable as (= *Str* (parse-failure)) where *Str* is any YACC structure.

7. non-empty-structure?

Action: returns true if the input component is a non-empty-list.

Type: (str (list A) B) → boolean

Comment: definable as (cons? (in-> Str)) where *Str* is a YACC structure.

8. hds

Action: the first element of the input component I of a YACC structure is returned.

Type: (str (list A) B) → A

Comment: definable as (head (in-> *Str*)) where *Str* is a YACC structure.

9. tls

Action: a 1-place function that takes a YACC structure S_1 and returns a YACC structure S_2 with the first element t of the input component of S_1 removed.

Type: (str (list A) B) → (str (list A) B)

Comment: the standard action when t has been successfully matched in the input. Definable as (comb (tail (in-> *Str*)) (<-out *Str*))

10. ccons?

Action: the first element of the input component I of a YACC structure is tested to see if it is a non-empty list.

Type: (str (list A) B) → boolean

Comment: definable as (cons? (hds *Str*)).

11. <e>

Action: a 1-place function that takes a YACC structure S_1 and returns a YACC structure S_2 composed of the input component of S_1 with the empty list as the output component.

Type: (str (list A) B) → (str (list A) (list C))

Comment: Definable as (comb (in-> *Str*) [])).

296

12. <!>

Action: a 1-place function that takes a YACC structure S_1 and returns a YACC structure S_2 composed of the empty list as the input component of S_1 with the output component as the input component tof S_1.

Type: (str (list A) B) $\rightarrow$ (str (list C) (list A))

Comment: Definable as (comb [] (in-> *Str*)).

13. <end>

Action: a 1-place function that takes a YACC structure S_1 and returns S_1 if the input component of S_1 is the empty list else returns parse failure.

Comment: Definable as (if (empty? (in-> *Str*)) *Str* (parse-failure)).

Type: (str (list A) B) $\rightarrow$ (str (list A) B)

14. compile

Action: a 2-place higher-order function that takes a function f that returns YACC structure S_2 from a YACC structure S_1 and returns the output component of S_2.

Type: (((list A) ==> B) $\rightarrow$ (list A) $\rightarrow$ B

Comment: this function is external to the Shen package

22.6* The Concrete Implementation

The concrete implementation of a YACC structure is a two element list. A parse failure is signalled by the return of the failure object. The concrete definitions of the first 13 abstract operators are obvious realisations of the abstract specification.

```
(define =hd?
  [[X | _] _] X -> true
  _ _ -> false)

(define parse-failure
  -> (fail))

(define parse-failure?
  X -> (= X (fail)))

(define comb
  X Y -> [X Y])
```

```
(define hds
  [[X | _] _] -> X)

(define tls
  [[_ | X] Y] -> [X Y])

(define ccons?
  [[[_ | _] | _ _ ] -> true
   _ -> false)

(define in->
  [X _] -> X)

(define <-out
  [_ X] -> X)

(defcc <e>
  [X _] -> [X []])

(defcc <!>
  [X _] -> [[] X])

(defcc <end>
  [[] X] -> [[] X]
  _ -> (parse-failure))

(define compile
  F L -> (let Compile (F [L ignore-me])
           (cases  (parse-failure? Compile)  (error "parse failure~%")
                   (cons? (in-> Compile))  (error "syntax error here: ~R~% ..."
                                                   (in-> Compile))
                   true (<-o Compile))))
```

Figure 22.4 The concrete implementation of the YACC primitives

The action of the compile function is to receive F and L and to apply F to a YACC structure formed by combining L with ignore-me. The ignore-me is a place-filler which is, of course, not consulted in the parse.   After the compilation is performed the result is locally assigned to Compile. If Compile is a parse failure then a syntax error is signalled. If the input component has not been entirely consumed then a syntax error is also signalled showing where the parse failed to complete. In all other cases the output component of Compile is returned.

22.7* The Compilation of YACC Rules

The compilation of a YACC grammar rule *R* begins by rendering it into an *internal form* which is a list [*x y*]. This internal form reflects the structure of a YACC rule into a syntactic component *x* (to left of the :=) and a semantic component *y* (to the right of the :=).   A guarded rule of the form *x* := *y* where *p*; is mapped to [*x* [where *p y*]].

The syntax component of the internal form is compiled first which is where the heavy lifting occurs. The syntax processing function takes four arguments

1. The type of the function in which R is found; this is used to optimise the code for type checking.
2. A formal parameter (variable) Str which will be bound to a YACC structure when the compiler is run.
3. The syntax component x of the internal form.
4. The semantics component y of the internal form.

The action of the syntax processing function is to recurse through the syntax component until the syntax component is exhausted and then hand control over to the semantics component to process the semantics. A item i encountered on the syntactic component falls into one of five types.

1. i is a non-terminal; that is, a symbol enclosed in <...>.
2. i is a variable.
3. i is a wildcard.
4. i is a terminal
5. i is a non-empty list.

Figure 22.5 gives the kernel code for the syntax processing function.

```
(define yacc-syntax
    Type Structure [] [where P Semantics]
     -> [if P (yacc-syntax Type Structure [] Semantics) [parse-failure]]
    Type Structure [] Semantics -> (semantics Type Structure Semantics)
    Type Structure [SyntaxItem | Syntax] Semantics
     -> (cases (non-terminal? SyntaxItem)
                (non-terminalcode Type Structure SyntaxItem Syntax Semantics)
               (variable? SyntaxItem)
                (variablecode Type Structure SyntaxItem Syntax Semantics)
               (= _ SyntaxItem)
                (wildcardcode Type Structure SyntaxItem Syntax Semantics)
               (atom? SyntaxItem)
                (terminalcode Type Structure SyntaxItem Syntax Semantics)
               (cons? SyntaxItem)
                (conscode Type Structure SyntaxItem Syntax Semantics)))
```

Figure 22.5 Processing the syntactic component of a YACC rule

Let us look at the bolded cases in this function.

1. i is a non-terminal.

The function designated by i is applied to the YACC structure. If the result is a parse failure then parse failure is returned. If not then the YACC structure created becomes the new input for the rest of the syntactic component. The code is given in figure 22.6.

```
(define non-terminalcode
    Type Structure NonTerminal Syntax Semantics
    -> (let ApplyNonTerminal (concat (protect Parse) NonTerminal)
        [let ApplyNonTerminal [NonTerminal Structure]
        [if [parse-failure? ApplyNonTerminal]
        [parse-failure]
        (yacc-syntax Type ApplyNonTerminal Syntax Semantics)]]]))
```

Figure 22.6 Compiling a non-terminal

2. *i* is a variable.

If *i* is a variable then the following actions are made.

1. The input component *I* of the YACC structure is tested to ensure it is non-empty.
2. If it is non-empty then *i* is locally bound to the head (hds) of *I*.
3. If not then parse failure is returned.
4. A new structure is composed by removing the head of the input stream from the old stream – effectively applying tls.

```
(define variablecode
    Type Structure Variable Syntax Semantics
    -> (let NewStr (gensym (protect News))
        [if [non-empty-structure? Structure]
        [let Variable [hds Structure]
            NewStr [tls Structure]
            (yacc-syntax Type NewStr Syntax Semantics)]
        [parse-failure]]))
```

Figure 22.7 Compiling a variable

3. *i* is a wildcard

If *i* is a wildcard then the following actions are made.

1. The input component *I* of the YACC structure is tested to ensure it is non-empty.
2. If not then parse failure is returned.
3. A new structure is composed by removing the head of the input stream from the old stream.

```
(define wildcardcode
    Type Structure Variable Syntax Semantics
    -> (let NewStructure (gensym (protect News))
        [if [non-empty-stream? Structure]
        [let NewStructure [tls Structure]
            (yacc-syntax Type NewStructure Syntax Semantics)]
        [parse-failure]]))
```

Figure 22.8 Compiling a wildcard

4. *i* is a terminal.

If *i* is a terminal then the generated code does the following

1. a test is made to see if *i* is the head of *I*.
2. If not then parse failure is returned.
3. If it is then a new structure is composed by removing *i*.

```
(define terminalcode
    Type Structure Terminal Syn Sem
    -> (let NewStr (gensym (protect News))
        [if [=hd? Structure Terminal]
            [let NewStr [tls Structure]
                (yacc-syntax Type NewStr Syn Sem)]
            [parse-failure]]))
```

Figure 22.9 Compiling a terminal

5. *i* is a non-empty list.

If *i* is a non-empty list then the generated code does the following

1. a test is made to see if the head of *I* is a non-empty list.
2. If not then parse failure is returned.
3. If so, then a new structure *S* is created by combining the head of *I* with the output component of the old structure.
4. The syntax function then resumes with *i* as the syntax component after removing the conses from *i*. A test <end> is inserted at the end of *i* to ensure the input is consumed.
5. The other syntax components that follow *i* are pushed onto the semantics.

```
(define conscode
    Type Structure Cons Syn Sem
        -> [if [ccons? Structure]
            [let (protect SynCons) [comb [hds Structure] [<-out Structure]]
                (yacc-syntax Type
                    (protect SynCons)
                    (append (decons Cons) [<end>])
                    [pushsemantics [tlstream Structure] Syn Sem])]
            [parse-failure]])
(define decons
    [cons X Y] -> [X | Y]
    X -> X)
```

Figure 22.10 Compiling a list

The compilation of the semantics is straightforward; the semantics is searched for non-terminals and every non-terminal is replaced by a call to return the output component associated with it. A small wrinkle is that if syntactic actions have been pushed onto the semantics then these actions have to be discharged.

```
(define yacc-semantics
    Type _ [pushsemantics Structure Syntax Semantics]
    -> (yacc-syntax Type Structure Syntax Semantics)
    Type Structure Semantics
    -> (let Process (process-semantics Semantics)
            Annotate (use-type-info Type Process)
        [comb [in-> Structure] Annotate]))

(define use-type-info
    [{ [str [list A] C] --> [str [list A] B] }] Semantics -> [type Semantics B]
    _ Semantics -> Semantics)

(define process-yacc-semantics
    [X | Y] -> (map (fn process-yacc-semantics) [X | Y])
    X  -> [<-out (concat (protect Parse) X)]]  where (non-terminal? X)
    X -> X)
```

Exercise 22

1. Annotate this code from chapter 13 with types.

```
(defcc <asbs>
    <as> <bs> := (= (length <as>) (length <bs>));)

(defcc <as>
    a <as>;  a;)

(defcc <bs>
    b <bs>;  b;)

(defcc <len>
    _ <len> := (+ 1 <len>);
    <e> := 0)

(defcc <expr>
    <term> <op> <expr> := [<op> <term> <expr>];
    <term> := <term>;)

(defcc <term>
    N := N  where (number? N);
    E := (parse-term E);)

(defcc <op>
    X := X              where (element? X [+ - * /]);)

(define parse-term
    E -> (compile (fn <expr>) E))
```

2. The language MINIM has the following syntax. (++ and -- increment and decrement a global variable).

```
<program> := <statement> ; <program> | <statement> ;
<statement> := <assignment> | <conditional> | <print>
               <input> | <goto> | <tag>
<assignment> := <var> := <val> | ++<var> | --<var>
<print> := print string | print <var>
<input> := input <var>
<var> := symbol
<val> := number | <var>
<conditional> := if <test> then <statement> else <statement>
<test> := <var> <comp> <var> | <test> and <test>
             | <test> or <test> | not <test>
<goto> := goto <tag>
<tag> := symbol
<comp> := > | < | =
```

The following MINIM program adds two non-negative integers.

```
print "Add x and yc#13;";
print "Input x: ";
input x;
print "c#13;Input y: ";
input y;

main;
        if x = 0 then goto end else goto sub1x;
        sub1x;
        --x;
        ++y;
        goto main;
end;
print "c#13;The total of x and y is ";
print y;
```

Devise a type secure Shen YACC program that loads a MINIM program from a file and executes it. Show it works by loading and executing the above program.

3. Devise a Shen YACC program that reads a Standard ML program from a file and compiles it into untyped Shen. Your compiler will ignore ML type declarations and focus only on SML definitions. Show you can load SML files into Shen.

4. Devise a Shen YACC compiler that compiles a Turing equivalent subset of C into an internal form that can be assigned a type – say internal-C. Devise an interpreter for internal C programs that executes them and thus provides an emulator for your C subset. Your compiler will read a C program from a file in bytes and will have the type (list number) ==> internal-C.

Further Reading

Montague's seminal papers are Montague (1970) and Montague (1973). Montague semantics is discussed in Thayse (1989, 1990). MINIM was first posed by myself in 2007 as a challenge problem in the Lisp newsgroup; see https://groups.google.com/forum/?hl=en#!topic/comp.lang.lisp/exqzb11czgo for a variety of solutions in different languages.

23 A Model Checker

23.1 An Introduction to Model Theory

Logic can be studied either from the point of view of **proof theory** or of **model theory**. Proof theory approaches the meaning of a logical constant c by asking after the conditions under which a logical formula containing c used in proofs; this was the approach of chapter 18. The model theoretic approach is to explain c by giving the **truth conditions** of sentences containing it.

Most students who have done computer science are introduced to the logical constants of propositional calculus through model theory. Truth-tables supply a precise and mechanical way of not only testing for the validity of an argument in propositional calculus, but also a precise characterisation of the meaning of those constants.

In first-order model theory an interpretation for a propositional atom is a truth-value (true or false). An interpretation I of a first-order atom $P(t_1,...,t_n)$ requires a domain (non-empty set) **D**. I assigns to P an n-ary relation $I(P)$ drawn from **D** and an object $I(t_i)$ from **D** for each t_i. The truth-conditions can now be stated simply. $P(t_1,...,t_n)$ is true under I just when the tuple $<I(t_1),...,I(t_n)> \in I(P)$.

Thus if we fix **D** to the set of natural numbers and assign to the relation symbol R the relation $>$ occupied by all pairs of number $<m, n>$ such that $m > n$, and to a the number 5 and to b the number 3, then the resulting interpretation is true (is a model) for $R(a, b)$. From then on the model theory for the logical connectives follows the expected pattern.

$I(\sim p) = $ true if $I(p) = $ false
$I(\sim p) = $ false if $I(p) = $ true
$I(p \lor q) = $ true if $I(p) = $ true or $I(q) = $ true
$I(p \lor q) = $ false if $I(p) = I(q) = $ false
$I(p \mathbin{\&} q) = $ true if $I(p) = I(q) = $ true
$I(p \mathbin{\&} q) = $ false if $I(p) = $ false or $I(q) = $ false
$I(p \rightarrow q) = $ true if $I(p) = $ false or $I(q) = $ true
$I(p \rightarrow q) = $ false if $I(p) = $ true and $I(q) = $ false
$I(p \leftrightarrow q) = $ true if $I(p) = I(q)$
$I(p \leftrightarrow q) = $ false if $I(p) \neq I(q)$

When it comes to the quantifiers, first-order model theory introduces us to the idea of the **domain D** of a quantifier. $\exists x\, P(t_1,..., x,...,t_n)$ is true under I just when there is an object d in **D** such that $<I(t_1), ..., d,..., I(t_n)> \in I(P)$. $\forall x\, P(t_1,...,x,...,t_n)$ is true under I just when for every object d in **D** $<I(t_1), ..., d,..., I(t_n)> \in I(P)$.

Presented formally, this may seem forbidding, yet ordinary language operates on the idea of a domain of discourse. The sentence

'Everybody is talking with somebody'

uttered at a party transcribes as '$\forall x \exists y$ talking_with(x, y)' in first-order logic. However the statement is certainly false unless the domain of quantification is restricted to those present at the party. Similarly in physics the statement

'All solid objects accelerate at 9.8 m/s^2 in free fall.'

is true allowing for approximation. In first-order logic, we would perhaps write this as

$$\forall x\, (solid(x) \rightarrow free\_fall\_acceleration(x, 9.8 \text{ m/s}^2))$$

This statement is true – provided that we take the domain of the quantifier to be restricted to, say, dense objects less than 1000 feet from the surface of the Earth. If we were to consider objects over 100 miles above the surface of the Earth or objects dropped on other planets, the statement would be false. Therefore the truth or falsity of the statement depends on the domain of the quantifier.

To make our assertion clear we could write the domain of the quantifier into the assertion.

$$\forall x \in E\, (solid(x) \rightarrow free\_fall\_acceleration(x, 9.8 \text{ m/s}^2))$$

where E denotes the set of all dense objects less than 1000 feet from the surface of the Earth.

When the domain of the quantifier is finite in size, then every universally quantified assertion can be seen as a shorthand for a conjunction. Thus let MP be all the set of men at a party, then

$$\forall x \in MP\; wearing\_a\_tie(x)$$

asserts that every man at the party is wearing a tie.

If Tom, Dick and Harry are the only men, then this assertion is true if and only if

'$wearing\_a\_tie(Tom)$ & $wearing\_a\_tie(Dick)$ & $wearing\_a\_tie(Harry)$'

is true. In this situation every universally quantified formula is equivalent to, and can be unpacked into, a finite conjunction of assertions.

If we supply a finite set of objects as the domain of quantification, then a universally quantified statement is really a conjunction and an existentially quantified statement is really a disjunction. Thus if the party consists of Flo, Dick, Tom and Harry, and the domain of quantification '$\forall x \exists y$ talking_with(x, y)' is limited to the set {*Tom, Dick, Harry, Flo*}. The assertion that $\forall x \exists y$ talking_with(x, y) reduces to a conjunction

$\exists y$ talking_with(*Tom, y*) & $\exists y$ talking_with(*Dick, y*)
   & $\exists y$ talking_with(*Harry, y*) & $\exists y$ talking_with(*Flo, y*)

By parity of reasoning, each element of this conjunction reduces to a disjunction, '$\exists y$ talking_with(*Tom, y*)' reduces to

talking_with(*Tom, Tom*) $\vee$ talking_with(*Tom, Dick*)
    $\vee$ talking_with(*Tom, Harry*) $\vee$ talking_with(*Tom, Flo*)

and so on for the other three existentially quantified statements.

We can sum this up by saying that any quantified first-order statement Q can be reduced to a finite quantifier-free first-order statement P when the domain **D** for every quantifier in Q is **finite** and **effable**. That is, when **D** is finite and each of its elements has a name. Under such a reduction, P and Q will be materially equivalent i.e. they will have the same truth-value, though not necessarily the same meaning. The effability aspect is not a problem in computing because we can access objects only through their symbolic representation. Infinity however is a different matter which we will face later.

23.2 Implementing a Model Checker

Now let us turn to the implementation of first-order model theory in functional programming in the form of a **model checker**. The purpose of a model checker is to check through a series of interpretations of formula f to see if they are models of f. The formulae we are concerned with are formulae of first-order logic and the main focus will be on the proper treatment of quantification. A simple encoding of quantification in Shen reduces it to two higher order functions.

```
(define exists
  {(list A) --> (A --> boolean) --> boolean}
  [ ] P -> false
  [X | Y] P -> (or (P X) (exists Y P)))

(define forall
  {(list A) --> (A --> boolean) --> boolean}
  [ ] P -> true
  [X | Y] P -> (and (P X) (forall Y P)))
```

Figure 23.1 Quantification in Shen

So (some [8 9 10 11 12 13] prime?) returns true (since some member of {8,9,10,11,12,13} is prime), whereas (all [11 12] prime?) returns false. The structure of these definitions reflects the idea that a quantified statement is simply a disjunction or conjunction.

However the expressive scope of this treatment of quantification is less than that found in first-order logic. In first-order logic with equality we can state that two distinct numbers in a domain are prime.

where $\mathbf{D} = \{8,9,10,11,12,13\}$; $\exists x \in \mathbf{D}\ \exists y \in \mathbf{D}\ prime(x)\ \&\ prime(y)\ \&\ (\sim (x = y))$

Not only does our functional version suffer from not finding a place for a bound variable, it is not immediately apparent how to introduce such a concept. Writing something like

(let D [8 9 10 11 12 13]
  (exists x D (exists y D (and (prime? x) (prime? y) (not (= x y))))))

fails because, even if the quantifier definition is changed, the expression (and (prime? x) (prime? y) (not (= x y))) returns an error because x and y are not a numbers.

However the situation is not hopeless. Functional programming does have an idea of a bound variable. Lambda abstractions bind variables - can we use this mechanism to implement quantification? Yes. If we do the assertion will look like this.

(let D [8 9 10 11 12 13]
  (exists D (/. X (exists D (/. Y (and (prime? X) (prime? Y) (not (= X Y))))))))

This works nicely and allows us to use our original definitions of exists and forall. The main problem is that our notation is not as easy to read as the first-order notation. We can arrange for a 'logic macro' to make the syntax closer to first-order logic using the standard model theoretic interpretation of the logical constants.

(defmacro logic-macro
   [exists Variable Domain Wff] -> [exists Domain [/. Variable Wff]]
   [forall Variable Domain Wff] -> [forall Domain [/. Variable Wff]]
   [~ P] -> [not P]
   [P & Q] -> [and P Q]
   [P v Q] -> [or P Q]
   [P => Q] -> [or [not P] Q]
   [P <=> Q] -> [and [P => Q] [Q => P]]
   [X R Y] -> [R X Y]   where (element? R [= > < >= <= + - / *]))

Figure 23.2 A logic macro

308

A quick test shows that this works.

```
(32+)  (let D [8 9 10 11 12 13]
          (exists X D (exists Y D ((prime? X) & ((prime? Y) & (~ (X = Y))))))))
true : boolean
```

This looks great, but our program falls down when we want to compute solutions for infinite domains. Here is an example involving *twin primes*. Twin primes are primes whose difference is 2. 3 and 5 are twin primes and so is 11 and 13. How could we express and test the following conjecture?

There are twin primes greater than 10^3.

First order logic copes with this; where **D** = the set of natural numbers > 10^3;

$$\exists x \in \mathbf{D} \; \exists y \in \mathbf{D} \; prime(x) \; \& \; prime(y) \; \& \; (x + 2) = y$$

But here the domain of quantification is infinite, so not even a computer can store these items. Some rethinking is necessary.

23.3 Dealing with Infinity

Since antiquity, two strands of thought have dominated discussions of infinity - that of Plato and that of Aristotle. The Platonist conception of infinity is that an infinite collection is like any other collection, but simply bigger - infinitely big in fact. The Aristotelian conception is that completed infinite collections do not exist as such. When we say that the collection of natural numbers is infinitely big, what we mean is that no matter how many natural numbers we list, it is possible for somebody to add a new one.

Aristotle's conception of infinity as an endlessly extendable list is more useful in the context of computing than Plato's. We can use it to represent infinity in the computer by giving the rules by which such lists can be made. To do this we assume that the domain D of the quantifier is **effectively enumerable,** meaning that there is

1. A first element *b*.
2. A means *s* of generating the next element of D.
3. A test *t* for determining when the last element (if any) of D has been generated and ...
4. ... that every element of D can be generated by applying *s* *n* times to *e* for some value of *n*.

Our domain D is given by a triple $<e, s, t>$ where e is the initial element, s is the successor function that generates the next element and t is a boolean function that returns true or false depending on whether an element is the last element of the enumeration of D. Let's refer to such a structure as a **progression**. In terms of types this corresponds to a parametric type over triples.

```
(datatype progression

B : A; S : (A --> A); T : (A --> boolean);
=============================
[B S T] : (progression A);)
```

The advantage of using progressions is that we can easily create domains by choosing the appropriate values for b and t. So the domain of all primes greater than 1000 is given by [1009 (fn next-prime) (/. X false)] while the domain of all primes between 1000 and 10000 is given by [1009 (fn next-prime) (< 10001)]. We define three functions over progressions.

```
(define force
  {(progression A) --> A}
  [B _ _] -> B)

(define delay
  {(progression A) --> (progression A)}
  [B S T] -> [(S B) S T])

(define end?
  {(progression A) --> boolean}
  [B _ T] -> (T B))
```

Any finite progression can be unpacked into a list.

```
(define unpack
  {(progression A) --> (list A)}
  [B S T] -> (if (T B) [] [B | (unpack (delay [B S T]))]))
```

exists and forall become;

```
(define exists
  {(progression A) --> (A --> boolean) --> boolean}
  Progression _ -> false    where (end? Progression)
  Progression P -> (or (P (force Progression)) (exists (delay Progression) P)))

(define forall
  {(progression A) --> (A --> boolean) --> boolean}
  Progression _ -> true    where (end? Progression)
  Progression P -> (and (P (force Progression)) (forall (delay Progression) P)))
```

Our conjecture becomes

(exists X [1009 (fn next-prime) (/. X false)] (prime? (X + 2)))

Now let's look at Goldbach's conjecture from chapter 3. This conjecture states that every even number > 2 is the sum of two primes. In first-order logic this could be stated as

$$\forall x \ (even(x) \ \& \ x > 2) \rightarrow \exists y \exists z \ prime(y) \ \& \ prime(z) \ \& \ x = (y + z)$$

If we write this in our notation it comes out as

```
(define even?
  {number --> boolean}
  N -> (integer? (/ N 2)))
```

```
(let N [0 (+ 1) (/. M false)]
  (forall X N (((even? X) & (X > 2))
    => (exists Y N (exists Z N ((prime? Y) & ((prime? Z) & (X = (Y + Z)))))))))
```

which triggers an infinite loop. When X is bound to 4, our model checker looks a model of (exists Y N (exists Z N ((prime? Y) & ((prime? Z) & (4 = (Y + Z)))))). The Y is bound to zero and the computer then tries to satisfy (some Z N ((prime? 0) & ((prime? Z) (= 4 (+ 0 Z)))))) by higher and higher values of Z. If we fix the domain of X to be the evens > 2 and the domain of Y and Z to be the domain of primes ....

```
(let E [4 (+ 2) (/. M false)]
  P [2 (fn next-prime) (/. M false)]
  (forall X E (exists Y P (exists Z P (X = (Y + Z))))))
```

... then this triggers an infinite loop too. When the progression E generates the number 6, the model checker attempts to solve

(let P [2 (fn next-prime) (/. M false)] (exists Y P (exists Z P (6 = (Y + Z)))))

The existentially quantified Y generates 2 and then the inner quantified Z seeks to satisfy (6 = (2 + Z)) from the domain of all primes which must fail. Again the computer simply recurses through the primes looking for higher and higher values of Z.

The problem here is that the domains of the inner existential quantifiers need to be linked to the domain of the universal quantifier; we can call them **dependent domains.**

Figure 23.4 uses dependent domains to cut off the runaway computation by limiting the search to a threshold not greater than the even number being tested. It begins by stating the progression being searched – the set of even numbers > 2

311

by using the progression [4 (+ 2) (/. N false)]. The successor function on the other progression finds the next largest prime. The outer universal quantifier recurses through the even numbers while the inner existential quantifiers search those primes whose greatest value is the value of X.

```
(let Evens [4 (+ 2) (/. N false)]
    (forall X Evens
      (let UpperBound (/. M (> M X))
        Primes [2 (fn next-prime) UpperBound]
        (exists Y Primes (exists Z Primes (X = (Y + Z)))))))))
```

Figure 23.3 Using dependent domains to test Goldbach's conjecture

This program, written in the notation of the model checker, is much shorter than the list-based encoding of Goldbach's conjecture in chapter 4.

23.4 Super Quantification

Super quantifiers begin from an observation. The code for forall and exists is very similar; one uses true as the final value and the other false, one uses or and the other and. Suppose we parameterise these definitions to extract the common content - we get the code for **super quantification**.[78]

```
(define super
    {(progression A) --> (A --> B) --> (B --> C --> C) --> C --> C}
    [B S T] P F Y -> (if (T B) Y (F (P B) (super [(S B) S T] P F Y))))
```

Figure 23.4 Super quantification

What does this function do and why is it so super? Well first we can define the other quantifiers forall and exists in it.

```
(define forall
    {(progression A) --> (A --> boolean) --> boolean}
    Progression P -> (super Progression P (fn and) true))
```

```
(define exists
    {(progression A) --> (A --> boolean) --> boolean}
    Progression P -> (super Progression P (fn or) false))
```

Super quantifiers also allow us to tie together a lot of diverse processes apart from universal and existential quantification, including FOR loops and filters.

---

[78] Haskell programmers will recognise the code for super quantification as a close relative of their *foldr* function. The main difference is that there are 4 and not 3 arguments to the function..

```
(10+) (define for
        {(progression A) --> (A --> B) --> number}
        Progression P -> (super Progression P (fn do) 0))
(fn for) : ((progression A) --> ((A --> B) --> number))

(11+) (for [0 (+ 1) (= 100)] (fn print))
0123456789101112131415161718192021222324252627282930313233343 5
3637383940414243444546474849505152535455565758596061626364656 6
6768697071727374757677787980818283848586878889909192939495969 7
98990 : number
```

Figure 23.5 A for loop with super quantification

Filtering a progression gathers all elements of a certain kind and with super quantification, filtering over progressions is easy. Here is the definition which we use to find all the even numbers between 1 and 99.

```
(13+) (define filter
        {(progression A) --> (A --> boolean) --> (list A)}
        Progression P -> (super Progression (/. X (if (P X) [X] []))
                                 (fn append) []))
(fn filter) : ((progression A) --> ((A --> boolean) --> (list A)))

(14+) (filter [1 (+ 1) (= 100)] (/. X (integer? (/ X 2))))
[2 4 6 8 10 12 14 16 18 20 22 24 26 28 30 32 34 36 38 40 ... etc] : (list number)
```

Figure 23.6 Filtering with super quantification

One source of annoyance. Our encoding of super quantifiers uses strict evaluation because a higher-order call will be strict in its evaluation and this is also the case with super. Unfortunately, when we pass lazy functions to super like or we want the evaluation in super to be lazy too. The type secure solution is to create **lazy super quantifiers** which are defined by the following definition

```
(define super
  {(progression A) --> (A --> B) --> (B --> (lazy C) --> C) --> C --> C}
  [B S T] P F Y -> (if (T B)
                       Y
                       (F (P B) (freeze (super [(S B) S T] P F Y)))))
```

Figure 23.7 Lazy super quantification

Our quantifier definitions use special versions of and and or which are defined to take a lazy boolean; only if needed is this argument thawed to deliver a boolean.

313

```
(define forall
   {(progression A) --> (A --> boolean) --> boolean}
   Progression P -> (super Progression P (fn and') true))

 (define exists
   {(progression A) --> (A --> boolean) --> boolean}
   Progression P -> (super Progression P (fn or') false))

(define and'
   {boolean --> (lazy boolean) --> boolean}
   false _ -> false
   _ Lazy -> (thaw Lazy))

(define or'
   {boolean --> (lazy boolean) --> boolean}
   true _ -> true
   _ Lazy -> (thaw Lazy))
```

Figure 23.8 First-order quantification with super quantification

In 23.9 we test out our model checker based on lazy super quantification. In input 60, we define a function that always returns true, but which allows us to see the value of a bound variable *v* by printing a message stating the binding. We then test the conjecture that there is a whole number between 1 and 100 divisible by 9 which is a perfect square. The response lends confidence to our belief that the model checker is actually computing the correct values.

```
(60+) (define show
         {string --> A --> boolean}
         String X -> (do (output "~A ~S~%" String X) true))
(fn show) : (string --> (A --> boolean))

(61+) (exists M [1 (+ 1) (= 100)] (exists N [10 (+ 1) (= 100)]
         (((integer? (N / 9)) & (N = (M * M))) & (show "N =" N))))
N = 36
true : boolean
```

23.9 Working with super quantification

23.5 Proof and Computability

There is a class of undecidable problems which even the model checker cannot help us with; these are characterised by mixed existential and universal quantifiers which both range over infinite domains. Here is an example.

There is no greatest prime number.

314

Though the truth of this sentence has been known over 2,000 years, the model checker will not return any verdict on it. Written in first-order notation the sentence appears as

$$\forall x\, prime(x) \to \exists y\, prime(y)\ \&\ (y > x)$$

Suppose the statement is true. Since it uses a universal quantifier over an infinite domain, the model checker will never return a positive answer. Suppose it is false, then the model checker will eventually find the greatest prime and spend forever looking for a bigger one. In either case, the program is silent. The example reminds us of what we learnt in the section on dependent types - that there is a gap between what is *provable* and what is *computable*.

Exercise 23

1. Encode the following conjectures in the language of the model checker.

    a.   any natural number can be represented as the sum of four integer squares.[79]
    b.   Every integer greater than 1 has a unique factorisation into primes.[80]

2. Use macros to change the model checker so that instead of returning *just* true or false, it returns messages of the kind shown in 20.11.

Further Reading

Mendelson (2009) contains an exposition of first-order model theory. Our quantifier machine abuts on the area of model checking, which concerns the use of these techniques to automatically verify properties of systems. Baier and Katoen (2008) provides an introduction. Abelson and Sussman (1996) provide an excellent discussion on the use of progressions (called *streams* in their book) in programming.

---

[79] Lagrange's 4 square theorem.

[80] Known as the 'fundamental theorem of arithmetic'.

24 An Interpreter for Kλ

24.1 Formal Semantics

In the first part of this book we studied Shen as a programming language, taking for granted the basic operating principles of the language. Such features as pattern matching were introduced by example, rather than being formally defined. From a pedagogic view this makes sense. However in the specification of a language, it is often important to define these operating principles formally and not just by example. The study of how to do this belongs to **formal semantics**.

There are three approaches to formal semantics; operational, denotational and axiomatic. An **operational semantics** for a language L provides the rules by which programs in L are executed. **Denotational semantics** provides a meaning for L programs by mapping then to a denotation which is held to be the meaning of the program. An **axiomatic semantics** for L provides a meaning by mapping the programs in L to some description within a formal language, of which first-order logic is one example. An examination of Shen from all these perspectives would require a book of comparable size to this one, and so for reasons of space we will limit ourselves to examining Shen from the operational perspective.

We asserted that an operational semantics is important without explaining why. There are two reasons for constructing a formal semantics for a computer language L. The first is to provide a formal basis for making proofs or predictions about L programs. The second is to provide some accurate model for implementing L.

In this chapter we will be concerned with providing a model of how to implement Kλ based on the SECD machine of Peter Landin. Since Kλ is in essence a very simple Lisp based on applicative order evaluation, we take as read the semantics of Kλ from our understanding of lambda calculus. Nevertheless we shall cover enough significant ground to show how the SECD machine can be turned into a vehicle for giving the semantics of Kλ. In chapter 28 we cover operational semantics of $\mathcal{L}$ from chapter 15 from the other perspective – as a ground for proving the correctness of the type checking algorithm in Shen.

24.2 The Environment Model of Evaluation

Recall from chapter 15 that Kλ definitions have the form (defun *f* (*parameters*) *expr*). This is a sugared way of associating an abstraction with a symbol. We can write total as

I. (defun total (x)
       (if (= () x) 0
         (+ (hd x) (total (tl x)))))

or as

II. (defun total ()
  (lambda x (if (= () x) 0
         (+ (hd x) ((total) (tl x))))))

What happens when we apply total in II. to a list – as in ((total) [1 2 3])? Following the model supplied by the lambda calculus, we replace or **unfold** (total) by the abstraction it designates to derive

((lambda x (if (= () x) 0
       (+ (hd x) ((total) (tl x)))))) [1 2 3])

Then by β reduction we derive

(if (= () [1 2 3]) 0
  (+ (hd [1 2 3]) ((total) (tl [1 2 3]))))))

(= () [1 2 3]) is false so this reduces to

(+ (hd [1 2 3]) ((total) (tl [1 2 3])))))

which simplifies to

(+ 1 ((total) (tl [1 2 3])))))

And so on. By repeatedly evaluating this expression by the rules for Kλ and using unfolding we derive the final answer, 6. If we follow the definition in I. the process is very similar. We associate the value [1 2 3] with the formal parameter x to derive

(if (= () [1 2 3]) 0
  (+ (hd [1 2 3]) (total (tl [1 2 3]))))

and proceed in much the same way to derive the same answer.

This substitution model of evaluation which we are using here is extremely inefficient. The substitution arises from carrying β reduction into our computational model and β reduction involves traversing a symbolic expression and replacing free variables within that expression. An alternative to replacing a free variable is simply to note that the free variable is now associated with a value and to use that association whenever that variable is encountered. This is the basis of the **environment** model for evaluating functional expressions which is the one that functional languages actually use.

An environment can be seen as a set of variable-value associations in which expressions are evaluated. Thus instead of assessing

(if (= () [1 2 3]) 0
    (+ (hd [1 2 3]) (total (tl [1 2 3])))))

We can choose to represent it like this

{x |→ [1 2 3]} (if (= () x) 0
                    (+ (hd x) (total (tl x))))

This composite object, an expression and the environment in which it is evaluated is called a **closure**. The name arises from the fact that the addition of an environment to an open lambda expression like the one above has the same effect as replacing the free variable in that expression by a closed term. We have effectively created a closed expression from an open one.

When we base our evaluation model on the use of environments we encounter a problem. When we unfold the next call to total and apply the body of that definition the x is then associated with [2 3]. We now have two inconsistent associations.

The inconsistency is solved by the use of **frames**. A frame is a consistent set of associations and an environment is a linked series of frames created in temporal order with the foremost being the most recently created. When we want to know the value of a variable we look in the most recent frame. If it does not occur there we look in the next frame in the series until we find a value. Therefore in the next call to total, a new frame is created in which x is associated with [2 3].

Our model takes unfolding as a separate action from variable association, but the environment model can cope with unfolding too. We suppose that in addition to those frames which are dynamically created as our program executes, there is also a frame that persists from one user input to another. This is often called the **global environment** and it contains associations between function symbols and the definitions attached to them. It stands in contrast to the **local environment** which does not persist between user inputs. When unfolding is called for, the global environment is searched for the appropriate association.

24.3 The Basic SECD Machine

Landin's SECD (Stack-Environment-Control-Dump) machine is based on the environment model for the evaluation of functional expressions. The SECD machine arose out of a landmark paper (Landin (1964)) in which he explained a method for evaluating a restricted lambda calculus. The SECD later proved to be immensely influential in the design of functional language compilers.

One potential for confusion needs to be cleared up: *Landin's 'environment' is really a frame in modern parlance* and in the SECD the linked series of frames is kept as a list of past environments on the dump. In the following sections we use 'environment' in the sense that Landin used it.

The fundamental datatypes which are processed by the SECD are those of the lambda calculus plus closures. Closures in the SECD machine follow the pattern of the previous section, but they are triples, $<E, v, x>$ where E is an environment, v is a free variable wrt x, and x is any lambda expression. We'll understand the logic of this construction when we come to study the SECD machine in detail. We'll refer to lambda expressions and SECD closures as objects or *obs*. They form a type given by the following sequent calculus rules.

```
E : environment; X : symbol; Y : ob;
============================
[closure E X Y] : ob;

X : symbol; Y : ob;
==============
[lambda X Y] : ob;

X : ob; Y : ob;
==========
[X Y] : ob;


X : symbol;
X : ob;
```

The other objects of the SECD, the stack, environment, control and dump are constructions out of *obs*, using standard type constructs.

```
(synonyms  stack (list ob)
           environment (list (symbol * ob))
           control (list ob)
           dump (list (stack * environment * control)))
```

The SECD machine begins by placing the expression to be evaluated on the control and a series of transitions then ensue in which this expression is evaluated. The stack is the work area of the SECD and the dump is an historical record of the past states of the SECD. When the control is empty and so is the dump, the element left on the stack is returned as the normal form.

The SECD is most conveniently viewed as a program and so to explain the SECD, we will code directly into Shen. We begin with a version of the SECD directed to pure λ calculus expressions using applicative order evaluation.

```
(define evaluate
 {ob --> ob}
 X -> (secd [] [] [X] []))

(define secd
 {stack --> environment --> control --> dump --> ob}
 [V] _ [] [] -> V
 [V] _ [] [(@p S E C) | D] -> (secd [V | S] E C D)
 S E [[lambda X Y] | C] D -> (secd [[closure E X Y] | S] E C D)
 S E [[X Y] | C] D -> (secd S E [Y X @ | C] D)
 [[closure E* X Y] Z | S] E [@ | C] D
    -> (secd [] [(@p X Z) | E*] [Y] [(@p S E C) | D])
 S E [X | C] D ->(if (bnd? X E) (secd [(lookup X E) | S] E C D) (secd [X | S] E C D)))

(define bnd?
 {ob --> environment --> boolean}
 X [] -> false
 X [(@p Y _) | _] -> true  where (== X Y)
 X [_ | Y] -> (bnd? X Y))

(define lookup
 {ob --> environment --> ob}
 X [] -> X
 X [(@p Y Z) | _] -> Z  where (== X Y)
 X [_ | Y] -> (lookup X Y))
```

Figure 24.1 An SECD machine for pure lambda calculus

The computation is initiated by evaluate which places the expression to be evaluated on the control and passes the computation to secd. The transitions of the SECD machine can be described by a function evaluate of type stack → environment → control → dump → ob. The first line states the base case; that if the stack contains one element and the control and dump are empty, then the head of the stack is returned as the value.

[V] _ [] [] -> V

The second line states that if the stack and dump are non-empty, but the control is empty, that the dump is to be used to restore the previous values of S, E, and C.

[V] _ [] [(@p S E C) | D] -> (secd [V | S] E C D)

The third line states if the control is fronted by an abstraction, then a closure is to be formed from the bound variable of the abstraction, its body and the current environment and placed on the stack.

S E [[lambda X Y] | C] D -> (secd [[closure E X Y] | S] E C D)

320

Fourth, if the control is headed by an application then the elements of the application are placed in reverse order on the control followed by the application symbol @. If the operator is placed after the operands in this manner then the notation is said to be in postfix or **reverse Polish**. The reason for this move is that in applicative order evaluation the argument Y must be evaluated first and hence it is placed on top of the stack.

S E [[X Y] | C] D -> (secd S E [Y X @ | C] D)

Fifth, if the stack is topped by a closure an followed by an *ob*, and the leading symbol of the control is @ (indicating that an application on the stack is to be evaluated) then the leading variable of the closure is to be bound to the argument in the environment and the body of the closure becomes the new control, the stack is emptied and the previous states of S, E and C are placed on the dump.

[[closure E* X Y] Z | S] E [@ | C] D -> (secd [] [(@p X Z) | E*] [Y] [(@p S E C) | D]))

Last if a *ob* is found at the head of the control, and the *ob* is bound in the environment, then the value of the *ob* is placed on the stack. If *ob* is unbound, then the *ob* itself is placed on the stack.

S E [X | C] D -> (if (bnd? X E) (secd [(lookup X E) | S] E C D) (secd [X | S] E C D))

24.4 Computing with the SECD Machine

To view the SECD in action we'll add some code to our program to give a window on the evaluation process (bolded code, figure 24.2). The secd function acquires a help function to perform evaluations while the secd function itself prints a history of the computation.

```
(define secd
   {stack --> environment --> control --> dump --> ob}
    S E C D -> (do (output "~%~%S = ~R~%E = ~R~%C = ~R~%D = ~R"  S E C D)
                (read-byte (stinput))
                (secd-h S E C D)))

(define secd-h
   {stack --> environment --> control --> dump --> ob}
    [V] E [] [] -> V
    [V] _ [] [(@p S E C) | D] -> (secd [V | S] E C D)
    S E [[lambda X Y] | C] D -> (secd [[closure E X Y] | S] E C D)
    S E [[X Y] | C] D -> (secd S E [Y X @ | C] D)
    [[closure E* X Y] Z | S] E [@ | C] D -> (secd [] [(@p X Z) | E*] [Y] [(@p S E C) | D])
    S E [X | C] D ->(if (bnd? X E) (secd [(lookup X E) | S] E C D) (secd [X | S] E C D))
    S E C D -> (error "~%cannot compute S = ~R, E = ~R, C = ~R, D = ~R~%"
                        S E C D))
```

Figure 24.2 Creating a window on the SECD.

321

Case 1: evaluate $((\lambda\, x\, x)\, a)$

The following is a trace of the basic SECD machine with a commentary.

(evaluate [[lambda x x] a])

S = ()
E = ()
C = (((lambda x x) a))
D = ()

The first action is to transfer the expression to the control C.

S = ()
E = ()
C = (a (lambda x x) @)
D = ()

The second action splits the application into parts using reverse Polish.

S = (a)
E = ()
C = ((lambda x x) @)
D = ()

The argument is placed on the stack.

S = ((closure () x x) a)
E = ()
C = (@)
D = ()

The abstraction is removed from the control and a closure is pushed on the stack.

S = ()
E = ((@p x a))
C = (x)
D = ((@p [] (@p [] [])))

The fifth action evaluates the application of the closure, the variable x is associated with a in the new environment and the history of the computation is pushed onto the dump.

S = (a)
E = ((@p x a))
C = ()
D = ((@p [] (@p [] [])))

The variable x is replaced by its value under E and that value is pushed onto the stack.

S = (a)
E = ()
C = ()
D = ()

The old values of S, E, C are retrieved from the dump. The values are all () so the answer is returned.

a : ob

Case 2: evaluate (λ x x)

(evaluate [lambda X X])

S = ()
E = ()
C = ((lambda x x))
D = ()

S = ((closure () x x))
E = ()
C = ()
D = ()

[closure [] x x] : ob

Here the SECD machine issues an *ob* which is not a lambda expression, whereas in λ calculus the input would be returned as a normal form.

Case 3: evaluate (x y)

(evaluate [x y])

S = ()
E = ()
C = ((x y))
D = ()

S = ()
E = ()
C = (y x @)
D = ()

S = (y)
E = ()
C = (x @)
D = ()

S = (x y)
E = ()
C = (@)
D = ()
cannot compute S = (x y), E = (), C = (@), D = ()

The SECD machine cannot compute the normal form of (x y) which is (x y). Compare however Shen,

(2-) (x y)
fn: x is undefined

This raises the question; given that the SECD does not always produce a lambda expression as an output. (as in case 2) and that it may fail to compute lambda expressions which have a normal form (as in case 3), what are the exact relations between the SECD machine and the lambda calculus interpreters of chapter 14?

The answer is that the SECD implements applicative order evaluation to WHNF for **closed** lambda expressions. This is a usable model for adapting lambda calculus to functional programming.

In the case where an SECD closure [closure E v x] is returned as normal form, in order to get the equivalent lambda expression, it is necessary to translate the closure back into conventional lambda calculus by replacing the variable v in x by its value in E. Where v has no value in E, then the result should be $(\lambda v x)$. Hence in case 2 of the previous page, [closure [] x x] translates back into $(\lambda x x)$.

Here is one last example from chapter 14.

Case 4: evaluate the normal form of (*if* t a b) where t is proxy for *true* and the definition of t and *if* proceeds according to the equivalence given in 14.4.

$t = (\lambda x (\lambda y x))$
$if = (\lambda z (\lambda x (\lambda y ((z x) y))))$.

(let If [lambda z [lambda x [lambda y [[z x] y]]]]
    True [lambda x [lambda y x]]
    (evaluate [[[If True] a] b]))

S = ()
E = ()
C = (((((lambda z (lambda x (lambda y ((z x) y)))) (lambda x (lambda y x))) a) b))
D = ()

S = ()
E = ()
C = (b (((lambda z (lambda x (lambda y ((z x) y)))) (lambda x (lambda y x))) a) @)
D = ()

324

S = (b)
E = ()
C = ((((lambda z (lambda x (lambda y ((z x) y)))) (lambda x (lambda y x))) a) @)
D = ()

S = (b)
E = ()
C = (a ((lambda z (lambda x (lambda y ((z x) y)))) (lambda x (lambda y x))) @ @)
D = ()

S = (a b)
E = ()
C = (((lambda z (lambda x (lambda y ((z x) y)))) (lambda x (lambda y x))) @ @)
D = ()

S = (a b)
E = ()
C = ((lambda x (lambda y x)) (lambda z (lambda x (lambda y ((z x) y)))) @ @ @)
D = ()

S = ((closure () x (lambda y x)) a b)
E = ()
C = ((lambda z (lambda x (lambda y ((z x) y)))) @ @ @)
D = ()

S = ((closure () z (lambda x (lambda y ((z x) y)))) (closure () x (lambda y x)) a b)
E = ()
C = (@ @ @)
D = ()

S = ()
E = ((@p z [closure [] x [lambda y x]]))
C = ((lambda x (lambda y ((z x) y))))
D = ((@p [a b] (@p [] [@ @])))

S = ((closure ((@p z [closure [] x [lambda y x]])) x (lambda y ((z x) y))))
E = ((@p z [closure [] x [lambda y x]]))
C = ()
D = ((@p [a b] (@p [] [@ @])))

S = ((closure ((@p z [closure [] x [lambda y x]])) x (lambda y ((z x) y))) a b)
E = ()
C = (@ @)
D = ()

S = ()
E = ((@p x a) (@p z [closure [] x [lambda y x]]))
C = ((lambda y ((z x) y)))
D = ((@p [b] (@p [] [@])))

S = ((closure ((@p x a) (@p z [closure [] x [lambda y x]])) y ((z x) y)))
E = ((@p x a) (@p z [closure [] x [lambda y x]]))
C = ()
D = ((@p [b] (@p [] [@])))

S = ((closure ((@p x a) (@p z [closure [] x [lambda y x]])) y ((z x) y)) b)
E = ()
C = (@)
D = ()

S = ()
E = ((@p y b) (@p x a) (@p z [closure [] x [lambda y x]]))
C = (((z x) y))
D = ((@p [] (@p [] [])))

S = ()
E = ((@p y b) (@p x a) (@p z [closure [] x [lambda y x]]))
C = (y (z x) @)
D = ((@p [] (@p [] [])))

S = (b)
E = ((@p y b) (@p x a) (@p z [closure [] x [lambda y x]]))
C = ((z x) @)
D = ((@p [] (@p [] [])))

S = (b)
E = ((@p y b) (@p x a) (@p z [closure [] x [lambda y x]]))
C = (x z @ @)
D = ((@p [] (@p [] [])))

S = (a b)
E = ((@p y b) (@p x a) (@p z [closure [] x [lambda y x]]))
C = (z @ @)
D = ((@p [] (@p [] [])))

S = ((closure () x (lambda y x)) a b)
E = ((@p y b) (@p x a) (@p z [closure [] x [lambda y x]]))
C = (@ @)
D = ((@p [] (@p [] [])))

S = ()
E = ((@p x a))
C = ((lambda y x))
D = ((@p [b] (@p [(@p y b) (@p x a) (@p z [closure [] x [lambda y x]])] [@]))
       (p [] (@p [] [])))

S = ((closure ((@p x a)) y x))
E = ((@p x a))
C = ()
D = ((@p [b] (@p [(@p y b) (@p x a) (@p z [closure [] x [lambda y x]])] [@]))
       (p [] (@p [] [])))

S = ((closure ((@p x a)) y x) b)
E = ((@p y b) (@p x a) (@p z [closure [] x [lambda y x]]))
C = (@)
D = ((@p [] (@p [] [])))

326

S = ()
E = ((@p y b) (@p x a))
C = (x)
D = ((@p [] (@p [(@p y b) (@p x a) (@p z [closure [] x [lambda y x]])] []))
    (@p [] (@p [] [])))

S = (a)
E = ((@p y b) (@p x a))
C = ()
D = ((@p [] (@p [(@p y b) (@p x a) (@p z [closure [] x [lambda y x]])] []))
    (@p [] (@p [] [])))
S = (a)
E = ((@p y b) (@p x a) (@p z [closure [] x [lambda y x]]))
C = ()
D = ((@p [] (@p [] [])))

S = (a)
E = ()
C = ()
D = ()

a : ob

24.5 Adding δ Rules to the SECD Machine

The SECD machine has no provision to doing basic arithmetic unless we use something like the Barendregt's representation of chapter 14. This representation is of no practical use and so we are driven to consider how native arithmetic rules can be added to the SECD machine. These 'extracurricular' rules are known as δ rules. To prepare the ground we need to extend the type of all *obs* to include booleans, strings and numbers.

X : boolean;
X : ob;

X : number;
X : ob;

X : string;
X : ob;

A primitive function is a extracurricular function, of which we can include the successor and predecessor functions and a zero test. An extra rule is added to secd-h which states that if an application of a primitive function is found on the stack, that the designated function is to be applied to the argument. The new code is bolded in figure 24.3.

```
(define secd-h
  {stack --> environment --> control --> dump --> ob}
  [V] E [] [] -> V
  [V] _ [] [(@p S E C) | D] -> (secd [V | S] E C D)
  S E [[lambda X Y] | C] D -> (secd [[closure E X Y] | S] E C D)
  S E [[X Y] | C] D -> (secd S E [Y X @ | C] D)
  [F X | S] E [@ | C] D -> (secd [(apply F X) | S] E C D) where (prim? F)
  [[closure E* X Y] Z | S] E [@ | C] D -> (secd [] [(@p X Z) | E*] [Y] [(@p S E C) | D])
  S E [X | C] D ->(if (bnd? X E) (secd [(lookup X E) | S] E C D)  (secd [X | S] E C D))
  S E C D -> (error "~%cannot compute S = ~R, E = ~R, C = ~R, D = ~R~%"
                              S E C D))
```

```
(define prim?
  {ob --> boolean}
  F -> (element? F [succ pred zero?]))
```

Figure 24.3   The SECD machine with δ rules

This leaves apply to be coded.   The following definition

```
(define apply
  {ob --> ob --> ob}
  X -> (+ X 1)   where (number? X)
  pred X -> (- X 1)    where (number? X)
  zero? X -> (= X 0)  where (number? X))
```

checks under the rule

(number? X) : verified >> X : number;

Here we evaluate (*succ* (*succ* (*succ* 3))).

(evaluate [succ [succ [succ 3]]])

```
S = ()
E = ()
C = ((succ (succ (succ 3))))
D = ()

S = ()
E = ()
C = ((succ (succ 3)) succ @)
D = ()

S = ()
E = ()
C = ((succ 3) succ @ succ @)
D = ()
```

```
S = ()
E = ()
C = (3 succ @ succ @ succ @)
D = ()

S = (3)
E = ()
C = (succ @ succ @ succ @)
D = ()

S = (succ 3)
E = ()
C = (@ succ @ succ @)
D = ()

S = (4)
E = ()
C = (succ @ succ @)
D = ()

S = (succ 4)
E = ()
C = (@ succ @)
D = ()

S = (5)
E = ()
C = (succ @)
D = ()

S = (succ 5)
E = ()
C = (@)
D = ()

S = (6)
E = ()
C = ()
D = ()
```

6 : ob

24.6 Adding Lazy Evaluation to the SECD Machine

Our revised SECD machine operates using applicative order evaluation. As we saw in chapter 14, there is a problem defining recursive definitions using applicative order evaluation, in that both limbs of a conditional are evaluated. This leads to runaway behaviour where the function continues to recurse even when it has encountered the base case.

There are various solutions to this problem but the simplest is to suspend applicative order evaluation in the case of conditionals and introduce a new rule for *if* which follows the common method of evaluating the test condition first and which, depending on the result of the evaluation, evaluates the *then* expression or the *else* expression exclusively. We need to extend the type of *obs* to cope with a new expression.

```
Test : ob; Then : ob; Else : ob;
========================
[if Test Then Else] : ob;
```

The SECD machine will reverse the order of the terms, placing the Test first on the stack. Depending on the result of evaluating the Test, the SECD will execute the appropriate action. The changes are bolded in figure 24.4.

```
(define secd-h
  {stack --> environment --> control --> dump --> ob}
  [V] E [] [] -> V
  [V] _ [] [(@p S E C) | D] -> (secd [V | S] E C D)
  S E [[if Test Then Else] | C] D -> (secd S E [Test if Then Else @ | C] D)
  [true | S] E [if Then Else @ | C] D -> (secd S E [Then | C] D)
  [false | S] E [if Then Else @ | C] D -> (secd S E [Else | C] D)
  S E [[lambda X Y] | C] D -> (secd [[closure E X Y] | S] E C D)
  S E [[X Y] | C] D -> (secd S E [Y X @ | C] D)
  [F X | S] E [@ | C] D -> (secd [(apply F X) | S] E C D) where (prim? F)
  [[closure E* X Y] Z | S] E [@ | C] D -> (secd [] [(@p X Z) | E*] [Y] [(@p S E C) | D])
  S E [X | C] D -> (secd [(lookup X E) | S] E C D)
                        where (and (atom? X) (not (== @ X)))
  S E C D -> (error "~%cannot compute S = ~R, E = ~R, C = ~R, D = ~R~%"
                        S E C D))
```

Figure 24.4 The SECD machine with lazy conditionals

(evaluate [if [zero? 1] a b])

```
S = ()
E = ()
C = ((if (zero? 1) a b))
D = ()

S = ()
E = ()
C = ((zero? 1) if a b @)
D = ()

S = ()
E = ()
C = (1 zero? @ if a b @)
D = ()
```

```
S = (1)
E = ()
C = (zero? @ if a b @)
D = ()

S = (zero? 1)
E = ()
C = (@ if a b @)
D = ()

S = (false)
E = ()
C = (if a b @)
D = ()

S = ()
E = ()
C = (b)
D = ()

S = (b)
E = ()
C = ()
D = ()
```

b : ob

24.7 Adding Global Definitions to the SECD Machine

Our SECD machine contains no provision for defining Kλ function definitions. To accommodate these, we have first to extend the concept of an *ob* to include definitions.

F : symbol; Params : (list symbol); Body : ob;
==================================
[defun F Params Body] : ob;

Since definitions inhabit the global environment and persist between evaluations, we need a global variable to function as the holder of these definitions. This variable is initialised to the empty list.

(value *global*) : environment;

(set *global* [])

The evaluate function is changed to update the global environment if a Kλ definition is entered.

```
(define evaluate
  {ob --> ob}
  [defun F Params Y] -> (do (update-global-environment F (reverse Params) Y) F)
  X -> (secd [] [] [X] []))

(define update-global-environment
  {symbol --> (list symbol) --> ob --> environment}
  F [] Z      -> (set *global* [(@p F Z) | (value *global*)])
  F [X | Y] Z -> (update-global-environment F Y [lambda X Z]))
```

The effect of update-global-environment is to map a Kλ definition to an abstraction and to associate the name of that function with the abstraction in the global environment. secd-h contains one small change. The penultimate rule in secd-h is changed from

```
S E [X | C] D ->(if  (bnd? X E)  (secd [(lookup X E) | S] E C D)  (secd [X | S] E C D))
```

to

```
S E [X | C] D -> (cases (bnd? X E) (secd [(lookup X E) | S] E C D)
                        (bnd? X (value *global*))
                                    (secd S E [(lookup X (value *global*)) | C] D)
                        true  (secd [X | S] E C D) )
```

The significance of searching the global environment after the local environment can be grasped by the following Kλ definition.

```
(defun f (reverse) (reverse ()))
```

If we suppose the global environment is searched first, then a call to f returns () (i.e. the empty list). If the local environment is searched first, then a call to f returns the result of applying the argument to f to the empty list. Hence under the first arrangement, (f (lambda x (cons 1 x))) will return [] and under the second [1]. The usual arrangement with functional languages is that the local environment is searched first and this is the case with Kλ.

```
(evaluate [defun plus [x y] [if [zero? x] y [[plus [pred x]] [succ y]]]])
plus : ob
```

```
(evaluate [[plus 3] 4])
```
.

. (88 transitions)

.

7 : ob

There is a conceptual connection between variable assignment and function definition that was touched on in chapter 7. A function definition can be seen as

332

an assignment of a lambda expression to a symbol. Thus (defun f (x) (g x y)) can be seen as syntactic sugar for (set f (lambda x (g x y))).

In some languages like Scheme and Python, this is precisely true. A consequence is that if an expression like (defun f (x) (g x y)) is entered followed by (set f 7), then the assignment overwrites the function definition. In such languages, a symbol may have only meaning and within the Lisp community these are known as **Lisp-1** languages.

In Common Lisp, (setq f 7) and (defun f (x) (g x y)) coexist without interference marking Common Lisp as a **Lisp-2** language. In a Lisp-2 language a symbol may have more than one denotation. In the design of Shen there arose the choice between following Lisp-1 and Lisp-2. Because symbols are inert and 'do nothing unless told', the denotation of the symbol depends on the use made by the programmer. If we want to get at the function denoted by the symbol then fn is used; if the intent is to get at the value assigned to it then value is appropriate. Shen effectively chose to follow Common Lisp and Lisp-2. It is fairly easy to divide the global environment in this program to support a Lisp-2 convention and the coding is left as an exercise to this chapter.

24.8 Quotation and Lexical Scope

Consider these two Kλ functions.

```
(defun f (x y) (g x))
(defun g (x) y)
```

Reasoning by λ calculus and by experiment in the Shen REPL, (f *a b*) returns y for any *a* and *b*. However if we compute say, (f 1 2) in our SECD machine, the answer comes out as 2. Here is a trace.

```
(evaluate [defun f [x y] [g x]])
f : ob

(evaluate [defun g [x] y])
g : ob

(evaluate [[f 1] 2])

S = ()
E = ()
C = (((f 1) 2))
D = ()

S = ()
E = ()
C = (2 (f 1) @)
D = ()
```

S = (2)
E = ()
C = ((f 1) @)
D = ()

S = (2)
E = ()
C = (1 f @ @)
D = ()

S = (1 2)
E = ()
C = (f @ @)
D = ()

S = (1 2)
E = ()
C = ((lambda x (lambda y (g x))) @ @)
D = ()

S = ((closure () x (lambda y (g x))) 1 2)
E = ()
C = (@ @)
D = ()

S = ()
E = ((@p x 1))
C = ((lambda y (g x)))
D = ((@p [2] (@p [] [@])))

S = ((closure ((@p x 1)) y (g x)))
E = ((@p x 1))
C = ()
D = ((@p [2] (@p [] [@])))

S = ((closure ((@p x 1)) y (g x)) 2)
E = ()
C = (@)
D = ()

S = ()
E = ((@p y 2) (@p x 1))
C = ((g x))
D = ((@p [] (@p [] [])))

S = ()
E = ((@p y 2) (@p x 1))
C = (x g @)
D = ((@p [] (@p [] [])))

334

S = (1)
E = ((@p y 2) (@p x 1))
C = (g @)
D = ((@p [] (@p [] [])))

S = (1)
E = ((@p y 2) (@p x 1))
C = ((lambda x y) @)
D = ((@p [] (@p [] [])))

S = ((closure ((@p y 2) (@p x 1)) x y) 1)
E = ((@p y 2) (@p x 1))
C = (@)
D = ((@p [] (@p [] [])))

S = ()
E = ((@p x 1) (@p y 2) (@p x 1))
C = (y)
D = ((@p [] (@p [(@p y 2) (@p x 1)] [])) (@p [] (@p [] [])))

S = (2)
E = ((@p x 1) (@p y 2) (@p x 1))
C = ()
D = ((@p [] (@p [(@p y 2) (@p x 1)] [])) (@p [] (@p [] [])))

S = (2)
E = ((@p y 2) (@p x 1))
C = ()
D = ((@p [] (@p [] [])))

S = (2)
E = ()
C = ()
D = ()

2 : ob

The problem arises when the SECD machine evaluates the symbol y which was bound to 2 in the evaluation of the call to f. Reaching into the subconscious memory of its past computation, the SECD retrieves the value 2 and returns it.

The computation is an example of the dangers of **dynamic scope**. The scope of the binding of y in f extends beyond the **lexical scope** of the expression in which it is introduced to include all free occurrences of this symbol within functions called by and subsequent to f; a feature called **dynamic binding**. In contrast, working according to lexical scope, the binding of y only has force within f and the binding is **lexical binding**.

In the history of Lisp, dynamic binding was used in all early implementations and the author's first experience with Lisp, DEC-10 Lisp in 1986, shared this feature.

Dynamic binding can be useful if there is a need to create symbol-value associations which are dynamically made or unmade depending on the state of the computation. Earlier work implementing Prolog in Lisp (Stickel, 1986) used dynamic binding through the PROGV command which survived in Common Lisp as a medium for dynamic binding.

However with the advent of Steele's work (Sussman and Steele, 1974) on Scheme, the vogue for dynamic binding came to an end. It was recognised that dynamic binding made the behaviour of programs hard to fathom and made formal reasoning about them almost unfeasible. Lexical binding reinstated the idea that functional programming should reflect the lambda calculus.

Another wart is that in our model, as soon as a symbol acquires a binding to a lambda expression, then it is evaluated to such. Thus if we define map as before then the expression [john read the map] (suitably rendered in cons form) will not evaluate to itself but will evaluate to a list in which the final element is the lambda definition of map. In languages like Python, this is in fact standard behaviour. As soon as a symbol acquires a definition it is fixed to that definition. However in Kλ, and in Shen, symbols moonlight in various roles and the principle rules that if we want to give a job to a symbol, we have to say exactly what that job is.

A single convention of **quotation** actually solves both of these problems. Quotation was used in the very first Lisp, Lisp 1.5, as a means of allowing the user to manipulate symbols or lists without being obliged to evaluate any binding of the symbol or (in the case of lists) to evaluate their contents. The device occurs in nearly all members of the Lisp family (though not in Shen). A short discursion on quotation in Common Lisp will help to cement understanding.

In Common Lisp, if a symbol is typed into the REPL, say howdy, then unless the symbol is bound an error is raised. In other words, symbols standing on their own (and not bound in definitions or by lambda etc.) are required to denote something.

This behaviour is a nuisance if the intent is to work just with the symbol itself. Since Common Lisp, like Shen, is designed to be a symbolic processing language, Lispers developed the idea of quotation to facilitate symbol and list manipulation. When a symbol S (or indeed any object) is quoted then the evaluation process stops short of evaluating S and what is returned is simply what is quoted. The function that performs this is quote. Hence though howdy will return an error (unless it is assigned a value), (quote howdy) will return howdy. Generally Lispers use a convenient shorthand for quote – the single quote – and (quote howdy) is written as 'howdy. The list [John reads the map] is written in Lisp as '(John reads the map).

Kλ and Shen obviously follow a different convention. Symbols 'do not do anything unless told' and evaluate to themselves unless the programmer specifically shows that they are to be treated otherwise. howdy evaluates to howdy. We can say that in Kλ and Shen, idle symbols are implicitly quoted. Syntactically an idle symbol is any symbol that is not lambda bound or used as a function (i.e. placed at the front of a parenthesised expression). Since idle symbols can be determined lexically, it is easy for the compiler to insert the missing quotes.

To adapt our SECD program to quotation we insert a function that walks through the Kλ definition, inserting quotes over idle symbols.

```
(define evaluate
  {ob --> ob}
  [defun F Params Y] -> (let Quote (quote-free-variables Params Y)
                             Update (update-global-environment F
                                          (reverse Params) Quote)
                          F)
  X -> (secd [] [] [X] []))
```

The quote -free-variables function walks through the body of the definition carrying with it a list of variables that are bound in the definition. When it encounters a symbol *s* that is not bound, the symbol is quoted as [quote *s*].

```
(define quote-free-variables
  {(list symbol) --> ob --> ob}
  Bound [lambda X Y] -> [lambda X (quote-free-variables [X | Bound] Y)]
  Bound [if Test Then Else] -> [if (quote-free-variables Bound Test)
                                   (quote-free-variables Bound Then)
                                   (quote-free-variables Bound Else)]
  Bound [X Y] -> [X (quote-free-variables Bound Y)]   where (symbol? X)
  Bound [X Y] -> [(quote-free-variables Bound X) (quote-free-variables Bound Y)]
  [V | Vs] X -> X     where (== V X)
  [_ | Vs] X -> (quote-free-variables Vs X)
  [] X -> [quote X]     where (symbol? X)
  _ X -> X)
```

An extra rule is added to secd-h that dictates a 'hands-off' policy to quoted *ob*s. The code is bolded in figure 24.5.

```
(define secd-h
 {stack --> environment --> control --> dump --> ob}
 [V] E [] [] -> V
 [V] _ [] [(@p S E C) | D] -> (secd [V | S] E C D)
 S E [[if Test Then Else] | C] D -> (secd S E [Test if Then Else @ | C] D)
 [true | S] E [if Then Else @ | C] D -> (secd S E [Then | C] D)
 [false | S] E [if Then Else @ | C] D -> (secd S E [Else | C] D)
 S E [[lambda X Y] | C] D -> (secd [[closure E X Y] | S] E C D)
 S E [[quote X] | C] D -> (secd [[quote X] | S] E C D)
 S E [[X Y] | C] D -> (secd S E [Y X @ | C] D)
 [F X | S] E [@ | C] D -> (secd [(apply F X) | S] E C D) where (prim? F)
 [[closure E* X Y] Z | S] E [@ | C] D -> (secd [] [(@p X Z) | E*] [Y] [(@p S E C) | D])
 S E [X | C] D -> (cases (bnd? X E) (secd [(lookup X E) | S] E C D)
                        (bnd? X (value *global*))
                          (secd S E [(lookup X (value *global*)) | C] D)
                        true  (secd [X | S] E C D) )
 S E C D -> (error "~%cannot compute S = ~R, E = ~R, C = ~R, D = ~R~%" S E C D))
```

Figure 24.5 The SECD adapted for quoted expressions

Repeating the computation now delivers a result consistent with actual Kλ behaviour.

(evaluate [[f 1] 2])

```
S = ()
E = ()
C = (((f 1) 2))
D = ()

S = ()
E = ()
C = (2 (f 1) @)
D = ()

S = (2)
E = ()
C = ((f 1) @)
D = ()

S = (2)
E = ()
C = (1 f @ @)
D = ()

S = (1 2)
E = ()
C = (f @ @)
D = ()
```

```
S = (1 2)
E = ()
C = ((lambda x (lambda y (g x))) @ @)
D = ()

S = ((closure () x (lambda y (g x))) 1 2)
E = ()
C = (@ @)
D = ()

S = ()
E = ((@p x 1))
C = ((lambda y (g x)))
D = ((@p [2] (@p [] [@])))

S = ((closure ((@p x 1)) y (g x)))
E = ((@p x 1))
C = ()
D = ((@p [2] (@p [] [@])))

S = ((closure ((@p x 1)) y (g x)) 2)
E = ()
C = (@)
D = ()

S = ()
E = ((@p y 2) (@p x 1))
C = ((g x))
D = ((@p [] (@p [] [])))

S = ()
E = ((@p y 2) (@p x 1))
C = (x g @)
D = ((@p [] (@p [] [])))

S = (1)
E = ((@p y 2) (@p x 1))
C = (g @)
D = ((@p [] (@p [] [])))

S = (1)
E = ((@p y 2) (@p x 1))
C = ((lambda x (quote y)) @)
D = ((@p [] (@p [] [])))

S = ((closure ((@p y 2) (@p x 1)) x (quote y)) 1)
E = ((@p y 2) (@p x 1))
C = (@)
D = ((@p [] (@p [] [])))
```

```
S = ()
E = ((@p x 1) (@p y 2) (@p x 1))
C = ((quote y))
D = (((@p [] (@p [(@p y 2) (@p x 1)] [])) (@p [] (@p [] []))))

S = ((quote y))
E = ((@p x 1) (@p y 2) (@p x 1))
C = ()
D = (((@p [] (@p [(@p y 2) (@p x 1)] [])) (@p [] (@p [] []))))

S = ((quote y))
E = ((@p y 2) (@p x 1))
C = ()
D = (((@p [] (@p [] []))))

S = ((quote y))
E = ()
C = ()
D = ()
```

[quote y] : ob

24.9 List Processing in the SECD Machine

Our SECD machine contains no provision for either equality or for list operations, both of which are central to Kλ. It is true that the lambda calculus provides tuples, but this representation, like the lambda calculus representation of natural numbers, is both cumbersome to write and inefficient to use. We therefore turn our attention to the representation of lists.

In Lisp the list [1 2 3] is represented as (quote (1 2 3)) or '(1 2 3) in the accepted shorthand. It is possible to use to form a list of any length. This suggests that the type for quoted expressions can usefully be extended to allow us to quote sequences of *obs*.

```
X : (list ob);
===========
[quote | X] : ob;
```

Let us nominate $ to stand proxy for the empty list in our implementation. A non empty list is thus signified by an expression of the form [quote ...] where what fills the ... are one or more *obs* followed by $. We exempt $ from needing quotation (bolded code below).

```
(define quote-free-variables
  {(list symbol) --> ob --> ob}
  Bound [lambda X Y] -> [lambda X (quote-free-variables [X | Bound] Y)]
  Bound [if Test Then Else] -> [if (quote-free-variables Bound Test)
                                   (quote-free-variables Bound Then)
                                   (quote-free-variables Bound Else)]
  Bound [X Y] -> [X (quote-free-variables Bound Y)]   where (symbol? X)
  Bound [X Y] -> [(quote-free-variables Bound X) (quote-free-variables Bound Y)]
  _ $ -> $
  [V | Vs] X -> X      where (== V X)
  [_ | Vs] X -> (quote-free-variables Vs X)
  [] X -> [quote X]    where (symbol? X)
  _ X -> X)
```

We add cons and = as dyadic *ob* forming functions to our type theory.

```
X : ob; Y : ob;
===========
[cons X Y] : ob;

X : ob; Y : ob;
==========
[= X Y] : ob;
```

We add hd and tl to our list of primitive functions.

```
(define prim?
  {ob --> boolean}
  F -> (element? F [succ pred zero? hd tl]))
```

To our apply function we add the code for the hd and tl functions.

```
(define apply
  {ob --> ob --> ob}
  succ X -> (+ X 1)    where (number? X)
  pred X -> (- X 1)    where (number? X)
  zero? X -> (= X 0)   where (number? X)
  hd [quote X Y | _] -> X
  tl [quote X $] -> $
  tl [quote X Y | Z] -> [quote Y | Z])
```

We also add to our swelling secd-h function, the code needed to deal with list construction and equality tests.

341

```
(define secd-h
 {stack --> environment --> control --> dump --> ob}
 [V] E [] [] -> V
 [V] _ [] [(@p S E C) | D] -> (secd [V | S] E C D)
 S E [[= X Y] | C] D -> (secd S E [Y X = @ | C] D)
 [= X Y | S] E [@ | C] D -> (secd [(= X Y) | S] E C D)
 S E [[cons X Y] | C] D -> (secd S E [Y X cons @ | C] D)
 [cons X Y | S] E [@ | C] D -> (secd [(mycons X Y) | S] E C D)
 S E [[if Test Then Else] | C] D -> (secd S E [Test if Then Else @ | C] D)
 [true | S] E [if Then Else @ | C] D -> (secd S E [Then | C] D)
 [false | S] E [if Then Else @ | C] D -> (secd S E [Else | C] D)
 S E [[lambda X Y] | C] D -> (secd [[closure E X Y] | S] E C D)
 S E [[quote X] | C] D -> (secd [[quote X] | S] E C D)
 S E [[X Y] | C] D -> (secd S E [Y X @ | C] D)
 [F X | S] E [@ | C] D -> (secd [(apply F X) | S] E C D) where (prim? F)
 [[closure E* X Y] Z | S] E [@ | C] D -> (secd [] [((@p X Z) | E*] [Y] [(@p S E C) | D])
 S E [X | C] D -> (cases (bnd? X E) (secd [(lookup X E) | S] E C D)
                       (bnd? X (value *global*))
                         (secd S E [(lookup X (value *global*)) | C] D)
                       true  (secd [X | S] E C D) )
 S E C D -> (error "~%cannot compute S = ~R, E = ~R, C = ~R, D = ~R~%" S E C D))

(define mycons
 {ob --> ob --> ob}
 X [quote | Y] -> [quote X | Y]
 X Y -> [quote X Y])
```

Figure 24.6 The SECD adapted for equality tests and list processing

Our next session shows the evaluation of the append function in our extended SECD machine.

```
(evaluate [tl [tl [quote 1 2 $]]])

S = ()
E = ()
C = ((tl (tl (quote 1 2 $))))
D = ()

S = ()
E = ()
C = ((tl (quote 1 2 $)) tl @)
D = ()

S = ()
E = ()
C = ((quote 1 2 $) tl @ tl @)
D = ()
```

S = ((quote 1 2 $))
E = ()
C = (tl @ tl @)
D = ()

S = (tl (quote 1 2 $))
E = ()
C = (@ tl @)
D = ()

S = ((quote 2 $))
E = ()
C = (tl @)
D = ()

S = (tl (quote 2 $))
E = ()
C = (@)
D = ()

S = ($)
E = ()
C = ()
D = ()

$: ob

(evaluate [defun append [x y] [if [= x $] y [cons [hd x] [[append [tl x]] y]]]])
append : ob

(evaluate [[append [quote 1 2 3 $]] [quote 4 5 6 $]])
.
. (104 transitions)
.
[quote 1 2 3 4 5 6 $] : ob

Further extensions to this program for Kλ are left as exercises to this chapter.

Exercise 24

1. Write a type secure Kλ interpreter based on the substitution model of evaluation.

2. Write a type secure Kλ interpreter based on the environment model of evaluation.

3. Augment the SECD machine to handle Kλ zero place functions.

4. Augment the SECD machine to handle >, <, >=, <=, *, /, -, + and number?.

5. Augment the SECD machine to handle cons?, and and or.

6. Augment the SECD machine to handle let.

7. In the SECD model of Kλ, set up a Lisp-2 convention with respect to global assignments and implement set and value.

8. Augment the SECD machine to handle the primitive vector creation, vector assignment and vector access functions used in Kλ.

9. Implement trap and error-to-string for the SECD machine.

10. Implement Kλ I/O for the SECD machine.

11. Destructive Shen is Shen that only uses global assignments, destructive vector operations and retrievals, and atoms. Implement an SECD interpreter in destructive Shen.

12. If you have not already done so, type check your answer to 10. Ensure your vectors are composed of homogenous items.

13. If you can solve 11, then write your SECD program in a procedural language such as C.

14. Our SECD machine is an interpreter that relies on storing every definition d of each user function f. To build a compiler we would need to compile d to a series s of SECD instructions so that when f is invoked then s is executed without consulting d. Read either Cardelli's (1985) Functional Abstract Machine (FAM) or Bailey's (1985) FP/M (Functional Programming Machine) and code a design in destructive Shen.

15. Implement your answer to 14. in C so that the SECD instructions emerge as C commands. If you add a garbage collector to this implementation you have a fully fledged low level implementation of Kλ.

Further Reading

Landin (1964) is the original paper, but clearer accounts are to be found in Field and Harrison (1988) and Danvy (2003). Quiennec (1996) contains a detailed account of Scheme compilation including actual C code. The standard introduction to C is Kernighan and Richie (1988).

Web Sources

https://www.cs.tufts.edu/comp/150FP/archive/luca-cardelli/functional-abstract-achine.pdf contains the pdf for Cardelli's paper. Danvy's (2003) paper can be found at https://www.brics.dk/RS/03/33/BRICS-RS-03-33.pdf.

25 Shen Prolog

25.1 A Short History of Prolog

Prolog (short for **pro**gramming in **log**ic) is a programming language developed in 1972 in a collaboration between Colmeraur and Kowalski at the University of Marseille. Prolog introduced a new perspective on programming by which computation was essentially a process of deduction. A Prolog program is a list of assumptions, an input to a Prolog program is a query and the Prolog response is the answer to the question deduced from the assumptions given.

Marseille Prolog was the first Prolog, originally written in Fortran and the performance was poor. Prolog implementations were measured in term of logical inferences per second or **LIPS** and Marseille Prolog executed at a speed of 200 LIPS on the IBM 360/67 mainframe. This was too slow to be practical as a programming language. In 1978 David Warren working at Edinburgh implemented a compiler on the DEC-10 mainframe which compiled Prolog to DEC-10 assembly.

At 40 KLIPS or 40,000 LIPS, **DEC-10 Prolog** fixed the standard notation for Prolog which became known as **Edinburgh notation** and was the first practical Prolog. In 1983 Warren moved to SRI and developed the **Warren Abstract Machine** or **WAM**, a virtual machine that linked Prolog programs to address instructions. The WAM allowed Prolog to run at 4 KLIPS/MHz on machines other than the DEC.[81] Since then, Prolog performance increased due to refinements of the WAM and better hardware so that the commercial Sicstus Prolog is capable of 50 KLIPS/MHz.

In Shen, Prolog is the language into which type declarations are compiled and it is the Prolog inference engine in Shen that makes the inferences that drive the type checking process. Shen Prolog is, in turn, compiled into Shen and Shen into Kλ. Unlike WAM-based Prologs that compile directly into assembly or microcode, the performance characteristic of an implementation like Sicstus Prolog is absent and under SBCL about 150 LIPS/MHz would be normal.

---

[81] One being the the Sun 3/50 workstation. The 3/50 ran at a clock speed of 15.7 MHz, about 100x slower than a conventional laptop of 2020 giving WAM Prolog a speed of 60 KLIPS on this machine.

Certain corners were cut in commercial Prologs like Sicstus to boost performance and one of these was the **occurs check** which we will come to later. Without this constraint type checking can fail to produce the correct result and so Shen Prolog reinstated this aspect. Unlike stand-alone Prologs like Sicstus or SWI Prolog, Shen Prolog was designed to integrate with Shen. A grasp of Prolog is essential is we wish to understand the relations between sequent calculus and Prolog and how sequent rules are compiled. We begin with looking at Horn clause logic.

25.2 Horn Clause Logic

The syntax rules of Horn clause logic are rather numerous when stated formally but the underlying idea is simple. Horn clauses are what result from Proplog when we allow Proplog atoms to be replaced by first-order atoms. The syntax rules are laid out in figure 25.1.

1. A Horn clause variable is a member of $V = \{x, y, z, x', y', z' \ .....\}$.
2. A propositional symbol p is any symbol p where $p \notin V \cup \{\&, \rightarrow\}$.
3. A predicate Φ is any symbol Φ where $\sigma \notin V \cup \{\&, \rightarrow\}$.
4. A name N is a symbol/string/number/boolean where $N \notin V \cup \{\&, \rightarrow\}$.
5. A functional symbol f is any symbol F where $f \notin V \cup \{\&, \rightarrow\}$.
6. A term is either
   a. A name or ...
   b. an element of V or
   c. an expression $(f\, t_1,...,t_n)$ consisting of a function symbol f followed by n ($n \geq 0$) terms.
7. $\Phi(t_1,..t_n)$ is a Horn clause if Φ is a predicate and $t_1,..,t_n$ ($n \geq 0$) are terms.
8. A propositional symbol on its own is a Horn clause.

   In cases 7 and 8 the Horn clause is a **Horn clause atom** or **fact**. If an expression is free of Horn clause variables then it is **ground.**

9. If A is an atom then it is a limiting case of a conjunction with only one limb. If A and B are conjunctions then (A & B) is a conjunction.
10. If B is an atom and A is a conjunction then the implication (A $\rightarrow$ B) is a Horn clause.

Figure 25.1 Horn clause syntax rules

In case 10 the Horn clause is a **Horn clause rule**. B is the **head** of the clause and A is the **body** of the clause.

In a Horn clause proof, the context (i.e. the set of assumptions used in the proof) is a list of rules and facts and the succeedent which is to be proved is a conjunction.

The first three sequent rules for Horn clause logic are almost exactly those of Proplog.

hyp

$$\overline{P \gg P};$$

$\rightarrow$-*left*
$$\frac{(P \rightarrow Q) \gg P;}{(P \rightarrow Q) \gg Q;}$$

&-*right*
where P *is ground*
$$\frac{P;\ Q;}{(P\ \&\ Q);}$$

The next two rules relate to variables. Let $P_{t/v}$ be the result of substituting all occurrences of a Horn clause variable v in P by a ground term t.

v-right
$$\frac{P_{t/v};}{P;}$$

v-left
$$\frac{P_{t/v}, P \gg Q;}{P \gg Q;}$$

The v-right and v-left rules are very similar to the $\exists$-*right* and $\forall$-*right rule* of first-order logic respectively. In fact the Horn clause variables in a sequent are implicitly quantified; a variable in a hypothesis is universally quantified and one occurring in the succeedent is existentially quantified.

Here is a problem in Horn clause logic (we relax bracketing for readability).

mammal(x) $\rightarrow$ *warm-blooded*(x),
mammal(*Socrates*),
bipedal(*Socrates*) $\gg$ *warm-blooded*(y) & *bipedal*(y).

Read in English

'All mammals are warm-blooded, Socrates is a mammal, also Socrates is bipedal therefore there is something that is warm-blooded and bipedal.'

Here is the proof of the validity of the argument in Horn clause logic.

Applying v-*right* and instantiating y to Socrates derives

mammal(x) → warm-blooded(x),
mammal(Socrates),
bipedal(Socrates) >> warm-blooded(Socrates) & bipedal(Socrates).

By *&-right*, two sequents are derived.

α   *(mammal(x) → warm-blooded(x))*,
           mammal(Socrates),
           bipedal(Socrates) >> warm-blooded(Socrates)

β   *(mammal(x) → warm-blooded(x))*,
           mammal(Socrates),
           bipedal(Socrates) >> bipedal(Socrates)

β is solved by *hyp.* By *v-left* applied to α, *x* is instantiated to '*Socrates*'.

mammal(Socrates) → warm-blooded(Socrates),
mammal(x) → warm-blooded(x),
mammal(Socrates),
bipedal(Socrates) >> warm-blooded(Socrates)

Hence by *→–left*.

mammal(Socrates) → warm-blooded(Socrates),
mammal(x) → warm-blooded(x),
mammal(Socrates),
bipedal(Socrates) >> mammal(Socrates)

which is solved by *hyp* and the proof is complete.

The importance of the ground restriction on the *&-right* rule is shown by the following 'poof'.[82]

man(Fred), woman(Flora) >> man(x) & woman(x)

Read in English

'Fred is a man, Flora is a woman therefore somebody is a man and a woman.'

By *&-right*, two sequents are derived

α   *man(Fred), woman(Flora) >> man(x)*
β   *man(Fred), woman(Flora) >> woman(x)*

---

[82] A term coined by Bundy to describe a purported proof which is not actually a proof at all.

Applying *v-right* to α and instantiating *x* to Fred gives

man(*Fred*), *woman*(*Flora*) >> *man*(*Fred*)

which is solved by *hyp* leaving β. Instantiating *x* to Flora in β gives

man(*Fred*), *woman*(*Flora*) >> *woman*(*Flora*)

which is solved by *hyp*.

The proof goes wrong because the initial *&-right* step does not respect the ground condition.

An important theoretical result is that when Proplog is extended to Horn clause logic then no complete and terminating theorem-prover can be found; that is to say, like first-order logic, Horn clause logic is undecidable.[83]

25.3 Unification

Since the rules for Horn clause logic are virtually identical to those of Proplog apart from the *v-left* and *v-right* rules, it follows that the automation of Horn clause logic will turn on the automating the choice of instances for variables. Once the correct instantiation is found, then a Horn clause problem reduces to a Proplog problem and for that there is already a program to hand.

One solution would be to assemble the set S of ground terms that can be formulated in the vocabulary of the Horn clause proof obligation and systematically test for each possible instantiation. If S is non-empty then S is the **Herbrand universe** H of the problem, and if S is empty then some arbitrary name *a* is introduced and H = {*a*}. Theorem-proving in Horn clause logic would then entail working through the Herbrand universe and testing each combination using the Proplog program.

The Davis-Putnam procedure (1961) was a very early work in the area of automated reasoning which used an approach that approximated to this suggestion. It has several disadvantages; the main being that the number of combinations can grow exponentially even if H is finite. If function symbols are introduced then H is infinite. The Herbrand universe of the following problem.

jewish(*mother_of*(*x*)) → *jewish*(*x*) >> *jewish*(*Albert*)

is H = {*Albert, mother_of*(*Albert*), *mother_of*(*mother_of*(*Albert*)) ...}. In this case the testing process would not terminate.

---

[83] The easiest way to do this is to encode some standard model of computability in Horn clause logic such as a Turing machine – see http://en.wikipedia.org/wiki/Prolog.

Another more promising line is to use pattern-matching as used within Shen. Given

$man(x) \rightarrow mortal(x)$, $man(Socrates) >> mortal(Socrates)$

instead of first instantiating the x to '*Socrates*', and then applying $\rightarrow$-*left* we pattern match the *mortal(x)* to *mortal(Socrates)*. This works just fine except that there are cases where the matching has to occur not only from the rule to the succeedent, but also from the succeedent to the rule.

$likes(Ted, x) >> likes(y, Bill)$

Here '*Ted*' is matched to y and '*Bill*' to x. Unlike Shen pattern matching, pattern matching for Horn clause logic has to work in two directions. This bidirectional pattern matching is called **unification**.

Unification was introduced into computer science by Robinson (1965) who gave an algorithm for the procedure. Two expressions **unify** when there is a uniform substitution for the variables in each expression that makes the two expressions the same.

'*likes(Ted, x)*' unifies with '*likes(y, Bill)*' since the substitution $\sigma = \{x \mapsto$ '*Bill*', $y \mapsto$ '*Ted*'\} makes the two identical. A set of associations that unifies two expressions e_1 and e_2 is a **unifier** of e_1 and e_2. The **most general unifier** or **MGU** of e_1 and e_2 is the smallest unifier needed to unify the two. Not every unifier is an MGU; '*likes(Ted, x)*' unifies with '*likes(Ted, x)*' under the unifier $\sigma = \{x \mapsto$ '*Bill*'\} which is not the MGU. The MGU here is \{\}.

The elements of a unifier are **bindings**, and process of substituting the variables in an expression by their values under a unifier is **dereferencing**. In the case of $\sigma = \{x \mapsto$ '*Bill*', $y \mapsto$ '*Ted*'\} '*Bill*' is said to be the **value** of x under this unification. Conventionally if σ is a unifier of two expressions then the result of dereferencing an expression e by σ is written $\sigma(e)$.

Robinson's algorithm for the unification of e_1 and e_2 begins with the **standardisation apart** of one of the two expressions if the set V_1 of variables in e_1 and the set V_2 of variables in e_2 is such that $V_1 \cap V_2 \neq \{\}$. Standardisation apart involves uniformly replacing the variables in either e_1 or e_2 so that $V_1 \cap V_2 = \{\}$. The motivation is shown in this example.

$likes(Ted, x) >> likes(x, Bill)$

Here unification cannot occur because the same variable x happens to be used in both the hypothesis and the succeedent. Replacing x by y allows the unification to go through. It is matter of choice which expression is standardised apart, but in logic programming it is always the hypothesis that is treated this way. Standardisation apart having been assumed, Robinson's algorithm takes as inputs two atoms $\Phi(s_1,..s_n)$ and $\Phi(t_1,..t_n)$. The algorithm (figure 25.2) is fairly straightforward, for $i = 1$ to n, each term s_i and t_i is compared using an accumulator M for the MGU.

1. If $s_i = t_i$ then i is incremented.
2. If s_i is a variable which does not occur in t_i then the substitution of t_i for s_i is made throughout both $\Phi(s_1,..s_n)$ and $\Phi(t_1,..t_n)$ and $s_i \mapsto t_i$ is added to M.
3. If t_i is a variable which does not occur in s_i then the substitution of s_i for t_i is made throughout both $\Phi(s_1,..s_n)$ and $\Phi(t_1,..t_n)$ and $t_i \mapsto s_i$ is added to M.
4. If s_i and t_i are complex terms of the form $f(a_1,..., a_m)$ and $f(b_1,...,b_m)$ then unification recurses within the two terms.
5. If none of the above hold then unification fails.

Figure 25.2 Robinson's unification algorithm

In the event of a successful unification, the algorithm has gone from $i = 1$ to n and M is returned as the result. Figure 25.3 gives the Shen code.

```
(define unify
  X Y -> (unify-loop X Y []))

(define unify-loop
  X X MGU -> MGU
  X Y MGU -> [[X | Y] | MGU]   where (and (variable? X) (occurs-check? X Y))
  X Y MGU -> [[Y | X] | MGU]   where (and (variable? Y) (occurs-check? Y X))
  [X | Y] [W | Z] MGU -> (let NewMGU (unify-loop X W MGU)
                              (unify-loop (deref Y NewMGU)
                                          (deref Z NewMGU)
                                          NewMGU))
  _ _ _ -> (error "unification failure"))

(define occurs-check?
  X X -> false
  X [Y | Z] -> (and (occurs-check? X Y) (occurs-check? X Z))
  _ _ -> true)

(define deref
  [X | Y] MGU -> (map (/. Term (deref Term MGU)) [X | Y])
  X MGU -> (let Binding (assoc X MGU)[84]
                (if (empty? Binding)
                    X
                    (deref (tl Binding) MGU))))
```

Figure 25.3 Unification in Shen

---

[84] See appendix A for assoc.

Figure 25.4 shows some sample inputs to the unification function.

```
(17-) (unify [f a] [f X])
[[X | a]]

(18-) (unify [f [g X]] [f X])
unification failure

(19-) (unify [f [g X] [h Y]] [f Z Z])
unification failure

(20-) (unify [f [g X] [h Y]] [f Z [h Z]])
[[Y g X] [Z g X]]
```

Figure 25.4 Running unification

Incorporating unification into the proof theory of Horn clause logic means that the *v-left* and *v-right* rules disappear and →-*left* is interpreted using unification. Since the *v* rules are gone, there is a problem with splitting conjunctions which, as we have seen, is safe only if the leading limb is ground. The solution is to avoid splitting and maintain a succeedent as a sequence of atoms and to dereference this sequence when unification is made. For convenience it is useful to make the body of a Horn clause a sequence of atoms too. Hence instead of

If B is an atom and A is a conjunction then $(A \rightarrow B)$ is a Horn clause.

we have

If B is an atom and A is a sequence of atoms then $(A \rightarrow B)$ is a Horn clause.

This gives us three rules to work with; the first *finish*, simply states when the list of atoms in the succeedent is empty, we can consider the proof finished.

finish

$$\overline{[];}$$

The other two are *hyp* and →-*left* interpreted with unification

hyp
where $\sigma(P, Q_1)$ is defined

$$\frac{P >> \sigma([....Q_n]);}{P >> [Q_1,...,Q_n];}$$

→-*left*
where $\sigma(Q_0, Q_1)$ is defined and $P + [...Qn]$ is the result of appending P to $[...Qn]$

$$\frac{(P \rightarrow Q_0) >> \sigma(P + [...Qn]);}{(P \rightarrow Q_0) >> [Q_1,...,Q_n];}$$

352

However if we allow that if (A → B) is a Horn clause it is permissible for A to be an empty sequence of atoms, then we can amalgamate facts and rules. A fact then becomes a rule whose body is empty. The significance of this identification is that the *hyp* rule then disappears and our version of Horn clause logic contains only two rules – *finish* (which is only invoked once) and →-*left*. Our →-*left rule* is a thinly disguised and restricted form of what Robinson called **resolution**. His achievement was to show that most inferencing in first-order logic could be reduced to the repeated application of this single rule of resolution. His 1965 work paved the way for the development of logic programming.

25.4 Programming in Horn Clause Logic

Logic programming is based on Horn clause logic. In logic programming the context is a **Prolog program** and the succeedent is a **Prolog query**. The model is that a logic program consists of a series of Horn clauses – rules and facts and the input to a program is a query - that is, a series of Horn clause atoms posed as the succeedent. The response returned by the Horn clause theorem prover to the query is the output of the program.

There is one thing missing with this picture. Logically the only thing that a Horn clause prover can do is return either 'yes' (I can prove that) or 'no' (I cannot prove that). This range of responses is too narrow for general programming and Horn clause logic seems an even more unlikely candidate for a programming language than lambda calculus. There was in fact a missing element required to make Horn clause logic work.

Green (1967) supplied this missing element in the form of an **answer literal**. The answer literal A is an atom that is tagged on to the end of the succeedent for the purpose of being able to deliver information. A contains all the variables in the succeedent and upon floating to the front of succeedent, the answer literal prints these variables together with their bound values. These values represented the answer to the query.

To illustrate, let's look at the problem we examined before

mammal(x) → *warm-blooded*(x),
mammal(*Socrates*),
bipedal(*Socrates*) >> *warm-blooded*(y) & *bipedal*(y)

Writing the problem in the new format this comes out as

mammal(x) → *warm-blooded*(x),
→ *mammal*(*Socrates*),
→ *bipedal*(*Socrates*) >> *warm-blooded*(y), *bipedal*(y).

The first step suggested by Green, is to add an atom to the succeedent – the so-called answer literal.

mammal(*x*) → *warm-blooded*(*x*),
→ *mammal*(*Socrates*),
→ *bipedal*(*Socrates*) >> *warm-blooded*(*y*), *bipedal*(*y*), *answer*("*y*", *y*).

The step of →-*left* unifies '*warm-blooded*(*x*)' with '*warm-blooded*(*y*)'; we can bind *x* to *y* or *y* to *x* here, but generally logic programming prefers to bind the hypothesis variable – we bind *x* to *y*. '*mammal*(*x*)' is added to the succeedent and dereferenced to '*mammal*(*y*)'.

mammal(*x*) → *warm-blooded*(*x*),
→ *mammal*(*Socrates*),
→ *bipedal*(*Socrates*) >> *mammal*(*y*), *bipedal*(*y*), *answer*("*y*", *y*).

Here '*mammal*(*Socrates*)' is unified with '*mammal*(*y*)' with *y* bound to '*Socrates*' and the result is

mammal(*x*) → *warm-blooded*(*x*),
→ *mammal*(*Socrates*),
→ *bipedal*(*Socrates*) >> *bipedal*(*Socrates*), *answer*("*y*", *Socrates*).

'*bipedal*(*Socrates*)' is eliminated by → *bipedal*(*Socrates*) and the answer literal remains.

mammal(*x*) → *warm-blooded*(*x*),
→ *mammal*(*Socrates*),
→ *bipedal*(*Socrates*) >> *answer*("*y*", *Socrates*).

This is printed out as

y = *Socrates*

With answer literals, it is possible to do list processing. The following two Horn clauses describe the append relation between lists. [1] is represented as (*cons* 1 $) with $ being proxy for the empty list.

→ *append*($, *x*, *x*)
append(*y*,*w*,*z*) → *append*((*cons x y*), *w*, (*cons x z*))

Suppose the query is *append*((*cons* 1 $), (*cons* 2 $), *x'*). This can be interpreted as a request to append (*cons* 1 $), and (*cons* 2 $) i.e. [1] and [2]. The result should be (*cons* 1 (*cons* 2 $)). The proof obligation is

→ *append*($, *x*, *x*)
append(*y*,*w*,*z*) → *append*((*cons x y*), *w*, (*cons x z*))
>> *append*((*cons* 1 $), (*cons* 2 $), *x*')

Adding an answer literal we have

→ *append*($, *x*, *x*)
append(*y*,*w*,*z*) → *append*((*cons x y*), *w*, (*cons x z*))
>> *append*((*cons* 1 $), (*cons* 2 $), *x*'), *answer*("*x*'", *x*')

Resolving by the second rule for append we get

→ *append*($, *x*, *x*)
append(*y*,*w*,*z*) → *append*((*cons x y*), *w*, (*cons x z*))
>> *append*($, (*cons* 2 $), *z*), *answer*("*x*'", (*cons* 1 *z*))

Resolving by the fact → *append*($, *x*, *x*)

→ *append*($, *x*, *x*)
append(*y*,*w*,*z*) → *append*((*cons x y*), *w*, (*cons x z*))
>> *answer*("*x*'", (*cons* 1 (*cons* 2 $)))

x' = (*cons* 1 (*cons* 2 $))

25.5 Programming in Prolog

Prolog is essentially a computational embodiment of Horn clause logic with answer-literals, unification and resolution that uses the same search strategy for solving problems that Proplog does. The other additions to Prolog are the equivalent of the δ rules for lambda calculus i.e. provision for the usual arithmetic operations and I/O operations that any language needs. Prolog is almost always written in Edinburgh notation. In this notation variables, as in Shen, are symbols beginning in uppercase. Facts are written in form *predicate*(*terms*) just as in our version of Horn clause logic except that a full stop is used to terminate the fact.

A rule in Edinburgh notation is not written in the form *body* → *head*, but in the form *head* :- *body*. again terminating with a full stop. Lists are written exactly as they are in Shen using [...] and | plays the same role as it does in Shen. A small note is that commas have to be used in Prolog to separate list items so [1 2 3] in Shen is [1, 2, 3] in Prolog.

SWI Prolog is a free Prolog using standard notation with a good interface and the following shows a session under Windows.

Prolog contains an arithmetic engine. X is (4 + 7) returns 11. Notice the full stop at the end of the query. = compares for equality using unification.

```
1 ?- X is (4 + 7).
X = 11.

2 ? X = a.
X = a
```

It is possible to write programs into Prolog, but it is more civilised to use an editor and load the program here. Here I create a file prologtest.pl and load it into SWI Prolog.

```
4 ? consult(prologtest.pl).
%c:/Users/Mark Tarver/tests.pl compiled 0.00 sec, 1,092 bytes
```

The contents of my file include two simple Prolog programs. One enumerates a list and the other gives the Cartesian product of two lists. As in Shen, an underscore functions as a wildcard.

```
enum(L, E) :- enum_help(L, E, 1).

enum_help([], [], _).
enum_help([X | Y], [[X, N] | E], N) :- M is N+1, enum_help(Y, E, M).
```

Figure 25.4 A simple Prolog program

Here I ask to number the list [a, b ,c]. I then ask to find a value that enumerates to [[a, 1], [b, 2], [c, 3]].

```
3- ? enum([a, b, c], E).
E = [[a, 1], [b, 2], [c, 3]].

4-? enum(L, [[a, 1], [b, 2], [c, 3]]).
L = [a, b, c]
```

append is a system predicate. I query values for X and Y which when appended together give [1, 2, 3], Typing ; to each solution prompts a search for the next.

```
6 ?- append(X,Y,[1,2,3]).
X = [],
Y = [1, 2, 3] ;

X = [1],
Y = [2, 3] ;

X = [1, 2],
Y = [3] ;

X = [1, 2, 3],
Y = [] ;

false
```

This is a brief introduction to Prolog programming in standard Edinburgh notation. For readers interested in becoming proficient in Prolog, the further reading section and the texts by Sterling and Shapiro and Bratko are relevant.

25.6 Shen Prolog

Shen Prolog is a version of Prolog that provides the object code for the sequent calculus rules of Shen. The syntax of Shen Prolog is based on that of Shen itself, with three differences.

1. defprolog is used instead of define.
2. <-- is used instead of -> or <-. In the clause *xxx* <-- *yyy*; the place of *xxx* is taken by a series of terms and *yyy* by a series of literals represented as function calls. Note the semi-colon terminates a clause.
3. Pattern-matching takes place only with respect to lists.

In Edinburgh syntax these facts

woman(martha).
woman(joan).

are written in Shen Prolog as

(defprolog woman
  martha <--;
  joan <--;)

To pose a Prolog query, the macro prolog? is used.

```
(3-) (prolog? (woman martha))
true

(4-) (prolog? (woman jean))
false

(5-) (prolog? (woman X))
true

(6-) (prolog? (man martha))
APPLY: undefined function man
```

Figure 25.5 Invoking Prolog

Note that repeated variables in Shen Prolog programs are interpreted using occurs-check unification (in most implementations of Prolog this is not true). (occurs-check -) disables automatic compilation with occurs-check unification. (occurs-check +) restores the default. This declaration also extends to the compilation of data types in Shen Prolog.

The predicate return ends the Prolog computation returning the value of its argument. Here the first value for which (woman X) is true is returned.

```
(7-) (prolog? (woman X) (return X))
martha
```

Figure 25.6 Returning a value from a Prolog call

To find all the values for which (woman X) is true, findall is used. This predicate takes three terms.

1. A variable x.
2. An Prolog call p.
3. A variable y.

and returns bound to y all the values of x for which p is provable.

```
(8-) (prolog? (findall X (woman X) Y) (return Y))
[martha joan]
```

Figure 25.7 Returning a list of values from a Prolog call

The predicate is, as in (is x t), unifies x to the result of evaluating t.

```
(12-) (prolog? (is X (+ 1 1)) (return X))
2
```

Figure 25.8 Assigning a value to a variable

The Bible program of chapter 2 can be written in Shen Prolog as follows.

```
(11-) (defprolog lived
          "Adam" 930 <--;
          "Seth" 912 <--;
          "Enos" 905 <--;
          "Ca-i'nan" 910 <--;
          "Mahal'aleel" 895 <--;
          "Jared" 962 <--;
          "Enoch" 365 <--;
          "Methu'selah" 969 <--;
          "Lamech" 777 <--;)
(fn lived)

(12-) (defprolog begat
          "Adam" "Seth"  <--;
          "Seth" "Enos" <--;
          "Enos" "Ca-i'nan" <--;
          "Ca-i'nan" "Mahal'aleel" <--;
          "Mahal'aleel" "Jared" <--;
          "Jared" "Enoch" <--;
          "Enoch" "Methu'selah" <--;
          "Methu'selah" "Lamech" <--;)
(fn begat)

(13-) (prolog? (findall Age (lived Person Age) Ages)
              (return (sum Ages)))
7625
```

Figure 25.9 Computing the total ages of the patriarchs (version 1)

Figure 25.9 uses the Shen system function sum to total the ages. We can also define sum in Shen Prolog.[85]

```
(14-) (defprolog total
      [] 0 <--;
      [X | Y] N <-- (total Y M) (bind N (+ M X));)
(fn total)

(15-) (prolog? (findall Age (lived Person Age) Ages)
              (total Ages Total)
              (return Total))
7625
```

Figure 25.10 Computing the total ages of the patriarchs (version 2)

The predicate when enables boolean tests to be used; (when *b*) where *b* is a boolean test, succeeds if *b* evaluates to true.

---

[85] When the first argument to is is *known* to be a variable, it is faster to use bind, which dispenses with unification in favour simply binding the variable. .

359

```
(16-) (prolog? (when (> 6 7)))
false

(17-) (prolog? (when (> 16 7)))
true
```

Figure 25.11 Calling a boolean test within Prolog

Shen Prolog allows function expressions to be embedded into the arguments of literals within the tails of clauses. Thus

```
(defprolog f
  X <-- (return (* 2 X));)
```

creates a Horn clause procedure that receives an input and doubles it, passing the result to the top level.

Calling Shen from Prolog is easy. Calling Prolog from Shen is only a little more difficult. The following shows a way *not* to call Prolog from Shen.

```
(1-) (define foo
      X -> (prolog? (is Y (* X X)) (return Y)))
(fn foo)

(2-) (foo 9)
The value #(shen.pvar 2) is not of type REAL

(3-) (define foo
      X -> (prolog? (is Y (* (receive X)  (receive X))) (return Y)))
(fn foo)

(4-) (foo 9)
81
```

Figure 25.12 Calling Prolog from Shen

Here in the first attempt to call Prolog, the X is treated as a free variable in the Prolog call, and Prolog tries to multiply the variable X by itself which raises an error. The correct approach is to delineate X as a variable whose value is to be received from *outside* the Prolog call using receive.

A basic control mechanism for trimming search space in Prolog is the **cut**. The cut, written as ! in Edinburgh Prolog and Shen Prolog, alters the backtracking behaviour of a Prolog program and occupies the position of an atom in the tail of a Horn clause. When the cut is called it always succeeds; however if control backtracks to a cut, then the effect of the cut is to cut off all consideration of choices after the clause in the Horn clause procedure in which it is invoked. As an example, we will use a case written in Shen Prolog itself.

360

```
(defprolog woman
  X <-- ! (married-to X john);
  martha <--;)

(defprolog married-to
  joan john <--;)
```

The first clause states that X is a woman if X is married to john. The intrusion of the cut in that clause commits Prolog to solving the query by looking under the married-to predicate. If that search fails, then the cut will block any attempt to look at further clauses in the woman procedure. Hence the query (woman joan) succeeds, but (woman martha) fails.

```
(22-) (prolog? (woman joan))
true

(23-) (prolog? (woman martha))
false
```

Figure 25.13 The cut in operation within Prolog

call functions as a higher-order aspect for Shen Prolog. Given an atom, the atom is turned into a goal by being called. Here it is used to define ~ as negation as failure; where (~ P) is provable (true) just when P is not provable (false).

```
(15-) (defprolog ~
         P <-- (call P) ! (when false);
  ~      _ <--;)

(16-) (prolog? (~ (woman susan)))
true
```

Figure 25.14 Defining negation as failure

fork does the job of the semi-colon in Edinburgh Prolog; it succeeds if one of the literals following succeeds.

```
(defprolog f
  X <-- (g X) (h X);
  X <-- (g X) (i X);
  X <-- (g X) (j X);)
```

can be coded as

```
(defprolog f
  X <-- (g X) (fork (h X) (i X) (j X));)
```

361

Mode declarations suspend unification in favour of pattern-matching and are used only in the head of a clause. - enables pattern-matching.[86]

```
(24-) (defprolog f
      (- a) <--;)
f

(25-) (prolog? (f X))
false

(26-) (prolog? (f a))
true
```

Figure 25.15 Using mode declarations in Shen Prolog

The default mode is unification signalled by +. Mode declarations can be nested as in (- [f a (+ b)]). In this event the innermost declaration has priority. The above expression would thus perform pattern-matching with respect to all its elements save b which would receive unification. In sum, Shen Prolog contains the following extralogical predicates (figure 25.16).

predicate	description
(is! *x t*)	unify *x* and *t* with an occurs check.
(is *x t*)	unify *x* and *t* w.o. an occurs check.
(bind *x t*)	bind *x* to *t*.
(findall *x p y*)[87]	*x* is a variable, *p* a Prolog call, and *y* a variable; finds all values for *x* in *p* for which *a* is provable and binds the list of these values to *y*.
(when *t*)	*t* is evaluated to true or false and succeeds if it is true.
(call *p*)[88]	call *p*
(return *t*)	terminate Prolog returning the dereferenced value of *t*.
!	Prolog cut
(receive *x*)	receives a variable binding to *x* from outside Prolog
(var? *x*)	test for Prolog variable.
(fork p_1 .... p_n)[89]	succeeds if one of p_1 .... p_n succeeds.

Figure 25.16 The predicates of Shen Prolog

---

[86] Prior to Shen 30 (- a) was expressed as (mode a -). This idiom is also acceptable.

[87] Prior to Shen 30 *p* was a list. Note the Horn clause corresponding to the predicate in *p* has to be compiled **before** the fork literal is compiled.

[88] Prior to Shen 30 *p* was a list. Note the Horn clause corresponding to the predicate in *p* has to be compiled **before** the fork literal is compiled.

[89] Note the Horn clauses corresponding to the predicates in p_1 .... p_n have to be compiled **before** the fork literal is compiled.

25.7 Implementing a Horn Clause Interpreter

Since this is a book about Shen, let's close this chapter by building a type secure Horn clause interpreter in Shen, designed on the model described in this chapter. A Horn clause atom is a predicate (symbol) followed by terms.

(datatype atom

```
F : symbol; X : (list term);
===================
[F | X] : atom;)
```

A term is a symbol, number, string or boolean or a symbol heading a list of terms.

(datatype term

```
P : symbol;
P : term;

P : number;
P : term;

P : string;
P : term;

P : boolean;
P : term;

F : symbol; X : (list term);
==================
[F | X] : term;)
```

A Horn clause consists of a head followed by a body.

(datatype horn-clause

```
H : atom; B : (list atom);
=================
[H <= | B] : horn-clause;)
```

The typed version of the unification algorithm is a little longer than the untyped version but does the same job. Unification failure returns an error.

```
(define unify-atoms
  {atom --> atom --> (list (term * term))}
  P P -> []
  [F | X] [F | Y] -> (unify-terms X Y [ ])
  _ _ -> (error "unification failure!"))
```

```
(define unify-terms
  {(list term) --> (list term) --> (list (term * term)) --> (list (term * term))}
  X X Mgu -> Mgu
  [X | Y] [W | Z] Mgu
  -> (unify-terms Y Z (unify-term (dereference X Mgu)
                                  (dereference W Mgu)
                                  Mgu))
  _ _ _ -> (error "unification failure!"))

(define unify-term
  {term --> term --> (list (term * term)) --> (list (term * term))}
  X X Mgu -> Mgu
  X Y Mgu -> [(@p X Y) | Mgu]   where (occurs-check? X Y)
  X Y Mgu -> [(@p Y X) | Mgu]   where (occurs-check? Y X)
  [F | Y] [F | Z] Mgu -> (unify-terms Y Z Mgu)
  _ _ _ -> (error "unification failure!"))

(define occurs-check?
  {term --> term --> boolean}
  X Y -> (and (variable? X) (not (occurs? X Y))))

(define dereference
  {term --> (list (term * term)) --> term}
  [X | Y] Mgu -> [X | (map (/. Z (dereference Z Mgu)) Y)]
  X Mgu -> (let Val (lookup X Mgu)
             (if (= Val X) X (dereference Val Mgu))))

(define lookup
  {term --> (list (term * term)) --> term}
  X [] -> X
  X [(@p X Y) | _] -> Y
  X [_ | Y] -> (lookup X Y))

(define occurs?
  {term --> term --> boolean}
  X X -> true
  X [Y | Z] -> (or (== X Y) (some (/. W (occurs? X W)) Z))
  _ _ -> false)

(define some
  {(A --> boolean) --> (list A) --> boolean}
  _ [] -> false
  F [X | Y] -> (or (F X) (some F Y)))
```

The Horn clause interpreter top level follows next. The Prolog top level receives a list (stack) of goals and a Horn clause program. We begin by building an answer literal and inserting it onto the end of the goal stack and passing the problem to the prolog-help function which does the heavy lifting. Here the same technique of spreading the input that was used in 6.3 is employed.

```
(define prolog
  {(list atom) --> (list horn-clause) --> boolean}
  Goals Program -> (prolog-help (insert-answer-literal Goals)
                                Program
                                Program))

(define insert-answer-literal
  {(list atom) --> (list atom)}
  Goals -> (append Goals
                   (answer-literal
                     (mapcan (fn variables-in-atom) Goals))))

(define answer-literal
  {(list term) --> (list atom)}
  Vs -> [[answer | (answer-terms Vs)]])

(define answer-terms
  {(list term) --> (list term)}
  [] -> []
  [V | Vs] -> [(str V) V | (answer-terms (remove V Vs))])

(define prolog-help
  {(list atom) --> (list horn-clause) --> (list horn-clause) --> boolean}
  [] _ _ -> true
  [[answer | Terms]] _ _ -> (answer Terms)
  [P | Ps] [Clause | Clauses] Program
    -> (let StClause (standardise-apart Clause)
            H (hdcl StClause)
            B (body StClause)
            (or (trap-error
                  (let MGU (unify-atoms P H)
                       Goals (map (/. X (dereference-atom X MGU))
                                  (append B Ps))
                       (prolog-help Goals Program Program)) (/. E false))
                (prolog-help [P | Ps] Clauses Program)))
  _ _ _ -> false)
```

prolog-help returns true if the stack is empty and enters the answer routine if an answer literal pops up. Otherwise the head of the first clause of the program is unified with the leading goal.

1. If the unification fails, the error is trapped and the program recurses on the rest of the Horn clause program.
2. If unification succeeds, then the new goals Goals are assembled and the prolog-help function restores the Horn clause program and attempts to prove Goals. If this attempt fails, then the prolog-help function recurses down the Horn clause program.
3. In the final case, if the list of program clauses is empty then false is returned,

```
(define hdcl
  {horn-clause --> atom}
  [H <= | _] -> H)

(define body
  {horn-clause --> (list atom)}
  [_ <= | Body] -> Body)

(define dereference-atom
  {atom --> (list (term * term)) --> atom}
  [F | Terms] MGU -> [F | (map (/. T (dereference T MGU)) Terms)])
```

The answer routine returns false to an affirmative to computing more solutions.

```
(define answer
  {(list term) --> boolean}
  [ ] -> (not (y-or-n? "~%more? "))
  [String Value | Answer] -> (do (output "~%~A = ~S" String Value) (answer Answer)))
```

standardise-apart renames all the variables in a program clause.

```
(define standardise-apart
  {horn-clause --> horn-clause}
  Clause -> (st-all (variables-in-clause Clause) Clause))

(define variables-in-clause
  {horn-clause --> (list term)}
  [H <= | B] -> (append (variables-in-atom H) (mapcan (fn variables-in-atom) B)))

(define variables-in-atom
  {atom --> (list term)}
  [Predicate | Terms] -> (mapcan (fn variables-in-term) Terms))

(define variables-in-term
  {term --> (list term)}
  Term -> [Term]          where (variable? Term)
  [F | Terms] -> (mapcan (fn variables-in-term) Terms)
  _ -> [])

(define st-all
  {(list term) --> horn-clause --> horn-clause}
  [] Clause -> Clause
  [V | Vs] Clause -> (st-all (remove V Vs)
                             (replace-term-in-clause V (gensym (protect X)) Clause)))

(define replace-term-in-clause
  {term --> term --> horn-clause --> horn-clause}
  V NewV [H <= | B] -> [(replace-term-in-atom V NewV H) <=
                        | (map (/. A (replace-term-in-atom V NewV A)) B)])

(define replace-term-in-atom
  {term --> term --> atom --> atom}
  V NewV [F | Terms] -> [F | (map (/. T (replace-term V NewV T)) Terms)])
```

366

```
(define replace-term
  {term --> term --> term --> term}
  V NewV V -> NewV
  V NewV [F | Terms] -> [F | (map (/. T (replace-term V NewV T)) Terms)]
  _ _ Term -> Term)
```

Our implementation of answer literals prints off multiple solutions since typing y
to the request for more will cause the value false to be returned. This value will
in turn trigger a backtrack in search of new solutions. Here is an example

```
(3+) (prolog [[woman X]]
            [[[woman martha] <=]
             [[woman joan] <=] ])
X = martha
more? y

X = joan
more? y
false : boolean

(4+) (prolog [[append X Y [cons 1 [cons 2 [cons 3 $]]]]]
            [[[append $ X X] <=]
             [[append [cons X Y] W [cons X Z]] <= [append Y W Z]]])

X = $
Y = [cons 1 [cons 2 [cons 3 $]]]
more?  (y/n) y

X = [cons 1 $]
Y = [cons 2 [cons 3 $]]
more?  (y/n) y

X = [cons 1 [cons 2 $]]
Y = [cons 3 $]
more?  (y/n) y

X = [cons 1 [cons 2 [cons 3 $]]]
Y = $
more?  (y/n) y
false : boolean
```

Since our program constitutes an adequate inference engine for Horn clause logic,
why not use it as the basis of the Shen Prolog? The short answer is that the
performance of our Prolog interpreter is too slow for the requirements of type
checking, where it is usual to require thousands of inferences to prove a program
type secure. To attain the necessary speed whereby such a proof can be secured
in seconds rather than minutes requires the sort of compilation strategies covered
in the next chapters.

Exercise 25

1. Write a Prolog program that

   a. reverses a list l.
   b. tests if x is an element of list l.
   c. removes an element x from list l.
   d. substitutes x for y in z
   e. tests if every element of l_1 is an element of l_2.
   f. takes two lists l_1 and l_2 and produces a list l_3 whose elements are all those which are in l_1 but not in l_2.

2. Change the Prolog interpreter in section 25.6 so that it accepts the following Shen Prolog features.

   a. the cut.
   b. findall.
   c. is
   d. when

3. Build a loop detector into your Prolog so that a rule like [[brother X Y] <= [brother Y X]] does not cause an infinite loop.

4. Reading chapter 18 on propositional and first-order logic, how many of the rules in that chapter can be usefully added to Prolog to increase the expressiveness of the language? Argue your case and implement them

Further Reading

Prolog is discussed in Sterling and Shapiro (1994) and Bratko (2002); Lloyd (1990) provides the theory to Prolog while Hogger (1990) is a rather gentler introduction. Stickel (1984, 1986) describes an extension to Prolog that is complete for first-order logic. Robinson's 1965 unification algorithm remains the standard approach to performing unification. Martelli and Montanari (1973) describe a linear time and space algorithm for performing unification. Knight (1989) provides a good overview of the uses and ramifications of unification.

Web Sites

Roman Bartak (http://kti.ms.mff.cuni.cz/~bartak/constraints) maintains a site devoted to constraint programming. Free implementations of Prolog are easily obtained over the web. Sicstus Prolog (http://www.sics.se/sicstus) is one of the fastest versions of Prolog currently available, but is not freely available. SWI Prolog (http://www.swi.prolog.org) is another widely used implementation and is free. GNU Prolog (http://pauillac.inria.fr/~diaz/gnu-prolog) is a free Prolog implemented by Daniel Diaz that offers extra facilities for constraint satisfaction handling. Visual Prolog (http://www.visual-prolog.com) is available from the Prolog Development Centre and includes facilities for building graphical interfaces. A free download version for non-commercial purposes is available from the Web site.

26★ Compiling Sequent Calculus

26.1 The Anatomy of a Sequent Calculus Rule

The compilation of sequent calculus into efficient object code proceeds according to a two step process that begins with sequent calculus, generates Shen Prolog as an intermediate step and from this generates functional Shen code.

From chapter 18, we learnt that every sequent rule R has three parts; a list of side conditions (possibly empty), a set of premises[90] (possibly empty) and a conclusion which is mandatory (figure 26.2).

(datatype sorted

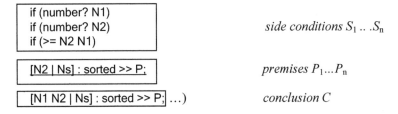

Figure 26.1 The structure of a derivation rule

Each premise and the conclusion has the form $x_1,...,x_n \gg y$ or simply $\gg y$. We'll call these **sequent schemes** or just **schemes** for short. $x_1,...,x_n$ are the **assumptions** of the scheme and y the **consequent** of the scheme. When the list of premises is empty and the conclusion S has an empty assumption list then the rule is an **axiom**.

---

[90] The word 'premise' is also used confusingly for an assumption that forms part of a sequent and the word 'conclusion' for what the sequent is attempting to prove from those assumptions. Logic is littered with the unfortunate consequences of overloading words ('soundness' for example, having three distinct though related meanings).

26.2 Sequent Calculus as a Source Language

The journey from sequent calculus into Shen begins with a distinction between the **surface syntax** of Shen sequent calculus and the **deep syntax**. The surface syntax of sequent calculus is given in appendix B of this book. The surface syntax is the two-dimensional presentation of a sequent calculus rules which we use for programming Shen and which is influenced by logical tradition. The deep syntax is the internal representation of the surface syntax and it is the deep syntax that is ultimately fed into the compiler.

Effectively connecting surface syntax to deep syntax requires some form of parsing and for this purpose we turn to Shen YACC as an executable specification language.   We assume that our datatype definition is passed to Shen YACC function <datatype> whose task it is to both to delimit the syntax of an acceptable datatype definition and to render it into a suitable form for computation.

```
(defmacro datatype-macro
 [datatype F | Rules]
   -> (let D (intern-type F)
         Compile (compile (/. X V (<datatype> X V)) [D | Rules])
         D))

(defcc <datatype>
  datatype D <datatype-rules> := (compile-datatype D <datatype-rules>);)
```

The macro says that a datatype definition is composed of the keyword datatype followed by a name D and a series of datatype rules. The action of the compiler is to compile that datatype.

```
(defcc <datatype>
  D <datatype-rules> := (let Prolog (rules->prolog D <datatype-rules>)
                         (remember-datatype D));)

(defcc <datatype-rules>
  <datatype-rule> <datatype-rules> := (append <datatype-rule> <datatype-rules>);
  <datatype-rule>             := <datatype-rule>;)

(define remember-datatype
  D -> (do (set *datatypes* (adjoin D (value *datatypes*)))
         (set *alldatatypes* (adjoin D (value *alldatatypes*)))
         D))
```

The datatype rules are composed of one or more elements each of which is a datatype rule. The <datatype> function compiles these rules into a Prolog function and rmembers the datatype submitted.   *datatypes* contains the list of datatypes in use whereas *alldatatypes* contains all the datatypes created.

```
(defcc <datatype-rule>
  <single>;
  <double>;)
```

A datatype rule is either a single rule (one in which the conclusion and the premises are seperated by a single line) or a double (LR) rule (one in which the conclusion and the premises are seperated by a double line).

```
(defcc <single>
  <sides> <prems> <sng> <conc>  := [[<sides> <prems> <conc>]];)
```

A single rule consists of a series of side conditions (possibly empty) followed by a series of premises (possibly empty) and a single line followed by a conclusion.

A single line is 3 or more concatenations of the underline.

```
(defcc <sng>
  X := X   where (sng? X);)
```

```
(define sng?
  S -> (and (symbol? S) (sng-h? (str S))))
```

```
(define sng-h?
  "___" -> true
  (@s "_" S) -> (sng-h? S)
  _ -> false)
```

The side conditions are zero or more objects each of which is a side condition.

```
(defcc <sides>
  <side> <sides> := [<side> | <sides>];
  <e> := [];)
```

A side condition is either a test (flagged by if) or a local assignment (flagged by let or let!). There are no restrictions on the syntax of these arguments to these keywords.

```
(defcc <side>
  if P    := [if P];
  let X Y := [let X Y]
  let! X Y := [let! X Y];)
```

The premises are patterned by each premise being seperated by a semi-colon. It is possible for the series of premises to be empty. If a formula is placed on its own, this indicates that the list of assumptions to that premise is empty.

```
(defcc <prems>
  <prem> <sc> <prems> := [<prem> | <prems>];
  <e> := [];)
```

```
(defcc <sc>
  X := skip   where (= X ;);)
```

A premise can either be a cut, or a sequent scheme composed of a series of assumptions followed by >> and another formula or a formula on its own.

```
(defcc <prem>
  !            := !;
  <ass> >> <formula>  := [<ass> <formula>];
  <formula>         := [[] <formula>];)
```

A series of assumptions is zero or more formulae seperated by commas.

```
(defcc <ass>
  <formula> , <ass> := [<formula> | <ass>];
  <formula>       := [<formula>];
  <e> := [];)
```

A formula is either a typing (an expression followed by a colon followed by a type or it is an expression on its own.

```
(defcc <formula>
  <expr> : <type> := [(curry <expr>) : (rectify-type <type>)];
  <expr>        := (curry <expr>);)
```

Expressions are curried and types are rectified.   Rectifying a type restores parentheses if necessary (so A --> B --> C becomes A --> (B --> C)) and rewrites types according to any synonym declarations made by the user.

An expression is anything that is not reserved for special use.

```
(defcc <expr>
  X := X where (not (key-in-sequent-calculus? X));)
```

```
(define key-in-sequent-calculus?
  X -> (or (element? X [>> ; , : <--]) (sng? X) (dbl? X)))
```

A type is an expression.

```
(defcc <type>
  <expr> := <expr>;)
```

The conclusion of a datatype rule has a very similar syntax to a premise, except that a cut is not allowed.

```
(defcc <conc>
  <ass> >> <formula> <sc> := [<ass> <formula>];
  <formula> <sc>        := [[] <formula>];)
```

372

A double rule has a series of (possibly empty) side conditions, a non-empty series of formulae, a double line and a concluding formula.

```
(defcc <double>
  <sides> <formulae> <dbl> <formula> <sc>
                   := (lr-rule <sides> <formulae> [[] <formula>]);)
```

Each formula is mapped to a sequent scheme whose assumption list is empty.

```
(defcc <formulae>
  <formula> <sc> <formulae> := [[[] <formula>] | <formulae>];
  <formula> <sc>            := [[] <formula>];)
```

A double line is a 3 or more equal signs joined together.

```
(defcc <dbl>
  X := X  where (dbl? X);)

(define dbl?
  S -> (and (symbol? S) (dbl-h? (str S))))

(define dbl-h?
  "===" -> true
  (@s "=" S) -> (dbl-h? S)
  _ -> false)
```

The double underline indicates that the rule is an LR rule. The function lr-rule takes the parsed content of this rule and generates and L rule and an R rule.

```
(define lr-rule
  Side Sequents [[] C] -> (let P (gensym (protect P))
                              LConc [[C] P]
                              LPrem [(coll-formulae Sequents) P]
                              Left [Side [LPrem] LConc]
                              Right [Side Sequents [[] C]]
                              [Right Left]))

(define coll-formulae
  [] -> []
  [[[] Q] | Sequents] -> [Q | (coll-formulae Sequents)])
```

In conclusion then, this Shen YACC procedure outputs the datatype rule as an object conforming to the deep syntax of the sequent calculus. The rules of this deep syntax are as follows:

1. A sequent rule is a triple [*S P C*] where *S* is a (possibly empty) list of side conditions, *P* is a (possibly empty) list of premises and *C* is the conclusion.
2. A side condition has the form [if *P*] or [let *X Y*] or [let! *X Y*] where *P*, *X* and *Y* are arbitrary.
3. A premise is a pair [*A R*] composed of a (possibly empty) list of formulae *A* and a formula *R* or the cut !.
4. A formula is either an expression or a typing [*X* : *Y*] where *X* is an expression and *Y* is a type.
5. A conclusion is a pair [*A R*] composed of a (possibly empty) list of formulae *A* and a formula *R*.

26.3 Enriched Horn Clause Logic as an Object Language

The source language for our compiler is the deep syntax of the previous section. The object language for our sequent calculus compiler is a list of enriched Horn clauses. The output conforms to the following syntax.

1. An enriched Horn clause is a pair [*H B*] where *H* is the head of the clause and *B* the body.
2. The head *H* is a list [$t_1...t_n$] where $t_1 ...t_n$ are head terms (*h* **terms**).
3. An *h* term is either an atom or and expression of the form [cons $t_1 t_2$] where t_1 and t_2 are *h* terms.
4. The body is a (possibly empty) list of literals.
5. A literal consists of a list [*f* $t_1...t_n$] where *f* is a predicate and $t_1 ...t_n$ are body terms (*b* **terms**).
6. A predicate is any symbol that can be used to name a Shen function.
7. A *b* term is either an atom or a list of *b* terms.

Notice the asymmetry between *h* terms and *b* terms. Every *b* term is an *h* term but not vice versa. An *h* term is essentially confined to describing lists and atoms. A *b* term is an arbitrary symbolic expression which can reflect any function call. This arrangement reflects the power of Shen Prolog to process lists in the head of the clause but to accommodate arbitrary function calls from within the body of the clause. This facility is needed to compile sequent calculus rules with side conditions.

26.4 Two Models for Compiling Sequent Calculus

There are two models for compiling sequent calculus; these are the *linked process model* and the *goal model*. These models represent different realisations of the same essential procedure. Every rule in our deep syntax is a three element list [*S P* [*As R*]] where *S* is the list of side conditions of the rule, *P* is the list of premises, *As* is the list of assumptions and *R* is the consequent.

The essential procedure is

1. First, match the consequent of the sequent to the conclusion trying to be proved.
2. Second, establish that any assumptions needed for the rule to apply are present in the list of hypotheses.
3. Third, ensure the side conditions are fulfilled.
4. If 1., 2., and 3. have been met, generate n proof obligations corresponding to the n premises in the rule.

At each stage from 1-2, the there is a list of constraints that must be passed forward. For example if our rule has the form

$$\dotfill$$

(f X Y) (f Y Z) >> (f X Z);

Then the value found for X in (f X Z) must be taken into the search for (f X Y) which in turn creates a binding for Y which together with the values for X and Z constrains the search for (f Y Z). *A constraint therefore is a variable, together with its value if it has one.* In what follows we refer to the constraint variables that occur within a search procedure as *being in the scope of that procedure.*

The difference between the linked process model and the goal model revolves around how these constraints are realised in our Horn clause logic. In the linked process model, the consequent R and the assumptions $A_1 \ldots A_n$ in As all generate seperate procedures ηR $\eta A_1, \ldots, \eta A_n$ and the flow of control is from ηR to $\eta A_1, \ldots, \eta A_n$.

The final procedure ηA_n (having succeeded and any side conditions having been met) generates the proof obligations from the premises. In the linked process model, each procedure passes forward the constraint variables that are fixed in its part of the search. The key defining characteristic of the linked process model is that each procedure *explicitly* calls its successor procedure if it succeeds.

This model is clean, simple and generates efficient code. It is suitable for compiling what might be called the *pure sequent calculus* as introduced in chapter 18. It is also generalisable to both logic programming and functional programming versions, but suffers from one problem; it does not support the use of the cut within a sequent calculus rule.

For example if a cut is placed in the position of the first premise, it will appear in the final procedure ηA_n whereas it should appear at the top level ηR. In a goal oriented architecture, there is no problem because though each goal is associated with a procedure, each procedure does *not* explicitly call the next procedure. The handover occurs because of the juxtaposition of the goals citing these procedures in ηR. Compiling a cut is trivial in this model, since the cut becomes part of the body of a clause in ηR.

In both models each procedure is responsible for the constraint variables within its scope. Wrt a constraint variable v, this responsibility is discharged in two ways.

1. If v is unbound then v is bound to a value which may be passed forward.
2. Or if v is already bound, then occurs-check unification is performed to see if any constraint attached to v is met.

The difference in the two cases is procedural; in fact unification suffices for both these cases, because if we assume that v is an unbound variable then unification must succeed in creating a binding.

The goal oriented model, unlike the linked process model, does not generalise to functional programming since unification via variable sharing is integral to this model. In place of the simple parameter passing of the continuation model, the goal oriented model is continually using occurs-check unification to transmit values forward in the computation. This is an expensive overhead and one that should be avoided if possible. An optimisation of the naïve procedure revolves around distinguishing the two cases cited above. If a variable is the scope of a procedure but does not occur within any prior procedure then v can simply be bound without recourse to occurs-check unification.[91]

26.5 Naïve Goal Oriented Compilation in Shen

To make the elucidation simpler, we will begin with the naïve procedure, which itself is reasonably complex, before adding the refinement suggested above. In what follows we will use ´assumption` to denote the assumptions in a rule. In our deep syntax notation, in a rule [S P [As R]], an assumption is a member of A. We´ll use the term ´hypothesis` to denote an object that can be matched by an assumption when the program is actually run.

The top level function here is rules->prolog which takes as arguments

1. The name D of the datatype defined. In figure 26.1 this is sorted.
2. A list of sequent rules in deep syntax.

---

[91] This adaption of the goal-oriented technique was introduced in 2021 in the S30 kernel and replaced the linked process model used in earlier kernels. In an experiment, the optimised goal-oriented compiler described in this chapter was run against an earlier linked process compiler. The code from each executed at the same speed within any reasonable measure of accuracy.

The function maps down the list of rules, converting them into clauses and organises the whole into a Prolog procedure.

```
(define rules->prolog
  D Rules -> (let Clauses (mapcan (/. Rule (rule->clause Rule)) Rules)
               (eval [defprolog D | Clauses])))
```

A rule is in deep syntax, having the form [*S P* [*As R*]]. The first step is to generate the list of constraints attached to this rule by extracting the list of variables used in it. The second step is to generate a list of new *hypothesis list variables* based on the length of *As*. Each goal generated by an assumption will generate a new list of hypotheses to be passed down the line and so we reserve a list of variables for that purpose.

A clause is then formed by compiling the consequent *R*, the code becoming the head of the clause and compiling the rest of the rule which becomes the body of the clause.

```
(define rule->clause
  [S P [As R]] -> (let Constraints (extract-vars [S P [As R]])
                       HypVs (nvars (+ 1 (length As)))
                       Head (compile-consequent R HypVs)
                       Goals (goals Constraints As S P HypVs)
                    (append Head [<--] Goals [(intern ";")])))

(define compile-consequent
  R [H | _] -> [(optimise-typing R) H])

(define nvars
  0 -> []
  N -> [(gensym (protect V)) | (nvars (- N 1))])
```

The conclusion *R* has to be processed into a form suitable for compilation into Prolog by placing terms into cons form. An optimisation wrt a typing *x : B* is that unification is performed over the *type B* and not the *term x*. So mode declarations are inserted to ensure this. Finally any mode declarations already present in *R* are compiler directives and need to be left alone.

```
(define optimise-typing
  [X : A]  -> [- (cons-form-with-modes [X : [+ A]])]
  X -> [+ (cons-form-with-modes X)])

(define cons-form-with-modes
  [- X] -> [- (cons-form-with-modes X)]
  [+ X] -> [+ (cons-form-with-modes X)]
  [mode X Mode] -> [Mode (cons-form-with-modes X)]
  [X | Y] -> [cons (cons-form-with-modes X) (cons-form-with-modes Y)]
  X -> X)
```

The goals are generated next.

377

```
(define goals
    Constraints As S P HypVs
                   -> (let GoalsAs (compile-assumptions As Constraints HypVs)
                           GoalsS (compile-side conditions S)
                           GoalsP (compile-premises P HypVs)
                           (append GoalsAs GoalsS GoalsP)))
```

The goals from the assumptions are generated by recursing down the assumptions list; each assumption A will generate code that receives a list of hypotheses and that code will generate a new list by removing a hypothesis that matches A.

```
(define compile-assumptions
    [] _ _ -> []
    [A | As] Constraints [H1 H2 | HypVs]
    ->  [(compile-assumption A H1 H2 Constraints)
         | (compile-assumptions As Constraints [H2 | HypVs])])
```

Compiling an assumption involves

1. Generating a search procedure F that looks for a hypothesis.
2. Returning a call to F in the form of a goal.

```
(define compile-assumption
    A H1 H2 Constraints
    -> (let F (gensym search)
            Compile (compile-search-procedure F A H1 H2 Constraints)
            [F H1 [] H2 | Constraints]))
```

The goal takes as parameters both H1 and H2, which are hypothesis list variables. H1 receives the hypotheses in play and H2 will be bound to the hypotheses returned if F succeeds. This hypothesis list will be passed on to the next goal. In addition there is a list of constraint variables, some of which may acquire bindings if the goal is met.

There is one other parameter, the empty list. This is associated in F with the list of hypotheses that have been unsuccessfully matched to the assumption A. Initially this is the empty list.

The search procedure consists of two clauses; a clause indicating that the assumption A has been found at the head of the hypothesis list and a clause that applies if it has not. A variable Past is generated to hold the hypotheses which have been searched; this variable will initially be bound to the empty list mentioned previously.

```
(define compile-search-procedure
    F A H1 H2 Constraints
    -> (let Past (gensym (protect Previous))
            Base (foundit! A H1 Past H2 Constraints)
            Recursive (keep-looking F H1 Past H2 Constraints)
            (eval [defprolog F | (append Base Recursive)])))
```

378

```
(define foundit!
   A H1 Past H2 Constraints
   -> (let Head  [[- [cons (optimise-typing A) H1]] Past H2 | Constraints]
          Body  [[bind H2 [append [1 Past] [1 H1]]]
      (append Head [<--] Body [(intern ";")]);))
```

The foundit! procedure generates a head in which the assumption A is matched to the head of the hypotheses. The action then is to bind the outgoing hypothesis list variable H2 to the hypotheses which were not matched; which is precisely the result of appending Past to H1. The expression [append [1 Past] [1 H1]] has a compiler optimisation for Shen Prolog which is explained in 27.19.

keep-looking generates a clause that matches the head X of the hypothesis list and pushes it on Past, recursing to call F.

```
(define keep-looking
   F H1 Past H2 Constraints
   -> (let X (gensym (protect V))
          Head  [[- [cons X H1]] Past H2 | Constraints]
          Body  [[F H1 [cons X Past] H2 | Constraints]]
      (append Head [<--] Body [(intern ";")])))
```

This concludes the densest part of the code. The rest is straightforward.

```
(define compile-side conditions
   S -> (map (/. X (compile-side condition X)) S))
```

The goals are a fairly direct transcription from the argot of sequent calculus into that of Shen Prolog.

```
(define compile-side condition
   [let X Y] -> [is X Y]
   [let! X Y] -> [is! X Y]
   [if P] -> [when P])
```

The code from the premises is created by mapping down the list of premises carrying the variable Hyp which is the last hypothesis list variable and it will be bound to the list of hypotheses current in the proof.

```
(define compile-premises
   P HypVs -> (let Hyp (hd (reverse HypVs))
                  (map (/. X (compile-premise X Hyp)) P)))
```

A premise may be a cut, in which case it is compiled as such; otherwise control is given to a help function.

```
(define compile-premise
   ! _ -> !
   [As R] Hyp -> (compile-premise-h (reverse As) R Hyp))
```

compile-premise-h then recurses through the list of assumptions attached to the premise and adds their instantiation under Constraints to the hypotheses bound to Hyp. After this process terminates, compile-premise-h then issues a call to system-S – the native code for the Shen type checker – with the conclusion R and the new list of hypotheses.

```
(define compile-premise-h
  [] R Hyp -> [system-S (cons-form R) Hyp]
  [A | As] R Hyp -> (compile-premise-h As R [cons (cons-form A) Hyp]))

(define cons-form
  [X | Y] -> [cons (cons-form X) (cons-form Y)]
  X -> X)
```

26.6 Refining Goal Oriented Compilation

Our naïve model uses occurs-check unification as a general tool for generating and checking constraints. The refinement consists of separating these two procedures and optimising for the former. The key section of the code is in foundit! where these constraints come into play. For convenience this code is repeated below.

```
(define foundit!
  A H1 Past H2 Constraints
  -> (let Head  [[- [cons (optimise-typing A) H1]] Past H2 | Constraints]
        Body  [[bind H2 [append [1 Past] [1 H1]]]
        (append Head [<--] Body [(intern ";")]);)
```

The list of constraint variables in Constraints can be subject to a tripartite division.

1. There are constraint variables which do not occur in A. We shall call these *bystanders*. These are simply passed as unused parameters and generate very little computational overhead.
2. There are constraint variables which do occur in A but not in any formula prior to A. We'll call these variables *passive*; they will receive values which place constraints on later procedures.
3. There are constraint variables which do occur in A and in some formula prior to A. We'll call these variables *active*; they actively place constraints on the match for A.

The proper action is to bind passive variables and use occurs-check unification on active variables. In order to do this we must suppose that foundit! receives a list Active of those variables which have been mentioned before A. Those variables which are in A but not in Active are passive variables.

380

The first step is to compute the list of passive variables and then to create a table in which each passive variable will be associated with a unique new variable.

```
(define foundit!
   A H1 Past H2 Constraints Active
   -> (let  Passive (passive A Active)
           Table (tabulate-passive Passive)
           Head  (head-foundit! A H1 Past H2 Constraints Table)
           Body (body-foundit! H1 Past H2 Table)
           (append Head [<--] Body [(intern ";")]);)
```

A passive variable is one that is not active.

```
(define passive
   [X | Y] Active -> (union (passive X Active) (passive Y Active))
   X Active -> [X]  where (passive? X Active)
   _ _ -> [])

(define passive?
   X Active -> (and (not (element? X Active)) (variable? X)))
```

A table is built by associating every passive variable with a proxy fresh variable.

```
(define tabulate-passive
   Passive -> (map (/. X [X | (gensym (protect V))]) Passive))
```

The head of the foundit! clause is constructed by replacing these passive variables by proxy variables from the table, thus preventing unification from being invoked on the passive variables.

```
(define  head-foundit!
   A H1 Past H2 Constraints Table
   -> (let Optimise (optimise-passive Constraints Table)
          [[- [cons (optimise-typing A) H1]] Past H2 | Optimise]))

(define optimise-passive
   Constraints Table -> (map (/. C (optimise-passive-h C Table)) Constraints))

(define optimise-passive-h
   C Table ->(let Entry (assoc C Table)
                  (if (empty? Entry) C (tl Entry))))
```

The body of the foundit! clause is constructed by using the same table to bind the proxy variables to the passive variables. When the table is exhausted, the final call in the body is exactly as in the naïve version – the output hypothesis list variable is bound.

```
(define body-foundit!
   H1 Past H2 [] -> [[bind H2 [append [1 Past] [1 H1]]]]
   H1 Past H2 [[C | V] | Table] -> [[bind V C] | (body-foundit! H1 Past H2 Table)])
```

This really wraps up the significant changes. The other changes arise from having to pass along the active variable list. Here is the code adapted from the previous section with the changes bolded.

```
(define rule->clause
  [S P [As R]] -> (let Constraints (extract-vars [S P [As R]])
                       HypVs (nvars (+ 1 (length As)))
                       Active (extract-vars R)
                       Head (compile-consequent R HypVs)
                       Goals (goals Constraints As S P HypVs Active)
                       (append Head [<--] Goals [(intern ";")])))

(define goals
  Constraints As S P HypVs Active
  -> (let GoalsAs (compile-assumptions As Constraints HypVs Active)
          GoalsS (compile-side conditions S)
          GoalsP (compile-premises P HypVs)
          (append GoalsAs GoalsS GoalsP)))

(define compile-assumptions
  [] _ _ _ -> []
  [A | As] Constraints [H1 H2 | HypVs] Active
  -> (let NewActive (append (extract-vars A) Active)
          [(compile-assumption A H1 H2 Constraints Active)
          | (compile-assumptions As Constraints [H2 | HypVs] NewActive)]))

(define compile-assumption
  A H1 H2 Constraints Active
  -> (let F (gensym search)
          Compile (compile-search-procedure F A H1 H2 Constraints Active)
          [F H1 [] H2 | Constraints]))

(define compile-search-procedure
  F A H1 H2 Constraints Active
  -> (let Past (gensym (protect Previous))
          Base (foundit! A H1 Past H2 Constraints Active)
          Recursive (keep-looking F H1 Past H2 Constraints)
          (eval [defprolog F | (append Base Recursive)])))
```

Further Reading

The compilation of sequent calculus within logic programming is something of a black art. Neal Alexander (https://github.com/Shen-Language/wiki/wiki/Sequent-Calculus) gives a summary of Shen's compilation technique for sequent calculus.

27 * Compiling Prolog

A **Horn clause procedure** P in a logic program L is the set of all clauses in L whose heads share the same n place predicate in the head. In Shen Prolog such clauses are gathered together under a defprolog definition which is compiled into a Shen function. It is the task of this chapter to explain how this is done.

Every n-place Horn clause procedure is compiled into an $n+4$ place Shen 'Horn clause' function. The extra four places are reserved for

1. The **binding vector**.
2. The **lock**.
3. The **key**.
4. The **continuation**.

The lock and the key are important in the compilation of the cut and are explained in section 27.17.

27.1 The Binding Vector

The task of the binding vector V_n is to maintain the variable-value associations that are made during the course of the Prolog computation. V_n is a standard vector which initially consists of the vector size (in index 0) and a **ticket number** (in index 1) which has the initial value 2. The ticket is handed out to new Prolog variables when they are created and it is incremented each time this happens. Indices > 2 are initially set to the default value -null- which indicates that there is no value to be found in this index. Prolog variables that point to such indices are therefore unbound.

The binding vector V_n contains all the needed information to maintain the bindings for the Prolog variables. Every Prolog variable v_i generated during the computation is generated as a print vector composed of

a. A tag in the zeroth place indicating that the non-standard vector is standing for a Prolog variable.

383

b. A unique positive integer i in the first place that determines the identity of the variable; (figure 26.7). The value of this variable is therefore found in index 713 of V_n

pvar	713

Figure 27.1 The vector anatomy of a Prolog variable Var713

The binding vector can either be **static**, which means that its size in fixed at the start of the computation or **dynamic** which means that its size can 'change' according to the requirements of the computation.[92] There are corresponding advantages and disadvantages of these arrangements.

A static vector does not require any tests to determine if it is running out of memory, and this speeds the computation, but at the expense of potentially running out of memory. A dynamic vector incurs overheads in checking for memory shortages and copying vectors but avoids 'out of memory messages' (which appear as system error messages signalling an out of bounds vector call).

Prior to 2019 Shen ran under dynamic vector management. In 2019 Shen was changed to run under static vector management and a method of recycling vector memory was developed which allowed Prolog computations to run for hours if needed but which required very little memory. This recycling method is generally referred to as **garbage collection** and is studied in section 27.13.

27.2 The Continuation

The continuation represents the unsolved part of the computation, or in our original interpreter-based model, the goal stack. However computationally it is more efficient to represent the continuation, not as a list, but as a lazy object which can be thawed when needed (the equivalent of popping the goal stack). The continuation, when thawed will eventually evaluate to an object which is the result of the computation. If this object is false, then the computation has failed and our Prolog backtracks. If not, then the object found is returned as the result of the Prolog computation.

27.3 Eager vs. Lazy Derefencing

We have seen that dereferencing is a process by which the value δ of any variable V is found by following a chain of pointers from that variable and replacing V by δ.   In **eager dereferencing**, the actual value is found, whereas in **lazy dereferencing** the chain of pointers is followed only as far as is needed to find an object that is not a bound variable.

---

[92] More accurately, when running short of memory a larger vector is created and the contents of the old vector copied over to the new.

To see the difference, consider a binding vector in which the variable V3 is bound to [V5 V6]. In binding vector terms this means that the third index is occupied by the list [V5 V6] (figure 27.2). V5 is in turn bound to a and V6 to b as signified by the presence of these elements in the fifth and sixth positions.

	...	[V5 V6]	...	a	b	...	...
1	2	3	4	5	6	7	8

Figure 27.2 A binding vector illustrating eager and lazy dereferencing

Using lazy dereferencing, V3 is dereferenced to [V5 V6] and the process ends because the result is not a variable. Using eager dereferencing, V3 is dereferenced to [a b]. Lazy dereferencing is obviously faster than eager, and since the structure of the computation often only requires that a non-variable result be used, lazy deferencing is used in Shen Prolog whenever possible.

27.4 Left Linear Horn Clauses

A Horn clause is left linear if no variable occurs more than once in its head. In the triple stack method discussed in chapter 15, left linearisation is an essential prerequisite for converting patterns into code. Likewise, compiling Prolog requires left linearising Prolog clauses. In the case of pattern matching this involves pushing an equality test onto the rule. In the case of Prolog the equality test is replaced by a unification test. Thus in

```
(defprolog member
  X [X | _] <--;
  X [_ | Y] <-- (member X Y);)
```

the first clause is not left-linear. We rename the duplicated variable Y and push a unification test ((is! X Y) in Shen Prolog) onto the (empty) body of the first clause. List expressions are presented in cons form. Wildcards offer room for optimisation, so these remain. The result looks like this:

```
(defprolog member
  X (cons Y _) <-- (is! X Y);
  X (cons _ Y) <-- (member X Y);)
```

By default Shen Prolog uses occurs-check unification and the occurs-check requires eager dereferencing. The occurs-check function (see Appendix A) allows this to be disabled and any code compiled under Shen Prolog is affected by this setting.

27.5 Implementing Unification

The conversion of clauses to left linear form leaves calls to unification in the body of the clause. is! is a two-place predicate that performs unification with respect to terms *x* and *y* and therefore compiles into a 6 place function that takes

385

x, y and the binding vector, lock, key and the continuation as arguments. The unification function steps through x and y, lazily dereferencing the arguments. If one argument is a variable, then the other argument is eagerly dereferenced to ensure the occurs check is met. lzy=! is a tree recursive function; the rightmost call is frozen and becomes part of the continuation.

```
(define is!
  X Y Bindings Lock Key Continuation
  -> (lzy=! (lazyderef X Bindings)  (lazyderef Y Bindings)
        Bindings
        Continuation))
```

```
(define lzy=!
  X X Bindings Continuation -> (thaw Continuation)
  X Y Bindings Continuation -> (bind! X Y Bindings Continuation)
            where (and (pvar? X) (not (occurs? X (deref Y Bindings))))
  X Y Bindings Continuation -> (bind! Y X Bindings Continuation)
            where (and (pvar? Y) (not (occurs? Y (deref X Bindings))))
  [X | Y] [W | Z] Bindings Continuation -> (lzy=! (lazyderef X Bindings)
                                       (lazyderef W Bindings)
                                       Bindings
                                       (freeze (lzy=! (lazyderef Y Bindings)
                                                (lazyderef Z Bindings)
                                                Bindings
                                                Continuation)))
  _ _ _ _ -> false)
```

```
(define occurs?
  X X -> true
  X [Y | Z] -> (or (occurs? X Y) (occurs? X Z))
  _ _ -> false)
```

Here is lazyderef.

```
(define lazyderef
  Tm Bindings -> (if (pvar? Tm)
                   (let Value (<-address Bindings (<-address Tm 1))
                     (if (= Value -null-) Tm  (lazyderef Value Bindings)))
                   Tm))
```

If Tm is a variable then the ticket number is taken from Tm and corresponding index on Bindings is searched. If the result is -null-, then Tm is unbound and Tm is returned. Otherwise the resulting binding is itself lazily dereferenced. With full dereferencing the ultimate value is chased down.

```
(define deref
  [X | Y] Bindings -> [(deref X Bindings) | (deref Y Bindings)]
  X Bindings -> (if (pvar? X)
                   (let Value (<-address Bindings (<-address X 1))
                     (if (= Value -null-) X  (deref Value Bindings)))
                   X))
```

```
(define bind!
  Tm Si PV GoTo -> (let Bind (bindv Tm Si PV)
                        Compute (thaw GoTo)
                        (if (= Compute false)
                            (unwind Tm PV Compute)
                            Compute)))
```

bind! thaws the continuation to the local variable Compute. If Compute fails then this binding is unwound. If not, then Compute is returned.

```
(define bindv
  PVar Si Bindings -> (address-> Bindings (<-address PVar 1) Si))
```

The bindv function grabs the ticket number from the term Tm and uses it to assign Si to the corresponding index in the binding vector.

```
(define unwind
  PVar Bindings Compute
  -> (do (address-> Bindings (<-address PVar 1) -null-)
         Compute))
```

The unwind function takes the ticket number form the variable and removes its binding by assigning -null- to that variable and returns Compute.

27.6 Coping with Exponential Code

An important difference between Prolog and Shen function definitions (SFDs) is the compilation of an atom a which is not a variable. In an SFD the appropriate action is to push an equality test onto the stack U. In the case of Prolog there are *two* ways that the computation can move forward successfully; either the relevant input is identical with a or it is a variable that can be bound to a.

Given n such atoms to be compared, there are 2^n successful computational paths constituting a binary tree. More precisely, there are 2^n successful computational paths for every Horn clause whose head contains n non-variable subterms. If we allocate code for each of these paths, then the amount of code generated can quickly exceed the capacity of the computer to compile it.

If we were to examine the code from this Prolog compiler, we would find that it was timewise efficient in execution, but prodigal with space.[93] Moreover we would also find, unsurprisingly, a great deal of repetition in the leaves of this 'code tree'. Compiler writers who work in lower level languages like assembly cope with these issues by creating low level procedures which are invoked as

---

[93] This was in fact a problem with all versions of Shen Prolog from 2011-2019 which were fast but bulky. The solution in these implementations was to cap the value of n to reasonable bounds and to use more or less clever techniques to massage the clause to a manageable form if n was too large. These techniques were supplanted in this fourth edition.

needed by **procedure calls** or **jumps**. Therefore instead of inlining all such calls, control is directed to the relevant procedure.

In functional programming we do not have jumps or procedure calls of this kind. However we do have something that can serve in this role; *lazy objects*. We can freeze a computation and store it in a local variable and then thaw it as needed and in this way we can gain the advantage of avoiding exponential code with only a little depreciation in performance as a cost.

Since we are on the subject of the space taken up by generated code, we should take note of the effects of mode declarations. Negative mode declarations have the effect of torching binary tree code, reducing the tree to a trunk. If an atom a lies in the scope of a negative mode declaration then the computer does not test to see if the input is a variable that can be bound to a. Hence we need to adapt to and take advantage of negative mode declarations by optimising the code generated from terms that fall under their scope.

27.7 The Twin Stack Method

The construction of the Kλ code from patterns in an SFD is a simple matter of *and*ing, the code generated from each pattern and for this purpose in the triple stack method we used a stack. In the compilation of Shen Prolog, these tests are interpolated in a complex way and a stack is not the appropriate data structure for that task. However stacks S and T do remain to keep in tandem, the comparison of the terms from the head of the clause and the elements of the formal parameters of the emerging function. Hence we refer to this as the **twin stack** method.

The complexity of the twin stack method is greater than the triple stack method used to compile SFDs. To describe it accurately, we need a computable specification language and for this purpose Shen is the logical choice.

To begin we need to regiment the structure of a Shen Prolog definition. Our left linearised version of member was as follows.

```
(defprolog member
  X (cons Y _) <-- (is! X Y);
  X (cons _ Y) <-- (member X Y);)
```

The compiler separates this into

1. A characterising predicate member.
2. A list L of head-body pairs $[H\ B]$ where H is the list of terms in the head of the clause and B is the list of literals in the body.

In the member case L would be

```
[        [[X [cons Y _]] [[is! X Y]]
          [[X [cons _ Y]] [member X Y]]        ]
```

The second element required is a list F of fresh formal parameters for the Shen function to be generated. There will be one such for every top level term to the characterising predicate. Here member has an arity of 2 and we'll use [V1 V2] as the list of formal parameters.

Remembering that, where the characterising predicate has an arity of n, the resulting Shen function has an arity of $n+4$, there are more arguments to be drawn into the compilation process. The first is the formal parameter designating the Prolog binding vector and we'll designate that by Bindings. The second is the continuation Continuation which will be constructed from the body B of the head-body pair. The other two arguments, Lock and Key we put aside for the moment.

The twin stack method steps through each element $[H\ B]$ of L in turn. The head H becomes the S stack, the list F of formal parameters becomes the T stack - these are the twin stacks. The other arguments are Bindings and Continuation. There is one final argument - the mode that is operating with respect to the terms being compiled. This is either + or -. This is represented as +m and -m inside the compiler.[94]

27.8 Compiling the Head of the Clause

The guts of our compiler is a function compile-head which compiles head-body pairs into code chunks. There are five inputs to compile-head.

1. The mode declaration that is operating; by default this is +, represented as +m inside the compiler.
2. The stack S which represents the list of n terms in the head H of the Horn clause. n is therefore the arity of the Prolog predicate.
3. The stack T of formal parameters which initially is F.
4. The name of the Prolog binding vector.
5. The **continuation code** which tells the computer what to do if the matching is successful. The continuation code is generated from the body B of the Horn clause.

Our base case is simple.

```
(define compile-head
   _ [] [] Bindings Continuation          -> Continuation
```

The base case says that if the stacks S and T are empty, then the continuation code has to be returned. We'll see shortly how the continuation code is generated, but for now we'll put this aside.

---

[94] More precisely, shen.m+ and shen.m-. The purpose of the renaming is to avoid any conflation with terms that contain + and - as actual function signs inside a clause.

389

The second and third rules deal with terms with mode declarations.

```
Mode [[+m Si] | S] T Bindings Continuation
-> (compile-head Mode [+m Si Mode | S] T Bindings Continuation)
Mode [[-m Si] | S] T Bindings Continuation
-> (compile-head Mode [-m Si Mode | S] T Bindings Continuation)
```

These rules say that when we encounter a term t embedded in a mode declaration on the S stack, we unpack the mode declaration and place that mode declaration in front of t and the current mode declaration after t.

The next two rules say that when a mode declaration is encountered on its own, that declaration becomes the new mode value carried by compile-head

```
_ [-m | S] T Bindings Continuation -> (compile-head -m S T Bindings Continuation)
_ [+m | S] T Bindings Continuation -> (compile-head +m S T Bindings Continuation)
```

The fifth rule says that if a wildcard is encountered then it is popped from the S stack and the corresponding term is popped from the T stack. No code is generated from a wildcard.

```
Mode [Si | S] [_ | T] Bindings Continuation
-> (compile-head Mode S T Bindings Continuation)      where (wildcard? Si)
```

The sixth rule says that if a variable is encountered then the code corresponding to the variable case is generated.

```
Mode [Si | S] T Bindings Continuation
-> (variable-case Mode [Si | S] T Bindings Continuation) where (variable? Si)
```

The seventh rule says that if the term is an atom (string, symbol, number, empty list or boolean) under a negative mode declaration then the code corresponding to a negative atom case is generated.

```
-m [Si | S] T Bindings Continuation
-> (atom-case-minus [Si | S] T Bindings Continuation)   where (atom? Si)
```

The eighth rule says that if the term is a cons structure (of the form $(cons\ x\ y)$) under a negative mode declaration then the code corresponding to a negative cons case is generated.

```
-m [[cons Sa Sb] | S] T Bindings Continuation
-> (cons-case-minus [[cons Sa Sb] | S] T Bindings Continuation)
```

The ninth and tenth rules deal with the positive atom and positive cons cases.

```
+m [Si | S] T Bindings Continuation
-> (atom-case-plus [Si | S] T Bindings Continuation)    where (atom? Si)
+m [[cons Sa Sb] | S] T Bindings Continuation
-> (cons-case-plus [[cons Sa Sb] | S] T Bindings Continuation)
```

390

27.9 The Variable Case

Here is the code for the variable case

```
(define variable-case
  Mode [Si | S] [Ti | T] Bindings Continuation
  -> (if (variable? Ti)
        (compile-head Mode S T Bindings (subst Ti Si Continuation))
        [let Si Ti (compile-head Mode S T Bindings Continuation)]))
```

Si must of course be a variable. The basic procedure is to test the corresponding Ti term on the *T* stack to see if it too is a variable. If so, the Si term is simply a place holder for Ti and so we substitute Ti for Si in the continuation code. If not, then Ti is locally assigned to Si.

27.10 The Negative Atom Case

```
(define atom-case-minus
  [Si | S] [Ti | T] Bindings Continuation
                    -> (let Tm (gensym (protect Tm))
                        [let Tm [lazyderef Ti Bindings]
                        [if [= Tm Si]
                            (compile-head -m S T Bindings Continuation)
                            false]]))
```

The code generated creates a local assignment in which Ti is lazily dereferenced. It is compared to Si and if it is identical then the resulting code from compile-head is executed. If not, then false is returned.

27.11 The Negative Cons Case

```
(define cons-case-minus
  [[cons Sa Sb] | S] [Ti | T] Bindings Continuation
  -> (let Tm (gensym (protect Tm))
        [let Tm [lazyderef Ti Bindings]
        [if [cons? Tm]
            (compile-head -m
                [Sa Sb | S]
                [[hd Tm] [tl Tm] | T]
                Bindings Continuation)
            false]]))
```

The code generated creates a local assignment Tm in which Ti is lazily dereferenced. If Tm passes the cons? test then compile-head recurses, placing Sa and Sb on the *S* stack and [hd Tm] and [tl Tm] on the *T* stack. If Tm fails the cons? test then false is returned.

27.12 The Positive Atom Case

Here is the code for the positive atom case.

```
(define atom-case-plus
  [Si | S] [Ti | T] Bindings Continuation
  -> (let Tm (gensym (protect Tm))
          GoTo (gensym (protect GoTo))
        [let Tm [lazyderef Ti Bindings]
              GoTo [freeze (compile-head +m S T Bindings Continuation)]
            [if [= Tm Si]
                [thaw GoTo]
                [if [pvar? Tm]
                    [bind! Tm (demode Si) Bindings GoTo]
                    false]]])))
```

The code generated creates a local assignment Tm in which Ti is lazily dereferenced as before. But an additional local variable GoTo is created which contains a frozen version of the code from compile-head.

Tm is compared to Si; if it is identical then the resulting code from compile-head is thawed. If not, then Tm is tested to see if it is a Prolog variable. If it is then Tm, Si, the binding vector PV and the frozen code GoTo are passed to bind. If not then false is returned.

The bind! function binds Tm to the demoded Si in the binding vector PV and thaws GoTo storing the result in a local variable Compute. Demoding involves removing any mode declarations. This is control information that does not belong inside any binding.

```
(define demode
  [+m X] -> (demode X)
  [-m X] -> (demode X)
  [X | Y] -> (map (/. Z (demode Z)) [X | Y])
  X -> X)
```

27.13 The Positive Cons Case

```
(define cons-case-plus
  [[cons Sa Sb] | S] [Ti | T] Bindings Continuation
  -> (let Tm (gensym (protect Tm))
          GoTo (gensym (protect GoTo))
          Vars (extract-vars [Sa | Sb])
          Tame (tame [cons Sa Sb])
          TVars (extract-vars Tame)
        [let Tm [lazyderef Ti Bindings]
            GoTo (goto Vars (compile-head +m S T Bindings Continuation))
          [if [cons? Tm]
```

```
(compile-head +m [Sa Sb] [[hd Tm] [tl Tm]] Bindings
                                    (invoke GoTo Vars))
[if [pvar? Tm]
   (stpart TVars [bind! Tm
                     (demode Tame)
                     Bindings
                     [freeze (invoke GoTo Vars)]] Bindings)
        false]]]))
```

The code again generated creates a local assignment Tm in which Ti is lazily dereferenced and an additional local variable GoTo which contains a version of the code from compile-head. But the code assigned to GoTo is more complex, because instead of being simply frozen it is generated from a function goto.

Freezing code generates an unparameterised procedure (effectively. a zero place procedure) whereas goto may generate a parameterised procedure. Parameterised procedures are necessary because the computation generated from the compilation of Sa and Sb will generate values for any variables inside those terms. These values need to be fed back into the computation when the stored procedure is called. Here is goto.

```
(define goto
  [] Procedure -> [freeze Procedure]
  Vars Procedure -> (goto-h Vars Procedure))
```

```
(define goto-h
  [] Procedure -> Procedure
  [X | Y] Procedure -> [lambda X (goto-h Y Procedure)])
```

These parameters become the parameters of a lambda function generated by goto. If $n = 0$, then a frozen expression is created. If $n > 0$, then these parameters pick up the values of the variables and transport them into the code generated by compile-head which represents the body of the lambda function.

Back to cons-case-plus; the first test to be performed on Tm is to determine if it is a cons expression.

```
[if [cons? Tm]
   (compile-head +m [Sa Sb] [[hd Tm] [tl Tm]] PV (invoke GoTo Vars))
```

If so, then the S terms Sa and Sb are placed on a new S stack and [hd Tm] and [tl Tm] on a new T stack and the compilation recurses. However this time the continuation code is contained in a function invoke. The job of invoke is to create an application in which the formal parameters of the GoTo procedure are applied to the variables from Sa and Sb.

```
(define invoke
  GoTo [] -> [thaw GoTo]
  GoTo Vars -> [GoTo | Vars])
```

393

invoke is essentially very simple; if there are no variables then the proper course is to thaw a frozen expression. If there are variables then an application is formed by applying the procedure to the (values of the) variables.

Suppose Tm is not a cons expression; then Tm is tested to see if it is a variable.

```
[if [pvar? Tm]
    (stpart TVars [bind! Tm (demode Tame)
                        Bindings
                        [freeze (invoke GoTo Vars)]] Bindings)
    false]
```

If Tm is a not a Prolog variable, then false is returned. If it is, Tm needs to be bound. There are two wrinkles to this process. First the mode declarations (if any) have to be removed from Sa and Sb.

Any wildcards inside [cons Sa Sb] are effectively fresh variables and must be treated as such. So the [cons Sa Sb] is 'tamed' first by removing the wildcards before the resulting expression Tame is searched for variables.

```
(define tame
  X -> (gensym (protect Y))   where (wildcard? X)
  [X | Y] -> (map (/. Z (tame Z)) [X | Y])
  X -> X)
```

The variables are extracted and each variable is assigned a new Prolog variable in stpart.

```
(define extract-vars
  [X | Y] -> (union (extract-vars X) (extract-vars Y))
  X ->[X]          where (variable? X)
  _ -> [])
```

```
(define stpart
  [] Continuation _ -> Continuation
  [X | Y] Continuation Bindings
    -> [let X [newpv Bindings] (stpart Y Continuation Bindings)]])
```

New Prolog variables are created by taking the ticket number N from the binding vector and creating a Prolog variable with that ticket number. The Nth index in the binding vector is set to -null- showing the variable is unbound and the ticket number in the binding vector is then incremented ready for the next new Prolog variable.

```
(define newpv
  Bindings -> (let N (ticket-number Bindings)
                   NewBindings (make-prolog-variable N)
                   NextTicket (nextticket Bindings N)
                   NewBindings))
```

394

```
(define ticket-number
  Bindings -> (<-address Bindings 1))

(define nextticket
  Bindings N -> (let NewVector (address-> Bindings N -null-)
                  (address-> NewVector 1 (+ N 1))))

(define make-prolog-variable
  N -> (address-> (address-> (absvector 2) 0 pvar) 1 N))
```

27.14 Garbage Collection

The action of the code so far described is that as the computation proceeds, the binding vector fills up until either the computation halts or the binding vector overflows. However we can reclaim vector space when failure gives us the opportunity to do so; a process called **garbage collection**. To do this we need to make a small adjustment in the code for stpart because it is here that new Prolog variables are manufactured. Here is the new code.

```
(define stpart
  [] Continuation _ -> Continuation
  [X | Y] Continuation Bindings -> [let X [newpv Bindings]
                   [gc Bindings (stpart Y Continuation Bindings)]])
```

The new code is bolded. The compiler introduces a function gc which performs garbage collection. Here is the definition.

```
(define gc
  Bindings Computation -> (if (= Computation false)
                             (let N (ticket-number Bindings)
                               (do (decrement-ticket N Bindings)
                                   Computation))
                             Computation))

(define decrement-ticket
  N Bindings -> (address-> Bindings 1 (- N 1)))
```

The gc function takes the binding vector and the result of the computation. If the computation fails then the ticket number in the Prolog variable is decremented which effectively releases a vector index to be reallocated. The computation is then returned. If the computation is successful then it is simply returned with no changes to the binding vector.

27.15 Constructing the Continuation

We now turn to the construction of the continuation as promised earlier. The construction of the continuation requires six inputs.

1. The head *H* of term in the head of the clause.
2. The body *B* of the clause.
3. The formal parameter Bindings denoting the binding vector.
4. The formal parameter Lock denoting the lock.
5. The fromal parameter Key denoting the key.
6. The formal parameter Continuation denoting the continuation.

The function continue constructs the continuation from these materials.

```
(define continue
  H B Bindings Lock Key Continuation
  -> (let HVs (extract-vars H)
         BVs (extract-vars B)
         Free (difference BVs HVs)
         ContinuationCode [do [incinfs]
                           (compile-body B Bindings Lock Key Continuation)]
       (stpart Free ContinuationCode Bindings)))
```

The first task of continue is to isolate the **free variables** in the body of the clause; these are the variables that occur in *B* but do not occur in *H*. Naïve reverse in Prolog exhibits free variables

```
reverse([],[]).
reverse([H|T], RevList) :- reverse(T, RevT), append(RevT, [H], RevList).
```

Here the variable RevT is a free variable because it does not occur in the head reverse([H|T], RevList).

These free variables are passed to the stpart function which generates new Prolog variables for them. The continuation itself is constructed using compile-body.

```
(define compile-body
  [] _ _ _ Continuation -> [thaw Continuation]
  [P] Bindings Lock Key Continuation
  -> (append (deref-calls P Bindings) [Bindings Lock Key Continuation])
  [P | Literals] Bindings Lock Key Continuation
  -> (let P* (deref-calls P Bindings)
         (append P* [Bindings
                     Lock
                     Key
                     (freeze-literals Literals
                                      Bindings
                                      Lock
                                      Key
                                      Continuation)])))
```

By cases, if the body *B* is empty then the desired action is to thaw the continuation. If the body consists of a single literal P then a function call is constructed by appending P to the additional arguments Bindings Lock Key Continuation. However there is one overhead - P must scanned by deref-calls.

What deref-calls does is to walk through the terms in P and dereference every variable in P that occurs in the scope of a function call other than cons. If a Prolog variable v is drawn into the scope of a function f ($f \neq$ cons) then the safe default course is for v to be eagerly dereferenced before f is applied to the result. For example this Prolog clause

```
(defprolog foo
  X <-- (bar (length X));)
```

calls the Shen length function on X. For this to work successfully the variable X may need to be eagerly dereferenced in the call to length.

deref-calls leaves the predicate of P alone and maps over the terms. If the literal is a call to fork, then the literals are subject to deref-calls and assembled into a list for fork to process.

```
(define deref-calls
  [fork | Literals] Bindings -> [fork (deref-forked-literals Literals Bindings)]
  [F | X] Bindings -> [F | (map (/. Y (function-calls Y Bindings)) X)])

(define deref-forked-literals
  [] _ -> []
  [Literal | Literals] Bindings -> [cons (deref-calls Literal Bindings)
                                         (deref-forked-literals Literals Bindings)]
```

If the term is a cons expression then function-calls recurses down the arguments. If it is a function application other than cons the default is for the variables inside the application to be eagerly dereferenced. In all other cases the term is returned untouched.

```
(define function-calls
  [cons X Y] Bindings -> [cons (fn-calls X Bindings) (function-calls Y Bindings)]
  [F | X] Bindings -> (deref-terms [F | X] Bindings)
  X _ -> X)
```

deref-terms inserts calls to eagerly deference variables. However the first two rules in deref-terms allow for the user to place control information which can affect eager dereferencing.[95]

```
(define deref-terms
  [0 X] _ -> (if (variable? X) X (error "attempt to optimise a non-variable ~S~%" X))
  [1 X] Bindings -> (if (variable? X)  [lazyderef X Bindings]
                        (error "attempt to optimise a non-variable ~S~%" X))
  X Bindings -> [deref X Bindings]        where (variable? X)
  [X | Y] Bindings -> (map (/. Z (deref-terms Z Bindings)) [X | Y])
  X _ -> X)
```

---

[95] These conventions and the ensuing possible program optimisations are discussed in section 27.19.

The remaining case of compile-body deals with the case where there is more than one literal in *B*. The relevant line is:

```
[P | Literals] Bindings Lock Key Continuation
            -> (let P* (deref-calls P Bindings)
                  (append P* [Bindings Lock Key
                    (freeze-literals Literals
                                     Bindings
                                     Lock
                                     Key
                                     Continuation)]))
```

The strategy here is to freeze the literals after P to form a frozen expression Freeze and to construct a function call to P as before but with Freeze rather than Continuation as the continuation argument. freeze-literals constructs a nested series of frozen expressions. Each one will be thawed at runtime if the computation is successful.

```
(define freeze-literals
   [] _ _ _ Continuation -> Continuation
   [P | Literals] Bindings Lock Key Continuation
   -> (let P* (deref-calls P Bindings)
          [freeze (append P* [Bindings Lock Key
                      (freeze-literals Literals
                                       Bindings
                                       Lock
                                       Key
                                       Continuation)])])))
```

27.16 Constructing a Horn Clause Procedure

It remains to fit the code from our Horn clauses into a coherent function. We have assumed that the clauses have been put into a canonical form as a list of pairs of the form [*H B*] where *H* is the head and *B* is the body. The operative function that does this job is prolog-fbody.

```
(define prolog-fbody
   [[H B]] Parameters Bindings Lock Key Continuation
      -> (let Continue (continue H B Bindings Lock Key Continuation)
             (compile-head +m H Parameters Bindings Continue))
   [[H B] | Clauses] Parameters Bindings Lock Key Continuation
      -> (let Case (protect (gensym C))
             Continue (continue H B Bindings Lock Key Continuation)
             [let Case (compile-head +m H Parameters Bindings Continue)
                [if [= Case false]
                   (prolog-fbody Clauses  Parameters
                                 Bindings  Lock
                                 Key
                                 Continuation)
                   Case]]))
```

This function receives six inputs.

1. the list Clauses of [*H B*] pairs.
2. the list Parameters of formal parameters.
3. the binding vector parameter Bindings.
4. the lock Lock
5. the key Key
6. the continuation parameter Continuation.

In the case where there is only one clause [[H B]] the continuation is constructed and passed to compile-head to generate the code. Where there is more than one clause, the leading clause is compiled in the same way and its evaluation locally assigned to Case. If Case evaluates to false then the code generated by the recursive call to prolog-fbody is evaluated, else the Case is returned.

To tie up the loose ends, the function body needs to be placed into a Shen function definition to be compiled. horn-clause-procedure takes the characterising predicate F, and a list of clauses and builds a Shen definition. First we compute the parameters to F.

```
(define prolog-parameters
  [[H | _] | _] -> (parameters (length H)))
```

```
(define parameters
  0 -> []
  N -> [(gensym (protect V)) | (parameters (- N 1))])
```

Next we pass this information to horn-clause-procedure to build a Shen function.

```
(define horn-clause-procedure
  F Clauses -> (let Bindings (gensym (protect B))
            Lock (gensym (protect L))
            Key (gensym (protect K))
            Continuation (gensym (protect C))
            Parameters (prolog-parameters Clauses)
            FBody (prolog-fbody Clauses Parameters
                    Bindings Lock Key Continuation)
            Shen [define F | (append Parameters
                      [Bindings Lock Key Continuation ->]
                      [FBody])]
          Shen))
```

27.17 Implementing the Cut

Before dealing with the complexities of the cut and Lock and Key, let's remind ourselves of how the cut works. When the ! is executed, it succeeds and causes two side effects:

1. backtracking cannot redo any of the subgoals to the left of the ! (i.e. the unifications made in the predicates to the left of the ! are frozen);
2. backtracking cannot use any other clause to satisfy the predicate that is the head of the clause containing the ! (i.e. clauses for the same predicate not yet used are pruned).

The cut thus functions as a one-way valve; it allows control to be freely transmitted through it but it interferes with that control when control passes back through the cut itself. Let's call 'backtracking through a cut', **cut failure**. When cut failure occurs, the cut locks the unification process until control further backtracks to the Horn clause procedure *H* which invoked the cut. *H* then fails; no other clauses in *H* are considered. However having failed, the lock is released by *H* and the computation proceeds normally.

The parameters Lock and Key control this process, Lock is a two element vector containing a **flag** and a **key**. A flag in computing terms is a boolean term which indicates whether a condition holds in a computation. The flag is either true (unlocked) or false (locked). The key is a positive integer which gives the means to unlocking the lock. The Horn clause procedure *H* which invoked the cut carries the key which is unique to that stage of the computation. If *H* creates a cut that fails, then unification is locked until control comes back to *H*. At that point *H* can use the key to unlock Lock and free the computation.

In sum then, when a Horn clause procedure *H* is invoked containing a cut then the following actions are initiated.

1. A unique key *K* is generated; this is a positive integer.
2. Any cut in *H* is handed this key.
3. There is a codicil inserted as a footnote to *H* that if control returns to *H* that the lock should be checked to see if the computation is locked, If so then the key *K* should be used to try to unlock the lock before failing.

Notice for this to work, we must suppose that Lock is consulted before any unification to the head of a program clause and that unification goes ahead only if the Lock is unlocked. This is in essence the method by which cuts are conducted in Shen Prolog. Let's now see how this affects the code in our Prolog compiler.

```
(define horn-clause-procedure
  F Clauses -> (let Bindings (gensym (protect B))
                    Lock (gensym (protect L))
                    Key (gensym (protect K))
                    Continuation (gensym (protect C))
                    Parameters (prolog-parameters Clauses)
                    HasCut? (hascut? Clauses)
                    FBody (prolog-fbody Clauses Parameters
                              Bindings Lock Key Continuation HasCut?)
                    CutFBody (if HasCut? [let Key [+ Key 1] FBody] FBody)
```

```
Shen [define F | (append Parameters
                       [Bindings Lock Key Continuation ->]
                       [CutFBody])]
       Shen))

(define hascut?
  ! -> true
  [X | Y] -> (or (hascut? X) (hascut? Y))
  _ -> false)
```

The changes are bolded. First we test for the presence of a cut. If there is no cut then the body of our Shen function remains unchanged. If there is a cut then code is inserted which increments the Key. This guarantees that the Key will be unique.

The flag Hascut? is sent to prolog-fbody as an extra parameter. Let's see what prolog-fbody does with that information; again the changes are bolded.

```
(define prolog-fbody
  [] _ _ Lock Key _ true -> [unlock Lock Key]
  [[H B]] Parameters Bindings Lock Key Continuation false
      -> (let Continue (continue H B Bindings Lock Key Continuation)
            [if [unlocked? Lock]
                (compile-head +m H Parameters Bindings Continue)
                false])
  [[H B] | Clauses] Parameters Bindings Lock Key Continuation HasCut?
      -> (let Case (protect (gensym C))
              Continue (continue H B Bindings Lock Key Continuation)
                  [let Case [if [unlocked? Lock]
                               (compile-head +m H Parameters Bindings Continue)
                               false]
                      [if [= Case false]
                          (prolog-fbody Clauses Parameters
                                      Bindings Lock Key Continuation HasCut?)
                          Case]]))
```

There is an additional base case to prolog-fbody. If the HasCut? flag is true then the final action of prolog-fbody, having compiled all the clauses in *H*, is to insert an instruction to unlock the Lock using the Key. The other change is that the Lock must be unlocked for any unification code to be activated.

Since the Lock is a two element vector where the flag is in the first index, checking to see if the Lock is locked just involves returning the flag.

```
(define unlocked?
  Lock -> (<-address Lock 1))
```

Unlocking the lock involves seeing if it is locked and then, if the key fits, using it to unlock the lock before failing.

401

```
(define unlock
  Lock Key -> (if (and (locked? Lock) (fits? Key Lock))
                 (openlock Lock)
                 false))

(define locked?
  Lock -> (not (unlocked? Lock)))

(define fits?
  Key Lock -> (= Key (<-address Lock 2)))

(define openlock
  Lock -> (do (address-> Lock 1 true) false))
```

This concludes the first batch of changes to the compiler. The second involves the treatment of cuts themselves. These changes occur in compile-body and freeze-literals. Again we bold these changes.

```
(define compile-body
  [] _ _ _ Continuation -> [thaw Continuation]
  [! | Literals] Bindings Lock Key Continuation
  -> (compile-body [[cut] | Literals] Bindings Lock Key Continuation)
  [P] Bindings Lock Key Continuation
   -> (append (deref-calls P Bindings) [Bindings Lock Key Continuation])
  [P | Literals] Bindings Lock Key Continuation
   -> (let P* (deref-calls P Bindings)
          (append P* [Bindings
                      Lock
                      Key
                      (freeze-literals Literals
                                       Bindings
                                       Lock
                                       Key
                                       Continuation)]))

(define freeze-literals
  [] _ _ _ Continuation -> Continuation
  [! | Literals] Bindings Lock Key Continuation
  -> (freeze-literals [[cut] | Literals] Bindings Lock Key Continuation)
  [P | Literals] Bindings Lock Key Continuation
  -> (let P* (deref-calls P Bindings)
         [freeze (append P* [Bindings
                             Lock
                             Key
                             (freeze-literals Literals
                                              Bindings
                                              Lock
                                              Key
                                              Continuation)])]))
```

The changes in these functions are very much the same; the exclamation mark is replaced by a zero-place predicate cut. Remembering that an *n* place predicate in Shen Prolog comes out as an *n*+4 place function, cut will actually be a 4 place function.

```
(define cut
  _ Lock Key Continuation -> (let Compute (thaw Continuation)
                                  (if (and (= Compute false) (unlocked? Lock))
                                      (lock Key Lock)
                                      Compute)))
```

The action of cut is to compute the continuation and to implement the following decision table (figure 27.3).

Compute	Lock	Action
not false	locked	return Compute
not false	unlocked	return Compute
false	locked	return Compute
false	unlocked	lock the Lock

Figure 27.3 A decision table for the cut function

The significant action occurs when the computation has returned false and the Lock is unlocked. In that case the Lock is locked. Locking the lock involves three actions.

1. The flag in the Lock is set to false; indicating that the Lock is locked.
2. The combination to opening the lock is inserted into the Lock using the Key.
3. false is returned.

```
(define lock
  Key Lock -> (let SetLock (address-> Lock 1 false)
                   SetKey (address-> Lock 2 Key)
                   false))
```

The Key is of course, supplied and held by the Horn clause procedure *H* from which the cut originated. It is the responsibility of *H* to unlock the computation when control returns to it.

27.18 Implementing findall

findall is a system predicate in Prolog that is resistant to any efficient Prolog implementation. It is very easy to print off all the solutions to a Prolog goal. For example

```
(defprolog findallwomen
  <-- (woman X) (is Show (print X)) (when false);)
```

403

will print off all values of X for which (woman X) is provable. However this program will not collect those results and this is what we want. Prolog struggles here because of a lack of global data structures which are preserved over backtracking. Here is a hand coded solution in Shen Prolog.

```
(defprolog findallwomen
  _ <-- (is Start (set *women* []))
        (woman X)
        (is Collect (set *women* [X | (value *women*)]))
        (when false);
  Women <-- (is Women (value *women*)) ;)
```

Here (prolog? (findallwomen Women) (return Women)) will return all women. However the use of a global variable is a blot, since it does not allow parallel Prolog processes and the approach does not lend itself to generalisation since several nested calls may be made to findall in the course of a computation.

The solution used in Shen Prolog is to use the binding vector and to create a fresh variable Store to hold the solutions. Store is **overbound**, that is additional values are added to the value of Store as the search for solutions continues. When the search fails then the value of Store is returned. Here is the code.

```
(defprolog findall
  In Literal Out <-- (is Store [])
                     (findall-h In Literal Out Store);)

(defprolog findall-h
  In Literal _ Store <-- (call Literal) (overbind In Store);
  _ _ Store Store <--;)
```

The overbind function overbinds the Store variable, dereferencing it and adding it to the existing list of solutions.

```
(define overbind
  In Store Bindings _ _ _
  -> (do (bindv Store [(deref In Bindings) | (lazyderef Store Bindings)] Bindings)
         false))
```

27.19 Optimising Shen Prolog Programs

Optimising any program generally requires good knowledge of the compiler underlying the programming language. Since we have now completed our survey of the Shen Prolog compiler, we are in a better position to receive advice as how to best optimise Shen Prolog programs. There are three main avenues open here.

1. *Replace occurs-check unification when possible.*

Occurs check unification is the Shen default. Whenever a variable is repeated in the head of a clause then occurs-check unification will be invoked. This can be globally changed by (occurs-check -). Alternatively, if a non-global solution is wanted, a non-left linear clause can be linearised and the repeated variable renamed. We saw examples of this style of programming in chapter 26.

2. *Use negative mode declarations when possible.*

Negative mode declarations result in faster code that also compiles more quickly. For instance if we scanning a list [X | Y], we are most unlikely to encounter a Prolog variable instead of a list. Hence (- [X | Y]) is useful.

3. *Take opportunities to use function calls to Shen in the body of a clause.*

Prolog is brilliant at deductive problems, but many computations do not benefit from Prolog. If, for instance, we are using an association list inside our Prolog program and this list does not require unification to search it then there is no advantage in using Prolog. If we have to search such a list then it is better to use assoc and bind in tandem.

```
(defprolog find-details
   Key DB Details <-- (bind Details (assoc Key DB));)
```

One overhead in invoking Shen function calls within the body of a Shen Prolog clause is that by default all variables within the scope of calls other than cons are eagerly dereferenced. Eager dereferencing is an expensive operation (it is one of the main overheads of occurs-check unification).

The pseudo-application (0 DB) is treated as an instruction to the Shen Prolog compiler not to try to attempt the dereferencing of DB. (1 DB) would instruct the compiler to only perform lazy dereferencing on DB. If we are simply passing a database direct to Prolog then we should avoid searching for Prolog variables inside it.

```
(defprolog find-details-fast
   Key DB Details <-- (bind Details (assoc (0 Key) (0 DB)));)
```

A pure Prolog version of this program with occurs check unification.is:

```
(defprolog find-details-slow
   Key [[Key | Details] | _] Details <--;
   Key [_ | DB] Details <-- (find-details-slow Key DB Details);)
```

find-details-slow is two orders of magnitude slower than find-details-fast.

27.19 Shen Prolog Performance

The performance of Prolog implementations is generally measured in LIPS or *logical inferences per second*. A logical inference is the act of successfully applying a Horn clause to a goal. This is not an exact measure because it ignores the complexity of the clause. However there are some standard benchmarks which are usefully applied to measure the performance of Prolog implementations. One of them is *Einstein's Riddle* which goes as follows.

There are five houses in five different colours in a row. In each house lives a person with a different nationality. The five owners drink a certain type of beverage, smoke a certain brand of cigar and keep a certain pet. No owners have the same pet, smoke the same brand of cigar, or drink the same beverage. This is what we know.

> the Brit lives in the red house
> the Swede keeps dogs as pets
> the Dane drinks tea
> the green house is on the left of the white house
> the green house's owner drinks coffee
> the person who smokes Pall Mall rears birds
> the owner of the yellow house smokes Dunhill
> the man living in the centre house drinks milk
> the Norwegian lives in the first house
> the man who smokes Blends lives next to the one who keeps cats
> the man who keeps horses lives next to the man who smokes Dunhill
> the owner who smokes BlueMaster drinks beer
> the German smokes Prince
> the Norwegian lives next to the blue house
> the man who smokes Blends has a neighbour who drinks water

The question is: *who owns the fish*? In Shen Prolog this problem is written

```
(defprolog riddle
  <-- (house A) (house B) (house C) (house D) (house E) (is Houses [A B C D E])
      (member [brit _ _ _ red] Houses)   (member [swede dog _ _ _] Houses)
      (member [dane _ _ tea _] Houses) (left [_ _ _ _ green] [_ _ _ _ white] Houses)
      (member [_ _ _ coffee green] Houses) (member [_ bird pallmall _ _] Houses)
      (member [_ _ dunhill _ yellow] Houses)
      (is C [_ _ _ milk _])   (is A [norwegian _ _ _ _])
      (next [_ _ blends _ _] [_ cat _ _ _] Houses)
      (next [_ horse _ _ _] [_ _ dunhill _ _] Houses)
      (member [_ _ bluemaster beer _] Houses)
      (member [german _ prince _ _] Houses)
      (next [norwegian _ _ _ _] [_ _ _ _ blue] Houses)
      (next [_ _ blends _ _] [_ _ _ water _] Houses)
      (who-owns-the-fish? Nationality Houses);)
```

```
(defprolog member
  X (- [X | _]) <--;
  X (- [_ | Z]) <-- (member X Z);)

(defprolog house
  [Nationality Pet Cigarette Drink Colour] <--;)

(defprolog next
  X Y List <-- (left X Y LIst);
  X Y List <-- (left Y X List);)

(defprolog left
  L R (- [L R | _]) <--;
  L R (- [_ | Houses]) <-- (left L R Houses);)

(defprolog who-owns-the-fish?
  Nationality Houses <-- (member [Nationality fish _ _ _] Houses)
                        (return Nationality);)
```

The solution to (prolog? (riddle)) is computed in 33,542 inferences in 0.047 seconds on a 4.7GHz machine (the answer is german). This gives Shen Prolog under SBCL a performance of about 150,000 LIPS/GHz. How does this compare with stand alone Prologs? If we run the program through the free SWI Prolog, it computes six times faster.[96] A really fast Prolog like the commercial Sicstus Prolog records 134MLIPS on a 2.8GHz machine on naïve reverse on 31 elements iterated 10^6 times (figure 27.4).

```
(defprolog nreverse
  [] [] <--;
  [X | Y] R <-- (nreverse Y RY) (nappend RY [X] R);)

(defprolog nappend
  [] X X <--;
  [X | Y] Z [X | W] <-- (nappend Y Z W);)

(define bench
  0 -> 0
  N -> (bench (do (prolog? (nreverse [1 2 3 4 5 6 7 8 9 10 11 12 13 14 15 16
                            17 18 19 20 21 22 23 24 25 26 27 28 29 30] X))
                  (- N 1))))

(14-) (time (bench 10000))

run time: 7.7920001220703125 secs
0
```

Figure 27.4 Naïve reverse in Shen Prolog

---

[96] These timings were gained from running Shen Prolog under SBCL with occurs-check unification which SWI Prolog does not use. Chez Scheme has proved itself somewhat faster than SBCL.

These speeds all come down to the optimisation of low level Prolog operations in languages like C, assembly and machine code (and the avoidance of occurs-check unification). Going down to the metal on these operations is the key to performance. That's why purpose-built Prologs are faster than ones built in high level languages like Shen. But this focus on LIPS misses two important points.

The first came from the lessons of the Fifth Generation Initiative project when the Japanese tried to base their programming development on Prolog. They found Prolog was amazing at certain kinds of problems requiring deduction, but it was missing ways of storing data in forms other than clauses. For this reason the modern approach is to embed Prolog within a programming environment.

The second point is that speed in LIPS is not an accurate measure of the speed of embedded Prolog programs. Shen Prolog gives the ability to reach down into Shen to tackle those problems which are amenable to functional programming. A single Shen 'logical inference' can contain a call to any random Shen function of any degree of complexity. Used skillfully this feature can enable the Shen programmer to construct Shen Prolog programs which are fully competitive in performance with most stand-alone Prologs.

Exercise 27

1. Here is a Prolog program

   p(1).
   p(2).

   If we submit p(X) to Prolog we get

   X = 1

   Typing semi-colon gets us another solution

   X= 2

   Typing semi-colon get us

   false

   showing there are no more solutions. Code a Shen Prolog procedure **answer** that given a variable, prints its value and poses a query **more?**. If **y** is entered it tries to find another solution for X. Show it works by using the above example.

2. Implement **fork** of chapter 25.

3. Shen Prolog uses the default control strategy of depth-first search. An interesting possibility is to compile Horn clauses into abstractions. Devise a means of so doing. If you apply a Horn clause abstraction to a goal then you get a list of goals or some object indicating failure. Show how you can create procedures which organise these Horn clause abstractions into search procedures such as depth-first search, breadth-first search, hill climbing etc.

4. Extend your treatment to create sequent abstractions. A sequent abstraction takes a sequent and maps it to a list of sequents. Encode the version of first order logic given in chapter 18 using sequent abstractions.

5. How easy or difficult is it to make your answers to 3. and 4. type secure? Explain your answer.

Further Reading

The first high performance compiler for Prolog was written for the DEC-10 by David Warren. He later generalised this to produce the Warren Abstract Machine (Warren 1983). A good account of Prolog compilation techniques is found in Maier and Warren (1988). *Principles of AI Programming* (Norvig 1992) explains how to compile Prolog into Lisp. WAM-CL https://github.com/TeamSPoon/wam_common_lisp implements Lisp in Prolog.

28* The Semantics of $\mathcal{L}$

28.1 An Overview of Our Approach

This chapter and the next two chapters, embark on the task of proving that **native Shen** is **type safe**. By 'native Shen' is meant Shen as it exists on startup, before any user types have been added to it. If a language is type safe then any type that it enforces on an expression E is an accurate representation of the actual type of E. The set of rules for enforcing types on expressions is the **type discipline** of the language.

In the previous chapters, the type discipline of Shen programs was enforced by sequent calculus. Naturally the type theory underlying Shen itself is expressible as a set of sequent calculus rules called system $\mathcal{S}$ and the goal of the next chapter is to present this system.

$\mathcal{S}$ is designed to typecheck programs written in the extended language $\mathcal{L}$ that we met in chapter 15, and not Shen itself. There are reasons for this, which are partly historical and partly naturally advantageous. The natural advantages are:

1. $\mathcal{L}$ is fully equivalent in expressive power to Shen and any Shen program can be computably mapped to an equivalent $\mathcal{L}$ program using the techniques of 15.4.
2. $\mathcal{L}$ is basically a sugared lambda calculus, and many of the rules for typing lambda calculus can be brought to bear. Since $\mathcal{L}$ is syntactically simpler than Shen (it is basically almost an orthodox Lisp in appearance), formulating type rules for $\mathcal{L}$ is easier than for Shen.[97]

How does this establish that Shen is type safe? Well, we achieve this through a series of staging posts.

---

[97] The compilation techniques for reducing $\mathcal{L}$ to Kλ are well established in functional programming. Historically these techniques were followed in Shen and $\mathcal{L}$ was the intermediate language for compiling Shen programs until the twin stack method was introduced in 2019. The twin stack method is however, only a procedural abstraction of the reduction mechanisms in $\mathcal{L}$ used to compile Shen to Kλ.

Staging Posts	Sections
1. First we establish an operational semantics for $\mathcal{L}$ which explains how $\mathcal{L}$ expressions are evaluated.	28.2
2. Second, we establish that under the compilation techniques for $\mathcal{L}$ used in 15.4, the resulting expression in Kλ will have the same behaviour as the $\mathcal{L}$ expression it originated from.	28.3
3. Third, we define a type discipline for $\mathcal{L}$ in sequent calculus, $\mathcal{S}$.	29.1-29.6
4. Fourth, we establish that under $\mathcal{S}$, if we can deduce that an $\mathcal{L}$ expression has a type then it really does have that type.	30.1

These are the most important results because they provide a means for proving that Shen programs are well-typed. Namely, translate them to $\mathcal{L}$ and use $\mathcal{S}$.

But supplying $\mathcal{S}$ does not in itself provide a typechecker for $\mathcal{L}$. This is probably not obvious to us because we have so far wallowed in the luxury of having Shen interpret our notation for us and insert the control information for our calculus rules using logic programming techniques.

So in addition to supplying a set of sequent calculus rules, we also need to supply a **proof procedure** for those rules which tells the computer how to apply them. To paraphrase Kowalski's famous dictum.

$$\text{typechecker} = \text{sequent calculus} + \text{control}$$

A very simple proof procedure used to do this for $\mathcal{L}$ and $\mathcal{S}$ is called $\mathcal{T}$. $\mathcal{T}$ is actually a composition of rule applications borrowed from S. In our parlance, $\mathcal{T}$ is an **animation** of $\mathcal{S}$. Since $\mathcal{T}$ is an animation of $\mathcal{S}$, it follows we can trust its conclusions as long as we can trust $\mathcal{S}$ and our reasoning says we can. Having defined $\mathcal{T}$ we will then prove

5. $\mathcal{T}$ is terminating	30.2

Having established $\mathcal{T}$, we will then show that there is a procedural abstraction of $\mathcal{T}$ called $\mathcal{T}^*$ (T star) which gives the same results as $\mathcal{T}$ but is much more efficient than $\mathcal{T}$ and which is friendly to the syntax of Shen.

6. $\mathcal{T}^*$ is equivalent to $\mathcal{T}$	30.3

This procedural abstraction of $\mathcal{T}$ to $\mathcal{T}^*$ is analogous to the performance-enhancing procedural abstractions that were made in the twin stack method.

28.2 An Operational Semantics for $\mathcal{L}$

We assume as $\mathcal{L}$ system functions, ++ (the successor function), -- (the predecessor function), @p, if, let, cases, where and cons. $\mathcal{L}$ contains two special symbols; $\perp$ designates the error condition and $\otimes$ the special error condition generated from unsuccessfully matching an extended abstraction to an input. A **primitive object** of $\mathcal{L}$ is a string, number, character, boolean or symbol which is not used as a system function. To save needless repetition, we shall not look at string and vector pattern matching in $\mathcal{L}$ because the logic of these operations is very much reflected in list pattern matching. $\mathcal{L}$ is nevertheless Turing complete.

The syntax rules for $\mathcal{L}$ are given in figure 29.1.

1. A primitive object is a formula of $\mathcal{L}$.
2. ( ) is a formula of $\mathcal{L}$.
3. $\perp$ and $\otimes$ are formulae of $\mathcal{L}$.
4. If x, y and z are formulae of $\mathcal{L}$, so is (if x y z), (cons x y), (@p x y), (where x y), (= x y), (x y).
5. If x is a variable and y and z are formulae of $\mathcal{L}$, then (let x y z) is a formula of $\mathcal{L}$.
6. If $x_i,\ldots,x_n$ ($0 \leq i \leq n$) are formulae of $\mathcal{L}$, so is (cases $x_i\ldots x_n$).
7. A primitive object is a pattern.
8. A variable is a pattern.
9. ( ) is a pattern.
10. If p_1 and p_2 are patterns then so is (cons p_1 p_2) and (@p p_1 p_2).
11. If p is a pattern and x is a formula of $\mathcal{L}$ then the abstraction (λ p x) is a formula of $\mathcal{L}$.
12. If v is a variable and the abstraction (λ v x) is a formula of $\mathcal{L}$ then (Y (λ v x)) is a formula of $\mathcal{L}$.

Figure 28.1 The syntax rules of $\mathcal{L}$

We assume that all patterns are linear; i.e. there are no repeated variables in a pattern. Next the rules giving the operational semantics of $\mathcal{L}$. The symbol $\Rightarrow$ means "rewrites to" and $\Downarrow$ indicates the normal form of an expression under rewriting; error(x) indicates x evaluates to $\otimes$ or $\perp$. Rules are applied in order of appearance.

Rule #1. (= x y) $\Rightarrow$ true if $\Downarrow x = \Downarrow y$ and not error($\Downarrow x$)
Rule #2. (= x y) $\Rightarrow$ false if $\Downarrow x \neq \Downarrow y$ and not error($\Downarrow x$) and not error($\Downarrow y$)
Rule #3. (= x y) $\Rightarrow \perp$ if error($\Downarrow x$) or error($\Downarrow y$)
Rule #4. ((λ p x) y) $\Rightarrow$ let σ be *match*(p, $\Downarrow y$); if $\sigma = \otimes$ then $\otimes$ else *sub*(σ, x)

Rule #5. (if x y z) $\Rightarrow$ if $\Downarrow x$ = true then y else if $\Downarrow x$ = false then z else $\perp$
Rule #6. (let x y z) $\Rightarrow$ ((λ x z) y)
Rule #7. (cons x y) $\Rightarrow$ if error($\Downarrow x$) or error($\Downarrow y$) then $\perp$ else (cons $\Downarrow x$ $\Downarrow y$)
Rule #8. (@p x y) $\Rightarrow$ if error($\Downarrow x$) or error($\Downarrow y$) then $\perp$ else (@p $\Downarrow x$ $\Downarrow y$)
Rule #9. (++ x) $\Rightarrow$ if $\Downarrow x$ is a number then $1 + \Downarrow x$ else $\perp$
Rule #10. (-- x) $\Rightarrow$ if $\Downarrow x$ is a number then $\Downarrow x$ - 1 else $\perp$
Rule #11. (cases x_1 ... x_n) $\Rightarrow$ if $\Downarrow x_1$ = $\otimes$ then (cases ... x_n) else $\Downarrow x_1$.
Rule #12. (cases) $\Rightarrow$ $\perp$
Rule #13. (where x y) $\Rightarrow$ (if x y $\otimes$)
Rule #14. (Y (λ v x)) $\Rightarrow$ $[x]_{v/(Y\ (\lambda\ v\ x))}$
Rule #15. (x y) $\Rightarrow$ if error($\Downarrow x$) or error($\Downarrow y$) then $\perp$ else ($\Downarrow x$ $\Downarrow y$)
Rule #16. $x \Rightarrow x$ for any primitive

The equations for *match* and *sub* are as follows.

Match #1. $match(x, x)$ = {} where x is a non-variable atom
Match #2. where x is a variable; $match(x, y)$ = {<x, y>}
Match #3. $match((\text{cons } x\ y), (\text{cons } w\ z))$
　　　　　　= let σ_1 be $match(x, w)$, let σ_2 be $match(y, z)$;

　　　　　　　if σ_1 = $\otimes$ or σ_2 = $\otimes$ then $\otimes$　else $\sigma_1 \cup \sigma_2$
Match #4. $match((@p\ x\ y), (@p\ w\ z))$
　　　　　　= let σ_1 be $match(x, w)$, let σ_2 be $match(y, z)$;

　　　　　　　if σ_1 = $\otimes$ or σ_2 = $\otimes$ then $\otimes$　else $\sigma_1 \cup \sigma_2$
Match #5. $match(x, y)$ = $\otimes$ in all cases not covered by Match #1-#4

Sub#1 $sub(\{\}, x)$ = x
Sub#2 $sub(\{<x, y>\} \cup S, z)$ = $sub(S, [z]_{y/x})$

We can use the rules of an operational semantics to hand-simulate an evaluation of a $\mathcal{L}$ expression. Figure 13.12 shows an example.

(let x 3 (if (= x 5) x (++ x)))
$\Rightarrow$ ((λ x (if (= x 5) x (++ x))) 3)
$\Rightarrow$ (if (= 3 5) 3 (++ 3))
$\Rightarrow$ (if false 3 (++ 3))
$\Rightarrow$ (++ 3)
$\Rightarrow$ 4

28.3 An Interpreter for $\mathcal{L}$

To show that our rules actually work, here is a complete interpreter for $\mathcal{L}$ written in Shen and based on our operational semantics. We begin by defining the datatypes of $\mathcal{L}$.

(datatype number

(number? X) : verified >> X : number;)

(datatype primitive_object

    X : symbol;
    X : primitive_object;

    X : string;
    X : primitive_object;

    X : boolean;
    X : primitive_object;

    X : number;
    X : primitive_object;

    [ ] : primitive_object;)

(datatype pattern

  X : primitive_object;
  X : pattern;

  P1 : pattern; P2 : pattern;
  ==================
  [cons P1 P2] : pattern;

  P1 : pattern; P2 : pattern;
  ==================
  [@p P1 P2] : pattern;)

(datatype number

(number? X) : verified >> X : number;)

414

```
(datatype l-formula

X : pattern;
X : l-formula;

X : l-formula; Y : l-formula; Z : l-formula;
==============================
[if X Y Z] : l-formula;

X : variable; Y : l-formula; Z : l-formula;
==============================
[let X Y Z] : l-formula;

X : l-formula; Y : l-formula;
====================
[cons X Y] : l-formula;

X : l-formula; Y : l-formula;
====================
[@p X Y] : l-formula;

X : l-formula; Y : l-formula;
====================
[where X Y] : l-formula;

X : l-formula; Y : l-formula;
====================
[= X Y] : l-formula;

X : l-formula; Y : l-formula;
====================
[X Y] : l-formula;

Xn : (list l-formula);
================
[cases | Xn] : l-formula;

P : pattern; X : l-formula;
===================
[/. P X] : l-formula;)
```

The code for the $\mathcal{L}$ interpreter now follows.

```
(define normal-form
 {l-formula --> l-formula}
  X -> (fix (fn ==>) X))
```

```
(define ==>
 {I-formula --> I-formula}
 [= X Y] -> (let X* (normal-form X) Y* (normal-form Y)
                     (cases (or (eval-error? X*) (eval-error? Y*)) "error!"
                            (= X* Y*) true
                            true false))
 [[/. P X] Y] -> (let Match (match P (normal-form Y))
                      (if (no_match? Match)
                          "no match"
                          (sub Match X)))
 [if X Y Z] -> (let X* (normal-form X)
                    (cases (= X* true)  Y
                           (= X* false)  Z
                           true  "error!"))
 [let X Y Z] -> [[/. X Z] Y]
 [@p X Y] -> (let X* (normal-form X) Y* (normal-form Y)
                  (if (or (eval-error? X*) (eval-error? Y*))
                      "error!"
                      [@p X* Y*]))
 [cons X Y] -> (let X* (normal-form X)  Y* (normal-form Y)
                    (if (or (eval-error? X*) (eval-error? Y*))
                        "error!"
                        [cons X* Y*]))
 [++ X] -> (successor (normal-form X))
 [- - X] -> (predecessor (normal-form X))
 [cases X1 | Xn] -> (let Case1 (normal-form X1)
                         (if (= Case1 "no match")
                             [cases | Xn]
                             Case1))
 [cases] -> "error!"
 [where X Y] -> [if X Y "no match"]
 [y-combinator [/. X Y]] -> (replace X [y-combinator [/. X Y]] Y)
 [X Y] -> (let X* (normal-form X)
               Y* (normal-form Y)
               (if (or (eval-error? X*) (eval-error? Y*))
                   "error!"
                   [X* Y*]))
 X -> X)

(define eval-error?
 {I-formula --> boolean}
 "error!" -> true
 "no match" -> true
 _ -> false)

(define successor
 {A --> I-formula}
 X -> (+ X 1) where (number? X)
 _ -> "error!")
```

416

```
(define predecessor
 {A --> l-formula}
 X -> (- X 1) where (number? X)
 _ -> "error!")

(define replace
 {pattern --> l-formula --> l-formula --> l-formula}
 V W [let V X Y] -> [let V X Y]
 X Y X -> Y
 V W [= X Y] -> [= (replace V W X) (replace V W Y)]
 V W [/. P X] -> [/. P (replace V W X)]  where (free? V P)
 V W [if X Y Z] -> [if (replace V W X) (replace V W Y) (replace V W Z)]
 V W [let X Y Z] -> [let X (replace V W Y) (replace V W Z)]
 V W [@p X Y] -> [@p (replace V W X) (replace V W Y)]
 V W [cons X Y] -> [cons (replace V W X) (replace V W Y)]
 V W [cases | Xn] -> [cases | (map (/. Xi (replace V W Xi)) Xn)]
 V W [where X Y] -> [where (replace V W X) (replace V W Y)]
 V W [X Y] -> [(replace V W X) (replace V W Y)]
 _ _ X -> X)

(define sub
 {[(pattern * l-formula)] --> l-formula --> l-formula}
 [] X -> X
 [(@p Var Val) | Assoc] X -> (sub Assoc (replace Var Val X)))

(define match
 {pattern --> l-formula --> (list (pattern * l-formula))}
 P X -> []                    where (== P X)
 P X -> [(@p P X)]      where (variable? P)
 [cons P1 P2] [cons X Y]
        -> (let Match1 (match P1 X)
             (if (no-match? Match1)
                 Match1
                 (let Match2 (match P2 Y)
                    (if (no-match? Match2)
                        Match2
                        (append Match1 Match2)))))
 [@p P1 P2] [@p X Y] -> (let Match1 (match P1 X)
                          (if (no-match? Match1)
                              Match1
                              (let Match2 (match P2 Y)
                                 (if (no-match? Match2)
                                     Match2
                                     (append Match1 Match2)))))
 _ _ -> [(@p no matching)])

(define no-match?
 {[(pattern * l-formula)] --> boolean}
 [(@p no matching)] -> true
 _ -> false)
```

```
(define free?
 {pattern --> pattern --> boolean}
  P P -> false
  P [cons P1 P2] -> (and (free? P P1) (free? P P2))
  P [@p P1 P2] -> (and (free? P P1) (free? P P2))
  _ _ -> true)
```

Figure 28.3 gives a short sample of our working interpreter.

```
(11+) (normal-form [[/. 3 5] 3])
5 : l-formula

(12+) (normal-form [[/. 73 5] 3])
"no match" : l-formula

(13 +) (normal-form [[[y-combinator
             [/. ADD [/. X [/. Y [if [= X 0] Y [[ADD [-- X]] [++ Y]]]]]] 3] 4])
7 : l-formula

(normal-form [[[y-combinator [/. APPEND [/. X [/. Y
       [if [= X [ ]] Y [cons [[/. [cons A B] A] X]
       [[APPEND [[/. [cons A B] B] X]] Y]]]]]] [cons 1 [ ]]] [cons 2 [ ]]])
[cons 1 [cons 2 [ ]]] : l-formula
```

Figure 28.3 The interpreter on some sample inputs

28.4 Compilation to Kλ and Semantics

Our next step is to prove that the semantics of £ is preserved under compilation to Kλ. Our compilation program is itself a function *co* where *e* is an expression of £ and *co(e)* an expression of Kλ. We require to prove that *e* and *co(e)* are semantically identical. By the semantics of an expression we mean in the case of a function, that the input-output behaviour of *co(e)* and *e* is the same and in the case where *e* is not a function, that the normal forms of *co(e)* and *e* are identical.

In order to facilitate this proof we will split it into two stages. First we describe the compilation process to a slightly enriched version of Kλ, Kλ+ with ++, --, cases and ⊗ as extra primitives (but not pattern matching). Then we show that following the compilation process through by reducing Kλ+ expression to Kλ preserves semantics.

A principle that we take as obvious, but is worth stating just to be clear, is that if *e* and *co(e)* are syntactically identical and evaluated by the same rules in £ and Kλ+ then *e* and *co(e)* have the same semantics. We'll simply say in these cases that the semantic equivalence is 'trivially proved' (*tp*).

418

Figure 28.4 sums up the normalisation rules for $\mathscr{L}$. As can be seen, c functions as the identity function in many of these cases and the semantics of $\mathcal{I}$ and Kλ+ are the same (*ditto*). In these cases we write *tp* to show that the proof of semantic equivalence is trivial. There are three cases which are not covered by *tp* and these cases need to be proved individually.

Semantics		
Language $\mathcal{I}$	Kλ+	Proof
$(= x\,y) \Rightarrow$ true if $\Downarrow x = \Downarrow y$ and not error$(\Downarrow x)$	*ditto*	*tp*
$(= x\,y) \Rightarrow$ false if $\Downarrow x \neq \Downarrow y$ and not error$(\Downarrow x)$ and not error$(\Downarrow y)$	*ditto*	*tp*
$(= x\,y) \Rightarrow \bot$ if error$(\Downarrow x)$ or error$(\Downarrow y)$	*ditto*	*tp*
$((\lambda\,p\,x)\,y) \Rightarrow$ let σ be *match*$(p, \Downarrow y)$; if $\sigma = \otimes$ then $\otimes$ else *sub*(σ, x)	**case 1**	**case 1**
$(\text{if } x\,y\,z) \Rightarrow$ if $\Downarrow x =$ true then y else if $\Downarrow x =$ false then z else $\bot$	*ditto*	*tp*
$(\text{let } x\,y\,z) \Rightarrow ((\lambda\,x\,z)\,y)$	*ditto*	*tp*
$(\text{cons } x\,y) \Rightarrow$ if error$(\Downarrow x)$ or error$(\Downarrow y)$ then $\bot$ else (cons $\Downarrow x\,\Downarrow y$)	*ditto*	*tp*
$(@\text{p }x\,y) \Rightarrow$ if error$(\Downarrow x)$ or error$(\Downarrow y)$ then $\bot$ else (@p $\Downarrow x\,\Downarrow y$)	*ditto*	*tp*
$(++ x) \Rightarrow$ if $\Downarrow x$ is a number then $\Downarrow x + 1$ else $\bot$	*ditto*	*tp*
$(-- x) \Rightarrow$ if $\Downarrow x$ and $\Downarrow y$ are numbers then $\Downarrow x - 1$ else $\bot$	*ditto*	*tp*
$(\text{cases } x_1 \ldots x_n) \Rightarrow$ if $\Downarrow x_1 = \otimes$ then (cases $\ldots x_n$) else $\Downarrow x_1$.	*ditto*	*tp*
$(\text{cases}) \Rightarrow \bot$	*ditto*	*tp*
$(\text{where } x\,y) \Rightarrow (\text{if } x\,y\,\otimes)$	**case 2**	**case 2**
$(\mathbf{Y}\,(\lambda\,v\,x)) \Rightarrow [x]_{v/(\mathbf{Y}\,(\lambda\,v\,x))}$	**case 3**	**case 3**
$(x\,y) \Rightarrow$ if error$(\Downarrow x)$ or error$(\Downarrow y)$ then $\bot$ else $(\Downarrow x\,\Downarrow y)$	*ditto*	*tp*
$x \Rightarrow x$ for any primitive	*ditto*	*tp*

Figure 28.4 The preservation of semantic equivalence under co

The proof is by structural induction over $\mathscr{L}$ expressions. The base case is where e is a primitive expression (a string, boolean, etc) and semantic equivalence is *tp*. If e is (if $x\,y\,z$), (cons $x\,y$), (@p $x\,y$), (++ x), (-- x), ($x\,y$), (let $x\,y\,z$), (= $x\,y$) and taking as the inductive hypothesis, that x, y and z preserve equivalence, then semantic equivalence of c and $co(e)$ is *tp* since syntax and semantics are preserved.

We pass on then, to the three cases.

Case 1: $e = ((\lambda\,p\,x)\,y)$

In this case p is a pattern. There are three subcases corresponding to the three cases of p.

Case 1.1: p is a variable; then $co(e) = ((\text{lambda } p\ x)\ y)$. lambda in $K\lambda$ and λ in $\mathcal{L}$ obey the same rules in this case. Both e and $co(e)$ are subject to conventional β reduction in $\mathcal{L}$ and $K\lambda$ which results in $x_{y/p}$ in both cases and by the inductive hypothesis the semantics of $x_{y/p}$ is the same in both $\mathcal{L}$ and $K\lambda$.

Case 1.2: p is a non-variable atom; then $co(e) = (\text{if } (= p\ y)\ x\ \otimes)$. The evaluation rule in $\mathcal{L}$ for e is

$$((\lambda\ p\ x)\ y) \Rightarrow \text{let } \sigma \text{ be } match(p, \Downarrow y); \text{ if } \sigma = \otimes \text{ then } \otimes \text{ else } sub(\sigma, x)$$

The applicative match rules are

A. $match(x, x) = \{\}$ where x is a non-variable atom
B. $match(x, y) = \otimes$ otherwise

Case 1.2.1 $p = \Downarrow y$; then $match$ rule A. applies and $\sigma = \{\}$. The sub rule that applies is:

$$sub(\{\}, x) = x$$

Hence under the assumption $p = y$, $((\lambda\ p\ x)\ y)$ evaluates to x in $\mathcal{L}$.

Case 1.2.2 $p \neq \Downarrow y$; then $match$ rule B. applies and e evaluates to $\otimes$.

Therefore the normal form of $((\lambda\ p\ x)\ y)$ under $\mathcal{L}$ is equivalent to $(\text{if } (= p\ \Downarrow y)\ x\ \otimes)$. This is identical to the $K\lambda$ compilation *modulo* the exchange of y for $\Downarrow y$. But by the inductive hypothesis, y in $K\lambda$ and y in $\mathcal{L}$ have the same semantics and share normal forms and we can substitute y for $\Downarrow y$.

Case 1.3 $p = (\text{cons } a\ b)$ for some a and b; then
$$e = ((\lambda\ (\text{cons } a\ b)\ x)\ y)$$
and

$$co(e) = (\text{if } (\text{cons? } y)\ co((\text{lambda } a\ (\text{lambda } b\ x))\ (\text{hd } y))\ (\text{tl } y))\ \otimes)$$

Here $co((\text{lambda } a\ (\text{lambda } b\ x))\ (\text{hd } y))\ (\text{tl } y))$ will be further reduced by β reduction.

The proof is by cases.

Case 1.3.1 $(\text{cons? } y)$ holds and so for some c and d, $y = (\text{cons } c\ d)$.

420

The evaluation rule in $\mathcal{L}$ for e is

$$((\lambda\, p\, x)\, y) \Rightarrow \text{let } \sigma \text{ be } match(p, \Downarrow y); \text{ if } \sigma = \otimes \text{ then } \otimes \text{ else } sub(\sigma, x)$$

by substitution, $p = (\text{cons } a\ b)$ and $y = (\text{cons } c\ d)$

$$((\lambda\, (\text{cons } a\ b)\, x)\, (\text{cons } c\ d)) \Rightarrow \text{let } \sigma \text{ be } match((\text{cons } a\ b), \Downarrow(\text{cons } c\ d)); \text{ if }$$
$$\sigma = \otimes \text{ then } \otimes \text{ else } sub(\sigma, x)$$

The applicative match rule is

$$match((\text{cons } a\ b), (\text{cons } c\ d))$$
$$= \text{let } \sigma_1 \text{ be } match(a, c), \text{ let } \sigma_2 \text{ be } match(b, d);$$
$$\text{if } \sigma_1 = \otimes \text{ or } \sigma_2 = \otimes \text{ then } \otimes \text{ else } \sigma_1 \cup \sigma_2$$

we know that $c = (\text{hd } y)$ and $d = (\text{tl } y)$, so we have

$$match((\text{cons } a\ b), y)$$
$$= \text{let } \sigma_1 \text{ be } match(a, (\text{hd } y)), \text{ let } \sigma_2 \text{ be } match(b, (\text{tl } y));$$
$$\text{if } \sigma_1 = \otimes \text{ or } \sigma_2 = \otimes \text{ then } \otimes \text{ else } \sigma_1 \cup \sigma_2$$

But the result of composing these two matches is equivalent β reducing the application $((\lambda\ a\ (\lambda\ b\ x))\ (\text{hd } y))\ (\text{tl } y))$ which is precisely the output of the *co* function. By the inductive hypothesis these share the same semantics.

Case 1.3.2 (cons? y) does not hold

In that case under *co* and in $\mathcal{L}$, $\otimes$ is returned.

Case 1.4 This is essentially a cut-and-paste of 1.3 with tuple? replacing cons? and fst and snd replacing hd and tl.

Case 2: $e = (\text{where } x\ y)$.

Here $co(\text{where } x\ y) = (\text{if } co(x)\ co(y)\ \otimes)$ and according to the semantics for $\mathcal{L}$

$$(\text{where } x\ y) \Rightarrow (\text{if } x\ y\ \otimes).$$

By the inductive hypothesis $(\text{if } co(x)\ co(y)\ \otimes)$ and $(\text{if } x\ y\ \otimes)$ are equivalent.

Case 3: $e = (\mathbf{Y}\ (\lambda\ v\ x)) \Rightarrow [x]_{v/(\mathbf{Y}\ (\lambda\ v\ x))}$

In compilation to Kλ+, the Y-combinator case is handled by explicit recursion to a named function f. $co(e) = [x]_{v/f}$ where f is defined as $(\lambda\ v\ x)$.

In the second stage we extend the action of *co* to eliminate the need for ++, --, cases and ⊗. (++ *x*) and (-- *x*) are trivially eliminable by (+ *x* 1) and (- *x* 1). We are interested only in those expressions of Kλ+ which could issue from the compilation of Shen. We do not consider, for instance, pattern matching abstractions outside of function definitions or the possibility of encountering the match error object ⊗ existing on its own. Hence *co* is thus a partial function with respect to Kλ+ because it only deals with Kλ+ functions that could arise from compiling Shen.

Under this restriction, the match error object ⊗ must occur in the scope of a cases expression e = (cases x_1 ... x_n) and cases is eliminated in favour of cond, $co(e)$ = (cond $co(x_1)$ ... $co(x_n)$). If ⊗ does occur then the context is in the form (if P Q ⊗) which is compiled to (P Q) eliminating the ⊗. We now have to show that the resulting expression, which is free of cases and ⊗ is semantically equivalent to the original.

The semantics under ℒ is

$$(\text{cases } x_1 \ldots x_n) \Rightarrow \text{if } \Downarrow x_1 = \otimes \text{ then (cases } \ldots x_n) \text{ else } \Downarrow x_1.$$
$$(\text{cases}) \Rightarrow \bot$$

Consider the base case, $co(\text{cases})$ = (cond (true $\bot$)) = $\bot$ where $\bot$ is an error condition reporting failure of a partial function. Equivalence is preserved. Now consider the inductive case e = (cases x_1 ... x_n) where $co(e)$ = (cond $co(x_1)$ ... $co(x_n)$). Assume equivalence is preserved for ... $co(x_n)$ and we prove that adding to this series with $co(x_1)$ preserves equivalence. $co(x_1)$ originates from x_1 = (if P Q ⊗) and $co(x_1)$ = (P Q). Either P holds or it does not. If P holds then Q is returned in both instances. If P does not hold then ⊗ is returned in Kλ+ which forces the evaluation of (cases ... x_n). If P does not hold then in Kλ the evaluation of (cond ... $co(x_n)$) is forced which by hypothesis is semantically equivalent to (cases ... x_n).

29* System ẟ

29.1 Type Checking Applications

Our first set of rules (figure 29.1) enables applications to be type checked.

Sequents	Application	Primitive
	F : (A → B); X : A;	if X is base and A ∈ τ(X)
$\overline{\rule{3cm}{0.4pt}}$ X : A >> X : A;	(F X) : B;	X : A;

Figure 29.1 The rules for type checking applications

The *Sequents Rule* is obvious. The *Rule of Application* states that an application (F X) has the type B provided F has the type A → B for some A and X has the type A. The *Primitive Rule* assumes that there is a function τ from the set of all base expressions of Shen (i.e. numbers, symbols, function symbols and the rest) into the powerset of all types such that A ∈ τ(e) when A is a type of e; thus τ(1) = {number}, τ("1") = {string}, τ(+) = {number → (number → number), symbol}.

The *Primitive Rule* states that given a typing e : A to prove, we may prove it if e is a base object where A ∈ τ(e). From these rules, we can establish the types of applications.

Here is an example; the goal is to prove that (* 1 0) : number. To adopt the curried form required by the *Rule of Application* we write (* 1 0) as ((* 1) 0).

Proof: by the *Rule of Application* ((* 1) 0) : number is proved if there is a type A such that (* 1) : A → number and 0 : A. Let A be the type number. Then we need to prove (* 1) : number → number and 0 : number. 0 : number follows by the *Primitive Rule*. By the *Rule of Application* (* 1) : number if there is some type B such that * : B → (number → number) and 1 : B. Let B be the type number; * : number → (number → number) and 1 : number are proved by the *Primitive Rule*.

The preceding proof could be easily mechanised on a computer except for the problem of choosing values for variables. Consider the case in the preceding proof where it was necessary to decide a value for 'B' such that '* : B → (number → number)' was solvable. The *Primitive Rule* can show that * : number →

423

(number ⊔ number)The problem is to match '* : number → (number → number)' to the conclusion '* : B → (number → number)'. These two typings match completely except where 'B' is matched to 'number'.

In order to agree that the two typings match, an extended notion of "match" must be used and unification provides this notion. Unification is used within type checking to perform the needed substitutions. The typings * : B → (number → number) and * : number → (number → number) are unified to find their MGU σ and the instantiation is given by σ(B). Here σ(B) = number.

In Shen, all the rules of its type system (including those entered by the user) are interpreted *modulo* unification with respect to types. We shall adopt this approach in all the subsequent proofs in this chapter.

29.2 Type Checking Abstractions

The *Rule of Abstraction* says that $(\lambda\ V\ X)$ has the type $A \rightarrow B$ if, where c is arbitrary object of type A, $[X]_{c/v}$ (the result of replacing all free occurrences of V by c throughout X) is of the type B (figure 29.2).

$$Abstraction$$

where c is fresh
$$\underline{c : A >> [X]_{c/v} : B;}$$
$$(\lambda\ V\ X) : (A \rightarrow B);$$

Figure 29.2 The rule for type checking abstractions

Here is a proof of $(\lambda\ x\ ((*\ 3)\ x)) :$ number → number, demonstrating the use of the *Abstraction* and *Sequents Rules*

Proof: by the *Abstraction Rule*, $(\lambda\ x\ ((*\ 3)\ x)) :$ number → number is provable if $a :$ number >> $((*\ 3)\ a) :$ number is provable (a is our fresh symbol). By the *Rule of Application*, $a :$ number >> $((*\ 3)\ a) :$ number is provable if both

$a :$ number >> $(*\ 3) : A \rightarrow$ number
$a :$ number >> $a : A$

are provable for some type A. The second sequent is solved using the *Sequents Rule* with unifier $\{A \mapsto$ number$\}$. The first sequent now becomes

$a :$ number >> $(*\ 3) :$ number → number.

By the *Rule of Application* again, this splits into two subproblems

$a :$ number >> $* : B \rightarrow$ (number → number).
$a :$ number >> $3 : B$

424

Both these problems are solved by the *Primitive Rule* using the unifier {B $\mapsto$ number}.

These three rules define the type theory of the **simply typed lambda calculus** (STL) and are implicit in all typed functional languages. This type theory is extremely basic; in fact it is provable that expressions that are well-typed according to STL are guaranteed to have terminating evaluations; a property called **strong normalisation**. The price for this property is that certain expressions like the Y-combinator cannot be type checked within the STL. Shen requires additional rules to operate as a practical language for programming. We next look at the rules for polymorphic types.

29.3 Polymorphic Functions

When we say that the polymorphic function ($\lambda\, x\, x$) has the type A $\to$ A, this is a shorthand for asserting that for *all* values of A, ($\lambda\, x\, x$) inhabits A $\to$ A, or in logical notation ($\forall$A (A $\to$ A)). The *Rule of Generalisation* enables proofs of the types of polymorphic functions. To prove that X : ($\forall$A B), we must prove that, where t is any arbitrary type, X : $B_{C/A}$ (where $B_{C/A}$ is the result of substituting all occurrences of A by C). The concept of arbitrary is defined in the same way as previously - by the introduction of a fresh symbol.

Where t is fresh and c is any type.

Generalisation	*Specialisation*
X : [B]$_{t/v}$;	X : [B]$_{c/v}$, X : ($\forall v$ B) >> P;
X : ($\forall v$ B);	X : ($\forall v$ B) >> P;

Figure 29.3 The rules for type checking with polytypes

Here is a proof that ($\lambda\, x\, x$) : ($\forall$A (A $\to$ A)).

Proof: Applying the *Rule of Generalisation* to the problem derives ($\lambda\, x\, x$) : $a \to a$, (a is our fresh symbol). Applying the *Rule of Abstraction* to ($\lambda\, x\, x$) : $a \to a$ derives $b : a >> b : a$ (b is our fresh symbol) which is solved by the *Sequents Rule*.

The *Rule of Specialisation* is obvious; if we have shown that X : ($\forall v$ B), then we can conclude that X : $B_{c/v}$ for any type C we care to choose. Here is a proof of that [ ] : ($\forall$A (list A)), remove : ($\forall$A (A $\to$ ((list A) $\to$ (list A)))) >> ((remove 1) [ ]) : (list number).

Proof: By the *Rule of Specialisation* applied twice, we derive

[ ] : $\forall$A (list A), [ ] : (list number),
remove : (number $\to$ ((list number) $\to$ (list number))),
remove : $\forall$A(A $\to$ ((list A) $\to$ (list A))) >> ((remove 1) [ ]) : (list number).

425

Let Δ be the assumptions in this sequent. We have to prove

$\Delta \gg ((\text{remove } 1) [\ ]) : (\text{list number})$.

By the *Rule of Applications* we have two sequents to prove; $\Delta \gg (\text{remove } 1) : (\text{B} \rightarrow (\text{list number}))$ and $[\ ] : \text{B}$. Applying the *Rule of Applications* to the first sequent we derive a total of three sequents;

1. $\Delta \gg \text{remove} : (\text{C} \rightarrow (\text{B} \rightarrow (\text{list number})))$
2. $\Delta \gg 1 : \text{C}$.
3. $\Delta \gg [\ ] : \text{B}$

The first is solved by unification using the *Sequents Rule* ($\{\text{C} \mapsto \text{number}, \text{B} \mapsto (\text{list number})\}$). The second ($1 : \text{C}$, with $\text{C} \mapsto \text{number}$) is solved by *Primitive* and $[\ ] : \text{B}$ is solved by the *Sequents Rule* with $\text{B} \mapsto (\text{list number})$.

In the implementation of Shen, the *Specialisation Rule* is not used, since its purpose is only to allow us to specialise the $\forall$-bound symbols. Instead, unification is used. The objects $\perp$ and $\otimes$ have the type ($\forall$ A A).

$$\frac{\rule{2cm}{0.4pt}}{\perp : (\forall \text{ A A})}; \qquad\qquad \frac{\rule{2cm}{0.4pt}}{\otimes : (\forall \text{ A A})};$$

Figure 29.4 The rules for error objects

29.4 Special Forms

Certain expressions of Shen are special forms - they cannot be curried and they have their own typing rules (figure 14.6).[98]

Cons Rule (left)
$$\frac{X : A, Y : (\text{list A}) \gg P;}{(\textbf{cons } X\ Y) : (\text{list A}) \gg P};$$

Cons Rule (right)
$$\frac{X : A; Y : (\text{list A});}{(\textbf{cons } X\ Y) : (\text{list A})}$$

@p Rule (left)
$$\frac{X : A, Y : B \gg P;}{(\textbf{@p } X\ Y) : (A * B) \gg P};$$

@p Rule (right)
$$\frac{X : A; Y : B;}{(\textbf{@p } X\ Y) : (A * B)}$$

Local Rule
where c is fresh
$$\frac{Y : B; \ c : B \gg [Z]c/X : A;}{(\textbf{let } X\ Y\ Z) : A};$$

Figure 29.5 The rules for special forms

---

[98] Other expressions which have their own typing rules are @s, @v, error, input+, make-string and output.

426

Here is a proof that (let X 6 (if (= X 5) 0 1)) : number. By the *Local Rule*, (let X 6 (if (= X 5) 0 1)) : number if both 6 : A and x : A >> (if (= x 5) 0 1) : number. The first problem is solved by the *Primitive Rule* with A $\mapsto$ number. The second problem dereferences to

$$x : \text{number} >> (\text{if} (= x\ 5)\ 0\ 1) : \text{number}$$

By the type for *if*, this problem is solvable if the following are solvable.

1. x : number >> (= x 5) : boolean;
2. x : number >> 0 : number
3. x : number >> 1 : number

2. and 3. are solvable by the *Primitive Rule* and 1. decomposes to

4. x : number >> x : B
5. x : number >> 5 : B

4. is solved by the *Sequents Rule* with B $\mapsto$ number and 5. by the *Primitive Rule*.

29.5 Recursion, Cases, Patterns and Guards

The rules in this section deal with two important aspects - recursion and patterns The first rule deals with the **Y** combinator.

Combinator Rule
where c is fresh

$$\frac{c : A >> [Y]_{c/v} : A}{(Y\ (\lambda\ v\ Y)) : A}$$

Figure 29.6 The rule for type checking recursive functions

In chapter 14 we saw that that the combinator **Y** could be used to define recursive functions. The combinator rule allows us to type check the types of such functions. We define factorial as (λ x (if (= x 0) 1) ((* x) (*factorial* ((- x) 1))))); or expressed with **Y** - (**Y** (λ y (λ x (if (= x 0) 1 ((* x) (y ((- x) 1)))))))). We prove that this expression has the type number $\rightarrow$ number.

Proof Sketch:

We want to prove (**Y** (λ f (λ x (if (= x 0) 1 ((* x) (f ((- x) 1))))))) : number $\rightarrow$ number. By the *Combinator Rule*, this is provable if

f : number $\rightarrow$ number >> (λ x (if (= x 0) 1 ((* x) (f((- x) 1))))) : number $\rightarrow$ number

The reader can complete the proof. The next two rules deal with case statements and guards.

Cases Rule

For each i, $1 \leq i \leq n$
$\underline{\text{Case}_i : A;}$
(**cases** $\text{Case}_1 \ldots \text{Case}_n$) : A

Guard Rule
Guard : boolean;
$\underline{\text{Guard : verified} >> X : A;}$
(**where** Guard X) : A

Figure 29.7 The rules for type checking cases and guards

The first rule says that the body of a function definition (consisting of a series of cases) has the type A if every case in the body of the function has the type A. The second rule applies to guards and says that a guarded expression X has the type A if the guard has the type boolean and X has the type A under the assumption that the guard is verified. These rules are fairly straightforward.

The Patterns Rule is used to type check extended abstractions. We assume that $V_1 \ldots V_n$ are all the variables occurring in P, and $\phi_1, \ldots, \phi_n$ are fresh symbols, and $C_1, \ldots C_n$ are fresh variables. For any κ, the expression $[\kappa]_{<\phi_1 \ldots \phi_n>/<V_1 \ldots V_n>}$ indicates the replacement of the free occurrences of the variables $V_1 \ldots V_n$ in κ by $\phi_1, \ldots, \phi_n$.

Patterns Rule

$$\phi_1 : C_1, \ldots, \phi_n : C_n >> [P]_{<\phi_1 \ldots \phi_n>/<V_1 \ldots V_n>} : A;$$
$$\underline{[P]_{<\phi_1 \ldots \phi_n>/<V_1 \ldots V_n>} : A >> [X]_{<\phi_1 \ldots \phi_n>/<V_1 \ldots V_n>} : B;}$$
$$(\lambda\, P\, X) : (A \to B);$$

Figure 29.8 The rule for type checking extended abstractions

The *Patterns Rule* subsumes the *Abstractions Rule* as a special case. Thus given P is a variable then the sequent $\phi_1 : C_1, \ldots, \phi_n : C_n >> [P]_{<\phi_1 \ldots \phi_n>/<V_1 \ldots V_n>} : A;$ collapses into a problem equivalent to the trivial $P : C >> P : A$ (where C is a fresh variable). The second sequent is just the same as the problem posed by the *Abstractions Rule*.

We illustrate the action of these rules by reference to the example of chapter 15, which in the language of $\mathcal{X}$ with fixpoints is.

$(Y$ $(\lambda$ M $(\lambda$ A $(\lambda$ B (cases $(((\lambda$ V $(\lambda$ [ ] false)) A) B)

$\qquad\qquad\qquad\qquad\quad$ $(((\lambda$ X $(\lambda$ (cons U W) (where (= U X) true)) A) B)

$\qquad\qquad\qquad\qquad\quad$ $(((\lambda$ X $(\lambda$ (cons Z Y) ((M X) Y))) A) B))))))

Here is a proof that the function defined has the type $(\forall A$ $(A \rightarrow$ ((list A) $\rightarrow$ boolean))).

Proof: $(Y$ $(\lambda$ M $(\lambda$ A $(\lambda$ B (cases $(((\lambda$ V $(\lambda$ [ ] false)) A) B)

$\qquad\qquad\qquad\qquad\quad$ $(((\lambda$ X $(\lambda$ (cons U W) (where (= U X) true)) A) B)

$\qquad\qquad\qquad\qquad\quad$ $(((\lambda$ X $(\lambda$ (cons Z Y) ((M X) Y))) A) B))))))

$\qquad\qquad$: $(\forall A$ $(A \rightarrow$ ((list A) $\rightarrow$ boolean)))

By the *Generalisation Rule* this is provable if

$(Y$ $(\lambda$ M $(\lambda$ A $(\lambda$ B (cases $(((\lambda$ V $(\lambda$ [ ] false)) A) B)

$\qquad\qquad\qquad\qquad\quad$ $(((\lambda$ X $(\lambda$ (cons U W) (where (= U X) true)) A) B)

$\qquad\qquad\qquad\qquad\quad$ $(((\lambda$ X $(\lambda$ (cons Z Y) ((M X) Y))) A) B))))))

$\qquad\qquad$: $(c \rightarrow$ ((list c) $\rightarrow$ boolean))

By the *Combinator Rule* this is provable if

m : $(c \rightarrow$ ((list c) $\rightarrow$ boolean))

>> $(\lambda$ A $(\lambda$ B (cases $(((\lambda$ V $(\lambda$ [ ] false)) A) B)

$\qquad\qquad\qquad\qquad$ $(((\lambda$ X $(\lambda$ (cons U W) (where (= U X) true)) A) B)

$\qquad\qquad\qquad\qquad$ $(((\lambda$ X $(\lambda$ (cons Z Y) ((m X) Y))) A) B))))

$\qquad\qquad\qquad\qquad\qquad\qquad\qquad$: $(c \rightarrow$ ((list c) $\rightarrow$ boolean))

By the *Abstractions Rule* this is provable if

a : c, m : $c \rightarrow$ ((list c) $\rightarrow$ boolean)

>> $(\lambda$ B (cases $(((\lambda$ V $(\lambda$ [ ] false)) a) B)

$\qquad\qquad\qquad$ $(((\lambda$ X $(\lambda$ (cons U W) (where (= U X) true)) a) B)

$\qquad\qquad\qquad$ $(((\lambda$ X $(\lambda$ (cons Z Y) ((m X) Y))) a) B))) : ((list c) $\rightarrow$ boolean)

By the *Abstractions Rule* this is provable if

b : (list c), a : c, m : $c \rightarrow$ ((list c) $\rightarrow$ boolean)

>> (cases $(((\lambda$ V $(\lambda$ [ ] false)) a) b)

$\qquad\qquad$ $(((\lambda$ X $(\lambda$ (cons U W) (where (= U X) true)) a) b)

$\qquad\qquad$ $(((\lambda$ X $(\lambda$ (cons Z Y) ((m X) Y))) a) b)) : boolean

Let $\Delta = \{b$: (list c), a : c, m : $c \rightarrow$ ((list c) $\rightarrow$ boolean)$\}$, then by the *Cases Rule*, three cases remain to be proved.

1. $\Delta \gg (((\lambda \ V \ (\lambda \ [\ ] \ \text{false})) \ a) \ b) : \text{boolean}$
2. $\Delta \gg (((\lambda \ X \ (\lambda \ (\text{cons U W}) \ (\text{where} \ (= U \ X) \ \text{true})) \ a) \ b) : \text{boolean}$
3. $\Delta \gg (((\lambda \ X \ (\lambda \ (\text{cons Z Y}) \ ((m \ X) \ Y))) \ a) \ b) : \text{boolean}$

<u>Case 1</u> $\Delta \gg (((\lambda \ V \ (\lambda \ [\ ] \ \text{false})) \ a) \ b) : \text{boolean}$

By the *Applications Rule* this is provable if

$\Delta \gg ((\lambda \ V \ (\lambda \ [\ ] \ \text{false})) \ a) : D \rightarrow \text{boolean}$
$\Delta \gg b : D$

The second problem is solved by *Sequents* with $D \mapsto (\text{list } c)$. We are left with

$\Delta \gg ((\lambda \ V \ (\lambda \ [\ ] \ \text{false})) \ a) : (\text{list } c) \rightarrow \text{boolean}$

By the *Applications Rule* this is provable if

$\Delta \gg (\lambda \ V \ (\lambda \ [\ ] \ \text{false})) : E \rightarrow ((\text{list } c) \rightarrow \text{boolean}))$
$\Delta \gg a : E$

The second problem is solved by *Sequents* with $E \mapsto c$. We are left with

$\Delta \gg (\lambda \ V \ (\lambda \ [\ ] \ \text{false})) : c \rightarrow ((\text{list } c) \rightarrow \text{boolean})$

By the *Abstractions Rule* this is provable if

$v : c, \Delta \gg (\lambda \ [\ ] \ \text{false}) : (\text{list } c) \rightarrow \text{boolean}$

By the *Patterns Rule* this is provable if

$v : c, \Delta \gg [] : (\text{list } c)$
$v : c, [] : (\text{list } c), \Delta \gg \text{false} : \text{boolean}$

which are both solved by the *Primitive Rule*. The proof of the remaining cases is left to the reader.

Internal forms are all ephemeral objects that exist during the compilation of Shen functions and do not appear in the resulting object code. Consequently it is not possible to execute some of these internal forms as actual procedures.

29.6 Global Variables

The *Global Rule* states that an assignment of X to a global variable G has the type A just when G is a symbol and it is provable that both the current value of G has the type A and so does X. Since Shen contains no rules to enable the conclusion (value G) : A to be proved, it is left to the user to enrich the type system by a rule stating the kind of object assigned to G in the way explained in chapter 19. set is also a special form.

where g is a symbol

$$\underline{(value\ G) : A;\ X : A;}$$
$$(set\ G\ X) : A;$$

Figure 29.9 The rule for type checking global assignments

Exercise 29

1. Prove that the following functions have the following types:

   a. plus of chapter 3 has the type number → (number → number).
   b. fibonacchi of chapter 3 has the type number → number.
   c. join of chapter 4 has the type ∀A (list A) → ((list A) → (list A))
   d. rev of chapter 4 has the type ∀A (list A) → (list A).
   e. powerset of chapter 4 has the type ∀A (list A) → (list (list A))
   f. converge of chapter 6 has the type ∀A (A → A) → (A → A).

2. Suggest sequent rules for & and v, where $x : (\alpha \vee \beta)$ just when $x : \alpha$ or $x : \beta$; and $x : (\alpha$ & $\beta)$ just when $x : \alpha$ and $x : \beta$.

3. What happens when you try to implement your answer to 4 in Shen and why?

4. *Implement a type secure program that allows you to interactively do proofs in ⴶ. This is called a **proof assistant**.

5. Extend your proof assistant to allow the system to receive new sequent rules which can be named. Add to the system your answers to 2.

6. Read Barendregt's article on the lambda cube and implement the vertices of the cube within the proof assistant.

7. *Read Thompson on Martin-Lof type theory and implement that system. Show that any two natural numbers have a sum and synthesise a program that adds them together.

8. Why cannot the Y-combinator be given a type in simply typed lambda calculus?

Further Reading

An axiomatisation for a typed functional language was described by Cardelli (1984); our system is closely modelled around Cardelli's axiomatisation. Discussions of alternative type systems can be found in Diller (1988), Girard (1989), Odifreddi ed. (1990), Turner (1991), Thompson (1991), Barendregt (1992), Gunter (1992) and Peirce (2002). Cerrito and Kesner (1999) describe a type system for an extended lambda calculus based on pattern-matching.

30* Type Safety

30.1 The Correctness of 𝕾

The goal of this section is to prove that Shen is type safe by proving that 𝕾 is correct. In order to do that it is necessary to give some account of what 'correct' means in this context.

1. If 𝕾 assigns a type τ to an 𝓛 expression *x*, and *x* evaluates to *y* then 𝕾 assigns τ to *y*. This is called the **subject reduction** property.
2. That if 𝕾 assigns a type τ to an 𝓛 expression *x* which is a normal form then *x* really does have the type τ.

We define a **primitive data structure** (p.d.) as a symbol, boolean, number, string, list or tuple of p.d.s. The expression '>> *e* : A' is taken to mean '*e* : A is provable in 𝕾'.

Our proof of the correctness of 𝕾 is covered in 3 theorems. In the first theorem, we demonstrate that if *e* is an p.d. of 𝓛 and >> *e* : A, then *e* : A. In the second theorem, we demonstrate the **subject reduction property**, namely;

$$\text{if} >> e : A \text{ and } e \Rightarrow e^* \text{ then } >> e^* : A.$$

The third theorem is a consequence of both these theorems; namely that if >> *e* : A, then the evaluation of *e* to a p.d. *e** will produce an expression of type A.

Notice that it is not true that if *e* ⇒ *e** and >> *e** : A then >> *e* : A. The expression (if (= 1 0) a "a") evaluates to "a", but although >> "a" : string, it is not a theorem that (if (= 1 0) a "a") : string.

Theorem 1: if *e* is a p.d. and >> *e* : A then *e* : A.

Proof: Suppose *e* is a p.d. and >> *e* : A; then *e* is either

(a) a primitive expression (symbol, boolean, number or string), or

432

(b) a list of p.d.s, or
(c) a tuple of p.d.s.

Suppose (a), then the type of e is determined by τ, so that e : string iff string $\in \tau(e)$ etc. The only type rule in $\mathcal{L}$ for proving the type of e is the *Primitive Rule* which establishes e : A only if A $\in \tau(e)$. Hence if $>> e$: A then A $\in \tau(e)$ and so e : A.

Suppose (b), then e is a list and the proof proceeds by induction. Let the **ultimate length** (υ) be defined as follows.

$\upsilon(x) = 1$ where x is a primitive object.
for any list l, $\upsilon(l) = \Sigma(\upsilon(i))$ where i is an element in l.

Base Case: $\upsilon(e) = 0$

then $e = []$; according to the *Primitive Rule*, which is the only applicable rule, $>>$ e : $\forall$A (list A). By the inhabitation rule for lists (chapter 17);

$$\forall A(e : (\text{list A}) \leftrightarrow (\forall x \text{ element } (x,e) \supset x : A))^{99}$$

Since $\sim\exists x$ element(x,e) then e : $\forall$A: (list A).

Inductive Case: the theorem holds for all lists l where $\upsilon(l) \le$ n.

Let $e = [X \mid Y]$ be a list expression of ultimate length n + 1. Then if e has a type under Shen, it has the type (list A) for some A and so $>> e$: (list A). This can only be established by the *Cons (right) Rule* and so $>> X$: A and $>> Y$: (list A). By the inductive hypothesis we conclude that X : A and Y : (list A). In which case $[X \mid Y]$: (list A) and so e : (list A).

Suppose (c), then e is a tuple (@p x y). Let the **tuple size** (σ) be defined as follows.

$$\sigma(x) = 0 \text{ if } x \text{ is not a tuple.}$$
$$\sigma(@p\ x\ y) = 1 + \sigma(x) + \sigma(y).$$

The proof is by induction on the size of $\sigma(e)$.

---

[99] A potential for confusion exists between the use of $\to$ for logical implication and $\to$ for the function space type operator. Rather than relying on context alone to disambiguate the intended meaning, the proof uses the older $\supset$ for logical implication and $\to$ for the type operator.

Base Case: $\sigma(e) = 1$

Suppose $>> e : A$; then for some B, C, A = (B * C) and $>>$ (@p $x\ y$) : (B * C). But if $>>$ (@p $x\ y$) : (B * C) then $>> x$: A and $>> y$: B. But since $\sigma(x) = \sigma(y) = 0$, x and y are not tuples and are primitive, x : B and y : C. By the inhabitation rule for tuples:

$$((@p\ x\ y) : (B * C)) \leftrightarrow ((x : B) \,\&\, (y : C))$$

Since the RHS of this equivalence is true, then (@p $x\ y$) : (B * C) and so $e : A$.

Inductive Case: the theorem holds for all tuples t where $\sigma(t) \le n$.

Suppose $\sigma(e) = n + 1$ and $>> e : A$; then for some B, C, A = (B * C) and $>>$ (@p $x\ y$) : (B * C). But if $>>$ (@p $x\ y$) : (B * C) then $>> x$: A and $>> y$: B. Also $\sigma(x) \le n$ and $\sigma(y) \le n$ and so by the inductive hypothesis, x : B and y : C. By the inhabitation rule for tuples:

$$((@p\ x\ y) : (B * C)) \leftrightarrow ((x : B) \,\&\, (y : C))$$

Since the RHS of this equivalence is true, then (@p $x\ y$) : (B * C) and so $e : A$.

Theorem 2: if $|- e :$ A and $e \Rightarrow e*$ then $|- e* :$ A.

The proof proceeds by cases. The reduction of e to $e*$ must be one of the rules #1-16 in the semantics for $\mathcal{L}$.

By rule #1; then $e = (= x\ y)$, by the signature for $=$, $>> e :$ boolean and since $e* =$ true then $>> e* :$ boolean.

By rule #2, then $e = (= x\ y)$, by the signature for $=$, $>> e :$ boolean and since $e* =$ false then $>> e* :$ boolean.

By rule #3; then $e = (= x\ y)$ and suppose $>> e :$ A. By rule #3, $e* = \bot$ or $e* = \otimes$ and by the rules for error conditions, $e^* :$ A.

By rule #4; then $e = ((\lambda\ p\ x)\ y)$. Assume $>> e :$ A, then by the *Applications Rule* for some B
$$>> (\lambda\ p\ x) : B \rightarrow A$$
$$>> y : B$$

Either *match*$(p, y) = \otimes$ or *match*$(p, y) \ne \otimes$. Assume *match*$(p, y) = \otimes$, then $e*$ $= \otimes$ and $>> e* :$ A (since $>> \otimes : (\forall\ A\ A)$).

Assume $match(p, y) \neq \otimes$, then either

(a) p is a constant and $p = y$ and so $e^* = x$. We have $>> (\lambda\, p\, x) : B \to A$ which by the *Patterns Rule* is provable only if $>> p : B$ and $p : B >> x : A$. But if $>> p : B$ then $p : B >> x : A$ iff $>> x : A$. Hence $>> e^* : A$.

(b) p is a variable; then $e^* = [x]_{y/p}$. We have $>> (\lambda\, p\, x) : B \to A$ which by the *Patterns Rule* is provable only if

$z : C >> z : B$ where z is any arbitrary name and C is a fresh type variable.
$z : B >> [x]_{z/p} : A$

Note: the sequent $z : C >> z : B$ is trivially soluble by unification of B with the fresh C. In this case the *Patterns Rule* just acts like the *Abstractions Rule* in Simply Typed Lambda calculus.

But if $z : B >> [x]_{z/p} : A$ for any arbitrary z, then certainly $y : B >> [x]_{y/p} : A$ and given $>> y : B$ then $>> [x]_{y/p} : A$ and so $>> e^* : A$.

(c) p is a pattern of the form (cons $v\, w$) or (@p $v\, w$); then since $match(p, y) \neq \otimes$ then $match(p, y)$ is a set σ of bindings. Each element $<v, b>$ of σ is an association of a variable v with a value b. We know from the *Patterns Rule* that $(\lambda\, p\, x) : B \to A$ is provable only if

    1. $N_1 : A_1, ... N_n : A_n >> p^* : B$;
    2. $p^* : B >> x^* : A$;

where $N_1...N_n$ are fresh names and $A_1...A_n$ are fresh type variables, p^* results from p by replacing all the variables $x_1,..,x_n$ in p by $N_1...N_n$ and x^* results from x by replacing all the free variables from $x_1,..,x_n$ by $N_1...N_n$.

$p^* : B >> x^* : A$ states that assuming an arbitrary substitution instance of the variables in p (i.e. p^*) to be of type B, that same substitution applied to the free variables in x produces an object (i.e. x^*) that can be proved to be of type A. Since $match(p, y)$ succeeds y is a substitution instance of p.

So we have

$\sigma(p) : B >> \sigma(x) : A$

But $\sigma(p) = y$ and $\sigma(x) = e^*$. So we have

$y : B >> e^* : A$

But given $>> y : B$ then $>> e^* : A$

By rule #5; then e = (if x y z); and e^* = y or e^* = z or e^* = $\perp$. Assume that $\gg e$: A, then this is provable by the type of *if* and so $\gg y$: A and $\gg z$: A. Since $\gg \perp$: A, then $\gg e^*$: A.

By rule #6; then e = (let x y z), suppose $\gg e$: A. Then by the *Local Rule* for some B, where x^* is fresh; $\gg y$: B and x^* : B $\gg z_{x^*/x}$: A

Here e^* = ((λ x z) y); by the *Applications Rule* e^* : A if for some B;

$\gg y$: B and
$\gg$ (λ x z) : (B $\to$ A)

By the *Patterns Rule*, $\gg$ (λ x z) : (B $\to$ A) just when, where x^* is fresh and C is a fresh type variable.

x^* : C $\gg x^*$: B and
x^* : B $\gg z_{x^*/x}$: A

Since x is a variable the first sequent is easily soluble (unify C with B). So $\gg e^*$: A if both the following are provable.

$\gg y$: B and
x^* : B $\gg z_{x^*/x}$: A

By hypothesis these are both provable, hence $\gg e^*$: A.

By rule #7; then e = (cons x y) and $\gg e$: A and either e^* = $\perp$ or e^* = (cons $\Downarrow x$ $\Downarrow y$). If e^* = $\perp$ then $\gg e^*$: A. Suppose e^* = (cons $\Downarrow x$ $\Downarrow y$). We write '$e \Rightarrow_n e^*$' when e can be normalised to e^* using n rewrite rules. The proof of subject reduction is by induction on n. Suppose n = 0; then e = e^* and the proof is immediate. Suppose that subject reduction holds when n rules are used; i.e. we assume if $\gg e$: A and $e \Rightarrow_n e_n$, then $\gg e_n$: A as an inductive hypothesis. We wish to show $\gg e$: A and $e \Rightarrow_{n+1} e_{n+1}$, then $\gg e_{n+1}$: A. In this case we need to show only that each individual rule of our semantics preserves subject reduction where no further normalisation is needed above what is performed in the rule itself. Such a proof is essentially nothing more than a reiteration of the cases already cited. In the case of rule #7, if no normalisation of x or y is required, then again e = e^* and the proof is immediate.

What our reasoning establishes is that the presence of the $\Downarrow$ symbol is irrelevant to the subject reduction property. Provided *every* rule preserves subject reduction in *every* case where no further normalisation is needed above what is performed in the rule itself, then subject reduction will obtain for the system overall. In future we will invoke this argument to banish the $\Downarrow$ by the phrase "by induction on the order of rewriting".

By rule #8; then $e = (@p\ x\ y)$ and $>> e$: A and either $e^* = \perp$ or $e^* = (@p\ \Downarrow x\ \Downarrow y)$. By induction on the order of rewriting, we drop the $\Downarrow$ and consider only $e^* = \perp$ or $e^* = (@p\ x\ y)$. If $e^* = \perp$ then $>> e^*$: A. If $e^* = (@p\ x\ y)$ then the proof is immediate.

By rule #9; then $e = (++\ x)$ and $>> e$: number. Either $e^* = \perp$ or $e^* = (1 + \Downarrow x)$. If $e^* = \perp$ then certainly $>> e$: number. If $\Downarrow x$ is a number then $1 + \Downarrow x$ is a number and by the *Primitive Rule*, $>> 1 + \Downarrow x$: number and so $>> e^*$: number.

By rule #10; then $e = (-\ -\ x)$ and $>> e$: number. Either $e^* = \perp$ or $e^* = (\Downarrow x - 1)$. If $e^* = \perp$ then certainly $>> e$: number. If $\Downarrow x$ is a number then $\Downarrow x - 1$ is a number and by the *Primitive Rule*, $>> \Downarrow x - 1$: number and so $>> e^*$: number.

By rule #11; then $e = (\text{cases}\ x_1\ \dots\ x_n)$ and $>> e$: A. Either $\Downarrow x_1 = \otimes$ or $\Downarrow x_1 \neq \otimes$. By induction on the order of rewriting, we drop the $\Downarrow$ and consider only the cases $x_1 = \otimes$ or not $x_1 = \otimes$.

If $x_1 = \otimes$ then $e^* = (\text{cases}\ \dots\ x_n)$. By the *Cases Rule*, $>> e$: A just when each x_i in $(\text{cases}\ x_1\ \dots\ x_n)$ is such that $>> x_i$: A. So certainly it must be true that $>> (\text{cases}\ \dots\ x_n)$: A and therefore $>> e^*$: A.
If $x_1 \neq \otimes$, then $e^* = x_1$ and since by the *Cases Rule* for each x_i in $(\text{cases}\ x_1\ \dots\ x_n)$, $>> x_i$: A then $>> x_1$: A and so $>> e^*$: A.

By rule #12; then $e^* = \otimes$ and since $>> \otimes : (\forall\ A\ A))$, subject reduction holds.

By rule #13; then $e = (\text{where}\ x\ y)$ and $e^* = (\text{if}\ x\ y\ \otimes)$. Suppose $>> e$: A, then by the *Guard Rule*, $>> x$: boolean and $>> y$: A. By the type of *if* to prove $>> e^*$: A, it suffices to prove $>> x$: boolean and $>> y$: A and $>> \otimes$: A. By hypothesis, the first two are provable and the third follows from $>> \otimes : (\forall\ A\ A))$.

By rule #14; in that case e is a combinator expression, $(Y\ (\lambda\ v\ x))$ and $e^* = [x]_{v/(Y\ (\lambda\ v\ x))}$. Assume e : A, then $(Y\ (\lambda\ v\ x))$: A and this is provable only if v : A $>> x$: A. Consider the proof tree for v : A $>> x$: A. For every subgoal of the form v : A, the assumption v : A will be used to solve it. Now replace this subgoal by $(Y\ (\lambda\ v\ x))$ and drop the assumption v : A. By the *Combinator Rule*, this is provable if v : A $>> x$: A, which by hypothesis *is* provable. Hence if there is a proof of v : A $>> x$: A then there is a proof of $[x]_{v/(Y\ (\lambda\ v\ x))}$: A and so $>> e^*$: A.

By rule #15; in that case e is an application $(x\ y)$. Suppose $>> e$: A and $e^* = \perp$ then $>> e^*$: A. Suppose $e^* = (\Downarrow x\ \Downarrow y)$. By induction on the order of rewriting, we drop the $\Downarrow$ and consider only the case $(x\ y)$ and the proof is trivial.

By rule #16; then $e = e^*$ and the proof is immediate.

Theorem 3: if $>> e$: A then, if $\Downarrow e$ is a p.d., then $\Downarrow e$: A.

Assume $>> e$: A and $\Downarrow e$ is a p.d.. We write '$e \Rightarrow_m e*$' when e can be normalised to $e*$ using m rewrite rules. The proof is by induction on m. If $e \Rightarrow_0 \Downarrow e$, then e is a normal form and by theorem 1, $\Downarrow e$: A.. Assume the theorem holds for n rewrites. Assume $e \Rightarrow_{n+1} \Downarrow e$; then for some $e*$, $e \Rightarrow e* \Rightarrow_n \Downarrow e$. By theorem 2 we know that if $>> e$: A then $>> e*$: A, and by the inductive hypothesis, we have if $>> e*$: A then $\Downarrow e$: A. So $>> e$: A implies $\Downarrow e$: A.

30.2 𝒯

𝒯 is a simple control strategy for creating a type checker from 𝓢. The easiest way to do this is to apply the rules of 𝓢 directly in the manner in which Shen conducts searches with sequent calculus theories.

Let $[s_1 \ ...s_n]$ be any ordering of the rules of 𝓢. Let $A = (apply\ s_i\ [S_1 \ ... \ S_x])$ be the application of any rule s_i of S to the solution of a list of sequents written in the notation of S. Either A will succeed, in the sense that the conclusion of s_i matches S_1 or it will not. If it does, then the output of A will be a new list of sequents. If not, then A behaves as the identity function. If all applications fail then control returns to the last choice point and resumes down the list $[s_1 \ ... \ s_n]$. If no such choicepoint exists then the search fails and a type error is recorded.

This strategy is essentially depth first search using chronological backtracking that is the default in Prolog. Fairly obviously, 𝒯 is sound (since it uses only the rules from 𝓢). We will also prove 𝒯 is terminating.

We first have to prove a theorem based on the nature of the type rules that 𝒯 uses. The type rules are of two kinds.

- A. Type rules that eliminate goals without producing subgoals.
- B. Type rules that generate subgoals but reduce the bracketing of an expression in the original goal.

We will call these 'A-rules' and 'B-rules' respectively. Let us say that a sequent system is an **AB system** if every rule in it is an A-rule or a B-rule. Intuitively, any proof procedure which uses an AB system by applying all the rules in it will eventually generate a fixpoint. In other words, it needs to be proved that there is no infinite chain of rule applications R_1, R_2, R_3, ... which can be successively applied to a series of goals G such that for all n, $R_n(...(R_1(G))) \neq R_{n+1}(...(R_n (R_1(G))))$. The theorem that states this is the **AB theorem**.

To prove this formally, we need a function, β, which returns a value based on the bracketing found in the expressions used in the proof procedure. We begin by

438

inductively defining β for typings. A typing is an expression of the form $x : \tau$, where x is an expression of $\mathcal{L}$ and τ is a type expression. Typings are effectively the well-formed formulae of a proof conducted by $\mathcal{T}$. Type expressions are defined inductively.

1. A symbol is a type expression.
2. If a is a type expression and b is a type expression and v is a variable, then $(a \to b)$, $(a * b)$, (list a), $(\forall v\ a)$ are type expressions.

The function β is defined inductively over typings as follows.

$\beta(x : \tau) = \beta(x) + 1$

For $\mathcal{L}$ expressions, β is defined as follows.

$\beta(x) = 0$ if x is a primitive object

$\beta(x_1 \ldots x_n) = \Sigma(x_i) + 1$ for i = 1 to i = n.

If $\beta(x) = n$ we say that the **B-value** of x is n. Given a sequent $\Delta >> C$, we associate it to the B-value of this sequent by the following equation.

$\beta(\Delta >> C) = \Sigma(\beta(x_i)) + \beta(C)$ for all x_i in Δ.

In other words to calculate the B-value of a sequent we simply total the B-values of its constituent wffs. We can now define a B-rule precisely.

A rule R is a B-rule just if whenever R is successfully applied to a tuple of goals $<G_0, G_1, \ldots, G_n>$, the resulting tuple of goals $<G^*_1, \ldots, G^*_m, G_1, \ldots, G_n>$ is such that $\beta(G^*_i) < \beta(G_0)$ for all i, where $1 \leq i \leq m$.

Theorem: all the rules of the type system for $\mathcal{L}$ are B-type rules with the exception of the Primitive, Sequents, Generalisation and Specialisation Rules.

Proof: the proof is long but straightforward. We will cover one case and leave it to the reader to complete the other cases.

The type rule for *if* states

X : boolean; Y : A; Z : A;
(if X Y Z) : A;

Let $<G_0, G_1, \ldots, .G_n>$ be a tuple of goals. Assume $\beta(G_0) = m$. Assume the Conditional Rule is successfully applied to $<G_0, G_1, \ldots, .G_n>$. If so, then G_0 is of the form $\Delta >> $ (if X Y Z) : A, and the output of the rule application is $<G_x, G_y, G_z, G_1, \ldots, .G_n>$ where G_x, G_y, and G_z are defined as follows.

$G_x = \Delta \gg X$: boolean
$G_y = \Delta \gg Y : A$
$G_z = \Delta \gg Z : A$

We have the following equalities

$\beta(G_0) = m = \beta(\Delta) + \beta((\text{if } X \ Y \ Z) : A)$
$\beta(G_x) = \beta(\Delta) + \beta(X : \text{boolean})$
$\beta(G_y) = \beta(\Delta) + \beta(Y : A)$
$\beta(G_z) = \beta(\Delta) + \beta(Z : A)$

But by the definition of β, the following inequalities hold.

$\beta(X : \text{boolean}) < \beta((\text{if } X \ Y \ Z) : A)$
$\beta(Y : A) < \beta((\text{if } X \ Y \ Z) : A)$
$\beta(Z : A) < \beta((\text{if } X \ Y \ Z) : A)$

Abbreviating $\beta(\Delta)$ by d and $\beta((\text{if } X \ Y \ Z) : A)$ by i, and $\beta(X : \text{boolean})$, $\beta(Y : A)$ and $\beta(Z : A)$ by x, y and z respectively, we have the following equalities.

$\beta(G_0) = m = d + i$
$\beta(G_x) = d + x$ where $x < i$
$\beta(G_y) = d + y$ where $y < i$
$\beta(G_z) = d + z$ where $z < i$

Hence $\beta(G_x) < \beta(G_0)$ and $\beta(G_y) < \beta(G_0)$ and $\beta(G_z) < \beta(G_0)$ and the Conditional Rule is a B-rule.

Theorem: the Primitive and Sequents Rules are A-rules.

Proof: by inspection of the rules.

Corollary: the type system for $\mathcal{L}$, excepting the Specialisation Rule, is an AB system.

The omission of the *Specialisation Rule* is generally not important in $\mathcal{T}$, since unification is used to bind variables. The omission of this rule and the *Generalisation Rule* will be discussed later.

An **AB series** is a series of lists of goals where (a) the first list contains a single goal (b) for any element G_n in the series, the immediate successor G_{n+1} is generated from G_n by the successful application of an A-rule or a B-rule. To prove the termination of $\mathcal{T}$, we have to prove that there is no infinite AB series.

440

Since the β function maps every sequent to its B-value, we can associate each element in an AB series with a list of numbers. Each number is the B-value of the sequent in the goal. Therefore we extend the concept of a B-value (and hence the domain of β) to embrace goals and AB series.

Let G be a goal, where $G = [s_1,\ldots,s_m]$ and let $\beta(s_1) = n_1,\ldots,\beta(s_m) = n_m$. The B-value of the goal G is the list of numbers $[n_1,\ldots,n_m]$. Let $G_0, \ldots,G_n$ be any series of goals. The B-value of this series is just the series $\beta(G_0),\ldots,\beta(G_n)$.

The B-value of an AB series is therefore a numeric representation of that series; it consists of a series of lists of numbers. Let us call such a series, an **AB_n series**. Since this series is derived by a mapping from an AB series, it has the following property.

Let L_n and L_{n+1} be elements of an AB_n series and let a be the number at the head of L_n. Then either

(a) L_{n+1} is the tail of L_n ($L_{n+1} = \text{tail}(L_n)$) or
(b) L_{n+1} is identical to the result of appending a list $[b_1,\ldots,b_k]$ to $\text{tail}(L_n)$ such that for each b_i, $b_i < a$.

In case (a) the inverse of L_{n+1} under β is derived from its predecessor by an A-operation. In the case of (b), the inverse of L_{n+1} under β is derived from its predecessor by a B-operation.

We will call the operation on L_n that corresponds to case (a) **the A_n operation**, and an operation that corresponds to case (b) **a B_n operation**. AB_n series are thus built up from a list containing a single number, by successively iterating A_n and B_n operations. Since the elements of an AB series are correlated 1-1 with elements of the corresponding AB_n series, we can show that there is no infinite AB series by proving the following theorem.

Theorem: There is no infinite AB_n series.

Let us say that an AB_n series is **protracted**, if there is no element L in the series that lacks a successor when an A_n or B_n operation could be successfully applied to L. We shall prove that there is no infinite AB_n series by proving the following result.

Theorem: If L_n is a non-empty list of numbers in a protracted AB_n series, then $\text{tail}(L_n)$ occurs in the series.

Proof: the proof proceeds by use of strong induction over the value of the first number a in L_n.

Base Case: $a = 0$. Then the only admissible AB_n operation that can be carried out on L_n is the A_n operation, and so $L_{n+1} = \text{tail}(L_n)$ and the theorem is proved.

Inductive Case: the theorem holds for all values for *a* less than *m*. Let $L_n = [m,....]$. Consider L_{n+1}. Either

    (a) L_{n+1} is derived from L_n by the A_n operation. If so, $L_{n+1} = tail(L_n)$ and the theorem is proved.

    (b) L_{n+1} is derived from L_n by a B_n operation. In which case $L_{n+1} = [b_1,...,b_k \mid tail(L_n)]$. Since each of the $b_1,...,b_k$ is less than *m*, the inductive hypothesis applies to each of $[b_1,...,b_k \mid tail(L_n)]$, $[b_2,...,b_k \mid tail(L_n)]$ ..... and so on to $[b_k \mid tail(L_n)]$. But if the inductive hypothesis applies to $[b_k \mid tail(L_n)]$, then $tail(L_n)$ occurs in the series and the theorem is proved.

Theorem: every protracted AB_n series is terminated by the empty list.

Proof: every AB_n series begins with a list containing a single number and the tail of that list is the empty list. Since no AB_n operation can be applied to the empty list, any protracted AB_n series terminates with the empty list.

Theorem: there is no infinite AB_n series.

Proof: assume X is an infinite AB_n series. Every infinite AB_n series must be protracted, since if it were not, it would terminate with a list to which an AB_n operation could be applied. So X is protracted and since every protracted AB_n series terminates with [ ], X is a terminating infinite series. By *reductio*, X does not exist.

The AB Theorem: there is no infinite AB series.

Proof: since the elements of every AB series are correlated 1-1 with every AB_n series, since there is no infinite AB_n series, there is no infinite AB series.

Hence we can finally assert.

Theorem: $\mathcal{T}$ is terminating.

Proof: If $\mathcal{T}$ failed to terminate, then an infinitely long AB series would exist.

30.3 Procedure $\mathcal{T}$*

The proof procedure $\mathcal{T}$ for type checking is depth-first search with chronological backtracking. We know that $\mathcal{T}$ is terminating in respect of the type rules we have stated. Another piece of good news is $\mathcal{T}$ is accurate, in the sense that if $\mathcal{T}$ says that an expression has a type, then it really does have that type.

The downside is that $\mathcal{T}$ is not particularly efficient. The *Cases Rule*, for instance, splits a proof of (cases Case$_1$ ... Case$_n$) : A into a number of subproofs that work on each $Case_i$. Since the type A is known and is variable-free, each $Case_i$ can be treated independently and there is really no need for backtracking between these subproofs of $Case_i$: A. Other rules offer opportunities for the elimination of choice points. The *Combinator Rule* is the only rule for checking combinators and so is a **committed choice** in the sense that if it can be applied, it should be and there should be no backtracking to reconsider this decision.

Another problem with $\mathcal{T}$ is that the procedure targets $\mathcal{L}$ expressions rather than Shen expressions, and this creates two problems. First, $\mathcal{L}$ expressions are generally larger and more deeply nested than Shen expressions, so the time spent on inferencing is proportionately greater. Second, any type errors detected are detected in $\mathcal{L}$ expressions and not in the Shen source, which makes it hard to raise a clear type error report.

The $\mathcal{T}^*$ procedure eliminates these disadvantages by type checking Shen source, and procedurally implements the role of many of the type rules used in $\mathcal{T}$. The Y-combinator, Pattern, Cases, Generalisation and Guard rules are redundant in $\mathcal{T}^*$. The bogus choice points are omitted. The $\mathcal{T}^*$ procedure operates on a typed Shen function definition. Such a definition generally has the form.

```
(define <function>
  {A₁ --> ... Aₙ --> B}
  ₐp₁ ... ₐpₙ -> rₐ
  ...................
  ₘp₁ ... ₘpₙ -> rₘ)
```

Each rule $_ip_1 \dots {_i}p_n \to r_i$ can be thought of as defining a sort of mini-function whose type is intended to be identical with the host function. Therefore to type check the entire function, it is enough to show that each rewrite rule obeys the type associated with its host function.

Under $\mathcal{T}^*$, the process of type checking a rewrite rule has two parts, corresponding to the two structural components of a rule. The first structural component is a sequence of patterns and the second is the result returned if the patterns match the inputs. The first job of the type checker is to show that each pattern p fits the type assigned to it. This we call **the integrity condition**. The second job is to show that, assuming the integrity conditions are met, that the result has the type expected of it. This we call the **correctness condition**. The two principles are defined below.

The Integrity Condition

An assignment of a type B to pattern p meets the integrity condition just when the sequent $\Delta >> p$: B is provable; where $\Delta = \{V, A \mid V : A\}$ where V is a variable in p and A is a fresh type variable.

The Correctness Condition

Assume a rule $p_1 \dots p_n \text{ -> } r$ is assigned the type $A_1 \rightarrow \dots A_n \rightarrow B$. Then this assignment meets the correctness condition just when the sequent $p_1 : A_1 \dots p_n : A_n \gg r : B$ is provable.

$\mathcal{T}^*$ verifies the type security of a function through establishing these two properties. Let's see what this means in concrete terms through an example. Here is a definition of a datatype details which represents the details about a person – her name, address and telephone number.

```
(datatype details

  \\ details right
  Name : string; Address : string; Phone : number;
  [Name Address Phone] : details;

  \\ details left
  Name : string, Address : string, Phone : number >> P;
  [Name Address Phone] : details >> P;)
```

The function address returns the address of a person given their details.

```
(define address
  {details --> string}
  [Name Address Phone] -> Address)
```

Represented in cons form; this definition appears as:

```
(define address
  {details --> string}
  (cons Name (cons Address (cons Phone []))) -> Address)
```

To establish the type details --> string, we have to satisfy the Integrity and Correctness Principles. The Integrity Principle requires that the following sequent be proved.

```
Name : A, Address : B, Phone : C
 >> (cons Name (cons Address (cons Phone []))) : details
```

The details right rule maps this sequent to three subgoals.

```
Name : A, Address : B, Phone : C  >> Name : string;
Name : A, Address : B, Phone : C  >> Address : string;
Name : A, Address : B, Phone : C  >> Phone : number;
```

These sequents are solvable under the assignments $A \mapsto$ string, $B \mapsto$ string, and $C \mapsto$ number. The Correctness Condition then requires that that the following sequent be proved.

(cons Name (cons Address (cons Phone []))) : details >> Address : string

The details left rule maps this sequent to an immediately soluble goal.

Name : string, Address : string, Phone : number >> Address : string

The Correctness Condition in its current form is adequate only for non-recursive functions. We define the expression 'r is recursive w.r.t. f' to mean that r occurs in a recursive definition of f and a recursive call to f occurs within r. The first revision to the Correctness Condition caters for such recursive calls.

The Correctness Condition (Revised)

Assume a rule p_1 ... p_n -> r is assigned the type $A_1 \rightarrow$ .... $A_n \rightarrow B$ and r is recursive w.r.t. f. Then this assignment meets the correctness condition just when the sequent $f : A_1 \rightarrow$ .... $A_n \rightarrow B, p_1 : A_1$ ... $p_n : A_n \gg r : B$ is provable.

Thus using the linear recursive definition of the factorial function.

```
(define factorial
  {number --> number}
  0 -> 1
  X -> (* X (factorial (- X 1))))
```

After currying, the proof obligations that the type checker generates are:

1. >> 0 : number;
2. 0 : number >> 1 : number;
3. X : A >> X : number;
4. X : number, factorial : (number --> number) >> ((* X) (factorial ((- X) 1)))) : number

Sequent 1. is generated by applying the Integrity Condition to the first rewrite rule and sequent 3. by applying the same condition to the second rewrite rule. Sequents 2. and 3. come from applying the Correctness Condition to the first and second rewrite rules respectively. Since the expression (* X (factorial (- X 1))) is recursive with respect to factorial, an extra assumption factorial : (number --> number) is required.

The Correctness Condition does not deal with guards or constructions using <-. The latter do not pose any special problem because they can be eliminated in favour of the forward arrow using the equivalences of chapter 12. The use of guards is also straightforward to type check. The rule

p_1 ... p_n -> r where g

445

has the type $A_1 \rightarrow \ldots A_n \rightarrow B$ just when the Integrity Condition and Correctness Conditions are met and g can be proved to be a boolean. In other words that is, all of the following conditions are met; for each p_i, let Δ_i be the set of typings $\{V, A \mid V : A\}$ where V is a variable in p_i and A is a fresh type variable.

1. $\Delta_i \gg p_i : A_i$ is provable for each i of $1,\ldots,n$.   (Integrity)
2. g : verified, $p_1 : A_1 \ldots p_n : A_n \gg r : B$ is provable.   (Correctness)
3. $p_1 : A_1 \ldots p_n : A_n \gg g :$ boolean is provable.   (Guard)

Here is an example using these conditions.

```
(define find_address
    {string --> (list details) --> string}
    Name [[Name Address Phone] | _] -> Address
    Name [_ | Details] -> (find_address Name Details))
```

The function contains no explicit guard, but it also contains a non-left linear rewrite rule in the first position. To render it left-linear for the purposes of type checking, we need to insert a guard. After doing this, the definition appears as below.

```
(define find_address
   {string --> (list details) --> string}
   Name1 [[Name2 Address Phone] | _] -> Address where (= Name_1 Name_2)
   Name [_ | Details] -> (find_address Name Details))
```

There are 8 proof obligations for type checking find_address (figure 30.3). The proof obligation Name1 : A >> Name1 : string is trivially solvable. Problems of this kind are always generated from patterns that are simply variables, and so $\mathcal{T}^*$ may omit these proof obligations because they are always solvable.

Rewrite Rule 1

Integrity Requirements

1. Name1 : A >> Name1 : string
2. Name2 : B, Address : C, Phone : D, Whatever : E
        >> [[Name2 Address Phone] | X] : (list details)

Correctness Requirements

3. Name1 : string, [[Name2 Address Phone] | X] : (list details),
        (= Name1 Name2) : verified >> Address : string

Guard

4. Name : string, [[Name2 Address Phone] | X] : (list details)
        >> (= Name1 Name2) : boolean

Rewrite Rule 2

Integrity Requirements

5. Name : string, [[Name2 Address Phone] | Whatever] : (list details)
          >> (= Name1 Name2) : boolean
6. Name : F >> Name : string
7. Detail : G, Details : H >> [Detail | Details] : (list details)

Correctness Requirements

8. Name : string, [Detail | Details] : (list details),
        find_address : string --> ((list details) --> string)
        >> ((find_address Name) Details) : string

Figure 30.3 The proof obligations from the find_address *function*

Finally only mutual recursion remains to be dealt with. The technique of handling a mutual recursion like

```
(define even?
   {number --> boolean}
   1 -> false
   X -> (odd? (- X 1)))

(define odd?
   {number --> boolean}
   1 -> true
   X -> (even? (- X 1)))
```

is to assume the typings odd? : number $\rightarrow$ boolean and even? : number $\rightarrow$ boolean in type checking the recursive calls. There are eight proof obligations generated by these two functions, but two are trivial and so we omit them. The remaining six are shown in figure 30.4.

even?

1. >> 1 : number;
2. 1 : number >> true : boolean;
3. X : number, odd? : (number --> boolean)
         >> (odd? ((- X) 1)) : boolean

odd?

4. >> 1 : number;
5. 1 : number >> false : boolean;
6. X : number, even? : (number --> boolean)
       >> (even? ((- X) 1)) : boolean

Figure 30.4 The proof obligations from the odd? and even? functions

The technique of $\mathcal{T}^*$ is to prove Integrity and Correctness for each rule of the function. There is no need for the Y-combinator, Pattern, Cases and Guard rules and these rules are no longer retained. Type variables in the type of a function are replaced by fresh terms at the start of the proof and so the Generalisation Rule is not required. $\mathcal{T}^*$ trades declarative purity for a reduction in the size of the type theory, and the elimination of bogus choice points, but delivers the same result in less time.[100]

We shall prove the equivalence[101] of $\mathcal{T}$ and $\mathcal{T}^*$ by showing how the rules not used by $\mathcal{T}$ are implemented procedurally within $\mathcal{T}^*$. The procedural equivalence is quite simple to show, except in the case of the Patterns Rule.

The efficiency gain in $\mathcal{T}^*$ comes from two sources.

1.   The elimination of rules that are used only once in the proof. Instead these rules are procedurally invoked early in the procedure and then not used again.

2.   The elimination of long stretches of proof that are purely mechanical and add to the search space without changing the result.

30.4 The Equivalence of $\mathcal{T}$ and $\mathcal{T}^*$

The easiest way to demonstrate the procedural equivalence of $\mathcal{T}$ and $\mathcal{T}^*$ is to work through the rules that $\mathcal{T}^*$ does not use and see why $\mathcal{T}^*$ does not use them.

First, the Generalisation Rule needs only to be used once in $\mathcal{T}$, at the beginning of a proof to remove the universal quantifiers binding the type variables. Since all types are shallow types, the Generalisation Rule is not needed after these quantifiers are removed. This is done automatically in $\mathcal{T}^*$, so the Generalisation Rule is not needed.

The Cases Rule requires that each case in the body of a definition obeys the type constraints of the whole function. The type constraints are free of shared variables, so that in effect, any proof using Cases can be split into n independent subproofs. In $\mathcal{T}^*$, this is exactly what happens, each rewrite rule is checked separately to ensure that it meets the type constraints. This means that the Cases Rule is not needed in $\mathcal{T}^*$.

---

[100] The improvement in performance is significant; using $\mathcal{T}$ to type check and compile one program took 77,453 inferences. Under $\mathcal{T}^*$, the same program was checked and compiled using 10,187 inferences. In cases where there are type errors, $\mathcal{T}^*$ is less likely than $\mathcal{T}$ to lose itself in combinatorial complexities.

[101] i.e.; that they both produce the same result for the same input.

The Y-combinator Rule is used in $\mathcal{T}$ to type check recursive functions. Effectively any abstraction $(\lambda\, x\, y)$ which amounts to the recursive definition of a function f is written as $(Y\, f\,(\lambda\, x\, y))$. The Y-combinator Rule, when applied to a problem of the form $(Y\, f\,(\lambda\, x\, y))$: A, gives f : A $>>$ $(\lambda\, x\, y)$: A. Thereafter the Y-combinator Rule plays no further part in the proof. A procedural optimisation assumes f : A and attempts to prove $(\lambda\, x\, y)$: A directly from the recursive definition, dispensing with the Y-combinator Rule which is not needed in $\mathcal{T}^*$.[102]

The optimisation of dispensing with the Patterns and Guard Rules is more delicate. Recall that in $\mathcal{T}$, the task of type checking a function begins with a problem of the form $(\lambda\, x_1\, ...(\lambda\, x_n\, y))$: $A_1 \rightarrow ... A_n \rightarrow A_{n+1}$. Each x_i is a variable, and by repeated applications of the Abstractions Rule, we generate a problem x_1 : $A_1,..., x_n$: $A_n >> y$: A_{n+1}. The body y of the former abstraction will consist of a series of cases c_1, ..., c_m each of which must be proved to be of type A_{n+1}. That is, our proof obligation breaks down into the following series.

x_1 : $A_1,..., x_n$: $A_n >> c_1$: A_{n+1}

....

x_1 : $A_1,..., x_n$: $A_n >> c_m$: A_{n+1}

Each c_i is an application composed of an n-place abstraction $(\lambda\, p_1\, ...\, (\lambda\, p_n\, z))$ applied to $x_1 ,..., x_n$ taking the form $(((\lambda\, p_1\, ...\, (\lambda\, p_n\, z))\, x_1)... x_n)$. Each p_i is a pattern. Thus the proof obligation for c_i is:

x_1 : $A_1,..., x_n$: $A_n >> (((\lambda\, p_1\, ...\, (\lambda\, p_n\, z))\, x_1)... x_n)$: A_{n+1}

Repeated use of the Applications Rule gives the following proof obligations; where $B_1\, ...\, B_n$ are free type variables

x_1 : $A_1,..., x_n$: $A_n >> x_1$: B_1

....

x_1 : $A_1,..., x_n$: $A_n >> x_n$: B_n

x_1 : $A_1,..., x_n$: $A_n >> (\lambda\, p_1\, ...\, (\lambda\, p_n\, z))$: $B_1 \rightarrow ... B_n \rightarrow A_{n+1}$

The proof obligation is

---

[102] In earlier versions of Shen, f : A was added as an explicit assumption in the proof. In later versions after 2020, f : A was procedurally encoded within a Prolog clause. The significant diiference is that where A is a polytype, the post 2020 version allows A to be instantiated in different ways within the same expression. In terms of system $\mathcal{J}$ this is equivalent to *first* applying the Y-combinator type rule before the Generalisation rule rather than the other ways round. The effect is to draw into the proof the assumption with the universal quantifiers in A intact rather than having a monotype. The universally bound type variables can then be instantiated in different ways. In Shen post-2020, the instantiation is of course done by unification. This change allows Shen post 2020 to typecheck certain functions which would have failed under the old regime.

$$x_1 : A_1,..., x_n : A_n \gg x_1 : B_1$$
$$\dots\dots\dots\dots\dots\dots\dots\dots\dots\dots\dots$$
$$x_1 : A_1,..., x_n : A_n \gg x_n : B_n$$

are trivially solvable by unifying each $x_i : B_i$ with the assumption $x_i : A_i$.

The final proof obligation is therefore

$$x_1 : A_1,..., x_n : A_n \gg (\lambda\, p_1 \dots (\lambda\, p_n\; z)) : A_1 \rightarrow \dots A_n \rightarrow A_{n+1}$$

The expressions $x_1 ,..., x_n$ do not occur anywhere within the conclusion of this sequent. Consequently they play no further part in the proof and may be thinned away. The proof obligation can now be simplified to

$$\gg (\lambda\, p_1 \dots (\lambda\, p_n\; z)) : A_1 \rightarrow \dots A_n \rightarrow A_{n+1}$$

n repeated applications of the Patterns Rule gives the following proof obligations. Each Δ_i is a series of typings of the form $v : C$, where v is a variable in p_i and C is a fresh type variable.

$$\Delta_1 \gg p_1 : A_1$$
$$\dots\dots\dots\dots\dots..$$
$$\Delta_n \gg p_n : A_n$$
$$p_1 : A_1 \dots p_n : A_n \gg z : A_{n+1}$$

Let us pause at this point and observe that the proof process so far is not only entirely mechanical, but is guaranteed to succeed merely by virtue of the syntactic structure of the language $\mathcal{L}$. In other words, type failure can only occur past this point, and reconsideration of the previous steps is a waste of time.

The second observation is that the proof obligations now facing us correspond precisely to the integrity and correctness checks required by $\mathcal{T}^*$. The integrity checks are contained exactly by the proof obligations

$$\Delta_1 \gg p_1 : A_1$$
$$\dots\dots\dots\dots\dots..$$
$$\Delta_n \gg p_n : A_n$$

while the correctness check is contained by the proof obligation

$$p_1 : A_1 \dots p_n : A_n \gg z : A_{n+1}$$

The advantage of $\mathcal{T}^*$ is that the mechanical and time-wasting steps required in $\mathcal{T}$ to get to this point are eliminated.

30.5 𝒯* in Shen

𝒯* is 260 lines of code in Shen. In this section we strip the program down to 150 lines of the essential code, indicating when needed, the functionality of missing functions. Here is the program, which is largely Shen Prolog, in its essentials.

```
(defprolog toplevel-forms
  (- [define F | X]) A   <-- ! (t* [define F | X] A);
  X A                    <-- (system-S [X : A] []);)
```

The highest level Prolog procedure is toplevel-forms which receives a term X and a type A and establishes if X has the type A. Generally A will be a variable and it is the task of toplevel-forms to assign A a value. toplevel-forms diverts control to different procedures depending on whether the expression is a Shen definition or not. system-S is directed towards expressions that are not definitions. t* is 𝒯* as we have studied it and presupposes system-S.

Let us begin with the simpler system-S procedure. system-S receives a conclusion P to be proved and a list of hypotheses Hyp with which to do it (this list is initially empty) and applies the rules of system 𝔖 to proving P. If P is a typing of the form X : A, it is assumed that X has been curried and that the type A has been rendered into canonical form; that is, any synonyms have been demodulated and any missing brackets restored (so that (A * B * C) is rendered as (A * (B * C)).)

```
(defprolog system-S
  _ _              <-- (when (maxinfexceeded?));
  (- [X : A]) Hyp <-- (when (type-theory-enabled?)) ! (system-S-h X A Hyp);
  P Hyp            <-- (when (value *spy*)) (show P Hyp);
  P Hyp            <-- (search-user-datatypes P Hyp (value *datatypes*));)
```

The first test determines if the number of inferences expended in type checking exceeds the set limit (by default 10^6 inferences).

```
(define maxinfexceeded?
  -> (if (> (inferences) (value *maxinferences*))
         (simple-error "maximum inferences exceeded")
         false))
```

If the threshold has been exceeded then an error is raised; if not then false is returned forcing the next clause to be considered.

(- [X : A]) Hyp <-- (when (type-theory-enabled?)) ! (system-S-h X A Hyp);

If a typing X : A is entered to be proved and Shen type theory is enabled (the default) then the program commits to proving that the term X has the type A. Supposing that either a typing is not entered or that Shen type theory is disabled then the next two clauses apply.

451

```
P Hyp        <-- (when (value *spy*)) (show P Hyp);
P Hyp        <-- (search-user-datatypes P Hyp (value *datatypes*));
```

The first clause directs the computer to show the current problem if spying is enabled. We shall not expend time on show; it merely displays the problem, returning false when the user hits RETURN. The final clause directs the computer to use user-defined rules to solve the problem.

The auxiliary procedure system-S-h hosts a lot of activity. It breaks down to a long list of cases which capture most of the rules of system ℑ.

```
(defprolog system-S-h
  X A Hyp                    <-- (when (value *spy*)) (show [X : A] Hyp);
  X A _                      <-- (when (not (cons? (0 X)))) (primitive X A);
  X A Hyp                    <-- (by-hypothesis X A Hyp);
  (- [F]) A Hyp              <-- (lookupsig F [--> A]);
  (- [fn F]) A _             <-- (lookupsig F A);
  (- [F X]) A Hyp            <-- (when (not (cons? (0 F))))
                                 (lookupsig F [B --> A])
                                 (system-S-h X B Hyp);

  (- [F X]) A Hyp            <-- (system-S-h F [B --> A] Hyp)
                                 (system-S-h X B Hyp);

  (- [cons X Y]) [list A] Hyp <-- (system-S-h X A Hyp)
                                 (system-S-h Y [list A] Hyp);

  (- [@p X Y]) [A * B] Hyp   <-- (system-S-h X A Hyp)
                                 (system-S-h Y B Hyp);

  (- [@v X Y]) [vector A] Hyp <-- (system-S-h X A Hyp)
                                 (system-S-h Y [vector A] Hyp);

  (- [@s X Y]) string Hyp    <-- (system-S-h X string Hyp)
                                 (system-S-h Y string Hyp);

  (- [lambda X Y]) [A --> B] Hyp <-- (bind New (freshterm (0 X)))
                                 (bind Z (beta (0 X) New (0 Y)))
                                 (system-S-h Z B [[New : A] | Hyp]);

  (- [let X Y Z]) A Hyp      <-- (system-S-h Y B Hyp)
                                 (bind New (freshterm (0 X)))
                                 (bind W (beta (0 X) (1 New) (0 Z)))
                                 (system-S-h W A [[New : B] | Hyp]);

  (- [open File D]) [stream D] Hyp <-- (when (element? (0 D) [in out]))
                                 (system-S-h File string Hyp);

  (- [type X A]) B Hyp       <-- ! (is! (rectify-type A) B)
                                 (system-S-h X B Hyp);

  (- [input+ A Stream]) B Hyp <-- (is! B (rectify-type A))
                                 (system-S-h Stream [stream in] Hyp);

  (- [set Var Val]) A Hyp    <-- (system-S-h Var symbol Hyp)
                                 (system-S-h [value Var] A Hyp)
                                 (system-S-h Val A Hyp);

  X A Hyp                    <-- (I-rules Hyp Normalised false)
                                 ! (system-S-h X A Normalised);

  X A Hyp                    <-- (search-user-datatypes [X : A] Hyp
                                   (value *datatypes*));)
```

The first line X A Hyp <-- (when (value *spy*)) (show [X : A] Hyp); is just the usual trace package that is activated by (spy +). It must fail and so we proceed to the second line.

The second line

X A _   <-- (when (not (cons? (0 X)))) (primitive X A);

attempts to prove that X : A according to the primitive rule of 𝔖 when X is an atom (number, string, boolean, symbol or the empty list). The definition of the primitive procedure is straightforward.

```
(defprolog primitive
  X number      <-- (when (number? (0 X)));
  X boolean     <-- (when (boolean? (0 X)));
  X string      <-- (when (string? (0 X)));
  X symbol      <-- (when (symbol? (0 X)));
  (- []) [list A]   <--;)
```

The third line

X A Hyp   <-- (by-hypothesis X A Hyp);

attempts to prove that X : A is provable by hypothesis. This requires searching the list of hypotheses.

```
(defprolog by-hypothesis
  X A (- [[Y : B] | _]) <-- (when (= X Y)) (is! A B);
  X A (- [_ | Hyp])    <-- (by-hypothesis X A Hyp);)
```

Searching the hypotheses to prove X : A requires finding a typing Y : B where X and Y are identical and A and B unify.

The fourth line

(- [F]) A Hyp   <-- (system-S-h F [--> A] Hyp);

is invoked if the term is an application of a zero place function.

The fifth line

(- [F X]) A Hyp   <-- (system-S-h F [B --> A] Hyp) (system-S-h X B Hyp);

invokes the Applications Rule.

The sixth, seventh, eighth and ninth rules all deal with rules for special forms.

```
(- [cons X Y]) [list A] Hyp  <-- (system-S-h X A Hyp) (system-S-h Y [list A] Hyp);
(- [@p X Y]) [A * B] Hyp     <-- (system-S-h X A Hyp) (system-S-h Y B Hyp);
```

```
(- [@v X Y]) [vector A] Hyp <-- (system-S-h X A Hyp)
                               (system-S-h Y [vector A] Hyp);
(- [@s X Y]) string Hyp      <-- (system-S-h X string Hyp)
                               (system-S-h Y string Hyp);
```

The tenth rule deals with an abstraction (lambda X Y) as a special form. It effectively invokes the Abstractions Rule; the bound occurrences of X in Y are replaced by a fresh term New by beta reduction to produce Z and New : A is added to the hypothesis list. The program recurses trying to prove Z : B from the new hypothesis list.

```
(- [lambda X Y]) [A --> B] Hyp <-- ! (bind New (freshterm (0 X)))
                                   (bind Z (beta (0 X) New (0 Y)))
                                   (system-S-h Z B [[New : A] | Hyp]);
```

The eleventh rule deals with local assignment (let X Y Z) : A as a special form. It attempts to prove Y has a type B and then, assuming X : B, that Z : A. Again renaming of bound variables is used to ensure that there is no accidental reuse of the same term.

```
(- [let X Y Z]) A Hyp        <-- ! (system-S-h Y B Hyp)
                                 (bind New (freshterm (0 X)))
                                 (bind W (beta (0 X) (1 New) (0 Z)))
                                 (system-S-h W A [[New : B] | Hyp]);
```

Rules twelve to fifteen deal with less common special forms. rectify-type renders the type into canonical form; that is, any synonyms are demodulated and any assumed brackets restored

```
(- [open File D]) [stream D] Hyp    <-- ! (when (element? (0 D) [in out]))
                                        (system-S-h File string Hyp);
(- [type X A]) B Hyp                <-- ! (is! (rectify-type A) B)
                                        (system-S-h X B Hyp);
(- [input+ A Stream]) B Hyp         <-- (is! B (rectify-type A))
                                        (system-S-h Stream [stream in] Hyp);
(- [set Var Val]) A Hyp             <-- ! (system-S-h Var symbol Hyp)
                                        (system-S-h [value Var] A Hyp)
                                        (system-S-h Val A Hyp);
```

The sixteenth rule encapsulates the L rules concerning inbuilt constructors. Thus the hypothesis (cons X Y) : (list A) is replaced by X : A and Y : (list A).

```
X A Hyp                             <-- (l-rules Hyp Normalised false)
                                    !
                                    (system-S-h X A Normalised);
```

The l-rules procedure carries a Flag? initially set to false. If an L rule is successfully applied then Flag? is set to true. When the procedure exhausts the hypothesis list, then it exits successfully only if the Flag? is set to true indicating that at least one successful L rule application has been achieved.

```
(defprolog I-rules
  (- []) Normalised (- true) <-- ! (bind Normalised []);
  (- [[[cons X Y] : [list A]] | Hyp]) Normalised _
          <-- ! (I-rules [[X : A] [Y : [list A]] | Hyp] Normalised true);
  (- [[[@p X Y] : [A * B]] | Hyp]) Normalised _
          <-- ! (I-rules [[X : A] [Y : B] | Hyp] Normalised true);
  (- [[[@s X Y] : string] | Hyp]) Normalised _
          <-- ! (I-rules [[X : string] [Y : string] | Hyp] Normalised true);
  (- [[[@v X Y] : [vector A]] | Hyp]) Normalised _
          <-- ! (I-rules [[X : A] [Y : [vector A]] | Hyp] Normalised true);
  (- [P | Hyp]) [Q | Normalised] Flag?
          <-- (bind Q P) (I-rules Hyp Normalised Flag?);)
```

The final rule requires that, if all the preceding rules have failed, that the list of rules supplied by the user be used.

```
X A Hyp          <-- (search-user-datatypes [X : A] Hyp (value *datatypes*));
```

search-user-datatypes recurses through the list of user-defined datatypes, calling each one.

```
(defprolog search-user-datatypes
  P Hyp (- [D | _]) <-- (call (D P Hyp));
  P Hyp (- [_ | Ds]) <-- (search-user-datatypes P Hyp Ds);)
```

This concludes the encoding for non-definitions. Now we embrace $\mathcal{T}^*$.

```
(defprolog t*
  (- [define F | X]) A    <-- ! (bind SigxRules (sigxrules [(0 F) | (0 X)]))
                              (bind Sig (fst (1 SigxRules)))
                              (bind Rules (snd (1 SigxRules)))
                              (bind FreshSig (freshen-sig Sig))
                              (t*-rules F Rules FreshSig 1)
                              (is Sig A);)
```

The initial part of t* parses the definition into a pair SigxRules where the first element is the signature Sig of the function (found in curly brackets and suitably rendered into canonical form) and the second element Rules is the list of rules in the definition. Each rule is a pair, composed of a list of left linear **patterns** (to the left of ->) and a **result** (to the right of ->). If <- is used then the equivalences of section 12.2 are used to represent the rule in terms of ->. A guarded rule 'p_1 … p_n -> r where g' is expressed as (@p [p_1 … p_n] [guard g r]).

The function freshen-sig replaces any variables in Sig by fresh terms since the proof must hold for all instances of the variables. Fresh terms are created using print vectors which are printed off as symbols but prefaced by &&.

```
(define freshen-sig
  Sig -> (let Vs (extract-vars Sig)
              Assoc (map (/. V [V | (freshterm (concat & V))]) Vs)
              (freshen-type Assoc Sig)))
```

```
(define freshen-type
  [] X -> X
  [[V | Fresh] | Assoc] X -> (freshen-type Assoc (subst Fresh V X)))
```

The name F of the function, the rules Rules and the signature Sig and a counter initialised to 1 are passed to t*-rules. If t*-rules succeeds, then the signature is unified to the original type A supplied to toplevel-forms.

```
(defprolog t*-rules
  _ (- []) _ _ <--;
  F (- [Rule | Rules]) A Counter <-- (bind Fresh (freshen-rule Rule))
                (t*-rule F Counter (fst (1 Fresh)) (snd (1 Fresh)) A)  !
                (t*-rules F Rules A (+ (0 Counter) 1));)
```

t*-rules recurses through the list of rules, incrementing the counter testing each rule by t*-rule. Following the reasoning of the previous section, each rule is treated as an independent test and the cut prevents backtracking after a failed test.

There is one other wrinkle to be observed; the variables in the type A and the patterns $p_1 \dots p_n$ are replaced by fresh terms. This avoids variable clash problems and unfortunate consequences that would arise from importing pattern variables as symbols into the proof. In particular since Shen variables are symbols, any variable could be 'proved' to be of type symbol by the primitive rule from $\mathfrak{I}$. To avoid this, the rule is 'freshened' before being passed forward to t*-rule.

```
(defprolog t*-rule
  _ _ Ps R A       <-- (t*-rule-h Ps R A);
  F Counter _ _ _ <-- (bind Err  (error "type error in rule ~A of ~A~%"
                (0 Counter) (0 F)));)
```

The t*-rule procedure passes on control to a help procedure; if the help procedure fails then the counter is printed as part of an error message. t*-rule-h receives a list Ps of patterns, a result R which is to be returned by Shen if the patterns fire and a type A. The task of t*-rule-h is to apply the integrity and correctness checks of section 30.3. A special case is where Ps = []. In that case the integrity test is skipped (since there are no patterns F must be a zero place function) and the control passes to t*-correct.

```
(defprolog t*-rule-h
  (- []) R (- [--> A])  <--  ! (t*-correct R A []);
  Ps R A         <--  (t*-integrity Ps A Hyps B) ! (t*-correct R B Hyps);)
```

The integrity test procedure t*-integrity performs integrity tests on the patterns and if these tests are successful, passes forward a set of hypotheses Hyps from these tests and the type B under which R is expected to fall if the Hyps are assumed. The system then performs a correctness test to verify that this is so. The correctness condition test is straightforward.

456

```
(defprolog t*-correct
  (- [where G R]) A Hyps <-- !  (bind CurryG (curry (0 G)))
                              (system-S-h CurryG boolean Hyps)  !
                              (t*-correct R A [[CurryG : verified] | Hyps]);
  R A Hyps              <-- (system-S-h (curry (0 R)) A Hyps);)
```

If the result R is guarded, then the system commits to proving that the guard G is boolean using system ℑ reasoning and if so, the hypothesis G : verified is added to the list of hypotheses. If R is not guarded then system ℑ is invoked on R. In all cases the expressions passed to system ℑ are curried.

```
(defprolog t*-integrity
  (- []) B [] B                            <--;
  (- [P | Ps]) (- [A --> B]) [Hyp | Hyps]  C    <--  (bind Hyp [P : A])
                                                   (p-hyps P PHyps)  !
                                                   (system-S-h P A PHyps)  !
                                                   (t*-integrity Ps B Hyps C);)
```

The t*-integrity predicate receives four inputs.

1. The list of patterns Ps.
2. The signature of the function.
3. A hypothesis variable Hyp which is eventually bound to the list of hypotheses needed to check R.
4. A variable C which is eventually bound to the expected type of R.

The procedure recurses over the list of patterns. In the base case where the list is empty, Hyp is bound to [] and C is bound to B which is the type of the result R. In the recursive case, p-hyps generates a list of hypotheses for testing the integrity of the first pattern P. This list is generated as the list of all typings $P_v : x$ where P_v is a fresh term in P (the site of a pattern matching variable) and x is a fresh Prolog variable. When this list of typings is generated, the procedure invokes system ℑ to test whether the integrity result holds

```
(defprolog p-hyps
  P PHyps <-- (when (freshterm? P)) ! (bind PHyps [[P : A]]);
  (- [X | Y]) PHyps <-- ! (p-hyps X XHyps)
                         (p-hyps Y YHyps)
                         (join XHyps YHyps PHyps);
  _ PHyps <-- (bind PHyps []);)
```

```
(defprolog join
  (- []) X X* <-- (bind X* X);
  (- [X | Y]) W [X* | Z] <-- (bind X* X) (join Y W Z);))
```

join is simply a Shen Prolog append, optimised here to avoid unnecessary occurs-check unifications.

457

Exercise 30

1. Melvin Micro types in the rules for binary numbers into Shen.

    (datatype binary

    > if (element? B [0 1])
    > _____
    > [B] : binary;
    >
    > B1 : binary; [B2 | Bs] : binary;
    > ========================
    > [B1 B2 | Bs] : binary;)

    and then types [(+ 1 0)] : binary and gets a type error. He is puzzled because (+ 1 0) is just 1 and [1] is a binary number. Explain why Melvin gets this error.

2. Melvin continues to experiment. He types in the definition of a function that removes all the internal [...]s from within a list.

    ```
    (define flat
      {(list (list A)) --> (list A)}
      [ ] -> []
      [[X | Y] | Z] -> (append (flat [X | Y]) (flat Z))
      [X | Y] -> [X | (flat Y)])
    ```

    and gets another type error. Why?

3. Melvin argues that this definition of complement is too long.

    ```
    (define complement
      [0] -> [1]
      [1] -> [0]
      [1 B | Bs] -> [0 | (complement [B | Bs])]
      [0 B | Bs] -> [1 | (complement [B | Bs])]
    ```

    He redefines it as

    ```
    (define complement
      {binary --> binary}
      [X] -> (if (= X 1) [0] [1])
      [X | Y] -> (if (= X 0) [1 | (complement Y)] [0 | (complement Y)]))
    ```

    He finds that with type checking disabled, this function works on binary numbers just like the old complement function does. However my_complement does not type check. Explain why.

Further Reading

The first practical type checking algorithm was incorporated into Edinburgh ML and is described in Milner (1975) and Field and Harrison (1988).

458

Appendix A

System Functions and their Types in Shen

- **absvector**

  Given a non-negative integer returns a vector in the native platform.

- **absvector?**

  A → boolean
  Recognisor for native vectors.

- **address->**

  Given an absolute vector A, a positive integer *i* and a value V places V in the A[*i*]th position.

- **<-address**

  Given an absolute vector A, a positive integer *i* retrieves V from the A[*i*]th position.

- **adjoin**

  A → (list A) → (list A)
  Conses an object to a list if it is not already an element.

- **and**

  boolean → boolean → boolean
  Boolean and.

- **append**

  (list A) → (list A) → (list A)
  Appends two lists into one list. Treated as polyadic by the reader.

- **arity**

  A → number
  Given a Shen function, returns its arity otherwise -1.

- **atom?**

  A → boolean
  Recognisor for atoms, i.e. symbols, strings, numbers, booleans and the empty list.

- **boolean?**

  A → boolean

  Recognisor for booleans.

- **bootstrap**

  string → string

  Given a filename to a Shen file pipes the Kλ code from the Shen code; returns the filename with a kl extension.

- **bound?**

  symbol → boolean

  Returns true if the variable is globally bound.

- **call**

  $\overline{}$

  A unary higher-order Prolog predicate that calls its argument.

- **cd**

  string → string

  Changes the home directory. (cd "Prog") causes (load "hello_world.txt") to load Prog/hello_world.txt. (cd "") is the default.

- **close**

  (stream A) → (list B)

  Closes a stream returning the empty list.

- **cn**

  string → string → string

  Concatenates two strings.

- **compile**

  (A ⇒ B) → A → B

  Applies a Shen YACC function to an input.

- **concat**

  $\overline{}$

  Concatenates two symbols or booleans.

- **cons**

  $\overline{}$

  A special form that takes an object *e* of type A and a list *l* of type (list A) and produces a list of type (list A) by adding *e* to the front of *l*.

- **cons?**
  A → boolean
  Returns true iff the input is a non-empty list.

- **declare**

  ‾
  Takes a function name *f* and a type *t* expressed as a list and gives *f* the type *t*.

- **destroy**
  symbol → symbol
  Receives the name of a function and removes its type from the environment.

- **difference**
  (list A) → (list A) → (list A)
  Subtracts the elements of the second list from the first.

- **do**
  A → (B → B)
  Returns its last argument; polyadic courtesy of the reader.

- **element?**
  A → (list A) → boolean
  Returns true iff the first input is an element in the second.

- **empty?**
  A → boolean
  Returns true iff the input is [ ].

- **enable-type-theory**
  symbol → boolean
  Takes + or - and enables/disables the Shen type system.

- **error**

  ‾
  A special form: takes a string followed by *n* (*n* ≥ 0) expressions. Prints error string.

- **error-to-string**
  exception → string
  Maps an error message to the corresponding string.

- **eval**

  ‾
  Evaluates the input.

461

- **eval-kl**

  Evaluates the input as a Kλ expression.

- **explode**
  A → (list string)
  Explodes an object to a list of strings.

- **external**
  symbol → (list symbol)
  Given a package name, returns the list of symbols external to that package.

- **factorise**
  symbol → boolean
  Takes + or - and enables/disables code factorisation.

- **fail**
  → symbol
  Returns the failure object – a symbol internal to the Shen package printed as ....

- **fix**
  (A → A) → (A → A)
  Applies a function to generate a fixpoint.

- **freeze**
  A → (lazy A)
  Returns a frozen version of its input.

- **fresh**

  Generates a print vector which is printed as a unique integer prefaced by &&t.
  This is used to generate arbitrary terms in type checking.

- **fst**
  (A * B) → A
  Returns the first element of a tuple.

- **gensym**
  symbol → symbol
  Generates a fresh symbol or variable from a symbol.

- **get-time**
  symbol → number
  For the argument *run* or *real* returns a number representing the real or run time elapsed since the last call. One of these options must be supported. For the argument *unix* returns the Unix time.

- **get**

  takes a symbol S, a pointer P and optionally a vector V and returns the value in V pointed by P from S (if one exists) or an error otherwise. If V is omitted the global property vector is used.

- **hash**
  A → number → number
  Returns a hashing of the first argument subject to the restriction that the encoding must not be greater than the second argument.

- **head**
  (list A) → A
  Returns the first element of a list; if the list is empty returns an error

- **hd**

  Returns the first element of a list; for [] the result is platform dependent.

- **hdstr**
  string → string
  Returns the first element of a string.

- **hdv**
  (vector A) → A
  Returns the first element of a standard vector.

- **if**
  boolean → A → A → A
  takes a boolean *b* and two expressions *x* and *y* and evaluates *x* if *b* evaluates to true and evaluates *y* if *b* evaluates to false.

- **implementation**
  → string
  Returns a string denoting the implementation on which Shen is running.

- **include**
  (list symbol) → (list symbol)
  Includes the datatype theories or synonyms for use in type checking.

- **include-all-but**
  (list symbol) → (list symbol)
  Includes all loaded datatype theories and synonyms for use in type checking apart from those entered.

- **inferences**
  → number
  Returns the number of logical inferences executed since the last call to the top level.

- **in-package**
  symbol → symbol
  Places the top level inside the package denoted by the input and returns the input.

- **input**

  $\overline{}$
  0-place function. Takes a user input *i* and returns the normal form of *i*.

- **input+**

  $\overline{}$
  Special form. Takes inputs of the form **<expr> <stream>**. If **<stream>** is not specified then defaults to standard input. *d*(**<expr>**) is the type denoted by the choice of expression (e.g. 'number' denotes the type number). Takes a user input *i* and returns the normal form of *i* given *i* is of the type *d*(**<expr>**).

- **integer?**
  A → boolean
  Recognisor for integers.

- **intern**

  $\overline{}$
  Maps a string to a symbol.

- **implementation**
  → string
  Returns the implementation of the language under which Shen is running.

- **intersection**
  (list A) → (list A) → (list A)
  Computes the intersection of two lists.

- **it**
  $\rightarrow$ string
  Returns the last input to standard input embedded in a string.

- **lambda**

  $\overline{}$
  Builds a lambda expression from a variable and an expression.

- **language**
  $\rightarrow$ string
  Returns a string denoting the language on which Shen is running.

- **length**
  (list A) $\rightarrow$ number
  Returns the number of elements in a list.

- **limit**
  (vector A) $\rightarrow$ number
  Returns the maximum index of a vector.

- **lineread**
  (stream in) $\rightarrow$ (list unit)
  Top level reader of read-evaluate-print loop. Reads elements into a list. **lineread** terminates with carriage return when brackets are balanced. $\wedge$ aborts lineread.

- **load**
  string $\rightarrow$ symbol
  Takes a file name and loads the file, returning **loaded** as a symbol.

- **macroexpand**

  $\overline{}$
  Expand an expression by the available macros.

- **map**
  (A $\rightarrow$ B) $\rightarrow$ (list A) $\rightarrow$ (list B)
  The first input is applied to each member of the second input and the results consed into one list.

- **mapcan**
  (A $\rightarrow$ (list B)) $\rightarrow$ (list A) $\rightarrow$ (list B)
  As map but the results appended into one list.

- **make-string**

  $\overline{}$
  A special form: takes a string followed by n ($n \geq 0$) well-typed expressions; assembles and returns a string.

- **maxinferences**

  number → number

  Returns the input and as a side-effect, sets a global variable to a number that limits the maximum number of inferences that can be expended on attempting to type check a program. The default is 10^6.

- **nl**

  number → number

  Prints *n* new lines.

- **not**

  boolean → boolean

  Boolean not.

- **nth**

  number → (list A) → A

  Gets the nth element of a list numbered from 1.

- **number?**

  A → boolean

  Recognisor for numbers.

- **n->string**

  number → string

  Given a number *n* returns a unit string whose ASCII number is *n*.

- **occurrences**

  A → B → number

  Returns the number of times the first argument occurs in the second.

- **occurs-check**

  symbol → boolean

  Receives either + or - and enables/disables occur checking in Prolog, datatype definitions and rule closures. The default is +.

- **open**

  Takes two arguments; the location from which it is drawn and the direction (*in* or *out*) and creates either a source or a sink stream.

- **optimise**

  symbol → boolean

  Takes either + or -. If + then Kλ code may be optimised to take advantage of type information.

- **or**

  boolean → (boolean → boolean)

  Boolean or.

- **os**

  → string

  Returns a string denoting the operating system on which Shen is running.

- **output**

  A special form: takes a string followed by n ($n \geq 0$) well-typed expressions; prints a message to the screen and returns an object of type string (the string "done").

- **package**

  Takes a symbol, a list of symbols and any number of expressions and places them in a package.

- **package?**

  symbol → boolean

  Returns **true** if the symbol names a package else returns **false**.

- **port**

  → string

  Returns a string denoting the version of the port under which Shen is running.

- **porters**

  → string

  Returns a string denoting the people who ported Shen.

- **pos**

  string → number → string

  Given a string and a natural number n returns the nth unit string numbering from zero.

- **pr**

  string → (stream out) → string

  Takes a string, a sink object and prints the string to the sink, returning the string as a result. If no stream is supplied defaults to the standard output.

- **preclude**

  (list symbol) → (list symbol)

  Removes the mentioned datatype theories and synonyms from use in type checking.

- **preclude-all-but**

  (list symbol) → (list symbol)

  Removes all the datatype theories and synonyms from use in type checking apart from the ones given.

- **print**

  A → A

  Takes an object and prints it, returning it as a result.

- **profile**

  (A → B) → (A → B)

  Takes a function represented by a function name and inserts profiling code returning the function as an output.

- **profile-results**

  (A → B) → ((A → B) * number)

  Takes a profiled function f and returns the total run time expended on f since profile-results was last invoked.

- **prolog-memory**

  number → number

  The size of the binding vector used in Shen Prolog.

- **protect**

  A → A

  The identity function but used to protect free variables.

- **ps**

  symbol → (list unit)

  Receives a symbol denoting a Shen function and prints the Kλ source code associated with the function.

- **put**

  3-place function that takes a symbol S, a pointer P (a string symbol or number), and an expression E. The pointer P is set to point from S to the normal form of E which is then returned.

- **read**

  (stream in) → unit

  Reads off the first Shen token from a stream; defaults with zero arguments to standard input.

- **read-byte**

  (stream in) → number

  As read but the token is a byte..

- **read-file**
  string → (list unit)
  Returns the contents of an ASCII file designated by a string.

- **read-file-as-bytelist**
  string → (list number)
  Returns the contents of an ASCII file designated by a string as a list of bytes.

- **read-file-as-string**
  string → string
  Returns the string contents of an ASCII file designated by a string.

- **read-from-string**
  string → (list unit)
  Reads a list of expressions from a string.

- **read-from-string-unprocessed**
  string → (list unit)
  Reads a list of expressions from a string without macroexpansion.

- **remove**
  A → (list A) → (list A)
  Removes all occurrences of an element from a list.

- **reverse**
  (list A) → (list A)
  Reverses a list.

- **simple-error**
  string → A
  Given a string, raises it as an error message.

- **snd**
  (A * B) → B
  Returns the second element of a tuple.

- **specialise**
  symbol → number → symbol
  Receives a symbol f, and $n = 0$, 1 or 2 and returns f. If $n = 0$, then f is treated as denoting a function. If $n = 1$, applications of f are not curried and f is not treated as denoting a function. If $n = 2$ noncurrying applies to all subexpressions in the scope of f.

- **spy**
  symbol → boolean
  Receives either + or − and enables/disables tracing the operation of $\mathcal{T}^*$.

469

- **step**
  symbol → boolean
  Receives either + or – and enables/disables stepping in the trace.

- **stinput**
  → (stream in)
  Returns the standard input stream.

- **stoutput**
  → (stream out)
  Returns the standard output stream.

- **str**
  A → string
  Given an atom (boolean, symbol, string, number) flanks it in quotes. For other inputs an error may be returned.

- **string?**
  A → boolean
  Recognisor for strings.

- **string->n**
  string → number
  Maps a unit string to its code point.

- **subst**

  Given (subst $x\ y\ z$) replaces y by x in z where z is a list or an atom.

- **sum**
  (list number) → number
  Sums a list of numbers.

- **symbol?**
  A → boolean
  Recognisor for symbols.

- **systemf**
  symbol → symbol
  Gives the symbol the status of an identifier for a system function; its definition may not be overwritten'. Returns the symbol itself.

- **tail**
  (list A) → (list A)
  Returns all but the first element of a non-empty list.

- **tc**

  symbol → boolean

  Receives either + or − and respectively enables/disables static typing.

- **tc?**

  A → boolean

  Returns true iff typechecking is enabled.

- **thaw**

  (lazy A) → A

  Receives a frozen input and evaluates it to get the unthawed result.

- **time**

  ‾

  Prints the run time for the evaluation of its input and returns its normal form.

- **tl**

  ‾

  Returns the tail of a list; for [] the result is platform dependent.

- **tlstr**

  string → string

  Returns the tail of a string.

- **tlv**

  (vector A) → (vector A)

  Returns the tail of a non-empty vector.

- **track**

  symbol → symbol

  Tracks the I/O behaviour of a function.

- **trap-error**

  A → (exception → A) → A

  Tracks the I/O behaviour of a function.

- **tuple?**

  A → boolean

  Recognisor for tuples.

- **type**

  ‾

  Takes an expression *e* and a type A; *e* is passed as type secure if *e* inhabits A.

- **undefmacro**
  symbol → symbol
  Removes a macro.

- **union**
  (list A) → (list A) → (list A)
  Forms the union of two lists.

- **unprofile**
  (A → B) → (A → B)
  Unprofiles a function.

- **unput**

  $\overline{\text{Given}}$ arguments x and y removes (put x y z) for any z.

- **untrack**
  symbol → symbol
  Untracks a function.

- **update-lambda-table**

  $\overline{\text{Takes}}$ a name of a function f and a positive integer n and sets the arity for f as n.

- **value**

  $\overline{\text{Applied}}$ to a symbol, returns the global value assigned to it.

- **variable?**
  A → boolean
  Applied to a variable, returns true.

- **version**
  string → string
  Changes the version string displayed on startup.

- **vector**
  number → (vector A)
  Creates a vector of size n.

- **vector?**
  A → boolean
  Recognises a standard vector.

- **vector->**

(vector A) → number → A → (vector A)

Given a vector V and an index *i* and object *o*, assigns *o* to V[*i*].

- **<-vector**

(vector Λ) → number → A

Given a vector V and an index *i* retrieves V[*i*].

- **warn**

As output but only outputs an error message if warnings are set.

- **warnings**

symbol → boolean

Takes + (default) or − and enables/disables warnings

- **write-byte**

number → (stream out) → number

Takes a byte as an integer *n* between 0 and 255 and writes the corresponding byte to the stream returning *n*.

- **write-to-file**

string → A → A

Writes the second input into a file named in the first input. If the file does not exist, it is created, else it is overwritten. If the second input is a string then it is written to the file without the enclosing quotes. The second input is returned.

- **y-or-n?**

string → boolean

Prints the string as a question and returns true for y and false for n.

- **@p**

Takes *n* (*n* > 1) inputs and forms the tuple.

- **@s**

Takes *n* (*n* > 1) strings and forms their concatenation

- **@v**

Takes *n* inputs, the last being a vector V and forms a vector of these elements appended to the front of V.

- **<e>**

(list A) ⇒ (list B)

Used by Shen YACC – indicates the ε (empty) expansion in a grammar..

473

- **<!>**

  (list A) $\Rightarrow$ (list A)

  Used by Shen YACC – consumes the remaining input and returns it.

- **<end>**

  (list A) $\Rightarrow$ (list A)

  Succeeds if the parse object has been consumed else fails.

- **+**

  number $\rightarrow$ number $\rightarrow$ number

  Number addition.

- **−**

  number $\rightarrow$ number $\rightarrow$ number

  Number subtraction.

- *****

  number $\rightarrow$ number $\rightarrow$ number

  Number multiplication.

- **/**

  number $\rightarrow$ number $\rightarrow$ number

  Number division.

- **>**

  number $\rightarrow$ number $\rightarrow$ boolean

  Greater than.

- **<**

  number $\rightarrow$ number $\rightarrow$ boolean

  Less than.

- **=**

  A $\rightarrow$ A $\rightarrow$ boolean

  Equal to.

- **==**

  A $\rightarrow$ B $\rightarrow$ boolean

  Equal to.

- **>=**

  number $\rightarrow$ number $\rightarrow$ boolean

  Greater than or equal to.

- **<=**

  number $\rightarrow$ number $\rightarrow$ boolean

  Less than or equal to.

Appendix B

The Shen Reader

The Shen reader reads in the user input from either file or keyboard in the same manner. Input is read as a stream of bytes (e.g. hello is read as 104 101 108 108 111) which are read in one by one and mapped to their character representation in Shen by the tokeniser. The reader behaves as the identity function except for the following cases where whitespace <ws> is inserted.

Chars	Reader Action
}	Read as <ws> } <ws>.
{	Read as <ws> { <ws>.
[	Read as <ws> [<ws>. See] below.
]	All tokens between] and the previous [are placed into cons form
;	Read as <ws> ; <ws>.
,	Read as <ws> , <ws>.
\\	Comment opener. Skip reading until the next carriage return
*	Comment opener. Skip reading until *\.
|	Read as <ws> bar <ws>
"	Suspend all special reader actions and read in the stream verbatim until the matching " is found.

Associative Functions

In the case of common associative functions Shen follows the usual mathematical practice in regarding them as polyadic and treating the internal parentheses as unwanted hair. The polyadic forms in Shen are +, *, and, or, append, /., @s, @p and let. Thus (and (and P Q) R) can be written as (and P Q R).

Syntax Rules for Shen Definitions

The syntax of Shen is presented as a context-free grammar in BNF notation annotated where necessary to explain certain context-sensitive restrictions. Terminals which represent parts of the Shen language are bolded, and in particular the bar | in Shen is bolded to **|** to distinguish it from the | used in the BNF to separate alternatives. For all X, the expansion $<X> ::= \varepsilon \mid \ldots$ indicates that $<X>$ may be expanded to an empty series of expressions.

<Shen def> ::= (**define** < lowercase > {<types>} <rules>)
           | (**define** <lowercase> <rules>)
           | (**defmacro** <lowercase> <rules>)
<lowercase> ::= any <symbol> not beginning in uppercase
<rules> ::= <rule> | <rule> <rules>
<rule> ::= <patterns> -> <item> | <patterns> <- <item>
       | <patterns> -> <item> **where** <item>
        | <patterns> <- <item> **where** <item>
<patterns> ::= ε | <pattern> <patterns>
<pattern> ::= <base> (except -> and <-)
              | [<pattern> <patterns> I <pattern>]
                | [<patterns>] | (**cons** <pattern> <pattern>)
                | (**@p** <pattern> <pattern> <patterns>)
                | (**@s** <pattern> <pattern> <patterns>)
                | (**@v** <pattern> <pattern> <patterns>)
<item> ::= <base> | [<items> I <item>] | [<items>]
         | <application> | <abstraction>
<items> ::= <item> | <item> <items>
<base> ::= <symbol> (except I) | <string> | <boolean> | <number> | ( ) | [ ]
<application> ::= (<items>)
<abstraction> ::= (/. <variables> <item>)
<variables> ::= <variable> | <variable> <variables>
<variable> ::= any <symbol> beginning in uppercase
<types> ::= ε | (<types>) | <types> --> <types> | <symbol>

<symbol> := <alpha> <symbolchars> | <alpha>
<symbolchars> := <alpha> <symbolchars>
                  | <digit> <symbolchars>
                  | <alpha>
                  | <digit>

<alpha> ::= a | b | c | d | e | f | g | h | i | j | k | l | m |
          n | o | p | q | r | s | t | u | v | w | x | y | z |
          A | B | C | D | E | F | G | H | I | J | K | L |
          M | N | O | P | Q | R | S | T | U | V | W | X | Y | Z | .
          = | - | * | / | + | _ | ? | $ | ! | @ | ~ | > | < | & | % | ' | # | ` | ; | : | { | }

<digit> ::= 0 | 1 | 2 | 3 | 4 | 5 | 6 | 7 | 8 | 9

<number> ::= <signs> <float> | <signs> <integer> | <signs> <e-number>
<signs> ::= ε | + <signs> | - <signs>
<float> ::= <digits> . <digits> | . <digits>
<integer> ::= <digits>
<digits> ::= <digit> | <digit> <digits>
<e-number> ::= <integer> **e** - <integer> | <integer> **e** <integer>
               | <float> **e** - <integer> | <float> **e** < integer>

476

Syntax Rules for Shen Datatype Definitions

\<datatype_definition\> ::= (**datatype** \<lowercase\> \<datatype-rules\>)
\<datatype-rules\> ::= \<datatype-rule\> | \<datatype-rule\> \<datatype-rules\>
\<datatype-rule\> :: = \<side conditions\> \<schemes\> \<underline\> \<scheme\>;
   | \<side conditions\> \<simple schemes\> \<double underline\> \<formula\>;
\<side conditions\> ::= ε | \<side condition\> | \<side condition\> \<side conditions\>
\<side condition\> ::= **if** \<item\> | **let** \< prolog-pattern\> \<item\>
                 | **let!** \< prolog-pattern\> \<item\>
\<underline\> ::= _ | one or more concatenations of the underscore _
\<double underline\> ::= = | one or more concatenations of =
\<simple schemes\> ::= \<formula\> ; | \<formula\> ; \<simple schemes\>
\<formula\> := \<item\> : \<item\> | \<item\>
\<schemes\> ::= ε | \<scheme\> ; \<schemes\>
\<scheme\> ::= \<assumptions\> >> \<formula\> | \<formula\>
\<assumptions\> ::= \<formula\> | \<formula\>, \<assumptions\>

Syntax Rules for Shen Prolog Definitions

\<prolog_definition\> ::= (**defprolog** \<lowercase\> \<clauses\>)
\<clauses\> ::= \<clause\> | \<clause\> \<clauses\>
\<clause\> ::= \<head\> **\<--** \<tail\>;
\<head\> ::= \<prolog-patterns\>
\<prolog-patterns\> ::= ε | \<prolog-pattern\> \<prolog-patterns\>
\<prolog-pattern\> ::= \<base\>
                | [\<prolog-pattern\> \<prolog-patterns\> | \<prolog-pattern\>]
                | [\<prolog-patterns\>]
                | (**cons** \<prolog-pattern\> \<prolog-pattern\>)
\<tail\> := ε | ! \<tail\> | \<application\> \<tail\>

Appendix C

The Next Lisp: Back to the Future

This talk was delivered in Milan in May 2009 to the European Symposium on Lisp and it was the first talk in which Shen was mentioned. It lays out fairly clearly the motivation for Shen and how the project was to be carried out. The criticisms of Common Lisp in this talk were not well received by the audience.

OK; from the title we're obviously going to talk about Lisp. It might seem tricky if I start off by debating exactly what we mean by 'Lisp'. But I'm going to do just that because it will shed a light on what I'm going to say. And I'm going to start off with a biological metaphor, and there will be a few of them in this talk. I hope any biologists out there will forgive me.

In biology there is a distinction between *genotype* and *phenotype*. The genotype of a person is the genetic legacy that the person carries. The phenotype is the way that genetic legacy expresses itself. So, for example, you might find that you carry a gene from your father for blue eyes and one from your mother for brown eyes. Your genotype is blue-brown, but your phenotype is the way your eyes appear which is brown.

Applied to languages the genotype of the language is the DNA of the language. It incorporates the essential ideas of the language. The phenotype is the actualisation of those ideas on a platform.

If we ask ourselves, 'What is the genotype of Lisp?', what is its DNA, its genetic legacy, I'd suggest that it is composed of the following five ideas.

1. Recursion as the primary mean of expressing procedure calling.
2. Heterogeneous lists for composing and dissecting complex data.
3. Programming by defining functions.
4. Garbage collection.
5. Programs as data.

So having defined Lisp as a genotype, we can now ask what we mean by 'Lisp'. Are we talking about a genotype - a particular set of ideas, or a phenotype, the way those ideas are represented on the computer? If we're talking about a genotype then Lisp is doing very well. Python, Ruby, NewLisp, Clojure and even TCL/tk are all inheritors of this genetic legacy. But I guess if I stood here and talked about Python for an hour nobody would be too pleased. So I have to talk about phenotypes, and the main one is Common Lisp and that is not doing so well.

What Went Wrong with Common Lisp?

To understand Common Lisp and what has gone wrong with it, we have to begin with Lisp 1.5. Lisp 1.5 was the brainchild of John McCarthy and his group and it was the first practical Lisp to incorporate all the ideas of the Lisp genotype. Lisp 1.5 was maybe 30 years ahead of the game in terms of programming language design. A lot of very bright guys ran with the idea and it mutated into a polyphony of Lisp dialects - Zeta Lisp, DEC-10 Lisp, InterLisp-D and so on. So Common Lisp was devised as an acceptable political solution for unifying the many tongues of Lisp. But now, 25 years on, it is not the dominant phenotype of the Lisp genotype. Why?

The answer is that quite a few mistakes were made with Common Lisp. The first was that it was too big. The drive was to make the language compatible with the previous dialects and the easiest way was to union these features together. This is generally what happens when you get a committee of guys each with their own input. The language specification explodes.

But for all the size of the CL spec, there are things that are missing from it. The foreign language interface is not defined. Calling the OS is possible in CL but every platform does it differently. Threads and concurrency are nowhere in sight (remember this is 1984).

The Common Lisp community has tried to deal with this through libraries. But these libraries are unsupported, and either undocumented or poorly so. I regard this as partly a weakness of the open source model, but of this another time. But the result is that CL has become unpopular with developers who want a good solution which is free and well supported. For that they turn to Python.

On the academic front CL is not popular as an introduction to functional programming and is the victim of early standardisation. To a degree, CL is a snapshot of functional programming in the '70s. Pattern-matching and static typing are not there. There is much in CL that is heavily procedural, too much so for teachers trying to convey the art of functional programming. The syntax is viewed as unattractive, Larry Wall's comment that 'Lisp has the visual appeal of oatmeal with finger nail clippings mixed in.' is funny and irreverent, but largely true. It's a great language but it doesn't look great.

I guess a review of past mistakes would be incomplete without a look at Lisp machines. In 'The Bipolar Lisp Programmer' I talked about brilliant failures and the Lisp machines were exactly that. The basic idea was simple: make Lisp run fast by making it run on special hardware. The problem was that in the mid-80s standard hardware was doubling in performance every 18 months. So a Lisp machine that promised at the design stage to be 10x faster than conventional hardware might be 5x faster by the time it appeared and that advantage would last only 2 years or so.

Symbolics woke up far too late that the real strength of the company lay in its ideas - in Genera. In our biological terms, they had got stuck on obsessing over the phenotype, and missed the significance of the genotype. So the DNA of Genera got trapped on a dying phenotype and today all that work is a lost investment. Imagine what the Lisp community would be like today if Symbolics had done what Torvalds did later and moved their ideas onto a PC!

When the CL community is exposed to criticism of CL their attitude is confrontational and conservative. For example, nearly every other newbie who hits CL for the first time complains about the brackets. And when they do they are told to shut up because they don't understand Lisp. Actually that response shows that the shushers don't understand Lisp, because the Lisp genotype is not hung on the idea of brackets. Guido van Rossum realised that in creating Python. Python is not new; it's just a sugaring on the Lisp genotype in favour of a syntax that people feel comfortable with. And look how far that idea went.

Along with all these ills went another - **macro laziness**. CL programmers think that macros are absolutely central whereas they are not. In Qi, the defmacro construction could be eliminated from the source without remainder by using the programmable reader. I've left them in because of laziness. But macro laziness arises when a challenge to CL is met by 'I could always write a macro to do that'. It's the same response of the slob on the sofa watching TV and saying 'I can always get into shape'. Actually being in shape and being able to get in shape are not the same. And since CL has stayed on the same sofa for 25 years, getting this fat specification from the supine position and into shape is not easy.

So what lessons do we learn from all this? I make about 7, which is a nice magical number.

1.   Don't bet the farm on a cumbersome language standard that is difficult to change and replace.
2.   Create a standard approach to common problems like concurrency, threads and OS calling.
3.   Hive off stuff into libraries.
4.   Absorb the lessons of programming development going on around you.
5.   Don't get trapped in a phenotype - whether machine or language.
6.   Listen to your critics - particularly newbies.
7.   Learn to communicate.

Qi

Now I want to talk a bit about my own work on Qi. By the way, I have pronounced it as 'Q Eye' for years which is wrong. I got the habit from my students. It really should be 'chee' which is the Taoist concept of life force. I'm a Taoist and hope to return to the mountains one day. But right now I'm here in the world of men and so I'll continue talking for a while.

Qi began life in the Laboratory for the Foundations of Computer Science in 1989. It owes its character from observing the activity with Standard ML, since the LFCS was the origin of that particular language. Essentially Qi is a harmonious fusion of three different paradigms; a functional one based on pattern-directed list handling and using sequent calculus to define types; a logic programming component based on Prolog and a language-oriented component based on compiler-compiler technology.

It's a powerful combination and it's not an accidental one. Each component has an important part to play in the coding of Qi. The compiler-compiler is used to frame the reader and writer, the Prolog compiles the sequent calculus to code and the functional language does nearly everything else. The result is that the source is amazingly small - about 2000 lines, but packs a punch like Bruce Lee who was built on the same scale.

The idea of Qi was to provide a programming environment based on CL but with the features of a modern functional programming environment. In fact, Qi is ahead of functional programming design in many of its features. Its generally efficient, being faster in execution than hand-coded native CL and has all the features of the Lisp genotype while being about 3x more compact for programming purposes than CL. It comes with a book and a collection of correctness proofs that nobody reads.

Qi is very powerful, but it is not computationally adequate as it stands. 'Computational adequacy' is a term I've coined to describe the characteristics that a language has when it is adequate for the needs of the programmers of the day. CL was computationally adequate in 1984 but is not today. Computational adequacy today means finding good answers to questions of how to provide threads, concurrency, FFI, GUI support and so on. Qi is not computationally adequate because it is written in CL which is itself not computationally adequate. I'm going to talk about what I've been doing to fix that, because it reflects back on the way that Lisp itself should go.

The general strategy of Qi development can be summed up in 6 aphorisms.

481

1. Grab the easy stuff.
2. Featurise out differences.
3. Infiltrate don't confront.
4. Isolate the core.
5. The genotype is always more important than the phenotype.
6. Educate people.

Since Qi is written in CL, grabbing the easy stuff meant grabbing the CL libraries and bits of the CL specification. **CLStrings**, **CLMaths** and **CLErrors** are all part of the Qi library and they bring type security to CL maths, string and error handling. CLHash and ClStreams are on the way. They are easy pickings. The combined sum is a lazy week's work.

Parts of the Qi library are not part of CL. **Qi/tk** is the biggest. The type theory of Qi/tk is 511 lines of Qi that generates over 200 rules and axioms of sequent calculus. This in turn generates over 27,000 lines of Common Lisp. But it's quick. A game program of 561 lines type checks and compiles in 5 seconds under CLisp (1-2 seconds under SBCL). It includes constraint propagation that allows you to dynamically link the properties of widgets to each other.

I've begun to featurise out the differences between CL implementations; there is one way to quit, one way to save an image and hopefully one day, one way to call the OS. Our goal is to make the Lisp platform invisible; and by 'Lisp' I'm talking about the Lisp genotype not the phenotype.

'CL is great and Blub is crap' has not worked as a strategy for selling Common Lisp. People invest years of their life learning Blub and don't want to hear this message. A strategy of infiltration is better. The **Q machines** are intended as a collection of machines that cross-compile Qi into any member of the Lisp genotype. Qi compiles into CL, but **Quip** compiles Qi into Python and that already exists. Clojure, Ruby, Perl are later targets. Qi can be used to provide optional type security for untyped languages like Python. The proper destination for Qi is as a universal metalanguage. Write once, run anywhere.

The Kernel Lisp Project: Back to the Future

When I started thinking of porting Qi to other members of the Lisp genotype I looked at the CL sources for Qi. They are amazingly small. About 8,500 lines from 2,000 lines of Qi. Because I'm a conservative coder nearly all of Qi is running on the Lisp 1.5 core. In all there are about 68 primitive functions in Qi and many of them like CADR are not really primitive. If we talk about 'kernel functions' meaning the stuff that is really primitive then we're down to about 50, if that.

This kernel defines a Lisp, call it **Kλ**, that is the kernel necessary to run Qi. Now the interesting bit is that Qi is mapped to Python etc. through a mapping from the Qi-generated Lisp source to the Python language. So by mapping Kλ to Blub, you get a version of Qi that runs under Blub.

Based on this idea, this opens the prospect of a new Lisp that would be effectively a virtual machine for the entire Lisp genotype. Kλ would and should be an enhanced version of Lisp 1.5, getting back to the roots of Lisp. By defining Kλ and running Qi and the Q machine cross-compilers on Kλ, we get a unified platform for the entire Lisp genotype with Qi functionality; state of the art thinking in functional programming across the genotype spectrum.

This process I call **kernelisation** is going to change the shape of a lot of computing in the next decade, in the way that RISC changed hardware in the '80s. In particular the profusion of different languages we have at the moment will be tamed through this technique. Kernelisation is really the computing analogue of **formalisation** - that expression of the mathematician's hunger for simplicity in the expression of formal systems; the fewest primitives and the fewest axioms needed to derive what we take as true. Formalisation issued in rich developments of mathematical logic like Zermelo-Frankel set theory and it was used to tame the wildness of C19 mathematics. Today I see us as poised to tame computing in the C21 in the same way.

Back to Lisp. What should Kλ look like? I've already given one answer relative to Qi; that it should incorporate all the functions necessary to run Qi. But Qi is itself not complete as a language specification. For example in *Functional Programming in Qi* I don't deal with how to interact with streams. The reason I don't deal with this and other such issues is that CL already deals with them and I assumed those people who wanted to learn how to do this would learn CL. But if Qi becomes portable across the Lisp genotype then that aspect will have to be addressed.

Hence the shape and the form of Kλ is not determined by Qi even though it should support Qi. But the general shape and form are, I think, reasonably clear. There has to be several components of Kλ.

1. **A Turing-equivalent subset based on classical functional programming.** This subset should be *really really* small. For instance you can build a decent functional model using if, = (generic equality), basic arithmetic and λ (for abstractions). Cons, car and cdr are all λ definable. All the utility functions go into a standard library.

2. **It should be dynamically typed but support detailed type annotations.** Qi can provide a wealth of detail about the types of Lisp

expressions which compilers can eat up. Kernel Lisp needs to be able to use this.

3. **It should support arrays, streams, concurrency, error handling in a straightforward way.** CLErrors is tiny but does what I need. One objection is that we still don't know how best to handle concurrency. But that does not matter, we can decide conventions on calling concurrency and leave it to developers to decide how to implement it.

4. **There should be an open source, freely available Kλ library for CL.** CL survives in library form. CL developers can load this library. Kλ would be an enormous help for implementers of CL. Right now there is too much reduplicated effort going on in a small community for CL to prosper. Putting all the stuff in a library would leave developers free to optimize Kλ and would improve Lisp performance no end.

To continue with the biological metaphor, Qi has wonderful viral characteristics; it is small and easy to move and because of its conservative encoding it will fit comfortably into Kλ. Once established on top of any instance of the Lisp genotype it forms a symbiotic relation with the host language improving the general well-being of the language it symbiotes. I hope with the help of the functional community we can make this dream happen.

(The Shen project was sponsored 18 months after this talk of May 2009 and the first version of Shen appeared in September 2011)

Bibliography

Abelson H. and Sussman G.J.
Structure and Interpretation of Computer Programs, 2nd edition, MIT Press, 1996.

Abramsky S., Gabbay D.M. and Maibaum T.S.
Handbook of Logic in Computer Science, vols. 1-6, Clarendon Press, Oxford, 1993-5.

Adams A. A.
"INDUCT: A Logical Framework for Induction over Natural Numbers and Lists built in SEQUEL", M.Sc. thesis, Leeds Computer Studies 1994.

Aho A.V. and Ullman J.D.
The Theory of Parsing, Translation and Compiling. Vol. 1 Englewood Cliffs, NJ: Prentice Hall, 1972.

Aiken A. and Murphy B.
"Static type inference in a dynamically typed language" In Proc. 18th ACM Symposium on Principles of Programming Languages, 1991.

Aiken A. et al.
"Soft typing with Dependent Types", In Proc. 18th *ACM Symposium on Principles of Programming Languages*, 1994.

Ait-Kaci H. and Podelski A.
"Towards a meaning of LIFE", *Journal of Logic Programming*, 1993.

Allen J.
The Anatomy of Lisp, McGraw-Hill, 1978.

Andrews P.B.
"Theorem Proving via General Matings", JACM 28, 2, 1981.

Aubin R.
"Mechanising Structural Induction", Theoretical Computer Science, 1979.

Baber R.L.
The Spine of Software: Designing Provably Correct Software, Theory and Practice, Chichester: Wiley, 1987.

Backhouse R.
"Constructive Type Theory: a perspective from computing science" in Dijkstra (ed.) 1990.

Backus J.
"Can Programming be liberated from the von Neumann style? A functional style and its algebra of programs", *CACM*, 1978.

Baeten J. and J. Bergstra
"Term Rewriting Systems with Priorities", in *Rewriting Techniques and Applications*, LNCS 256, Springer-Verlag, 1986.

Barendregt H.P.
The Lambda Calculus: its syntax and semantics, North Holland, 1984.

Barendregt H.P.
"Lambda Calculus with Types", in Abramsky, Gabbay and Maibaum, vol. 2, 1993.

Bartree T.
Digital computer Fundamentals, Tata-McGraw-Hill, 2004

Basin D.A. & Kaufmann M.
"The Boyer-Moore Prover and NuPrl: An Experimental Comparison", *Logical Frameworks*, CUP, 1991.

Beckert B. and Posegga J.
"leanT^{A}P: Lean Tableau-based Deduction", JAR 1997.

Bibel W.
"On matrices with connections", J. ACM 1981.

Bibel W. and Jorrand P.
Fundamentals of Artificial Intelligence: an advanced course, Springer-Verlag, 1986.

Bird R.S.
"The Promotion and Accumulation Strategies in Transformational Programming", *ACM Transactions on Programming Languages and Systems* 6, 1984.

Bird R. and Wadler P.
Introduction to Functional Programming, Prentice-Hall, 1998.

Blasius K.H. and Burckert H.J.
Deduction Systems in Artificial Intelligence, Ellis Horwood, 1989.

Bobrow D.G. and Winograd T.
"An Overview of KRL", *Cognitive Science* I, 1977.

Boolos G.S., Burgess J.P. and Jeffrey R.C.
Computability and Logic, 4th edition, Cambridge University Press, 2002.

Boyer R. S. and Moore J. S.
A Computational Logic, Academic Press, 1979.

Boyer R. S. and Moore J. S.
A Computational Logic Handbook, Academic Press, 1997.

Bove. A. and Dybjer P.
"Dependent Types at Work", *Language Engineering and Rigorous Software Development*, Springer, 2008.

Baier C. and Katoen J.
Principles of Model Checking, MIT Press, 2008.

486

Bratko I.
Prolog Programming for Artificial Intelligence, Addison-Wesley, 2000.

de Bruijn N.G.
"Lambda Calculus Notation with Nameless Dummies, a tool for automatic formula manipulation, with application to the Church-Rosser theorem", Indag. Math., 1972.

Bundy A.
The Mechanisation of Mathematical Reasoning, Academic Press, 1983.

Bundy A., Stevens A., Harmelen F., Ireland A., & Smaill A.
"Rippling: A heuristic for guiding inductive proofs", *Artificial Intelligence* 1993.

Burstall R. A and Darlington J.
"A Transformation Program for Developing Recursive Programs", *Journal of the ACM*, 24, 1977.

Burstall R.., MacQueen D., Sannella D.: HOPE: An Experimental Applicative Language. LISP Conference 1980:

Cardelli L.
"The Functional Abstract Machine", *Polymorphism*, vol. 1., #1, 1983.

Cartwright R. and Fagan M.
"Soft typing". In *Proc. SIGPLAN '91 Conference on Programming Language Design and Implementation*, 1991, 278--292.

Cerrito S. and Kesner D.
"Pattern Matching as Cut Elimination", *Logic in Computer Science*, 1999.

Chang C. and Lee R.
Symbolic Logic and Mechanical Theorem Proving, Academic Press, 1973.

Charniak E. and McDermott D.
Introduction to Artificial Intelligence, Addison Wesley, 1985.

Church A.
"A Note on the Entscheidungsproblem", *Journal of Symbolic Logic*, 1936.

Church A.
The Calculi of Lambda Conversion, Princeton University Press, 1941.

Codd E.
"Relational Completeness of Data Base Sublanguages". Database Systems: 65–98

Colby K.
Artificial Paranoia, New York: Pergamon Press, 1975.

Constable R.
Implementing Mathematics with the Nuprl Proof Development System, Createspace, 2012.

487

Cooke D.J. and Bez H.E.
Computer Mathematics, Cambridge University Press, 1984.

Crochemore M. and Hancart C., "Automata for matching patterns", in *Handbook of Formal Languages*, G. Rosenberg and A. Saloma, eds., volume 2, Linear Modeling, Springer-Verlag, 1997.

Date C. J. and Darwen H.
The SQL Standard, 4th edition, Addison-Wesley, 1996.

Darlington J., Henderson P., and Turner D.A.
Functional Programming and its Applications, an advanced course, Cambridge University Press, 1982.

Davis M. and Putnam H.
"A Computing Procedure for Quantification Theory", *Journal of the Association of Computing Machinery*, 1960.

DeMillo R., Lipton R., and Perlis A.
"Social Processes and Proofs of Theorems and Programs", *Communications of the ACM* 22, 1979.

Dijkstra E.W.
Formal Development of Programs and Proofs, Addison-Wesley, 1990.

Diller A.
Compiling Functional Languages, John Wiley, 1988.

Diller A.
Z: an Introduction to Formal Methods, John Wiley, 1990.

Dreyfus, H. L.
What computers can't do : a critique of artificial reason, New York: Harper & Row, 1972.

Dreyfus, H. L.
What computers still can't do: a critique of artificial reason Cambridge, Mass. London: MIT Press, 1992.

Duffy D.
Principles of Automated Theorem Proving, Wiley, 1991.

Eder E.
"An Implementation of a Theorem Prover Based on the Connection Method", *Artificial Intelligence*, ed. Bible and Petkoff, North-Holland, 1985.

Eisinger N. and Nonnengart A.
"Term Rewriting Systems", in Blasius and Burckert, 1989.

Emmer, M..
SNOBOL4+: The SNOBOL4 Language for the Personal Computer User. Englewood Cliffs, NJ: Prentice Hall, 1985

Faé M. I. and Tarver M.
"Wardrop's Principle Revisited: a multiagent approach", *ANPET 2002*.

Ferber J.
Multi-Agent Systems: An Introduction to Distributed Artificial Intelligence, Addison Wesley, 1999

Fetzer J.H.
Communications of the ACM 31, 1988.
Artificial Intelligence: its Scope and Limits, Kluwer Academic Publishers, 1990.

Field A. J. and Harrison P. G.
Functional Programming, Addison-Wesley, 1988.

Fitting M.
Proof Methods for Modal and Intuitionistic Logics, Synthese library, 1983.

Frost R.A.
Introduction to Knowledge Based Systems, Collins, 1986.

Futumara Y.
"Partial Computation of Programs", in Goto ed. *RIMS Symposia on Software Engineering and Science*, LNCS, Springer-Verlag 1983.

Gabbay D.M. and Robinson J.A.
Handbook of Logic in Artificial Intelligence and Logic Programming Hogger C.J. Vols 1-6, Clarendon Press, Oxford, 1993.

Gallier J.N., Plaisted D., Ecqstz S. and Snyder W.
"An algorithm for finding canonical sets of ground rewrite rules in polynomial time", *Journal of the ACM*, 1993.

Gabrial R.P.
"Lisp: Good News, Bad News, How to Win Big", *European Conference on Practical Applications of Lisp*, 1990.

Gardner M.
Logic Machines and Diagrams, University of Chicago Press, 1983.

Gentzen G.
Investigations into logical deduction (first published 1934) in *The Collected Papers of Gerhard Gentzen* (Szabo, ed.), Amsterdam, North Holland 1969.

Giarratano J.C. and Riley G. D.
Expert Systems: Principles and Programming (3rd edition), PWS, 1998.

Girard J.Y., Lafont Y. and Taylor P.
Proofs and Types, Cambridge University Press, 1989.

Gordon M.J.
Programming Language Theory and its Implementation, Prentice Hall, 1988.

Gordon M.J., Milner R. and Wadsworth P.
Programming in the Edinburgh LCF, Springer-Verlag, 1979

Gray P.
Logic, Algebra and Databases, Ellis-Horwood, 1984.

Green J. A.
Sets and Groups, Library of Mathematics, Routledge and Kegan Paul, 1965.

Green C.
Theorem-proving by resolution as a basis for question-answering systems, Machine Intelligence 4, 1969.

Grune D. and Jacobs C.J.H.
Parsing Techniques: a practical guide, Ellis Horwood, 1991.

Gunter C.
The Semantics of Programing Languages: Structures and Techniques, MIT Press, 1992.

Haack S.
Deviant Logic, Cambridge University Press, 1974.

Haack S.
Philosophy of Logics, Cambridge University Press, 1978.

Haynes C.
"Logic Continuations", *Journal of Logic Programming* 4, 1987.

Helman P. & Veroff R.
Walls and Mirrors, Addison-Wesley, 2005.

Hendrix G.
"Encoding Knowledge in Partitioned Networks" in *Associative Networks*, ed. N. Findler, Academic Press 1979.

Henglein F.
"Global tagging optimisation by type inference" in ACM Conference on LISP and Functional Programming, 1992.

Henkin L.
"Systems, Formal and Models of", in Edwards P. (chief editor), *The Encyclopaedia of Philosophy*, MacMillan and Free Press, 1967.

Henson M.C.
Elements of Functional Languages, Blackwell, 1987.

Hewitt C.E.
"PLANNER: A Language for Proving Theorems in Robots", *IJCAI* 1969.

Hindley J.R. and Seldin J.P
Introduction to Combinators and Lambda Calculus,. Cambridge University Press, 1986.

490

Hodges W.
Logic, Pelican, 1977.

Hogger C.J.
Introduction to Logic Programming, London, Academic Press, 1984.

Hogger C.J.
Essentials of Logic Programming, Oxford, Clarendon, 1990.

Holmes B.J.
Introductory Pascal, DP Publications, 1993.

Hughes G. E. and Cresswell M.J.
An Introduction to Modal Logic, Methuen, 1968.

Hughes G. E. and Cresswell M.J.
A Companion to Modal Logic, Methuen, 1984.

Hughes G.E. and Cresswell M.J.,
A New Introduction to Modal Logic, Routledge, 1996

Hughes J.
"Why Functional Programming Matters", in Turner D.A. (ed.), *Research Topics in Functional Programming*, Addison-Wesley, 1990.

Ito T. and Halstead R.H.
Parallel Lisp: Languages and Systems, LNCS 441, Springer-Verlag, 1989.

Jackson P.
Introduction to Expert Systems, International Computer Science Series, 1999.

Jones N.D., Sestoft P. and Sondergaard H.
"An Experiment in Partial Evaluation: The Generation of a Compiler Generator", in Jouannaud 1985.

Jorrand P.
"Term Rewriting as a Basis for the Design of a Functional and Parallel Programming Language", in W.Bibel and Jorrand P. (ed.) 1986.

Jouannaud J.P.
Rewriting Techniques and Applications, LNCS, vol. 202, Springer-Verlag 1985.

Kac M. and Ulam S.
Mathematics and Logic, Pelican, 1971.

Keene S.E.
Object-Oriented Programming in Common Lisp: A Programmer's Guide to CLOS, Addison-Wesley, 1989.

Kernighan B.W. and Plauger P. J.
"Ratfor – a Preprocessor for a Rational Fortran", *Software, Practice and Experience*, 1975.

Kleene S.C.
Introduction to Metamathematics, North Holland, 1952.

Knight K.
"Unification: a multidisciplinary survey", in *ACM Computing Surveys*, 1989.

Knuth D.E. and Bendix P.B.
"Simple Word Problems in Universal Algebras", in Leech (ed.), *Computational Problems in Abstract Algebras*, Pergamon Press, 1970.

Knuth D.E.
The Art of Computer Programming, Sorting and Searching, Addison-Wesley, Reading, Massachussetts, 1998

Kounalis E. and Rusinowitch M.
"Mechanising Inductive Reasoning", Bulletin of the European Association for Theoretical Computer Science.

Kowalski R.
Logic for Problem Solving, North Holland, 1979.

Kripke S.
"Identity and Necessity", in Munitz M. (ed.), *Identity and Individuation*, New York 1971.

Lajos G.
"Language Directed Programming in Meta-Lisp", *First European Conference on Practical Applications of Lisp*, 1990.

Landin P.
"The Mechanical Evaluation Of Expressions", *Computer Journal*, 6, 1964.

Lemmon E. J.
Beginning Logic, Hackett Publishing Co., 1978.

Lenat D. B. and Guha R. V.
"The Evolution of CYCL, the CYC Representation Language", *SIGART Bulletin*, 1991.

Linsky L. (ed.)
Reference and Modality , Oxford University Press, 1975.

Liu Y. and Staples J.
"btC: an Extension of C with Backtracking", *Proceedings of the Sixth International Conference on Symbolic and Logical Computing, Dakota State University*, 1993.

Lam C.W.H.
"How Reliable is a Computer Based Proof?" *Mathematical Intelligencer* 12, 1,1990.

Lipson J.D.
Elements of Algebra and Algebraic Computing, Benjamin Cummings, 1984.

Lloyd J.
Foundations of Logic Programming, Springer-Verlag, 1990.

Lopes R.H.C.
"Inductive Generalisation of Proof Search Strategies from Examples", Ph.D. thesis, School of Computer Studies, University of Leeds, 1998.

Loveland D. W. (ed)
Automatic Theorem Proving: After 25 years, American Mathematical Society, 1984.

Maier D. and Warren D.S.
Computing with Logic, Benjamin/Cummings, 1988.

Martelli A. and Montenari U.
"Unification in Linear Time and Space", Internal Report B76-16, Insituto di Elaborazione di Informatione, Pisa, Italy, 1973.

McCarthy J.
"Recursive Functions, Symbolic Expressions and their Computation by Machine", *Comm. of the ACM*, 1960.

McCarthy, J.
"History of Lisp". *ACM Sigplan Not.* 13,8 (Aug. 1978), 217-223.

McCarthy J.
"Circumscription: a form of non-monotonic reasoning", *Artificial Intelligence* 13, 1980.

McDermott D. and Doyle J.
"Non-monotonic logic", *Artificial Intelligence* 13, 1980.

McDermott D.
"A Critique of Pure Reason", *Computational Intelligence 3*, 1987.

Mendelson E.
Introduction to Mathematical Logic, Chapman and Hall, 2009.

Minsky M.
"A Framework for Representing Knowledge", in Winston P. (ed.), *The Psychology of Computer Vision*, McGraw-Hill, 1975.

Montague R. "Universal Grammar" (1970) and also "English as a Formal Language" (1970) and "The Proper Treatment of Quantification in Ordinary English" (1973) reprinted in *Formal Philosophy: Selected Papers by Richard Montague*, ed. Richmond H. Thomason, Yale University Press (1974).

Murch R. and Johnson T.
Intelligent Software Agents, Prentice Hall, 1998.

Nipkow T., Paulson L. and Wendel M.
Isabelle/HOL: A Proof Assistant for Higher-Order Logic, Springer, 2002.

O'Donnell M.J.
Equational Logic as a Programming Language, MIT Press, 1985.

Ousterhout, John K.; Jones, Ken
Tcl and the Tk Toolkit (2nd ed.). Addison Wesley, (2006).

Paulson L.
ML for the Working Programmer, Cambridge University Press 1996.

Paulson L.
Logic and Computation: Interactive Proof with Cambridge LC, CUP, 1990.

Peirce B.
Types and Programming Languages, MIT Press, 2002.

Pettorossi A.
"A Powerful Strategy for Deriving Efficient Programs by Transformation" *ACM Symposium on LISP and Functional Programming*, 1984.

Peyton-Jones S. and Lester D.
Implementing Functional Languages, Prentice-Hall, 1987.

Plaisted D.
"Equational Reasoning and Term Rewriting Systems" in Gabbay, Hogger and Robinson, vol. 1, 1993.

Post E.
"Formal Reductions of the General Combinatorial Decision Problem", American Journal of Mathematics, vol. 65, 1943.

Quillian M.R.
"Semantic Memory", in Minsky M. (ed.), *Semantic Information Processing*, MIT Press, 1968.

Reeves S. and Clarke M.
Logic in Computer Science, Prentice-Hall, 1990.

Reiter R.
"A Logic for Default Reasoning", *Artificial Intelligence* 13, 1980.

Reppy J.H.
Concurrent Programming in ML, Cambridge University Press, 2007

Robinson J.
"A Machine-Oriented Logic Based on the Resolution Principle", *Journal of the ACM*, 1965

Robinson J.A. and Sibert E.E.
"Logic Programming in Lisp", research report, School of Computer and Information Science, Syracuse University, New York, 1980.

Russell S. and Norvig P.
Artificial Intelligence: a modern approach, Prentice Hall Series in Artificial Intelligence, first edition 1995, second edition 2002.

Schwartz J.T., Dewar R.B.K., Dubinsky, E., and Schonberg, E
Programming with Sets: an introduction to SETL, Springer-Verlag, 1986.

Shrobe H.
"Symbolic Computing Architectures", *Exploring Artificial Intelligence*, ed. Shrobe and AAAI, Morgan Kaufmann, 1988.

Simon H.
Models of my Life, New York, Basic Books, 1991.

Sitaram D.
"Handling Control", Proceedings of the SIGPLAN Conference on Programming Language Design and Implementation, 1993.

Slater R.
Portraits in Silicon, MIT Press, 1989.

Sloman A.
"POPLOG: a multi-purpose multi-language program development environment", *Artificial Intelligence - Industrial and Commercial Applications. First International Conference*. 1985

Smullyan R.
First Order Logic, Springer-Verlag, 1968.

Smullyan R.
Theory of Formal Systems, Princeton University Press, 1960.

Steele G.
Common Lisp: the Language, Digital Press, 1990.

Sterling L. and Shapiro E.
The Art of Prolog, MIT Press, 1994.

Stickel M.E.
"A PROLOG Technology Theorem-Prover" in *New Generation Computing 2*, 1984.

Stickel M.E.
"A Prolog Technology Theorem Prover: Implementation by an extended Prolog Compiler", *CADE 8*, LNCS vol 230, Springer-Verlag, 1986.

Stickel M.E.
"An Introduction to Automated Deduction" in W. Bibel and P. Jorrand (ed.), 1986.

Sussman G. J. and Steele G. L., Jr.
"Scheme: An Interpreter for Extended Lambda Calculus" *AI Memos* (MIT AI Lab), 1975.

Tarver M.
"Towards a Unified Theorem Proving Language", M.Sc. thesis, *University of Leeds, School of Computer Studies*, 1989.

Tarver M.
"The World's Smallest Compiler-Compiler", *European Conference on Practical Applications of Lisp*, 1990.

Tarver M.
"A Rationalisation of Lisp", *University of Leeds, School of Computer Studies Report 90.19*, 1990.

Tarver M.
"An Algorithm for Inducing Tactics from Proofs", *University of Leeds, School of Computer Studies Internal Report,* 1992.

Tarver M.
"A Language for Implementing Arbitrary Logics", *IJCAI*, 1993.

Tarver M.
"Representing the Types of Polyadic Lisp Functions", in *International Lisp Conference* 2002.

Tarver M.
Logic, Proof and Computation, 2nd edition FastPrint, 2014.

Thayse A.
From Modal Logic to Deductive Datbases, Wiley, 1989

Thayse A.
From Natural Language Processing to Logic for Expert Systems, Wiley, 1990.

Tecuci G.
Building Intelligent Agents, Academic Press, 1998.

Thompson S.
Miranda: the Craft of Functional Programming (second Edition), Addison-Wesley, 1995.

Thompson S.
Haskell: the Craft of Functional Programming (second Edition), Addison-Wesley, 1999.

Thompson S.
Type Theory and Functional Programming, Addison-Wesley 1991.

Thompson S.
Haskell: the Craft of Functional Programming (second Edition), Addison-Wesley, 1999.

Torkel F.
Logic programming and the intuitionistic sequent calculus. SICS Research Report, 1988.

Turner D. A.
SASL Language Manual, University of St Andrews Dept. of Computer Science Report, 1976.

Turner D. A.
"A New Implementation Technique for Applicative Languages", in *Software Practice and Experience,* 1979.

Turner D. A.
"Recursion Equations as a Programming Language", in Darlington, Henderson and Turner, 1982.

Turner D. A.
"An Overview of Miranda" in Turner (ed.) 1990.

Turner D. A. (ed.)
Research Topics in Functional Programming, Addison-Wesley, 1990.

Walther C.
"Many-sorted unification", *Journal of the ACM,* 1988.

Wand M.
"Continuation Based Program Transformation Strategies", *Journal of the ACM,* 27, 1980.

Warren D. "An Abstract Prolog Instruction Set", Technical Note 309, SRI International,
Menlo Park, 1983.

Wikstrom A.
Functional Programming Using Standard ML, Prentice-Hall, 1987.

Winograd T.
"Understanding Natural Language", *Cognitive Psychology* 1972.

Wright A. and Cartwright R.
"A practical soft type system for Scheme", *1994 ACM Conference on LISP and Functional Programming,* 1994.

Index of System Functions Used in this Book

Index

fresh, 112, 179, 180, 185, 222, 223, 224, 424, 425, 427, 428, 435, 436, 443, 446, 448, 450, 462
fully qualified name, 113
Functional Abstract Machine, 11

G

garbage collection, 8, 9, 384, 395
generalisation rule, 425, 429, 448
Gentzen, 13, 214, 215, 230, 489
global, 81, 82, 196, 430, 466, 490
global environment, 82
global variable, 81, 82, 113, 236
goal, 32, 129, 130, 132, 141, 160, 224, 225, 228, 255, 275, 361, 364, 365, 374, 375, 376, 377, 378, 384, 403, 406, 408, 410, 423, 432, 438, 440, 441, 445, 482
goal state, 129, 130
Goldbach's conjecture, 45, 46, 57
Gordon, 11, 170, 213, 489, 490
graceful labeling problem, 139
grammar, 133, 134, 138, 143, 144, 146, 147, 153, 155, 291, 473, 475
grammatical, 132, 133, 134, 135, 136, 138
green macro, 120
guard, 42, 43, 45, 145, 146, 149, 179, 243, 428, 446, 455, 457

H

halting problem, 48, 162
Harrison, 18, 48, 489
hash, 14, 91, 92, 93, 463
hash table, 14, 91, 92
Haskell, 12, 18, 54, 71, 73, 125, 204, 214, 215, 312, 496
help function, 39
Henson, 47, 490
Hett, 139, 140, 212
Hewitt, 141, 490
Hickey, 13
higher-order, 9, 70, 74, 75, 76, 79, 80, 124, 130, 131, 144, 195, 209, 276, 292, 313, 361, 460

higher-order programming, 9, 195
Hilbert proof, 269, 271
Hindley, 156, 170, 490
Hodges, 18, 230, 491
home directory, 30, 31, 460
Horn clause, 214, 225, 226, 346, 347, 349, 350, 352, 353, 355, 360, 363, 364, 367, 383
Horn clause procedure, 360
Hughes, 1, 80, 491
hypotheses, 216, 220, 235, 240, 247, 251, 375, 377, 378, 379, 380, 451, 453, 456, 457

I

I/O, 99, 171, 471
idle symbol, 337
implicitly typed, 204
include, vii, 16, 69, 81, 98, 148, 165, 230, 243, 250, 256, 265, 276, 356, 463, 464
INDUCT, 485
inference rule, 216, 219, 223, 224
infinite, 3, 26, 37, 39, 60, 131, 229
infinity, 229, 309
infix, 21, 108, 109, 204
inlined, 111
integer, 20, 21, 22, 34, 35, 36, 37, 38, 42, 43, 46, 56, 66, 87, 96, 126, 140, 162, 202, 257, 264, 285, 286, 287, 309, 311, 315, 384, 400, 459, 462, 464, 473, 476
integrity condition, 443, 445, 446
internal, 114
internal expressions, 71
interpretation, 157, 178, 305
interpreter, 170, 200, 415
interval, 234
intuitionistic propositional calculus, 221
inverter, 31
isomorphic, 140

J

Java, 12, 13, 80

503

504

509

β

β-redex, 161
β reduction, 158, 159, 160, 161

δ

δ rules, 355

η

η conversion, 158, 160, 170

WS - #0072 - 070222 - C0 - 229/152/29 - PB - 9781915012111 - Gloss Lamination